The GARDENER'S HANDBOOK *and* DICTIONARY

The GARDENER'S HANDBOOK and DICTIONARY

JACK KRAMER

BARNES
&NOBLE
BOOKS
NEW YORK

Originally published as *The New Gardener's Handbook and Dictionary*

Copyright © 1992 by Jack Kramer

This edition published by Barnes & Noble, Inc.,
by arrangement with Jack Kramer

2000 Barnes & Noble Books

ISBN 0-7607-1984-5

Printed and bound in the United States of America

00 01 02 03 04 MC 9 8 7 6 5 4 3 2 1

MV

ACKNOWLEDGMENTS

It is difficult to thank individually all those who have contributed to this book, especially as it has taken so many years to write. In any case, I am most appreciative of the help I received from many mail-order plant suppliers and wholesale plant growers, and wish to thank the many plant-growing societies in the United States. I would also like to thank my good production editor, Nana Prior, who so capably assisted in turning out this book.

JJK

CONTENTS

3 KEEPING PLANTS HEALTHY AND BEAUTIFUL

FOREWORD

The principal purpose of a gardener's guide is to help the gardener. Therefore, I have had to make rather arbitrary choices in regard to what I should include—both which plants to discuss and what advice to give. To make these decisions, I have drawn on my many years of gardening and have thus listed in this guide only those plants with which I am familiar and that are reasonably easy to grow. The result is that rare and exotic plants, plants that are no longer popular, and plants that are difficult to grow have not been included.

When I began gardening, I was always hunting—usually unsuccessfully—for certain sources and information. In this handbook, therefore, I have included information to compile, essentially, a gardening manual, a gardening dictionary, and a reference sourcebook. In the latter you will find the names of suppliers, other useful gardening books, and various other bits of information that I think might be helpful to you.

In sum, I hope that this book will be of help to all ranks of gardeners, the novices as well as the more seasoned.

Please note that there are many plants in nature, and some of those mentioned in this book, that may be poisonous. Please act with caution when handling plants with which you are unfamiliar, and contact a local nursery to ensure your safety.

PREFACE

A good gardening guide is indispensable to amateurs and professionals alike. It should offer plant descriptions, growing specifications, troubleshooting tips, and information for both those needing to know about plants already in the garden and those selecting plants for a garden they are designing.

Gardeners should know that many of the plants now being sold in nurseries are *clones*. In 1965, the technique of *meristemming*, popularly known as cloning, was imported from France to the University of California at Davis, where it was refined. This technique enabled the propagation of endless copies of a plant—any plant. Whereas the production of *hybrids*—the revolutionary technique that preceded cloning—requires experimenting with and interbreeding two plants to produce a new, hybrid variety, meristemming allows growers to create new varieties from any felicitous mutation that might occur. Meristem propagation not only gives us a large stock of new, exotic plants at affordable prices, but it also produces unusually healthy plants. The industry has taken full advantage of this new technology: Since the 1970s, thousands of new plant varieties have appeared in nurseries across the country. Consequently, cloning now dominates the plant-propagating industry. Old varieties are disappearing, and cloned plants are taking over. And yet nowhere have growing instructions for and descriptions of these new plants been collected and made readily available. This guide is intended to meet this need. The encyclopedia section of this book covers many of the new cloned varieties as well as the older, more familiar ones.

Meristemming, or tissue culture, is thus a method of reproducing cells that (to oversimplify it) enables a grower to replicate hundreds of the same parent plant. Tissue culture also permits the exponential reproduction of plants; that is, four plants become sixteen, sixteen plants become sixty-four, and so on.*

The Gardener's Handbook and Dictionary also reflects the current thinking about and new approaches to pest control and watering. Since 1970, horticulturalists have moved away from using insecticides toward using biological (that is, environmentally safe) pest-control methods that take advantage of the pests' natural predators. Watering by means of drip-system irrigation, which delivers the water right to the roots rather than sweeping the cultivated area and which therefore conserves water, has come into favor as well.

HOW TO USE THIS BOOK

Part One: The Gardening Handbook has four chapters: 1: "Becoming a Gardener" provides introductory garden information for beginners; 2: "Deciding What to Plant" helps gardeners plan and plant specific kinds of gardens; 3: "Keeping Plants Healthy and Beautiful" offers instructions for maintaining an established garden; and 4: "The Plants" is an illustrated overview of the plants, flowers, trees, and shrubs covered in this book. Part Three supplies sources for more information and a quick-reference in which plants are arranged by soil and sun requirements. Each plant entry includes a description, use and growing specifications, troubleshooting tips, and information on ease or difficulty of growing. You may also refer to the following "English to SI Substitutions" chart if you are more comfortable using metric measurements.

---

*I wish to thank the Weyerhaeuser Tissue Culture Center, Florida, for information on the tissue culture process.

English to SI Substitutions

English	SI (Metric)

LIQUID MEASUREMENTS

English	SI (Metric)
1 gallon	4 liters
1 quart	1 liter
1 pint	500 milliliters
1 cup (8 oz.)	250 milliliters
1 ounce	30 milliliters
1 tablespoon	15 milliliters
1 teaspoon	5 milliliters

LENGTH MEASUREMENTS

English	SI (Metric)
1 yard	1 meter
1 foot (12 inches)	⅓ meter
1 inch	2.54 centimeters
1 mile	1.61 kilometers

PRESSURE

English	SI (Metric)
14.7 pounds per square inch (PSI)	1 atmosphere

Abbreviations

atmosphere = atm	liter = l
centimeter = cm	milliliter = ml
cup = c	meter = m
gallon = gal.	millimeter = mm
pint = pt.	kilometer = km
quart = qt.	yard = yd.
ounce = oz.	foot = ft.
tablespoon = T.	inch = in.
teaspoon = tsp.	

PART ONE:
THE
GARDENING
HANDBOOK

BECOMING A GARDENER

Gardening is more than digging holes and putting plants into them. To be a successful gardener, you must know something about how plants grow. You also must know how to buy plants. Unhealthy plants or the wrong plants for the garden you are planning will not result in a garden of which you can be proud. Assuming that you have bought healthy plants suitable for your region and particular location, you then must know how deep to dig those holes and how best to put the plants into them. Then, to tend your garden, you will need the proper tools. With them, gardening is a joy; without them, it can be a chore.

Your garden will either flourish or struggle to survive, depending on whether you have selected plants suitable for your region's climate, that is, its particular range of temperature, amount of rainfall, type of soil, and the like. As you no doubt know, plants need sufficient sun, water, and nutrients to grow. And so you must also take into account whether spring comes early or late in your area. Does your region receive a little or a lot of rain? It is not just the plants themselves with which you must be concerned. To find out more about your particular area, talk to your local nursery or university or state agricultural department (the last is listed in the back of this book).

A roof garden in San Francisco. Vegetables and herbs can thrive in almost any place and climate.

PLANTS

A plant consists of roots, stem or trunk, leaves, and flowers and fruit. The roots are the plant's feeding apparatus and its means of holding it in the ground. Roots absorb both water and nutrients. The root tip, or cap, is made of tough, flat cells that cut through the soil. There are few obstacles that can stop roots—think of the little plants that have pushed through the asphalt of

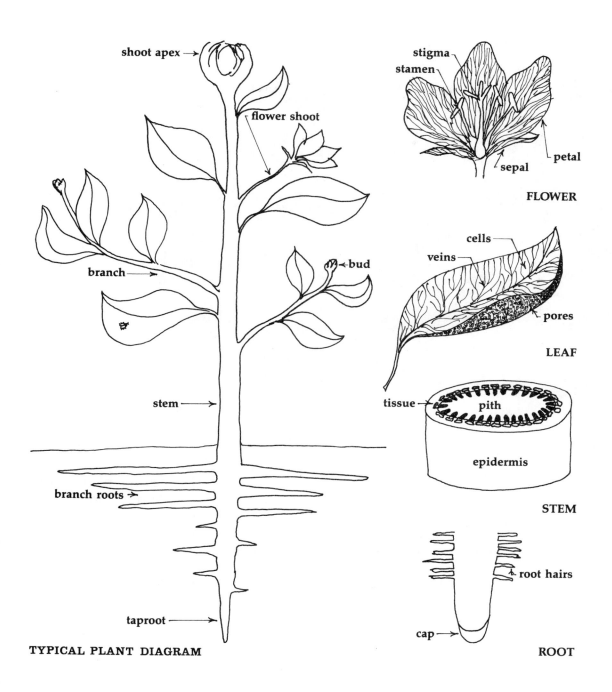

shoot apex →

flower shoot

branch →

← bud

stem →

branch roots →

taproot →

TYPICAL PLANT DIAGRAM

stigma

stamen

sepal

petal

FLOWER

cells

veins

pores

LEAF

tissue →

pith

epidermis

STEM

root hairs

cap →

ROOT

PLANT STRUCTURE

ADRIÁN MARTÍNEZ

A seedling ready to be planted. Note the intact root ball; this ensures a successful transplant. (Photo courtesy USDA)

a highway. Behind the root tip is the root's growing area, cells that are constantly dividing. The roots grow in tandem with the visible part of the plant. The plant's main roots send out smaller roots, which in turn give birth to even smaller ones, and so forth. The roots (actually feeding tubes) carry nutrients and water to the plant, and they also may store food.

Some plants, such as carrots and trees, have a long, central taproot from which smaller roots sprout. Plants with short stems and small leaves have fat roots that store food. Corms, rhizomes, and bulbs (lilies, onions, and such) have short feeding roots to absorb water and nutrients. Grass roots are shallow because they can collect food just below the surface of the soil, whereas the roots of a large tree grow both deep and wide, to absorb sufficient food and water and also to grip the soil and hold the tree in place.

A plant's stem or trunk processes and distributes the products of its leaves and roots. Each of the stem's cells must have a constant supply of water, nutrients, and air and also must store food for leaner times. The stem transports water and nutrients to the plant's buds, leaves, and flowers, and it returns to the roots the sugars manufactured in the leaves. The stem also supports the plant.

A plant's leaves transform sunlight, air, water, and the nutrients in the soil into organic food, through a process known as *photosynthesis*. The water that a plant absorbs is filtered through its leaves by means of *transpiration*, during which the water is changed into vapor. Thus when a plant does not obtain enough moisture, its leaves wilt, and eventually the plant will die if it is not rescued.

A plant's flowers contain its reproductive organs which produce seeds. The seeds await the proper mix of sun, water, and nutrients to begin sprouting, thereby setting in motion the growth of yet more plants.

GROWING PLANTS

Air. To stay healthy, plants need lots of fresh air circulating around them. Crowding plants robs them of necessary light; dusty and/or smoggy air hinders their growth by blocking air pores and cells. Although some plants do well in dry areas, generally plants like a fair amount of moisture in the air. Wind also increases the rate of water loss, modifies the water content of the plant cells, and thereby affects the plant's growth.

Sunlight. Sunlight is a main ingredient of photosynthesis and the production of chlorophyll. Most of the sunlight that strikes the leaves is changed into heat and thus raises the plant's temperature. Not surprisingly, thick leaves like sun, and thin leaves prefer shade.

Nutrients. The three most important nutrients in a plant's diet are nitrogen, phosphorus, and potassium. Nitrogen promotes leaf growth; phosphorus helps develop the roots and stem; and potassium stabilizes the plant's growth and intensifies its color. But a shortage of any one of these elements will hamper all of a plant's normal development.

Temperature. Temperature influences each of a plant's activities: photosynthesis, assimilation of nutrients, respiration, absorption of water, transpiration, and the formation of enzymes. Note that the ideal temperature for one of these processes may differ from that for another being carried out at the same time. Note, too, that temperature and water together determine the general distribution of all vegetation on this planet.

Water. Plants must have adequate water to thrive. If they do not, they will grow more slowly or even die. Although some plants do quite well with little water (drought-tolerant plants) and still others manage with very little (such as cacti), the majority do best with more generous amounts.

Climate. The word *climate* encompasses sunlight, rainfall, temperature, humidity, and wind—all of the environmental elements that determine how well, or even if, your plants will grow. Every region has a particular climate; indeed, even your garden may have separate "microclimates," based on shade, direction of the sun, and the like.

A window decorated with ferns and African violets.

You must plant and maintain your garden according to its particular climate (or climates, as the case may be). For example, if you live in a rainy area, you should make sure that your garden has sufficient drainage, and because the rain will leach away many of the soil's nutrients, you should fertilize your garden often. In hot, dry, sunny regions, consider situating your plants where they will receive some shade, perhaps near a large tree or on the north side of your house. Mulching the soil helps compensate for the lack of moisture. Wind also dries out the soil, and so plants exposed to lots of

Plants grown against house walls or fences can withstand cold temperatures better than those growing in the open.

wind need to be watered more often. Windbreaks such as trees, hedges, and fences help.

PLANT CLIMATE ZONES

The United States Department of Agriculture (USDA) issues a plant hardiness zone map. It is arranged with ten different climate zones for the United States. Most gardening books use this map to indicate which plants do well in each of the areas. The zone map can be found here at the beginning of the Appendix, and zone information for individual plants are listed in the Botanical Names/Common Names listing.

The map is useful but it can be awkward to flip from plant descriptions to the map to find the proper temperature range. For this reason, I have also included the temperatures suitable for the most common plants in the alphabetical Plant Dictionary.

PLANT NAMES

It is not enough to identify plants only by their common names, for one plant's common name to you may not be its common name to me. That is, one plant may be known by different names in different parts of the country. For example, blue marguerites are called felicias in one geographical area but asters in another. And some plants are available as either perennials or annuals, such as delphinium—a perennial—and larkspur—an annual. Only by identifying a plant by its botanical or Latin name can you be sure of getting what you want. Furthermore, when you know a plant's botanical name, you can order it with confidence from any plant catalog in the world.

Plants that have been bred to produce a superior color or form (or perhaps taste or some other such quality if it is edible) carry special variety names enclosed in single quotation marks that follow the species name, such as 'Golden Glow' or 'Celebrity'.

BUYING AND PLANTING PLANTS

SEEDLINGS

Of course you can grow plants from scratch or, rather, from seed, but except for some vegetables, it is far easier to plant plants that have already been started and have progressed to varying stages of growth. The smallest ready-to-grow plants are *seedlings*, which are often bought in *flats*, shallow wooden or plastic containers. Some of the plastic containers—six packs—resemble muffin tins, with each "cup" holding one seedling. The seedlings in a flat are ready to be put into the ground. If all the plants are together (that is, not in six packs), separate them with a kitchen knife or a trowel by cutting straight down around them. If the plants are in separate cups, hold the plant gently and tap or carefully squeeze the cup until the plant falls out. Dig holes large enough to accommodate the plant and its roots easily; don't try to force the roots into a too-small hole. Then, holding the plant gently, fill in the hole, and firm the soil around the plant's base. Make sure that the roots are covered, but don't bury the plant much deeper than that. Finally, form a well around the plant so that when you water it, the water will soak into the ground around the plant and not run off. If you have bought your seedlings in peat pots, set the plant, peat pot included, into the hole; the pot will be absorbed by the surrounding soil.

VARIOUS STAGES OF PEAT PELLETS

SEED CUBES

SHRUBS AND TREES

Shrubs and trees are sold either "bare root" or balled and burlapped (the tree is dug out of the ground with a ball of soil around its roots, which is then wrapped in burlap and tied at the top of the ball). Small deciduous fruit trees, shade trees, and certain shrubs are available in nurseries in bare-root form in early spring or sometimes even sooner. Bare-root plants cost less than do plants bought later in containers, and they often are healthier.

When buying a bare-root plant, check to make sure that its roots are plump and fresh. If the roots seem dry, soak the plant overnight in a bucket of water. When planting it, dig a hole big enough to accommodate the plant comfortably without forcing it. Never squeeze, bend, or cut the roots to make them fit the hole; make the hole bigger instead. If a training stake is needed, put it in *outside* the roots; in that way you won't damage them. Next, make a mound of soil on the bottom of the hole, and place the plant on top of the mound. Now fill in the hole and around the roots with soil. Don't pack it tightly; you want the roots to be able to breathe. Tie the plant in several places to the stake, if you are using one, with plastic or cloth ties. Make a well around the plant, and water the plant thoroughly. For the next few weeks, water the plant moderately, as bare-root or dormant plants require less water than do actively growing ones. When leaves begin appearing, start watering the plant regularly.

Large trees and shrubs are sold balled and burlapped and should not be handled unnecessarily roughly, although they do not need to be treated as gingerly as certain other plants do (such as bougainvillea). In any case, do not use the trunk as a handle; cradle the root ball in your hands or arms if you can. Do not drag the tree or shrub along the pavement, as you may damage its roots.

To plant a large tree or shrub, dig a deep hole—about twice the diameter of the root ball and at least half as deep as the height of the root ball. Make a mound of soil at the bottom of the hole, and then place the plant on top of the mound so that the base of the plant itself is slightly above the soil line. Pour in some water, and let the soil settle for a few moments. Now cut the twine or string holding the burlap, and spread out the burlap (it will eventually decompose). Fill in the hole, and make a water well around the base of the tree. Fill the well with water a few times, each time letting the water soak into the soil.

PLANTS IN CONTAINERS

Plants of all sizes are always available in containers at nurseries. When buying plants in containers, check to make sure that the roots are not

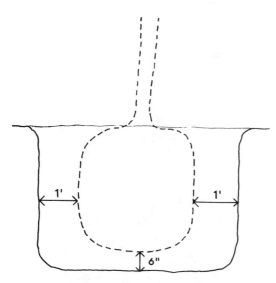

1. Size of hole varies with size of root ball.

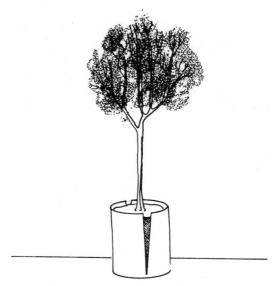

2. Carefully cut the can from the roots.

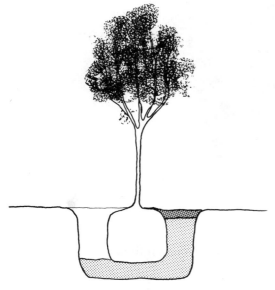

3. Fill with topsoil and 3 in. of mulch.

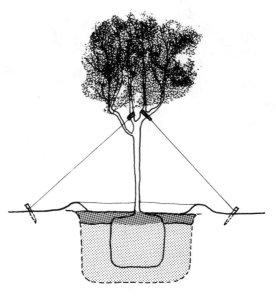

4. Support with guy wires, and then water.

HOW TO PLANT A TREE

Boxes newly planted with ivy and other ground covers.

growing out the bottom; such plants have outgrown their container and may not be healthy.

Many container plants at nurseries are raised in a loose soil mix to promote fast growth. Once in the ground, however, they will need much more soil around them. When planting container plants, dig a hole at least twice the diameter of the container. If the plant comes out of the container easily or with a minimum amount of persuasion, fine. If not, cut away the container. Crumble, or gently remove some of the old soil from the roots, and then follow the same procedure for planting as for balled-and-burlapped plants. If you cannot put the plant into the ground on the same day that you buy it, keep it cool and watered until you can.

SEED-STARTING KITS

Although you can plant seeds in the ground and hope for the best, the new seed-starting kits are almost foolproof. One kind is the polystyrene perforated block: You drop a few seeds into each hole in the block, set the block in the water tray provided, and then insert the perforated block of sterile peat moss held together with an organic binder. (The peat moss block is premoistened and ready to use.) Put the block in a place where it will get some sun, and keep it moist. When the seedlings are big enough to go into the ground, simply push out each cylinder from the bottom—the root balls will not crumble.

Other seed-starting kits are growing trays with holes in them; some have covers. Jiffy pots, which I use, have been on the market for years. They are inexpensive peat moss pots, two to three inches in diameter. You fill them with potting soil, drop in the seeds, and keep them watered. When the seedlings are big enough to move outdoors, plant the entire peat moss pot; it will dissolve into the soil.

TRANSPLANTING

Transplanting entails moving an entire plant factory to a new location. Although the job is simple for small plants, it becomes increasingly complicated with the size of the plant.

Move plants when they are dormant. That is, transplant spring-blooming plants in August or early September, summer-blooming plants in early spring when the danger of frost has passed.

When transplanting a tree or large shrub, first dig a trench around the outermost roots, and then begin uncovering the roots from there toward the trunk. Work carefully, making sure not to damage the principal roots, especially the taproot. Do not try to remove the soil clinging to the roots. A deciduous tree or large shrub or an evergreen should always be moved with a ball of soil around its root system. A few days before transplanting, soak the root ball so that it will hold together when you lift it. You will find that some plants have a dense root system that automatically holds the root ball together but that other plants, such as many junipers, have loosely arranged roots that do not form a root ball. Such plants are, of course, more difficult to move, as the root ball tends to break apart. If the root ball remains intact, the transplanting operation will usually be successful. But if it falls apart, as it might if it is in sandy soil, the chances of success will not be so good. If the root ball starts to crumble as you take the plant out of the hole, try to wrap some burlap around it and tie it around the trunk. This often is difficult to do, so be patient and don't give up.

Sometimes the hole that you have dug for the plant will not drain, thereby shutting off the plant's air supply, encouraging the growth of mold, and rotting the roots. (It thus may be a good idea to test the hole's drainage if you are unsure. Pour some water into the hole and see whether it is absorbed quickly.) To remedy this problem, dig a hole within the hole. That is, after you have dug the hole, tunnel down with a "posthole digger." Fill this second hole with fine sand or ground bark. If it is impossible to dig into the soil after you have finished digging the planting hole, at least try to loosen the soil at the bottom and mix it with mulch or organic matter, in order to aerate the soil. Then rough up the sides of the hole with the edge of your shovel so that the plant's roots can grasp onto them.

If you are thinking of transplanting a very large tree or shrub, call a professional tree service. Such a move requires ropes and pulleys and the like, and it is not a job for the fainthearted.

PRUNING

You must periodically trim and prune trees and shrubs to keep them shapely, to allow the free circulation of air and the penetration of sunlight, and to remove any dead branches and excess growth. The kind of pruning you should do depends on the particular plant and its age and development. Many trees and shrubs should be cut back a bit immediately after being planted, in order to encourage new growth. Others are best pruned after they flower, and still others (such as fruit trees) are usually trimmed in late winter.

In any case, do not needlessly prune plants. Trim them only with good reason, and plan what you are going to do before you pick up the shears; pruning is not an operation that you can reverse. Generally, cut only above a bud, a small side branch, or a main branch. Do not leave a small stub—it can be an invitation to decay. Cut branches in the direction in which you want new growth. Prune young shade trees to help them develop strong frames, by taking out any crossed branches or side branches that threaten to unbalance the tree's dominant shape. Cover all cuts with tree-wound paste.

Some deciduous shrubs and trees bloom only on old wood, whereas others flower only on new growth. Accordingly, shrubs that bloom on last year's wood should be pruned after they have flowered, and shrubs that bloom on new growth should be pruned in winter or early spring.

Always use only clean, sharp tools to prune plants.

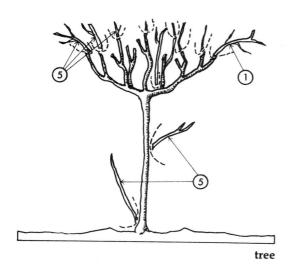

tree

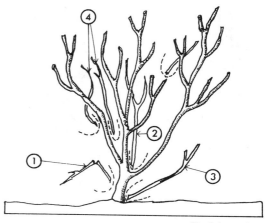

climbing vine

in the spring, prune

1. dead, damaged, or diseased canes.

2. old canes that have been replaced by new ones.

3. suckers that start below bud unions.

4. canes or twigs that cross and crowd one another.

5. canes and twigs to maintain the proper shape.

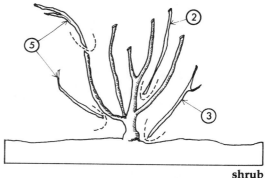

shrub

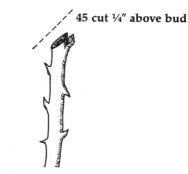

45 cut ¼" above bud

stem

PRUNING

ADRIÁN MARTÍNEZ

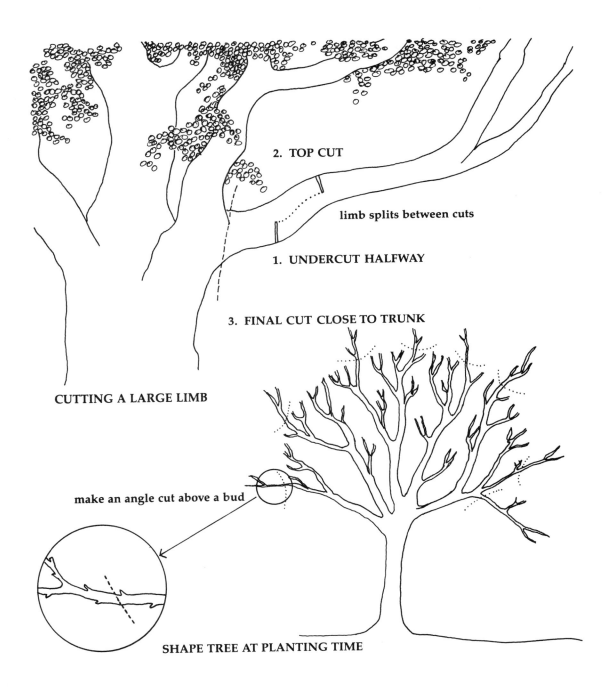

2. TOP CUT

limb splits between cuts

1. UNDERCUT HALFWAY

3. FINAL CUT CLOSE TO TRUNK

CUTTING A LARGE LIMB

make an angle cut above a bud

SHAPE TREE AT PLANTING TIME

PRUNING AND SHAPING

TOOLS

Most gardeners need only a few, basic gardening tools. You will use a *hand trowel* to plant, scoop soil, and remove weeds. Buy a scoop-and-spatula trowel, selecting one that feels comfortable in your hand.

You will need *shovels* to dig, mix, and lift soil. Buy a round-pointed, long-handled shovel for general purposes, and also buy a square-headed shovel if you will be moving large amounts of soil.

Use a *hoe* to break up crusted soil and to dig up weeds. The best one for most jobs is a standard hoe with a sturdy, securely attached handle.

There are various kinds of *rakes* for various purposes, such as working around shrubs, raking leaves, and cleaning up grass cuttings. I use a fan-shaped bamboo rake for most cleaning chores, and a level-headed rake for breaking up spaded soil and removing debris.

I have never found the perfect *weeder*. The palm of your hand and your fingers are still the best one available. But if you don't want to get your hands dirty, use a weeder with iron tines shaped like a claw or a flat-bladed weeder whose blade is at a right angle to the shaft. A fishtail weeder is the best choice for getting out deep roots.

Use shears to prune plants, either the scissors type or the anvil type (more durable). A pruning knife is handy for reaching those places that shears cannot.

Knives should be part of your tool kit, especially a small, sharp one for light pruning and for snipping flowers. A putty knife is useful for a variety of jobs, such as scraping off paint or dirt from tools.

Buy one very good *wheelbarrow*—you will find it useful for a variety of jobs. Be sure to get a heavy-duty, sturdy one. Forget those on sale; the good wheelbarrows are expensive, and worth it.

Finally, buy a pair of good garden gloves. They help keep your hands clean and protect them against spiders and other unexpected residents in your garage and soil. Leather gloves last longer than do cloth or plastic ones. Try them on before you buy them, as some gloves are available in only two sizes, large or small, which is frustrating if you wear a medium size.

Most important, keep all your tools clean. Dirty tools can rust or spread diseases among your plants. After using them, scrape off the dirt with a flat stick or a putty knife. Then "churn" the tool up and down in a bucket of oiled sand to remove any remaining dirt and to keep the surfaces free of rust. Keep all blades sharp, and store your tools away from rain and snow.

POWER TOOLS

Some gardening power tools are useless gimmicks, but others really do save time and make your work easier. If you have a relatively small garden, you will not need many, if any, power tools unless you just like to collect gadgets. One power tool that I find useful, however, is a multipurpose one that tills soil, pulls out weeds, edges, and even trims bushes and hedges. It is called a *Mantis* and is available at most garden stores. There are two models, either gasoline powered or electric powered. The electric-powered model is better because it does not have to be run at full throttle, as does the gasoline-powered one. Available attachments include a furrower, an edger, a lawn aerator, a lawn dehatcher, and a hedge trimmer. Another garden power tool that I like is a gasoline- or electric-powered blower to blow away and clean debris such as leaves, dirt, and dust. But because they are illegal in many areas, find out the regulations in your town before investing in one.

You probably won't need a large power saw for trimming trees or a large power mower with a seat unless you have a great deal of cultivated land. Likewise, mulchers, shredders, and compost makers are not necessary for a small garden; you probably will not have enough debris to justify the expense. A power tiller is mainly a tool for a landscape contractor, as it is costly and not practical in a small yard. You may, however, want a trimmer. Power trimmers have two round-toothed blades that work like scissors cutting in all directions. They do not throw rocks, as some string trimmers do, and they are excellent edgers. (See the list at the back of this book for sources.)

2

DECIDING WHAT TO PLANT

There are many kinds of gardens, ranging from formal to informal to flower to vegetable to a combination of these, a peculiarly American concept known as a *companion garden*. Such a garden contains a little bit of everything: flowers, herbs, vegetables, and fruits. Other kinds of gardens, such as vertical gardens and container gardens, are old concepts that have achieved new popularity, sometimes by necessity (less land) and sometimes by choice. What kind of garden you choose will, of course, depend on how much land you have, what kind of climate prevails in your region, how much time you want to spend maintaining your garden, what the purpose of your garden is (vegetables for the dinner table? flowers for the living room? herbs for the kitchen?), and your own personal desires.

DESIGNING YOUR GARDEN

When designing a garden, you must take into account the available space, the contour of the land, the particular shapes you want to feature, the mass you want to achieve, the garden's overall balance and rhythm, and its proportions. Before you even start to think about the details, walk around the property that you have designated as your future garden. Is the site rectangular, square, or, perhaps, pie shaped? Maybe it has no recognizable

This sky garden is a jumble of flowers, herbs, and even houseplants.

shape. That, too, you should know. The shape is important, for it will dictate the placement of the plants. Another important element is the contour of the land. If the land is flat, your garden can be of almost any design, but if it is hilly, you must plan accordingly.

Next, make a rough sketch of the site. Indicate the location of your house, the geographic directions (north, south, east, west), and the outside borders

LANDSCAPE SYMBOLS

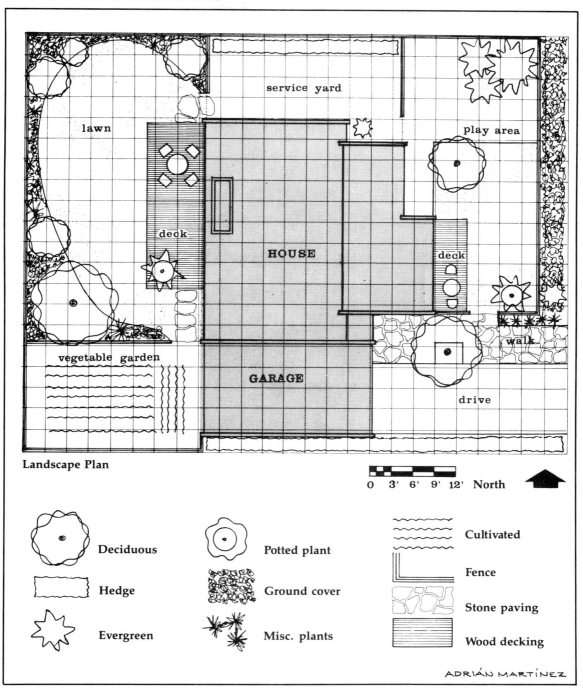

Landscape Plan

0 3' 6' 9' 12' North

Deciduous

Hedge

Evergreen

Potted plant

Ground cover

Misc. plants

Cultivated

Fence

Stone paving

Wood decking

ADRIÁN MARTÍNEZ

SPRING GARDEN

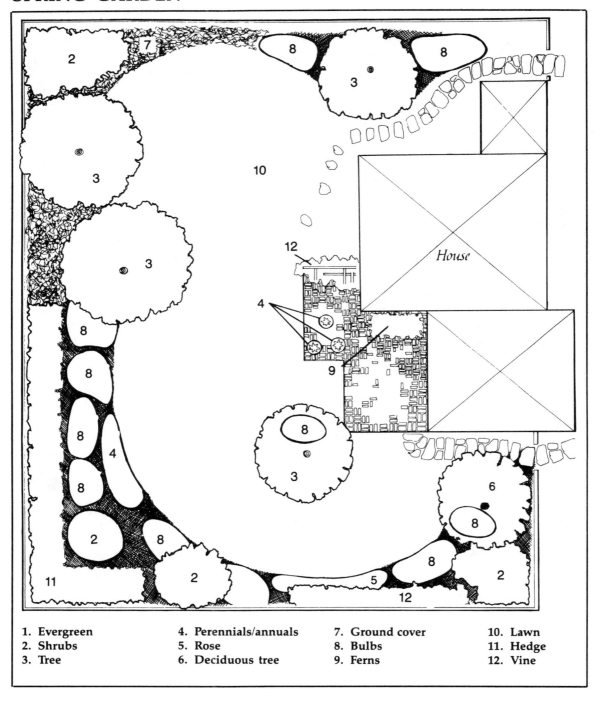

House

1. Evergreen
2. Shrubs
3. Tree
4. Perennials/annuals
5. Rose
6. Deciduous tree
7. Ground cover
8. Bulbs
9. Ferns
10. Lawn
11. Hedge
12. Vine

This landscape plan is both functional and simple. The shrubs provide privacy, and the island planting provides color.

of the proposed garden. Decide whether and/or where you will have fences, walls, trellises. These provide privacy, help block wind, support vertically growing plants, and add a decorative note. For the most effective sketch, try to draw it as a contour map. If the property has a uniform, gradual slope, draw equally spaced lines across the sketch. Indicate any ridges with lines curving toward you, any valleys with lines curving away from you. Drifts of plants (perhaps spring bulbs) belong in low-lying areas, to create mass. Hills and slopes should be planted with small trees and shrubs. Those areas where the ground is level can be designated as planting beds. A contour map can tell you whether a particular tree will be too tall and will obscure a view or whether it will be too short and thus not be readily noticed.

Now visualize your garden with vegetables, flowers, fruits, herbs, trees, and shrubs in it. For example, you could put the vegetables close to the house (for easy picking), as well as the flowers you will be cutting often. Fruit

LATE SUMMER/FALL GARDEN

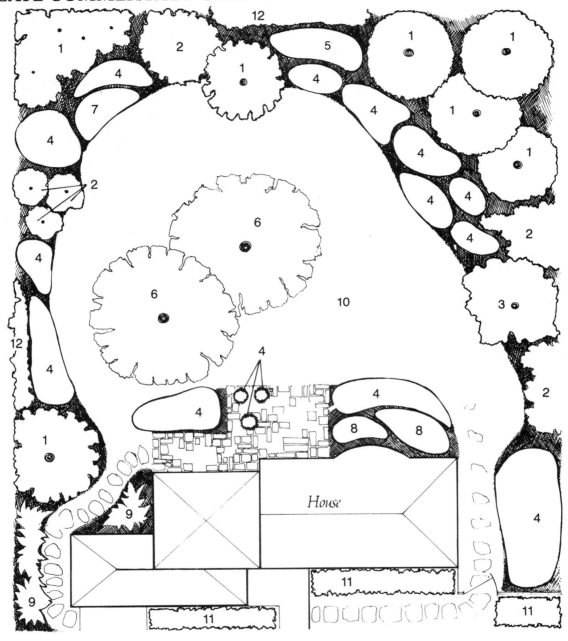

1. Evergreen
2. Shrubs
3. Tree
4. Perennial/annuals
5. Rose
6. Deciduous tree
7. Ground cover
8. Bulbs
9. Ferns
10. Lawn
11. Hedge
12. Vine

DROUGHT-RESISTANT GARDEN PLAN

This rectangle city garden is enclosed by a fence. The drought-resistant plants listed below suggest using trees, shrubs, and vines in a uniform color scheme of red to white.

1. Shrub—flowering quince (chaenomeles)
2. Shrub—rockrose (cistus), 5' high
3. Shrubs—deutzia, 6' high
4. Perennial—yarrow (achillea millefolium)
5. Tree—Arizona ash (fraxinus velutina) 25'
6. Perennial—pinks (dianthus—D. 'Allwoodii', carnations) 10"–24" high
7. Perennial—gas plant (dictamus), 3'
8. Tree-of-heaven (ailanthus altissima)
9. Vine—trumpet vine (clystoma)
10. Annual—rose moss (portulaca), 6"
11. Perennial—sea lavender (limonium)
12. Tree—flowering cherry (prunus)
13. Annual—sweet alyssum (lobularia)
14. Vine—morning glory (ipomea)
15. Ground cover—sandwort (arenaria verna caespitosa), 3" high

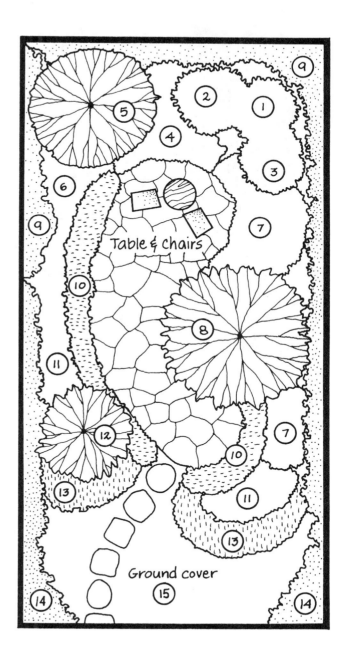

Table & chairs

Ground cover

A balance of vertical and horizontal elements and a repetition of square plantings to match the concrete walk.

trees make good borders. I usually begin by looking at the far-left or far-right corner of the plot and deciding what would go best there and then work inward. For instance, in the left-hand corner a somewhat large and concave arc would work well, to soften the straight lines of the corner (I will decide later what to put in the arc). Shrubs and vegetables or perhaps a flower bed could go in front. Along the fence or property border running to the right, I can see vegetables or herbs; in the right-hand corner, espaliered fruit trees would add an elegant touch.

But before you get carried away adding too many plants, be sure you plan your paths. Paths are necessary in order for you to reach the plants; they will not maintain themselves without your help.

At this point you can begin to think about the details. How about espaliered fruit trees along the left-hand border as well, a flower bed in the aforementioned arc, and an herb garden in front, near the house (for easy access)? Consider planting three large drifts of flowers, to add grace and dimension, proportion and balance. Where do they look best in the plan?

You now have straight-lined espaliered fruit trees, curves of shrubs, arcs of flowers, and an herb garden. Study your plan. Do you like it? If not, what about it don't you like? Rearrange the elements, perhaps discarding some and adding new ones. Always keep in mind the concave and convex arcs because they can make a garden especially handsome. If you want to include a lawn or other ground cover, by all means do, but remember that it will require regular maintenance.

BEDS AND BORDERS

An English-style flower border is an excellent way to define the boundaries of your garden site and to soften any severe angles. In an informal garden, vegetables and herbs may be mixed in with the flowers, with each enhancing the others. Keep in mind the following seven rules:

1. Place tall plants in the back, short plants in the front.
2. Do not use too many different colors.
3. Mix plants—mounds, verticals, creepers—to create variety and avoid monotony.
4. Select one or two types of plants, and use large masses of them to unify the landscape.
5. Select plants with the same soil and water requirements.
6. Construct paths so that you can easily reach your plants.
7. Have a flower bed in more than one area. One flower bed looks like an afterthought; two look better; and three look natural.

Don't forget to design your vegetable beds. Grow anything you want, but remember to put the tall plants in the back and the short ones in the front. Either annuals or herbs make a good front border.

Beds of plants do not have as dramatic an effect in smaller gardens as they do in larger ones, but they still are a necessary part of any garden. If you decide on a rectangular or square bed, place it some distance from the house, perhaps in the back of the garden separated by paths. When placed too close to the house, a bed of plants looks cramped. Also make the bed a manageable size—a bed ten feet by ten feet will be impossible to care for. Provide access to the plants from all sides, for maximum use.

Beds may contain the same plants as the borders do: tall-growing accents,

SUMMER/EARLY FALL GARDEN

1. Evergreen
2. Shrubs
3. Tree
4. Perennials/annuals
5. Rose
6. Deciduous tree
7. Ground cover
8. Bulbs
9. Ferns
10. Lawn
11. Hedge
12. Vine

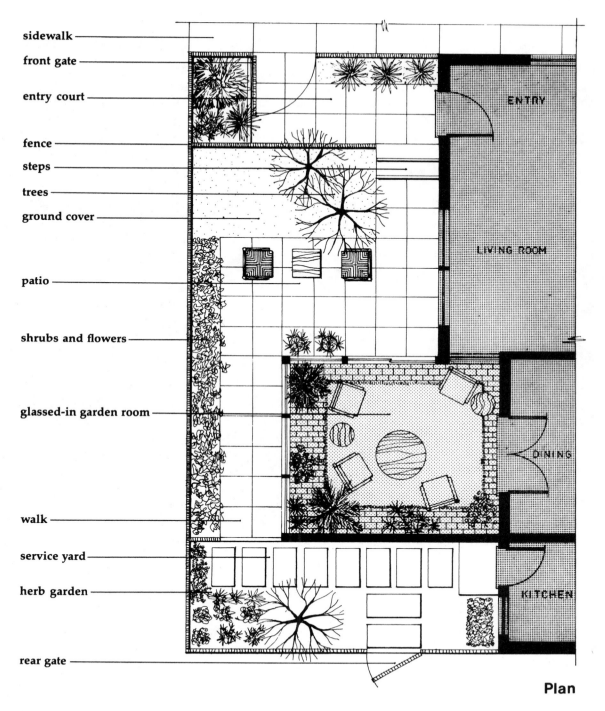

sidewalk

front gate

entry court

fence

steps

trees

ground cover

patio

shrubs and flowers

glassed-in garden room

walk

service yard

herb garden

rear gate

ENTRY

LIVING ROOM

DINING

KITCHEN

Plan

SIDE YARD

ADRIÁN MARTÍNEZ

Flowers and evergreens are mixed together in this unusual patio garden.

vegetables, herbs, and so on. Place the smallest plants around the perimeter of the beds, with the largest and/or tallest plants in the center. Raised or terraced plant beds bordered by brick, for example, offer additional definition and eye appeal. Raised beds also are a boon for gardeners who have trouble bending over for long periods of time.

NARROW BACKYARD

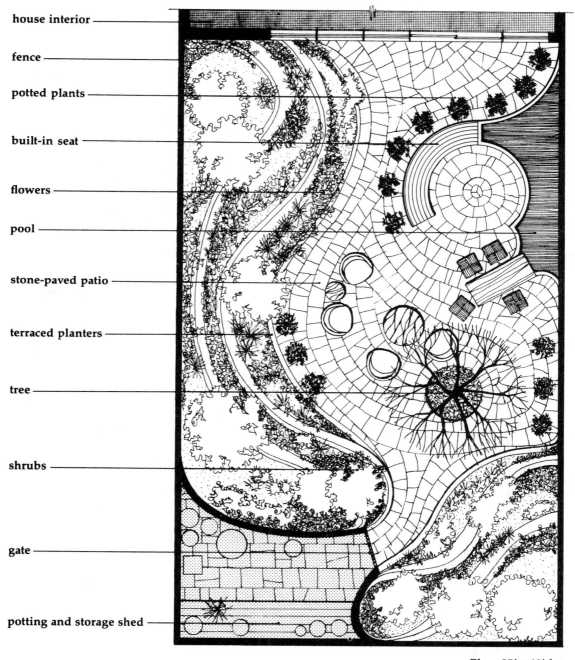

house interior

fence

potted plants

built-in seat

flowers

pool

stone-paved patio

terraced planters

tree

shrubs

gate

potting and storage shed

ADRIÁN MARTÍNEZ

Plan: 25' × 40' lot

FORMAL GARDEN

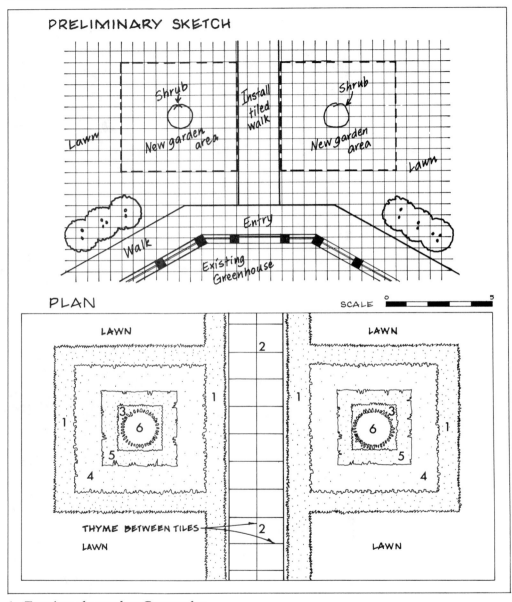

PRELIMINARY SKETCH

Shrub

Shrub

Lawn

New garden area

Install tiled walk

New garden area

Lawn

Entry

Walk

Existing Greenhouse

PLAN

SCALE 0   5

LAWN

LAWN

2

1

1

1

1

3

3

6

6

5

5

4

4

THYME BETWEEN TILES

2

LAWN

LAWN

1. *Teucrium chamsedrys* Germander
2. *Thymus serpyllum* Woolly thyme
3. *Anthemis nobilis* Roman chamomile
4. Artemisia schmidtiana Satiny wormwood
5. Caladium 'White Christmas'
6. Rosa 'Pascoli'

FORMAL GARDEN

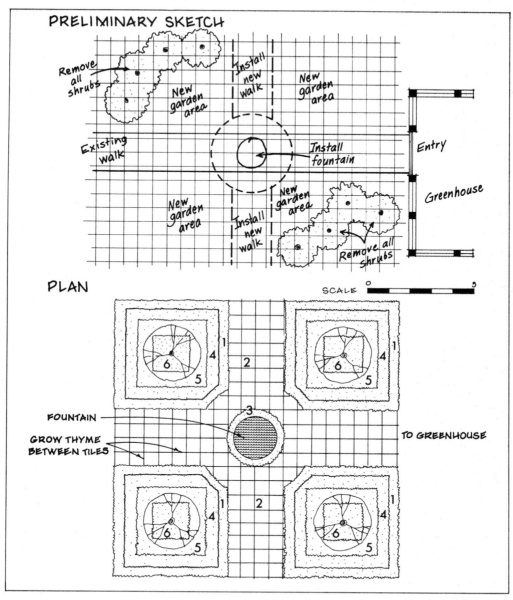

PRELIMINARY SKETCH

Remove all shrubs

Install new walk

New garden area

New garden area

Existing walk

Install fountain

Entry

Greenhouse

New garden area

Install new walk

New garden area

Remove all shrubs

PLAN

SCALE 0 5

FOUNTAIN

GROW THYME BETWEEN TILES

TO GREENHOUSE

1. *Tecurium chamaedrys* Germander
2. *Thymus serpyllum* Woolly thyme
3. *Anthemis nobilis* Roman chamomile
4. *Artemisia schmidtiana* Satiny wormwood
5. Caladium 'White Christmas'
6. Rosa 'Pascoli'

DRIFTS AND ARCS

A drift or arc lends a note of grace to a garden. A drift is an amoeboid- or kidney-shaped area; an arc is a concave shape.

In an arc arrangement, the shortest plants are placed around the perimeter, and the tallest plants are put in the center. The average arc is about fifteen feet long and two feet wide at the ends, broadening to about six feet wide in the middle. An arc can be used almost anywhere in a companion garden, but it is most effective in front of shrubs or tall-growing vegetables (perhaps those on trellises). Arcs look best when situated on the left or the right of the garden; if they are directly in the front of the view from the house, they may lose their gracefulness.

This garden offsets drifts and arcs of plants with brick pavement.

SOIL

Soil has two layers: topsoil and subsoil. The subsoil is the older of the two, having been in place for decades. The topsoil consists of disintegrated rock, stone particles with decomposing organic materials such as bacteria, fungi, and water. The topsoil contains dissolved minerals, salts, and air. Because most soils eventually lose their mineral content, they must constantly be revitalized. Thus if your soil is clayey or sandy, you must add loam (topsoil) to it. If you can afford to do so, you should mix into the old soil several pounds of fresh topsoil containing all the necessary microorganisms. The addition of new topsoil almost guarantees healthy plants.

To determine the condition of your soil, dig down about sixteen inches and bring up a shovelful of soil. Run your hand through it; it should be porous (contain holes) and feel mealy. If the soil is heavy and chunky (clayey), it needs to be aerated, and microorganisms should be added. If the soil is sandy (slips easily through your fingers), it needs topsoil.

Clayey soil is heavy and difficult to work with and warms up slowly in the spring when plants are eager to grow. Such soil also forms a crust, thereby

A terraced garden provides both dimension and interest.

preventing air and water from reaching the plants' roots. At the other extreme, sandy soil drains too quickly, and because it cannot hold moisture, plant nutrients are immediately lost through leaching.

SOIL ADDITIVES

Humus. Humus is animal manure, leaf mold, or any decayed organic matter. It adds nutrients to the soil and nourishes the living organisms that the soil houses. Humus also lightens clayey soil, enabling it to drain more easily, and it improves the physical structure of sandy soil, enabling it to retain moisture more easily. Humus is continuously being depleted, and so it must continuously be replaced. How much humus to add to soil depends on the condition of the soil and on the plants being grown in it. I generally add about one inch of humus to six inches of garden soil.

Compost. Compost is decayed vegetable matter such as leftover and scraps of food, grass clippings, leaves, and twigs. You can maintain your own compost heap in a homemade bin or a commercially made metal bin. Start the compost heap with accumulated twigs, leaves, grass clippings, and other garden debris. Periodically add food scraps. When the compost pile has grown a bit, add some manure and a sprinkling of lime. Keep it moist but never saturated. After a few months, turn the pile, bringing the sides to the top.

FERTILIZERS

To grow and thrive, plants need nitrogen (N), phosphorus (P), potassium (K), and, in smaller amounts, iron, boron, manganese, zinc, and other trace elements.

Nurseries sell inorganic fertilizers, in powdered, pellet, tablet, or liquid form. Sprinkle powdered or pellet fertilizers around the plants and then water them thoroughly. Dissolve fertilizer tablets in water and then pour the solution on the soil around the plants. Mix liquid fertilizer with water before spraying on the plants (you will need spraying equipment for this).

The first number on the bottle or bag of fertilizer indicates the percentage of nitrogen that the fertilizer contains; the second number, the percentage of phosphorus; and the third number, the percentage of potassium. This is the fertilizer's NPK ratio.

Organic fertilizers are made from the remains or by-products of once-living organisms. Examples are bone meal, manure, and cottonseed meal; urea is a synthetic organic fertilizer. Packages of organic fertilizers also list their NPK ratio, although most such fertilizers are dominant in just one of these elements.

WATER ABSORPTION CHART

depth	coarse sand	sandy loam	clay with loam
0			
6″			
12″	15 minutes	30 minutes	60 minutes
18″			
24″		60 minutes	
30″	40 minutes		
36″			
42″			
48″	60 minutes		

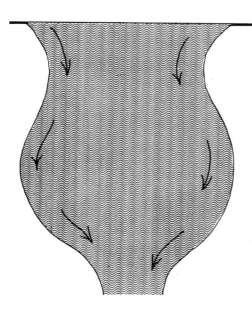

water moves laterally, not fanning out to any degree

SOILS

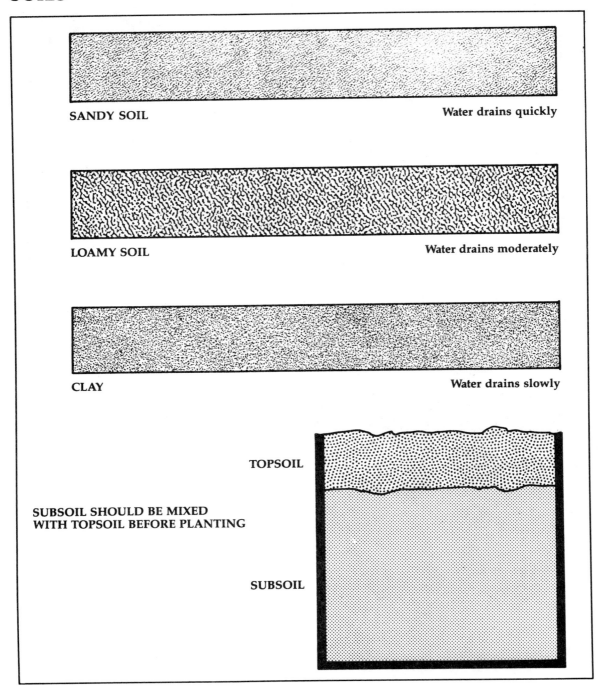

SANDY SOIL — Water drains quickly

LOAMY SOIL — Water drains moderately

CLAY — Water drains slowly

TOPSOIL

SUBSOIL SHOULD BE MIXED
WITH TOPSOIL BEFORE PLANTING

SUBSOIL

Whatever fertilizer you choose, feed your plants with the following guidelines in mind:

1. A weak solution or application of fertilizer is more effective than a strong one is, which may burn the plant.
2. Allow newly planted or transplanted plants to adjust to their new surroundings before fertilizing them.
3. Never feed sick plants; it won't make them well, it will only push them over the edge.
4. As the weather warms up in the spring, feed your plants more often.
5. Likewise, as the weather becomes colder in the fall, feed your plants less often.

For all plants but lawns, use a commercial 10-10-5 plant food, supplemented occasionally with cottonseed meal and manure. Add humus to the soil at least once a year, but do not use so-called soil conditioners. Although they do improve the soil's physical structure, they do not increase its nutrient content.

MULCHES

Mulches are made of either organic (leaves, hay or straw, grass clippings, ground fir bark, or sawdust) or inorganic (stones and gravel or shredded newspapers) materials. Organic mulches are absorbed into the surrounding soil, thereby improving it.

"Mulching" a plant—that is, spreading a mulch around its base—decreases the amount of moisture lost from the surface of the soil through evaporation. Mulches also protect the soil from the sun, thus keeping it cooler; indeed, they help protect the soil from any extreme swings from very hot to very cold weather. Mulches even help smother weeds, thereby showing themselves to be very useful additions to the garden.

Spread a two- to four-inch layer of mulch around your plants in the spring when the soil has warmed up and the plants have resumed growing. And in the fall, apply mulch after the soil has frozen.

Leaves make an especially good mulch because they are full of humus. Be sure that the leaves are chopped so that they form a porous layer rather than an impenetrable coat around the plants. *Cocoa beans* and *pecan shells* deteriorate slowly and are fairly heavy and easy to use. *Fir bark* is a favorite because it looks attractive, decomposes slowly, and adds nutrients to the soil. *Sawdust* sometimes forms a tight layer and prevents water from penetrating the soil, so mix it with some small pebbles. Acceptable inorganic mulches include

This is the persistent dock weed. (Photo courtesy USDA)

shredded newspapers, aluminum foil, polyethylene film, and plastic sheeting. But because they are not absorbed into the soil and add nothing to it, they are less desirable than organic mulches.

WATERING

Watering with a hose takes an average of one hour for the water to penetrate the soil to a depth of two feet (see table). Because the roots of most plants—especially trees and shrubs—extend much deeper into the soil than two feet and because the roots must receive water in order to grow, you would have to keep the hose running almost all day for the water to reach the roots.

MINUTES FOR WATER TO PENETRATE SOIL

SOIL DEPTH (INCHES)	COARSE SAND	SANDY LOAM	CLAYEY LOAM
12	15	30	60
24		60	
30	40		
48	60		

Planters can be arranged in all sorts of ways to accommodate all sorts of plants, and at waist level, watering is made somewhat easier.

SPRINKLERS

Unless you have several of them, you must constantly move around portable sprinklers because they generally deliver water only within a seven- to nine-foot radius. Permanent (buried) sprinklers deliver water to everything, even if it does not need it. If you have automatic sprinklers, it is best to set them to go on at night so that the least amount of water will evaporate before soaking in. In addition, the water pressure in the sprinkler is apt to fluctuate, thus watering the area unevenly and perhaps differently each time they go on.

DRIP IRRIGATION SYSTEMS

Drip irrigation is the frequent, slow application of water only to plants' roots. It is the system of watering that conserves the most water. Some drip systems also include misting and sprinkling devices that concentrate the water in a small area on and around the plants the system serves.

The basic drip system is a network of flexible plastic pipes of graduated

COMPONENT PARTS OF A DRIP SYSTEM

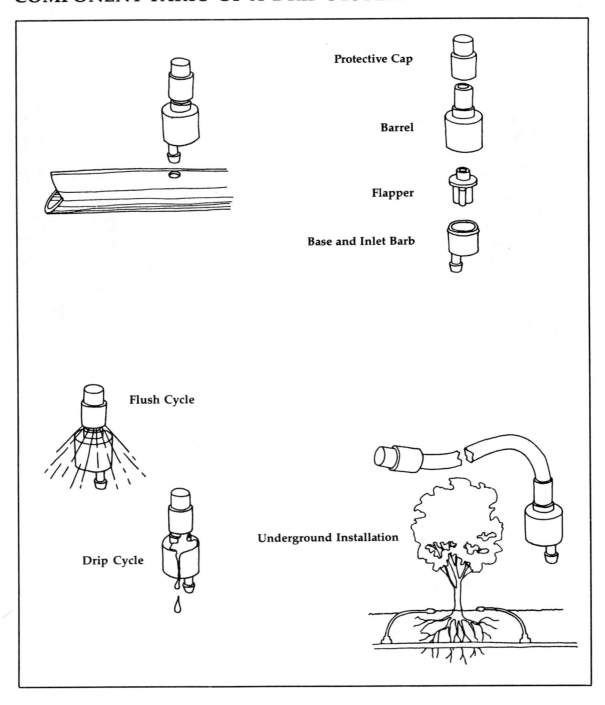

Protective Cap

Barrel

Flapper

Base and Inlet Barb

Flush Cycle

Drip Cycle

Underground Installation

TYPES OF DRIP SYSTEMS

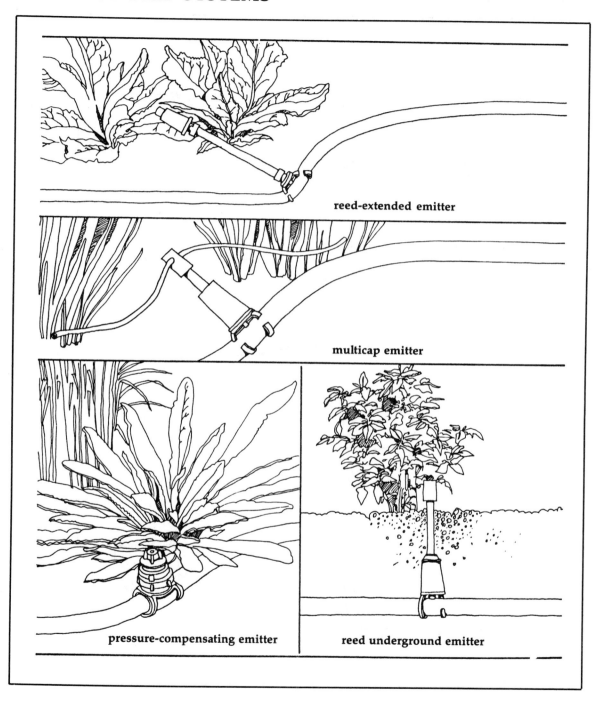

reed-extended emitter

multicap emitter

pressure-compensating emitter

reed underground emitter

TYPES OF EMITTERS

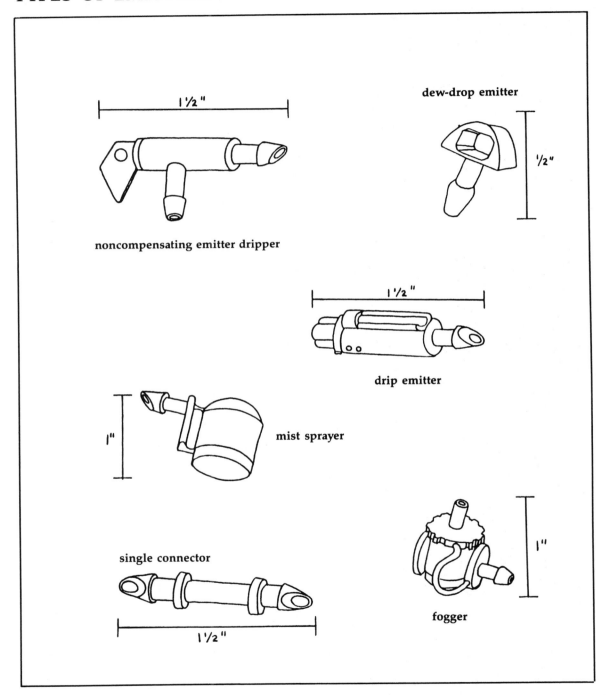

dew-drop emitter

1½"

½"

noncompensating emitter dripper

1½"

drip emitter

1"

mist sprayer

single connector

1"

1½"

fogger

WATER EMITTERS

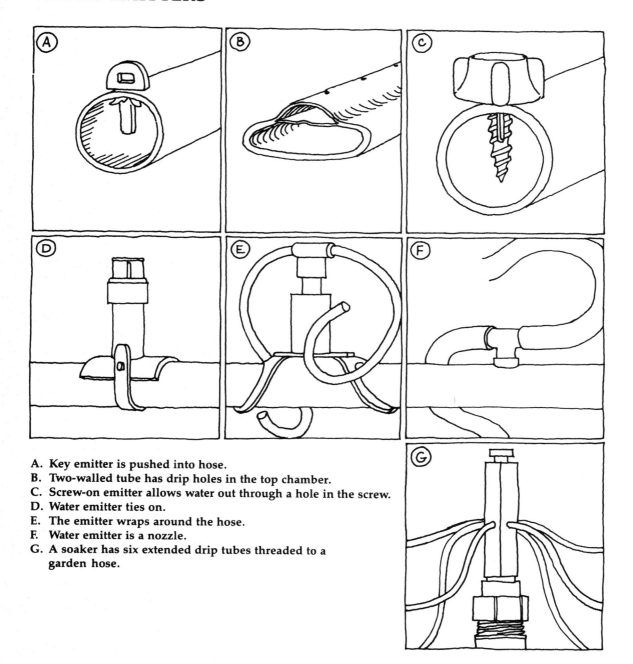

A. Key emitter is pushed into hose.
B. Two-walled tube has drip holes in the top chamber.
C. Screw-on emitter allows water out through a hole in the screw.
D. Water emitter ties on.
E. The emitter wraps around the hose.
F. Water emitter is a nozzle.
G. A soaker has six extended drip tubes threaded to a garden hose.

sizes. The main pipe (usually one-half inch in diameter) brings the water to the site; from this pipe extends a series of smaller lateral pipes (usually one-fourth to three-eighths inch in diameter). These lateral pipes are placed parallel to the plants on or just below the ground, and the water is discharged from them through emitters (holes). The emitters allow a slow trickle of water to moisten the immediately surrounding root zone.

The main concern when using a drip system is overloading it; that is, putting too many emitters in it. If the system has too many emitters, the regulated, steady flow of water will be interrupted. Although the system will still work, it will not work efficiently.

Another concern is that the water must be filtered so that any particulates it may contain will not clog the emitters. Most drip systems include filters, as well as pressure regulators or valves to control the flow of water. Drip systems come in either manual or automatic models and in a range of prices.

Planning the System. The best way to plan a drip system is first to sketch it on graph paper. Draw the garden to scale in feet and inches, and then sketch in the shrubs, trees, and various beds. You can drip water to almost any plant, even grass, although a soaker drip system is generally used for lawns rather than the conventional drip system with emitters.

On your sketch, draw in the various systems as they would apply: a row pattern in one area, perhaps (vegetables and flowers), and a point or grid pattern in another. The layout will depend on how many plants you have in your garden and the distances between them.

When determining how much water each group of plants will need, what is important is the *wet zone*, the area around the roots of the plant. The size and shape of the wet zone vary according to (1) the type of soil, (2) the rate at which the plant absorbs water from the soil in relation to the number of emitters used, and (3) the rate at which the emitters discharge water. Gravity pulls the water downward, and capillary action spreads it out in all directions. In fine soil, capillary forces are stronger than gravitational forces, and so the wet zone has a circular shape, whereas in coarse soil, the reverse is true, and the wet zone has an elliptical shape. The water should be applied slowly so that it will be absorbed and not run off. This can be avoided by shutting off the water and then turning it on later. The time interval here may be anywhere from one to sixteen hours; if it should be any longer than that, the number of emitters should be increased instead.

Drip systems come with guidelines as to how much water various groups of plants require, but these can only be very general. The actual amounts you will need depend on your particular climate, soil, and so forth.

Drip System Equipment. The main feature of a drip system is its monitoring device, that is, an emitter, that is situated close to the plant(s) to be irrigated. Some emitters are small mechanisms plugged directly into rigid or flexible tubing; others are one-eighth-inch tubing inserted into adapters on the main line. The emitter emits a very small amount of water (usually one to two gallons per hour) to the plant. The emitter regulates the water flow into the soil by decreasing the pressure from the inside to the outside of the lateral line, thus enabling the water to emerge as drops.

The water used for drip irrigation must be even cleaner than drinking water, and so it must be kept free of sediment, soil, and mineral deposits. Various types of sand filters, cartridge filters, and 100- to 200-mesh screens are used, separately or in combination. These filters and screens then must be cleaned periodically by hand or by a built-in back-flushing device.

Piston- and power-run injectors are used to introduce (liquid) fertilizers and such into the lines. The injectors are attached to the main line.

Automatic watering devices turn off the system when it is raining and turn it on when soil moisture falls below a certain point.

BUILDING A VERTICAL GARDEN

If you are short of space or just like the idea of planting up instead of out, consider building a vertical garden. Such a garden enables you to grow flowers, fruit, and vegetables—almost a complete garden—in a space as small as ten feet square. The trellises that make possible such a garden will become a permanent part of it, so you should plan them carefully. And you will have to, anyway, as you will probably end up constructing them yourself; few sturdy trellises are available ready-made.

CONSTRUCTING A TRELLIS

Build your trellis with laths, strips about three-eighths inch thick and one and five-eighths inches wide. They are sold in lengths of six, eight, and ten feet, in bundles of fifty. There are two grades of laths; one has knots and blemishes, and the other is surface lath, which is almost free of imperfections. The latter is what you should use for your trellis. Laths can also be made from one-by-one-inch or two-by-two-inch wood cut to size. These strips are heavier, more expensive, but also better looking. Redwood or cedar is the best wood to use, but if you decide to use the less expensive pine, apply a protective coating to shield it from rain and snow.

Now, to build your trellis, follow these rules:

1. Use one-by-two, two-by-two, and two-by-four laths.
2. Tape together bundles of the two-by-two laths, ten to a bundle, with the ends flush.

3. Across all the pieces draw parallel lines one inch apart.
4. For two-inch strips, put a strip of masking tape lengthwise on your saw, one inch above the cutting edge of the blade. Saw down to the tape, just inside the line.
5. With a small hammer, hit the wood between the saw cuts to knock out the chunk of wood, leaving a socket or groove.
6. Insert the one-by-one laths into the grooves; they should fit flush.
7. Nail the laths into the grooves.
8. When you make the lattice (usually a grid pattern, but it may be something more elaborate), be sure that the strips are evenly spaced, both for a pleasing pattern and to give the plants room to grasp the wood. Generally, for laths one-half inch to one-inch thick, you should allow three-fourths of an inch between the strips; for those two inches thick, allow one to two inches of space.
9. Construct the frame with the two-by-fours.

A vertical garden is the answer to a very small space.

FORMAL ESPALIERS

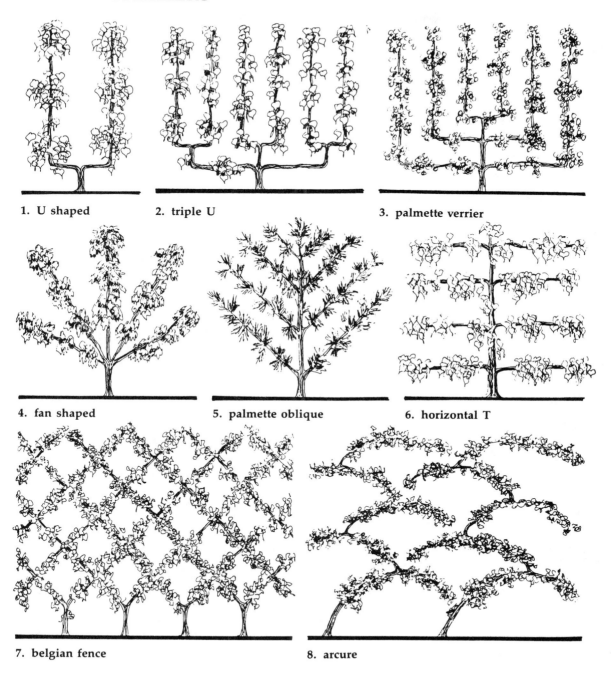

1. U shaped

2. triple U

3. palmette verrier

4. fan shaped

5. palmette oblique

6. horizontal T

7. belgian fence

8. arcure

ADRIÁN MARTÍNEZ

INFORMAL ESPALIERS

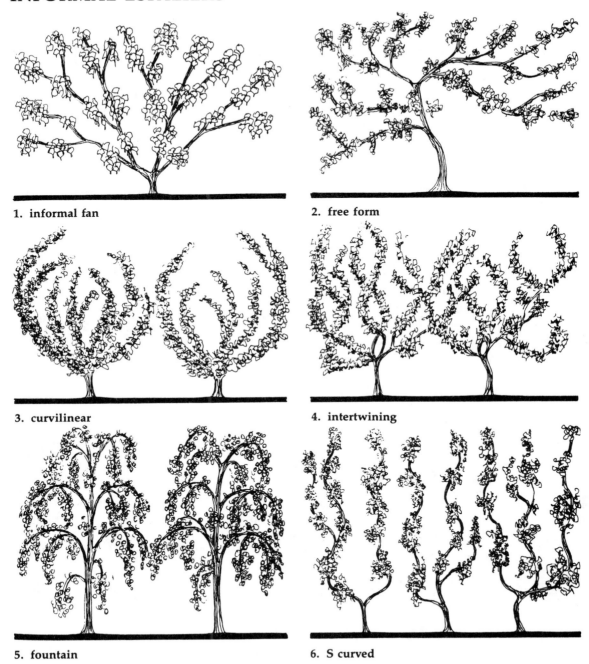

1. informal fan

2. free form

3. curvilinear

4. intertwining

5. fountain

6. S curved

ADRIÁN MARTÍNEZ

PATIO TRELLIS

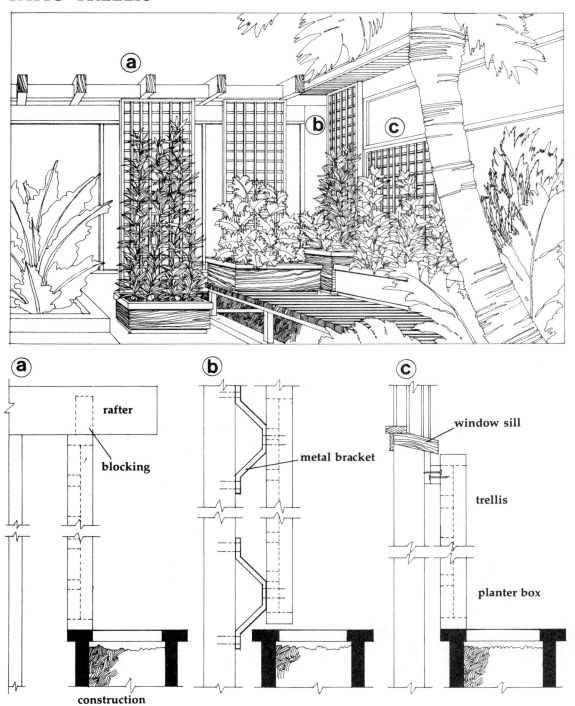

(a)

rafter

blocking

(b)

metal bracket

(c)

window sill

trellis

planter box

construction

ASSEMBLING A CONTAINER GARDEN

A container garden is especially good for flowers and vegetables. It also is fast gardening, as you can get plants started quickly in containers, and if the soil in your area is bad, you can easily correct that. Finally, you can rearrange your garden more or less at will (using a dolly if the containers are big).

A trellis used as a fence.

SOILS FOR CONTAINERS

The soils best for plants in containers are as follows:

General
2 parts garden loam
1 part sand
1 part leaf mold
1 teaspoon bone meal for an eight-inch pot

Begonias and ferns
2 parts garden loam
2 parts sand
2 parts leaf mold

Bulbs
2 parts garden loam
1 part sand
1 part leaf mold

If wooden containers are raised on slats, insects cannot crawl into the soil from underneath.

Cacti and succulents
2 parts garden loam
2 parts sand
1 part leaf mold
handful of limestone for an eight-inch pot

Bromeliads and orchids
medium-grade fir bark

Potting. Place drainage material (broken pot pieces, stones) in the bottom of the container to enable any excess water to run off. Spread a layer of soil over this material—about three inches for a container sixteen inches in diameter. Gently remove the plant from its original container, and center it in the pot. Fill in the container with soil, pressing it down with your fingers

Two wooden containers hold flowers on this porch.

PLANTER BOXES

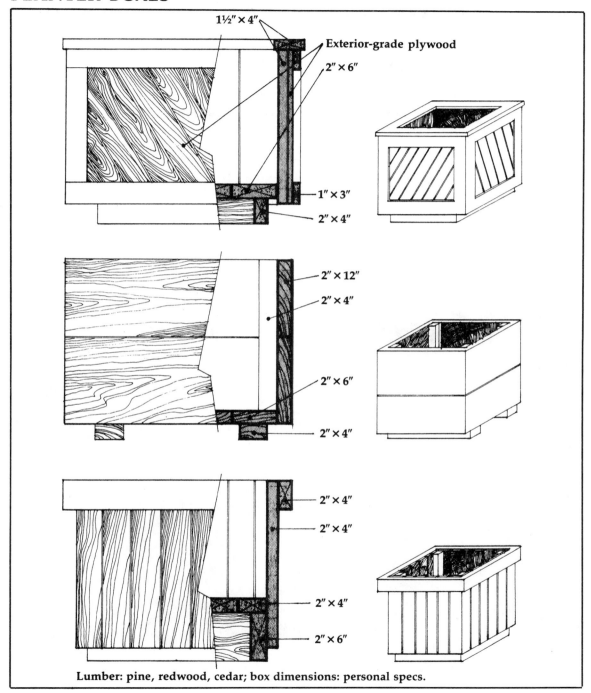

1½" × 4"

Exterior-grade plywood

2" × 6"

1" × 3"

2" × 4"

2" × 12"

2" × 4"

2" × 6"

2" × 4"

2" × 4"

2" × 4"

2" × 6"

2" × 4"

Lumber: pine, redwood, cedar; box dimensions: personal specs.

to eliminate any air pockets. Do not press it down too hard (you will smother or damage the plant), but make sure the soil is firmly in place. Fill the container to one inch from the rim. Water the plant thoroughly, place in a partially shaded area for a few days where it can get used to its new home, and then move it to its assigned area.

Be sure that the container is the right size for the plant. If the container is too large, the unused portions of the soil are apt to become waterlogged, thus harming the plant. If the container is too small, the plant will not have enough soil and space to grow.

Watering. Plants in containers generally dry out more quickly than do plants in the ground, depending, of course, on the particular pot and where it is situated. Large containers dry out faster than do small ones. Plants in glazed pots without drainage holes should be watched carefully and watered only when needed.

When you do water, soak the plant until water pours out of the drainage

These unusual wooden containers decorate the top of a garage with flowers.

hole. Then let it become somewhat dry before watering again. You often can kill plants more easily with too much water than with not enough. Occasionally hose down, or spray, the foliage to flush out any insects hiding in it and to remove dust from the leaves.

Feeding. Feed plants in containers with a 10-10-15 NPK fertilizer mixed weaker than directed but used more often. In general, during the summer, plants in large containers (eighteen to thirty-six inches in diameter) should be fed about four times, and those in smaller pots should be fed about once a month. Do not feed plants at all during the winter, but do give them a light meal once in the fall and early spring. Remember not to feed sick or newly potted plants.

PLANTS TO GROW IN CONTAINERS

Any kind of plant can be grown in a container. Small trees are good for a patio. A four-foot tree is the minimum size for a twenty-four-inch pot. Square or rectangular boxes are attractive for trees with bold foliage, whereas a round pot is best for trees with delicate leaves.

Decide whether you want a fast-growing or a slow-growing tree. And if the climate you live in is not mild year-round, be sure you have a place to put the tree in the winter. Some trees can be placed in a sunny window, others in an unheated but not freezing garage or porch, and still others in a basement with a little light. If your area has severe winters and you have no indoor space for the plant, select a hardy tree or shrub that can survive the winter outside. Ask your local nursery for advice.

3

KEEPING PLANTS HEALTHY AND BEAUTIFUL

Most people brighten when you mention the word *garden*, but they shudder at the word *gardening*. Yet keeping plants healthy and protecting them against invaders is not as arduous as it may seem. First, we now know how to combat pests and discourage weeds without drowning them in toxic chemicals. Second, the satisfaction you will receive from growing your own flowers, vegetables, fruit, or whatever should far outweigh any qualms you may have. Besides, gardening is good exercise!

PROTECTING YOUR PLANTS

Once you have spent time, effort, and expense to create a garden, you naturally will want to protect it from invaders and disease. Usually, the chance of your plants coming down with a disease is minimized if you regularly feed and water them. But no matter how much care you lavish on your plants, sometimes it only seems to encourage the pests.

The common dandelion weed.
(Photo courtesy USDA)

Aphids on gladioli. Their
nature enemies are lacewings
and ladybugs. (Photo
courtesy USDA)

INSECTS

To minimize the damage from insects, try to head them off at the pass; that is, try to discourage their choosing your garden in the first place, or at least make life unpleasant for them if they have decided to come anyway. Be vigilant—when you first see signs of, or the insects themselves, prepare for battle. Do avoid using harmful chemicals, as they also will kill the helpful insects—ladybugs, butterflies, and the like—and they may very well shorten your life too.

Aphids attack almost all types of plants, stunting their growth and deforming their leaves. Aphids come in several colors. *Beetles* love flowers and vegetables. *Borers* attack woody plants, wilting them and eating holes in their stems and branches. *Caterpillars* and *worms* eat all sorts of leaves, as do *grasshoppers*.

Spindly growth indicates pests at work.

COMMON LAWN WEEDS

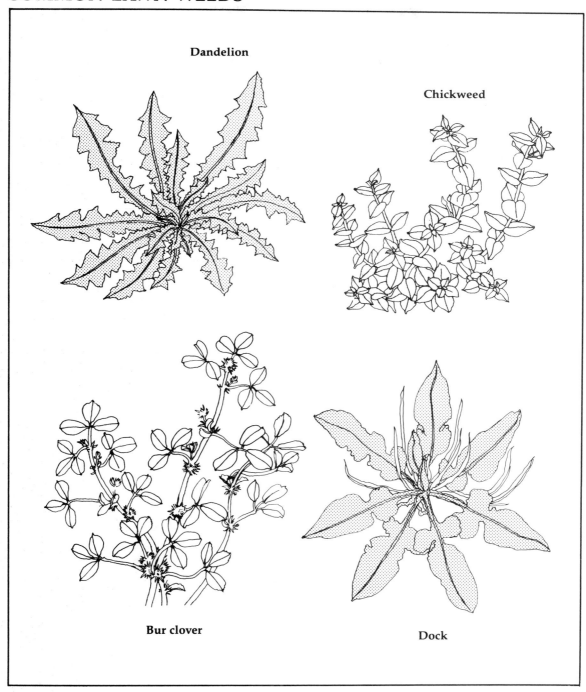

Dandelion

Chickweed

Bur clover

Dock

HELPFUL GARDEN INSECTS

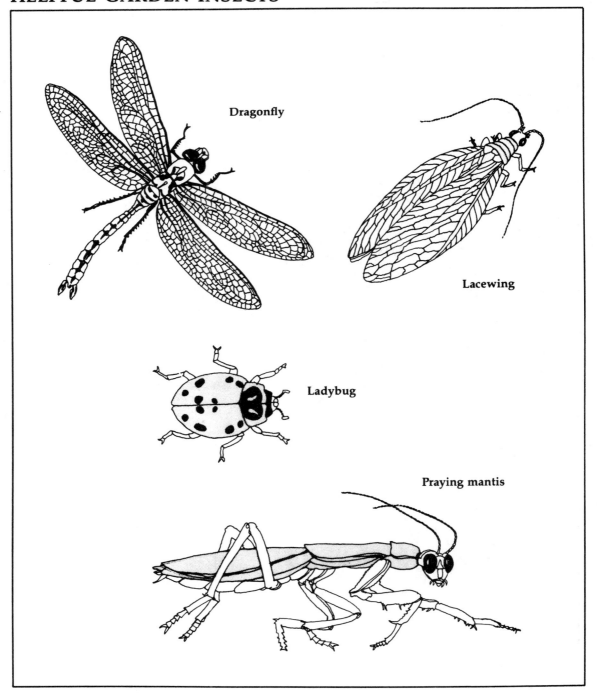

Dragonfly

Lacewing

Ladybug

Praying mantis

Leafhoppers are wedge shaped and stunt plant growth, leading to pale or brown leaves. *Leaf miners* make leaves spotted and blotched, and *leaf rollers* cause the leaves of deciduous plants to roll up. *Mealybugs* look like tiny cotton swabs; they stunt the growth of many kinds of plants. *Mites* suck on plants, causing their leaves to become discolored.

Nematodes are tiny worms that stunt the growth of many plants. *Scale* causes plants' leaves to turn yellow and drop off. *Snails* and *slugs* leave slimey trails and feast on leaves of all sorts.

Spittle bugs are variously colored and are wrapped in froth. They attack both plants and fruit. *Springtails* pit leaves, and *squash bugs* turn plants black and kill them. *Thrips* are winged and turn plants silvery, and *wireworms* work underground, killing flower and vegetable seedlings.

BOTANICAL INSECTICIDES

Botanical insecticides are safe for both you and your plants. They now are sold in spray form; just check to make sure that they have not been combined with toxic chemicals.

Pyrethrum is derived from a species of chrysanthemum whose flowers are toxic to insects (but not to people). Pyrethrum kills, on contact, aphids, whiteflies, leafhoppers, and thrips.

Rotenone comes from the derris root, which is ground into a powder that wards off spittle bugs, aphids, spider mites, chinch bugs, harlequin bugs, pea weevils, and even houseflies.

A dust or spray made from the roots and stems of *ryania*, although not lethal, incapacitates (perhaps paralyzes) many insects, such as squash bugs, Japanese beetles, and elm leaf beetles.

Finally, there is nicotine, which is derived from the tobacco plant. It is poisonous to mammals (as you know); it is also toxic to insects. Because it is harmful to the environment as a whole it should not be used. (You can however, substitute cigarette tobacco as an insect repellant. Steep the tobacco from one unused cigarette in a half-cup of water for a half-day and apply directly on insects with a cotton swab. This solution is effective against aphids, whiteflies, leafhoppers, and various other insects.)

OIL SPRAYS

When used properly, nontoxic oil-and-water sprays are effective against chewing and sucking insects such as aphids, mealybugs, scale, and red spiders. Oil sprays are used on orchard trees before the buds open, and some gardeners use them on shrubs and other plants as well. Such sprays form a film over insect eggs spending the winter in the trees, thereby

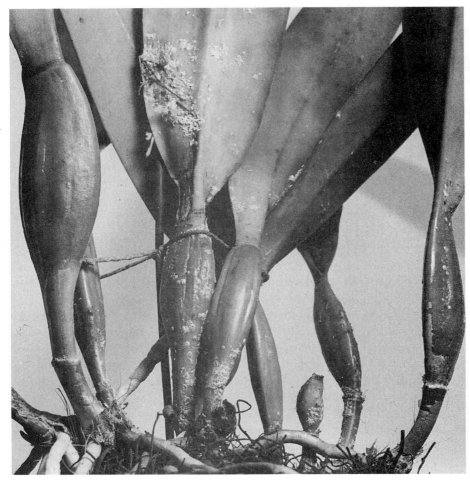

Scale has made deep inroads into this plant. Small skirmishes can be fought back, but heavy attacks such as this are difficult to repel, requiring artillery and good strategy. Observe plants daily, or nearly daily, for signs of insects, and take action immediately if you see any.

suffocating them. Obviously, these sprays should be used only on leafless trees.

Commercial oil sprays are sold at garden stores, but you can also make your own. Mix together one gallon of light-grade oil, one-half gallon of water, and one pound of fish-oil soap as an emulsifier. Boil the mixture, stirring until well blended. For the spray, use one part of this to about twenty parts of water. Because oil emulsions tend to separate after a while, use the spray as soon as possible.

If you use these amounts, oil sprays will not harm plants or soil, and although some insects develop a resistance to certain insecticides, they cannot to oil sprays. Remember, however, that oil sprays kill the good insects as well as the bad ones, and so use them sparingly.

INSECT TRAPS

Traps also catch both good and bad insects. With this in mind, however, you can construct a simple trap just by putting a board on the ground. Squash bugs, snails, and wireworms will crawl under it to hide; when you pick it up, you can easily destroy them. Trenches and ditches will stop the migrations of some insects, and earwigs will crawl onto paper or moss. Wireworms and snails are attracted to (cut) raw potatoes. Pickle jars filled with molasses and water have become the last resting place for many insects. Pine tar and molasses on a cardboard-band trap, or roofing tar or cement on a rope, entice crawling insects.

Mealybugs attacking grape ivy.

More sophisticated traps have lights, a small motor, and a fan that draw the insects down into a removable bag. The light may be white, blue, or yellow, depending on the kind(s) of insects it is meant to attract.

Black light, which is invisible to humans but inviting to insects, is also used in some traps. Some black-light traps suck in the insects; others use a wire grid that electrocutes them and they then fall into a tray. These traps are expensive. Some are portable; others must be permanently installed; and some have automatic timers to activate them at dusk.

Vacuum-net traps work like a portable vacuum cleaner, sucking insects off plants and depositing them in bags. But you must be the one to operate it; it will not move around unaccompanied.

STERILIZATION

Sterilization in this context refers to the method of sterilizing male insects and then releasing them en masse. The reasoning is that if the sterile males

Scale attacking plant.

outnumber the fertile ones, the latter will have less chance of reaching the females and thus will die without reproducing. Eventually, the females should lay so many infertile eggs that the insects will die out. Experiments with this method have so far been promising.

SEX ATTRACTANTS

According to the U.S. Department of Agriculture, sex attractants offer the greatest promise of controlling specific insects. These attractants may be insect lures, chemicals, or light—anything to draw specific (that is, not good ones) insects to their doom.

SOUND

Sound may be used to attract, to repel, or possibly to kill insects. Most insects react to sounds at frequencies too high for people to hear, and so, for example, a high-frequency sound could be emitted from a wire fence around a patio that would either repel insects or kill them.

MORE PRIMITIVE METHODS

Picking off insects by hand is a primitive means of control, but it is one of the best and safest. For example, I don't use snail bait because my dog thinks it is food. After one emergency visit to the veterinarian with him, I decided to pick up the snails instead, unpleasant though it is. Another remedy suggested by the U.S. Department of Agriculture is to put out small dishes or saucers of beer to attract the snails (making it easier to find and dispose of them). Sometimes this works, but not always; maybe they don't like the brand of beer I use. Just now I am trying a English snail bait (Snare-All™) that is not toxic to people or animals and seems to be effective.

Many insects and larvae can shaken off a small tree or shrub, after which you can stamp on them or dispatch them in any other way you see fit. But this method is hardly practical for anything more than a few bushes.

Aphids, red spiders, mealybugs, and scale can be discouraged by using soap (not detergent) and water. Use one-half pound of laundry soap to about two gallons of water. Spray this on the plants and then hose them off with clean water. It is not magic; it takes several applications to eliminate them, but it is worth the trouble because it is easy, cheap, and not poisonous.

Mealybugs can be eliminated by using rubbing alcohol on a cotton swab. Although it takes time and more than one application, it does work and is safe.

Here you can easily see the webs made by mealybugs.

SENDING IN THE CAVALRY

A more positive way to get rid of garden pests is to introduce hordes of hungry good insects (see the Appendix for sources). Ladybugs and ladybug larvae, green lacewings, and praying mantises are among the rescuers you can buy and release. Although they probably will not eliminate your garden pests, they will reduce the population, and even though there is no way to keep them in your yard, when they leave, you can be sure that they are helping your neighbors. This is definitely a beneficial, inexpensive, and effective way to combat undesirable insects. You can order them by mail. Be sure to follow the directions, as releasing them at the wrong time or in other than the prescribed ways can reduce their effectiveness.

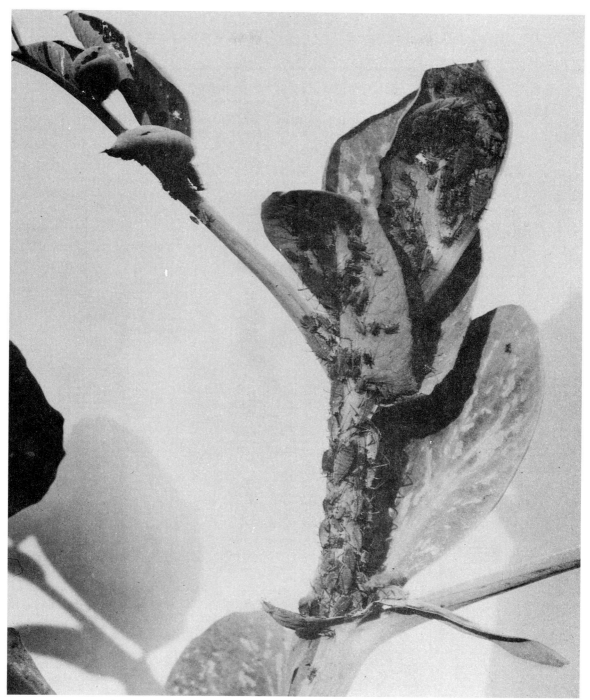

Close-up picture of aphid mites. (Photo courtesy USDA)

FLOWER INSECT AND DISEASE TABLE

ASTER

INSECT OR DISEASE	APPEARANCE OR SYMPTOMS	CONTROL
Blister beetle	Long legs, about one inch long, black or gray with yellow stripes. Eats leaves and flowers.	Handpick (wear gloves) or dust with lime and flour.
Tarnished plant bug	Tiny, oval, and brown mottled. Sucks juices from new shoots and buds.	Spends the winter in weeds and debris. Keep garden clean, and use botanical insecticides.
Aster wilt (disease)	Streaks on stems; plants wilt and die.	Do not grow plants in same soil every year, as diseased organisms can live in same soil for years.
Damping off (disease)	Affects plants in seedling stage; stems collapse and rot off at soil surface.	Eliminate excessive moisture; water lightly in the morning so plants can absorb water before nighttime.

CHRYSANTHEMUM

INSECT OR DISEASE	APPEARANCE OR SYMPTOMS	CONTROL
Borer	Worm. Wilted stems that topple.	Use light traps to collect borer moths.
Caterpillar	Chewed foliage.	Introduce stinkbugs to eat caterpillars in immature stage. Or use ground hot pepper and water, or handpick.
Gail midge	Slender, two-winged fly; larva forms a cone-shaped gall. Adult is tiny gnat whose only host is chrysanthemum. Twisted stems and deformed buds.	Use only clean cuttings; remove and burn infected plants.
Leaf nematode	Very tiny worm. Eats leaves, resulting in yellow, wedge-shaped spots; leaves wither and fall.	Remove and burn infected plants; use lots of humus in soil.
Ground mealybug	Smaller than regular mealybug; lives off roots in soil.	Use healthy cuttings and plant in different locations. Dry out soil bed for a month.

INSECT OR DISEASE	APPEARANCE OR SYMPTOMS	CONTROL
Aster yellows (disease)	Carried to chrysanthemum by leafhoppers and aphids. Stunted growth.	Control aphids with ladybugs.
Chrysanthemum stunt (disease)	Small flowers; leaves pale green or reddish.	Disease is carried in planting stock; thus buy only from reputable dealers.
Petal blight (disease)	Deformed flowers.	Allow adequate ventilation in flower bed, and dry out growing area.

DAHLIA

INSECT OR DISEASE	APPEARANCE OR SYMPTOMS	CONTROL
Borer	Worm. Wilted stems that topple.	Use light traps to collect borer moths.
Leafhopper	Small, green-yellow, wedge shaped; eats leaves.	Use pyrethrum, quassia, or ladybugs.
Tarnish plant bug	Tiny, oval, brown mottled; sucks juices from new shoots and buds.	Spends the winter in weeds and debris. Keep garden clean.
Black cucumber beetle	Eats leaves.	Spray with mixture of ground hot pepper and water.
Bacterial wilt (disease)	Sudden wilting and death of plant.	Bacteria lives in soil. Change soil and planting site yearly.
Powdery mildew (disease)	White powdery spots on leaves, caused by excessive moisture.	Provide ample ventilation.

DELPHINIUM

INSECT OR DISEASE	APPEARANCE OR SYMPTOMS	CONTROL
Stalk borer	Grayish brown larva with white stripes. Wilted, fallen stalks.	Keep old stalks and weeds out of growing area. Use light traps later in year to collect borer moths.
Cyclamen mite	White, microscopic insect. Distorted leaves and blackened leaves.	Mites travel fast from plant to plant. Keep plants well spaced to avoid infestation. Use rotenone if necessary.

INSECT OR DISEASE	APPEARANCE OR SYMPTOMS	CONTROL
Slugs and snails	Slugs are like snails without a shell. Both leave a slime trail and work at night, eating leaves and delphinium roots.	Use Snare-All™ or beer, or handpick.
Bacterial leaf spot (disease)	Black spots on leaves, stems, and buds.	Bacteria spend winter in soil on dead leaves and crowns of infected plants. Keep area clean of debris.
Crown and root rot (disease)	Discolored lower leaves; new shoots wilt.	Destroy infected plants.

GLADIOLUS

INSECT OR DISEASE	APPEARANCE OR SYMPTOMS	CONTROL
Borer	Worm. Wilted stems that topple.	Use light traps to collect borer moths.
Tarnished plant bug	Tiny, oval, brown mottled; sucks juices from new shoots and buds.	Spends winter in weeds and debris. Keep garden clean.
Gladioli thrip	Minute insect. Distorted flower bud.	Feeds on host plants, such as iris, lily, calendula, aster, and delphinium. Plant corms early in fall.
Dry rot (disease)	Small circles of decay on corm.	Inspect corms and destroy infected ones.
Hard rot (disease)	Rust spots on leaves; pinpricks on corms.	Inspect corms and destroy infected ones.
Gladioli bacterial blight (disease)	Attacks leaves and stems.	Use new soil; build up soil fertility.

IRIS

INSECT OR DISEASE	APPEARANCE OR SYMPTOMS	CONTROL
Iris borer	Black-headed worm. Attacks all plant parts.	Spends winter in egg stage in old iris leaves and debris. Keep garden clean.
Botrytis rhizome rot (disease)	Soft, foul-smelling rot in rhizomes.	Inspect rhizomes and destroy infected ones.
Leaf spot (disease)	Translucent spots on leaves.	Disease thrives on wetness, so curtail watering somewhat. Burn old leaves in fall.

LILY

INSECT OR DISEASE	APPEARANCE OR SYMPTOMS	CONTROL
(Rarely troubled by insects)		
Botrytis blight (disease)	Small, round, orange-red spots on leaves.	Make sure plants have good air circulation and drainage.
Basal rot (disease)	Attacks through roots; rots tip of leaves.	Disease is in soil. Plant in new site each year; destroy infected plants.
Gray mold (disease)	Oval or circular spots on leaves.	Thin out plants, enabling good air circulation, and destroy infected plant parts.

PANSY AND VIOLET

INSECT OR DISEASE	APPEARANCE OR SYMPTOMS	CONTROL
Crown and root rot (disease)	Discolored lower leaves; new shoots wilt.	Destroy infected plants.
Violet sawfly	Bluish black larva with white stripes. Leaves are skeletonized.	Apply rotenone.
Color breakdown (disease)	Streaks or blotches in flower color.	Aphids spread the disease; destroy infected plants.
Slugs and snails	Slugs are like snails without a shell. Both leave a slime trail and work at night, eating leaves.	Use Snare-All™ or beer, or handpick.

PETUNIAS
(Many varieties are resistant to both disease and insect attack.)

PHLOX

INSECT OR DISEASE	APPEARANCE OR SYMPTOMS	CONTROL
Beetle	Black or gold beetle most common. Leaves chewed or with holes.	Spends winter in debris. Keep garden clean.
Spider mite	Tiny, yellow, green, or red spider. Grayish speckled leaves.	Use strong pressure and spray underside of leaves with water.
Nematode	Worm. Knots or swellings on roots.	Mix lots of humus into soil; fungi in humus are natural enemies of nematodes.
Leaf spot (disease)	Leaves with gray centers and brown edges.	Sugar sprinkled on soil sometimes works.

INSECT OR DISEASE	APPEARANCE OR SYMPTOMS	CONTROL
Powdery mildew (disease)	White powdery spots on leaves.	Avoid excessive moisture if possible. Mixture of ground hot pepper and water sometimes helps.

MARIGOLD

INSECT OR DISEASE	APPEARANCE OR SYMPTOMS	CONTROL
Japanese beetle	Iridescent beetle with metallic green, copper, or brown wings. Eats leaves and flowers.	Doom milky disease spore powder

SNAPDRAGON

INSECT OR DISEASE	APPEARANCE OR SYMPTOMS	CONTROL
Spider mite	Tiny yellow, green, or reddish spider. Grayish speckled leaves.	Use strong pressure and spray underside of leaves with water.
Rust (disease)	Brown pustules on leaves and stems.	Use resistant varieties; mix lots of humus into soil.

STARTING SEEDS INDOORS

You can start growing your seedlings indoors to get a headstart on spring. Indeed, because many plants may have a longer growing season (the time required to come into flower and fruit) than your particular climate allows, starting them inside while it is still cold outside will give them the season they need.

FINDING THE RIGHT PLACE

Start your indoor garden in a place with ample room for containers, watering cans, and the like where they will not interfere with your everyday routine and be insightly. Try to keep all your plants together, as it will make your plant tending easier. "Enough" space means, on average, an area about five to six feet in width and two to three feet in length. Kitchen-counter height is ideal. Your chosen spot should have a constant temperature rather than a fluctuating one (perhaps not by a door to the outdoors) and natural light but not direct sunlight. (However, if you want to start your seeds under artificial

This plant has been invaded by a fungus.

Various kinds of agave grown in pots on a bed of gravel. These make good houseplants and may be grown outside in mild climates.

light, you can use an unused closet or a dark nook or cranny, or any area with some open space and easy access. Finally, if possible, choose an area near a water tap.

SELECTING THE RIGHT CONTAINERS

Your seed containers should be small enough so that they are easy to move but large enough to accommodate a minimum of ten to twenty seedlings. Wooden flats are the best, but if you cannot find any, plastic trays are fine. They should be about four inches deep, sixteen inches wide, and twenty

Decorative plant containers.

inches long. You can also use such household containers as aluminum frozen-roll cartons, milk cartons sliced lengthwise, one-pound coffee cans, bread pans, and plastic egg cartons. You can even use regular terra cotta or plastic plant pots; the shallow ones are best. Whatever you use, make sure that they have drainage holes at the bottom. Peat pots are good for starting vegetable seeds, and fiber seed trays and pots also are available.

CHOOSING THE RIGHT GROWING MEDIUM

Whatever growing medium you choose must be sterile; otherwise the fungus called "damping off" may find its way in. Nurseries carry the five most popular sterile growing media: milled sphagnum moss, vermiculite, perlite, peat moss and sand, and a mixture of equal parts of vermiculite, sphagnum, and perlite.

Milled sphagnum moss is one of the best growing media; just remember to keep it evenly moist. Vermiculite is expanded mica that retains moisture for a long time, and packaged vermiculite has additional ingredients. Perlite is volcanic ash. By itself, perlite tends to float and disturb the seed bed, and so you should mix it with a little sterilized soil (all packaged soil is sterilized). Perlite also retains moisture well. Try to avoid using packaged soil mixes, because they are too heavy for seeds. If you must use them, combine them with some fine and porous sterile soil.

Moisten all growing media a few hours before you start planting, or you will have a mess of mud on your hands. Last, always keep your growing medium moist (but not soggy) while the seeds are growing.

PLANTING THE SEEDS

Fill the container with a premoistened growing medium to within one-quarter inch of the top. If the planting bed is lower than one-quarter inch, the growing medium will not be exposed to enough good ventilation, which deters damping off.

If you bought seed packets, cut them open at one end. Tap out the seeds into the palm of your hand, and distribute them in the pots. Dustlike seeds will be inside another, smaller envelope. Slit this one open too, and sprinkle them, evenly if possible, over the growing medium. Both large and small seeds need room to grow; crowding them will encourage damping off. Do not worry about how far apart they should be; just allow some space between them.

Once you have scattered the seeds on the growing medium, they must either be buried slightly or pressed in lightly. Fine seeds, such as petunias, begonias, and snapdragons, should be pressed in lightly. Large seeds, like

SOWING SEED IN FLATS

1. Fill with sterile growing medium, and moisten.

2. Sow seeds according to directions on packet. Cover seeds lightly with soil, and mist them.

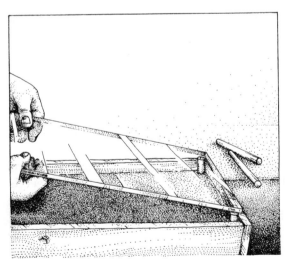

3. Cut dowels to lengths of one-half in. from top of flat; insert dowels in corners on both sides of flat. Top with glass panel or plastic covering to ensure humidity.

4. Remove seedlings for transplanting.

morning glories, should be buried slightly, just until they are no longer visible. Tree or shrub seeds with a very hard coating should be nicked before being planted.

Now that the seeds are in place, water them. Do not just dump a glass of water into the container, because then the seeds will float all over. And do not use a mister bottle, as you can actually blow them away. Instead, water them from the bottom. That is, slowly submerge the pots into a larger container of water (such as a sink), for 5 or 10 minutes, and then lift them out.

It is important to keep the seeds moist, but not wet. A good way to keep the medium moist is to cover the tray or containers with a clear plastic sheet propped up on four sticks, one in each corner of the container. Make sure that the plastic does not touch the growing medium. Punch a few small holes in the plastic so that air can circulate; otherwise, too much moisture will accumulate inside. When leaves have developed, remove the plastic.

While the seeds are growing, they should be in a bright but not sunny or dark spot. Try to maintain a constant temperature of about 75° F, as most seeds germinate at this temperature. If it is difficult to maintain a constant temperature, try using electric heating cables (you can buy them at nurseries). Put the cable at the bottom of the container before you put in the growing medium. You can also buy wooden containers with the cables already attached.

While they are germinating and growing, most seeds do not need to be fed, although some annual and perennial and tree and shrub seeds grow slowly after germinating and so must remain in their original containers for many weeks. Such seeds thus will need a very weak solution of plant food. Use a food like Rapid Gro or Hyponex, but make it half-strength. Feed these seedlings about once every ten days until they are ready to be transplanted.

TRANSPLANTING

Transplant your seedlings (that is, move them) only when the first set of true leaves—four leaves—has appeared. To remove the seedlings, use a blunt instrument like a wooden ladle or the handle of a teaspoon. The goal is to lift out the seedling with as much of its root ball as possible. Be gentle! If you yank it out, it will suffer great shock and probably die.

First, however, prepare the smaller, individual containers into which you will transplant the seedlings. Use a mixture of equal parts of soil, sand, and compost. Fill the containers to within one-quarter inch of the top, and lightly water the soil mixture until it is moist. Using the same ladle or spoon handle, make a slight indentation in the soil to accommodate the seedling's root ball. Make it big enough so that you do not have to squeeze or force it in; if you

PLANTING FROM FLATS

1. with a knife or trowel, cut out plants in squares.

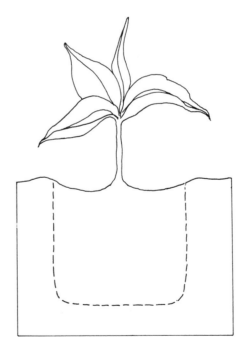

2. gently place the plant in the hole (don't force it in).

3. firm the soil and make a depression around it for water.

TRANSPLANTING SEEDLINGS TO POTS

1. When seedlings are about 2 in. high and have separate leaves, remove them for transplanting.

2. Taking as much of the root ball as possible, place the seedlings in small pots.

3. Keep the seedlings moist with a fine-mist spray of water.

4. After a few weeks, transplant the seedlings to larger pots and place them in their permanent positions at a window, or outdoors if for the garden.

Gazanias and petunias create a simple but easy-to-care-for garden.

do, you will damage it. Set the seedling in the pocket so that the root ball is beneath the surface. Fill in the hole gently but firmly so that the seedling is held in place. Water the soil immediately after transplanting, and put the containers in a bright but not sunny place for about a week to give the young plants a chance to recuperate from their move. Then move them into bright light.

You must keep the little plants growing in their new containers until you move them outdoors or into permanent indoor sites. Be sure to keep the soil moist at all times. If it is moist to the touch, fine. If not, water it immediately.

Do not dump water into the container; rather, apply it evenly and gently, and use tepid water, never icy cold or hot.

Feed the plants lightly about once every five days. Watch the new plants: If they are becoming leggy, pinch them back to encourage branching and more compact growth. To pinch back a plant, nip off the top growth with your thumbnail and index fingernail. This pinching is especially helpful to single-stemmed plants.

HARDENING OFF

Next you must acclimatize those plants that you are going to move outside, a period during which the plants become accustomed to outdoor conditions. To do this, place the plants in a protected area—porch, back steps—for a few days and nights before planting them in the garden. Make sure that the plants are out of the direct sun but are still getting some bright light. If the weather is very cold, move them back into the house until it warms up again, or they may die. After a few days, move the plants into stronger light and a more exposed area for a week or so. They should now be ready to go into the garden. Plant them in the ground according to the instructions in Chapter 1. Unless it rains, they probably should be watered every three days until they are established.

WINTER PROTECTION

Give your plants some protection against freezing and also against alternate freezing and thawing. Perennials and bulbs can be protected by a heavy layer of mulch, which should be spread over the ground after it has frozen. Cover both the roots and tops of woody plants. Spread a two-inch layer of straw, peat moss, or leaves over the soil, and wrap the top with burlap or evergreen boughs. In areas of heavy snow, tie together any tree branches that might be broken.

PROPAGATING YOUR PLANTS

DIVIDING THEM

You can divide perennials, many house plants, bulbs, and plants with clump growth such as ferns. It is easy. You divide the main plant into several smaller plants, either by pulling one clump free from another or by cutting the plant apart—roots and all—with a sharp knife, right down the middle.

Bulbs are sometimes divided after the first season and sometimes not until

WINTER PROTECTION METHODS

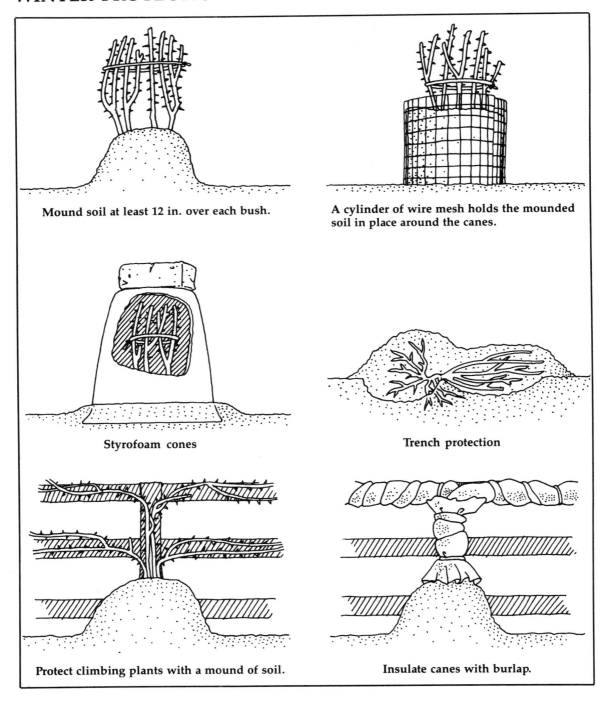

Mound soil at least 12 in. over each bush.

A cylinder of wire mesh holds the mounded soil in place around the canes.

Styrofoam cones

Trench protection

Protect climbing plants with a mound of soil.

Insulate canes with burlap.

PLANTING BARE-ROOT SHRUBS

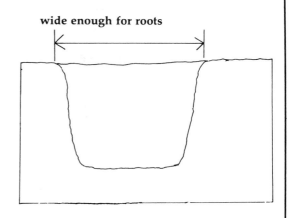

wide enough for roots

1. Prune and trim any broken roots and branches.

2. Soak roots for a few hours, and then dig hole wide enough for roots

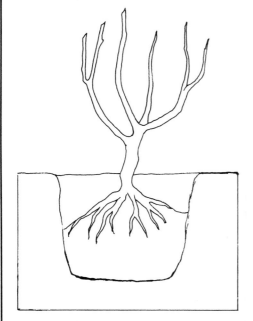

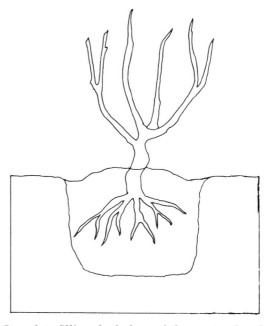

3. Mound the soil; and spread the roots over it.

4. Complete filling the hole, and then water the plant.

after a few seasons. They multiply in the ground, and so after you dig them up, you simply break off the small bulbs or rhizomes that have formed. Keep the biggest ones to replant, and discard the smallest, least promising ones.

The best time to divide plants is in the early spring or fall when they are dormant. After you have divided them, keep them moist and replant them as soon as possible.

AIR LAYERING THEM

Air layering a plant may sound difficult, but it actually is not. It is a good way of propagating plants that cannot be divided, and it usually works. Select a sturdy branch (at least one inch in diameter), and make a slanting cut in it about one-quarter inch deep. You can either hold the cut open by inserting a matchstick in it, or you can remove a ring of bark around it about three-fourths inch wide, scraping it down to the hard core at the center of the branch with a sterilized knife (you can sterilize the knife by running it through a match flame). Dust the open cut with a rooting hormone powder (get this at a nursery). Cover the cut with sphagnum moss, and wrap a piece of plastic (a plastic bag is fine) around the moss. Tie the plastic at each end.

It takes about a month or even longer for roots to form in the moss. When they are visible, cut off the new plant with a sharp knife, and plant it in a pot or in the ground. If the air layering does not work, it will not have harmed the plant, as the cut branch will eventually form a callous or scar that will seal it.

STARTING SEEDS OUTDOORS

Seeds are started differently outdoors than they are indoors in containers. Many vegetables, annuals, and perennials do better when begun outside. Nasturtiums, cosmos, and zinnias, and beets, carrots, and lettuce are examples of plants that germinate well in cold moist soil. In addition, these plants and some varieties of peas do not transplant well, which is another good reason for starting them in the ground.

The soil should be prepared as discussed in Chapter 1. Then you can deposit the seed, usually in rows. Space the seed according to the directions on the seed packet. Spacing big seeds is easy, but tiny ones can be difficult. Planting in rows gives you room to walk between them and to tend the plants, and it also helps you differentiate between the seedlings and weeds.

Be sure both that the soil is moist before you put in the seeds and that you label each row. Pull out the weeds as soon as they appear, as they will rob the seedlings of nutrients and water.

When the seedlings are about two to four inches high, you should thin

PROPAGATING PLANTS

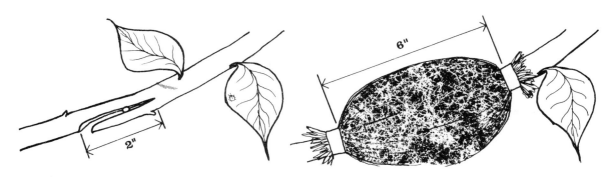

A. AIR LAYERING
cut; hold split open with pebble; cover with damp sphagnum moss; seal in plastic film
until roots sprout

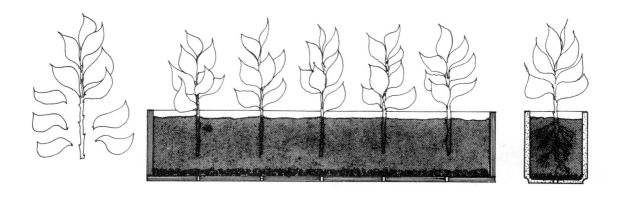

B. TAKING CUTTINGS
trim lower leaves; dip cuttings in root hormone; plant in flats in rooting medium;
water; pot after roots sprout

ADRIÁN MARTÍNEZ

GROWING SEEDS OUTDOORS

1. Preparing soil and rows.

2. Sow seeds in mounds and label.

3. Remove weeds as seeds grow.

4. Thin out weak plants.

them so that they will have room to grow. This means pulling up the smaller ones to give to your friends or to use in other areas. No matter how careful you are when you thin your seedlings, you will inevitably disturb those left in the ground, and so you should give extra attention to them. Make sure that the soil is moist both before (it will make pulling them up easier) and after you pull them. And remember that not all the seeds will germinate; some may be sterile, and others may not have just the right conditions. But you should have more than enough plants from your packet of seeds.

4

THE PLANTS

T his chapter is an illustrated overview of the plants, flowers, trees, and shrubs covered in this book. Following this chapter is *Part Two: The Gardening Dictionary,* an alphabetical list of almost two thousand garden plants: trees and shrubs, houseplants, annuals and perennials, vines, bulbs, and herbs. I have included those plants that I felt were the most widely used and the most easily grown. My judgment is based on twenty-three years of gardening in Chicago, San Francisco, and Miami, as well as on the many plants I have raised over these years. I have purposely omitted many obscure trees because space is limited in small gardens (the focus of this book) and, also, growing trees to maturity is quite difficult.

ANNUALS AND PERENNIALS

Annuals and perennials are the foundation of most gardens. They form the beds, borders, drifts, and arcs, offering an almost endless variety of shapes, colors, heights, and fragrances.

An *annual* completes its life cycle in one season—zinnias, marigolds, and petunias are examples. Although you can grow annuals from seed, it is easier to buy seedlings, ready to put into the ground.

A *perennial* returns from dormancy every spring, ready to resume growing. Therefore, once it has been planted and if it is properly cared for, it should last for years. Perennials are generally planted between October and April, and most of them should be dug up and divided every three or four years.

Geraniums in window box.

The focus of this landscape plan is a courtyard garden, with the sparse planting blending in well.

Landscaping the side of a house with false bamboo and Japanese maple.

A hedge of shrubs offers privacy but requires little maintenance.

This landscape plan for a desert house takes full advantage of the environment and thereby requires a little maintenance.

Here, a brick walk winds through a bed of annuals and perennials used mainly for cutting.

ANNUALS

Cleome spinosa

Gaillardia grandiflora

Godetia amoena

Cosmos bipinnatus

ANNUALS

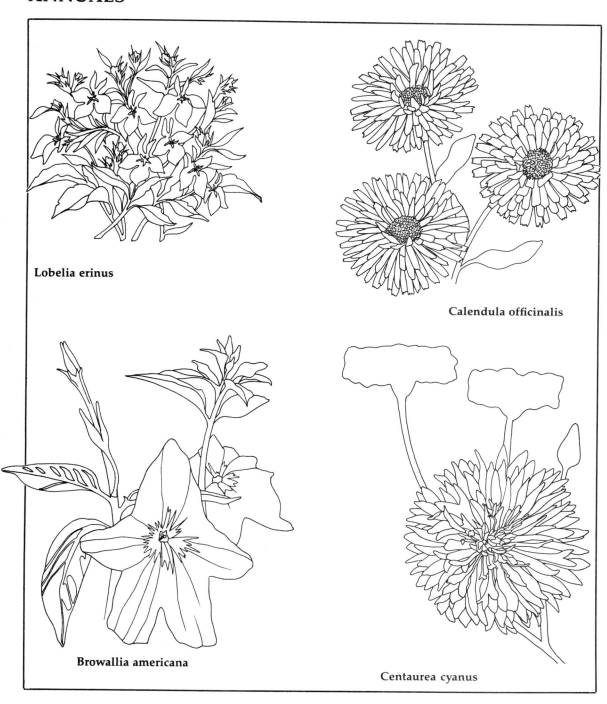

Lobelia erinus

Calendula officinalis

Browallia americana

Centaurea cyanus

ANNUALS

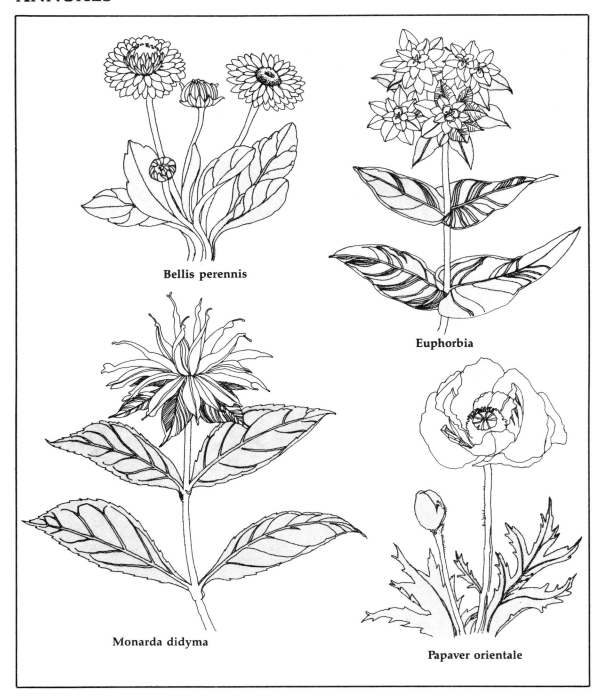

Bellis perennis

Euphorbia

Monarda didyma

Papaver orientale

PERENNIALS

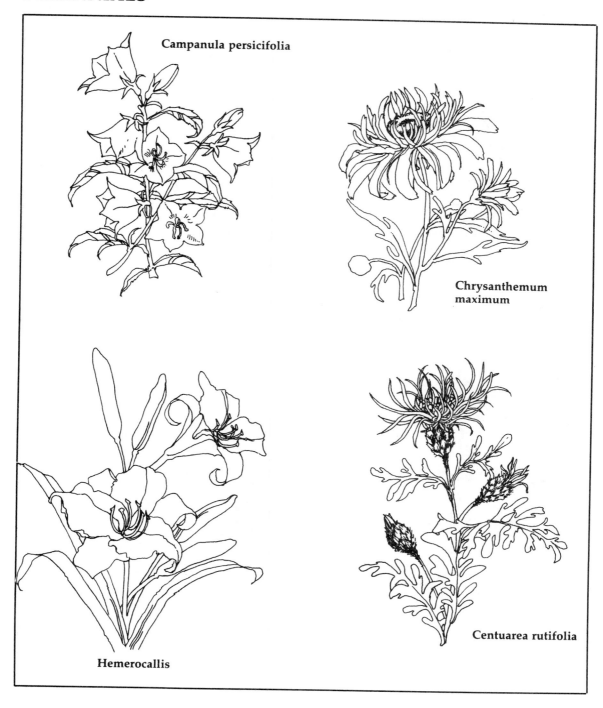

Campanula persicifolia

Chrysanthemum maximum

Hemerocallis

Centuarea rutifolia

PERENNIALS

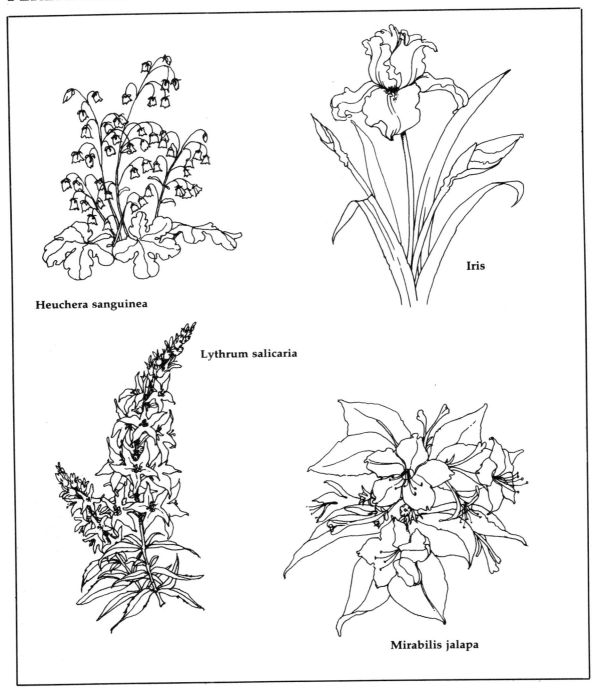

Heuchera sanguinea

Iris

Lythrum salicaria

Mirabilis jalapa

There also are a few *biennials,* plants that are put into the ground in early summer, bloom the following summer, and then die. But most biennials have been eclipsed by annuals and perennials.

TREES AND SHRUBS

Today, most gardens are much smaller than they used to be; the average garden is barely forty by sixty feet. Accordingly, two, three, or perhaps four big trees will be all that such a garden can accommodate. And because these

(Continued on page 106)

Try to incorporate trees in the landscape plan, as shown here, instead of taking them out.

HEDGES

side view | end view

Berberis wilsoniae (Barberry)

To 4 feet (trimmed)

Spiraea prunifolia plena (Bridal wreath)

To 6 feet (untrimmed)

Prunus laurocerasus (Cherry laurel)

To 12 feet plus (trimmed)

TREE FORMS

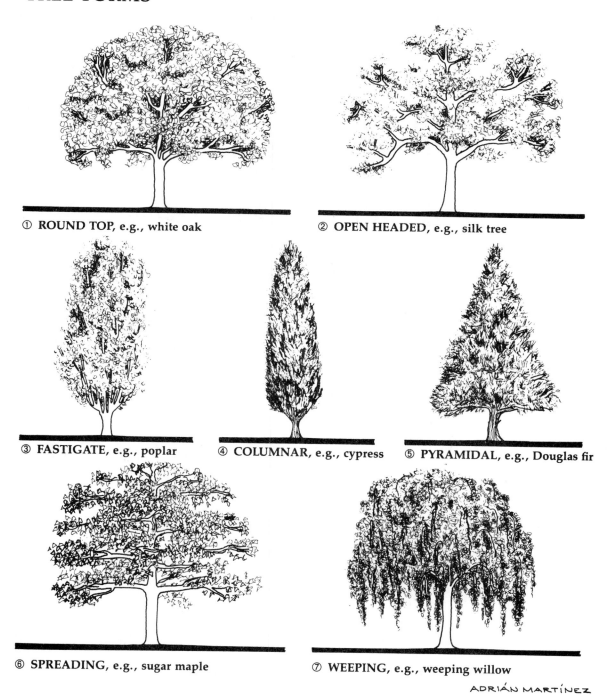

① **ROUND TOP**, e.g., white oak

② **OPEN HEADED**, e.g., silk tree

③ **FASTIGATE**, e.g., poplar

④ **COLUMNAR**, e.g., cypress

⑤ **PYRAMIDAL**, e.g., Douglas fir

⑥ **SPREADING**, e.g., sugar maple

⑦ **WEEPING**, e.g., weeping willow

ADRIÁN MARTÍNEZ

EVERGREEN TREES

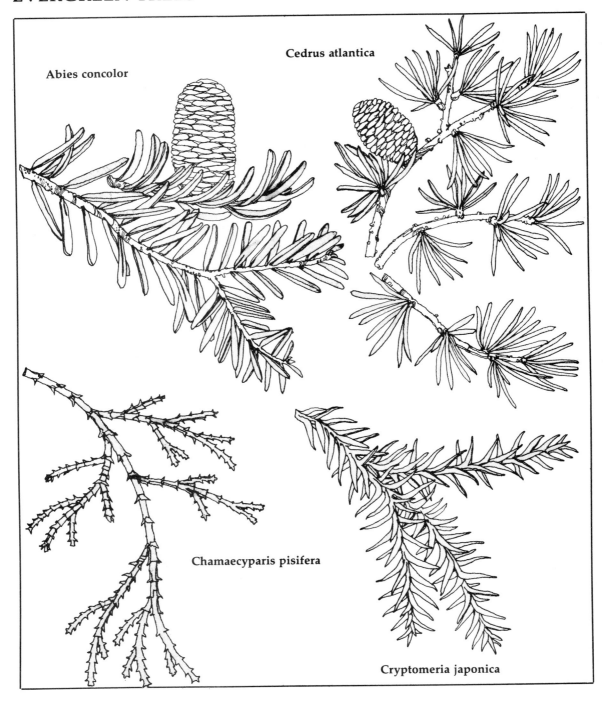

Abies concolor

Cedrus atlantica

Chamaecyparis pisifera

Cryptomeria japonica

SHRUBS

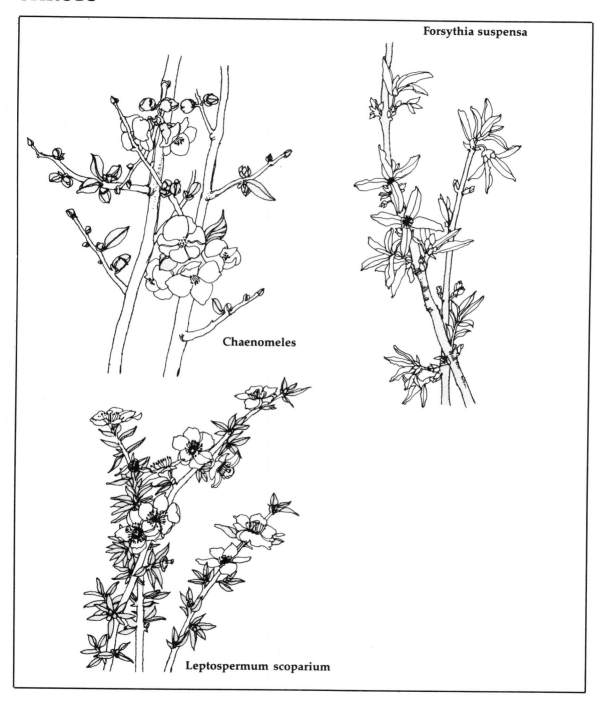

Forsythia suspensa

Chaenomeles

Leptospermum scoparium

(Continued from page 101)

trees usually will be with you for a lifetime, select them carefully, considering their eventual shape and height. It is important, too, to balance your garden with both deciduous and evergreen trees, to provide color and interest year-round. Autumn color should be taken into account as well.

Shrubs have become more popular than ever, perhaps because of the declining interest in trees. There now are more varieties from which to choose, both deciduous and evergreen.

GRASSES, GROUND COVERS, AND AQUATIC PLANTS

Only recently have Americans begun using ornamental grasses in their gardens. It is a shame that they have been neglected because some of them are very graceful and handsome when planted in large clumps. Grasses are not difficult to grow; once they are established, they are almost self-sufficient. Most grasses need moisture and a sunny location, although some can survive with less light and drier conditions. Indeed, some may be hard to control or even to eliminate.

Some ground covers are low, almost carpetlike, but others can grow to a foot or so. Ground covers are the answer to work-free gardening: They are easy to start, spread rapidly, and last for years. Most ground covers grow well in bright light or sun; a few tolerate shade. Ground covers like moisture and fertilizer in the spring. If you want a ground cover quickly, do not space the ground-cover plants as recommended; instead, place them close together, and you will have a plant carpet in no time.

Although water lilies are the most common aquatic plants, there are many more. Of course, aquatic plants can be used only in those gardens that have the conditions (very wet) and the space for them (a pond). There also, however, are "near-water" plants—those that do need very wet conditions but not necessarily a pond—such as cattails or Egyptian paper plants. Such plants need very moist conditions at their roots, but otherwise are easy to grow. If you have some areas in your garden where standing water is a problem or places that just accumulate too much water, consider growing aquatic plants there. Not only will they be attractive, but they also will resolve your excess-water problem.

VINES

Vines are probably the most underused plants in the garden, yet they offer a variety of colors and covers. There are annual and perennial vines and evergreen, semievergreen, and deciduous vines. But even though the choice is large, there seems to be little information in gardening books about

Once they are established, evergreen shrubs, ground covers, and ferns make an easy-to-maintain garden.

GROUND COVERS

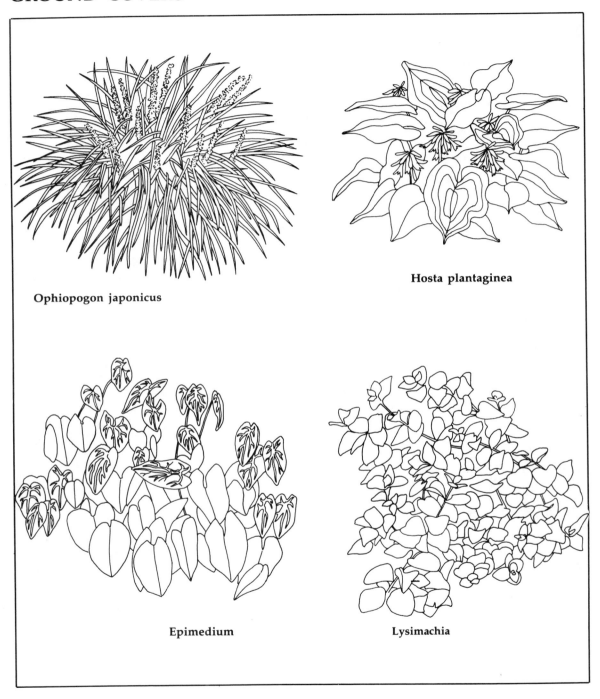

Ophiopogon japonicus

Hosta plantaginea

Epimedium

Lysimachia

Water lilies.

growing vines, which is probably the reason that gardeners forget about them.

Vines are not difficult to grow. They need the same care as do other plants, with one exception: They must be fed regularly with a 10-20-10 (NPK) fertilizer. Vines also should be pruned at certain times of the year, and they

Aquatic plants in a garden pool.

all need some support, such as a trellis. But once they are established, vines grow quickly and are good for covering unsightly walls or fences.

To keep vines in place on a fence or trellis, use U-shaped vine hooks or plastic ribbon. I usually prune my vines only when they look as though they need it—when they seem ungainly or appear to be taking over the garden.

Water lilies around a pool in a quiet garden of green.

A vertical garden with an arbor.

BULBS

Bulbs grown outdoors make good (if temporary) borders, and they look wonderful planted en masse in large drifts or beds. Bulbs are easy to grow: All you need to do is plant them and water them.

Most bulbs are planted in the fall, although some go in the ground in early spring and still others even later (such as gladioli). Furthermore, some can remain in the ground all year, but others must be dug up each year. When you plant them, first carefully prepare the ground, mixing into the soil a

What could be prettier than a field of tulips?

generous amount of humus and top soil. Then dig the hole at least twice as deep as the height of the bulb. After the bulbs have started to send up shoots, feed them a little bone meal and blood meal. Some bulbs need sun—such as daffodils—but others do well in shade—such as crocuses. After the bulbs have flowered and the leaves have begun to fade, don't cut them off, because at this stage the nutrients for next year are returning to the bulb. Not until the bulbs seem completely dead is it safe to trim them.

Irises grown in planter boxes.

Hyacinths grown indoors bring welcome color and fragrance during the winter. (Photo courtesy USDA)

Tuberous begonias come in many shapes and colors.

BULBS

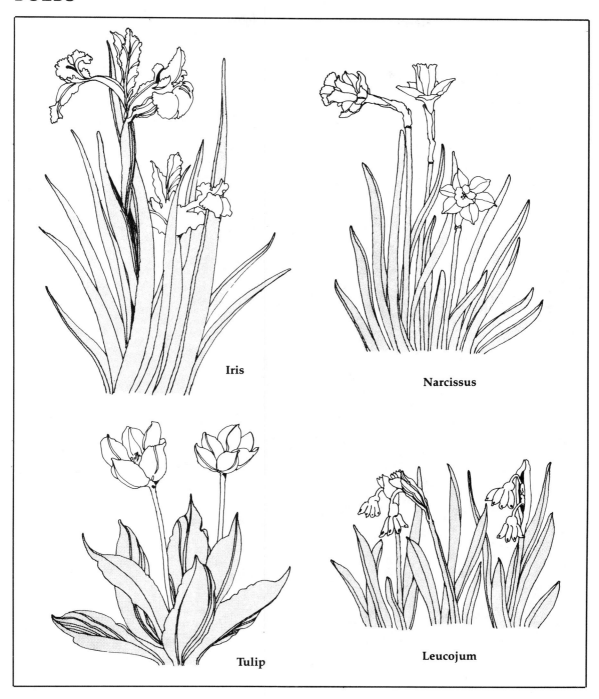

Iris

Narcissus

Tulip

Leucojum

A container of assorted Pteris ferns.

Dieffenbachia, with their multicolored leaves, are popular houseplants.

Columnar cacti make excellent corner decorations.

A group of handsome houseplants—*Crassula argentea, Agloanoma,* and *Ficus.*

A large *Euphorbia* and, behind it, the popular globe cactus *Echinocereus grusoni*.

The novelty bromeliad *Ananas cosmosus*.

A *Phalaenopsis* hybrid orchid.

An *Oncidium* hybrid orchid.

An *Epidendrum porpax* orchid.

A close-up of a miniature *Dendrobium* orchid.

The leaves of the bright Nasturtium adds a delicious peppery flavor to salads.

Aechmea fasciata is perhaps the most popular flowering bromeliad. It is easily grown and blooms for a long time.

PERENNIALS

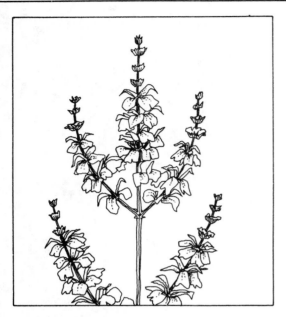

Salvia haematodes

Lobelia cardinalis

Rochea coccinea

VINES

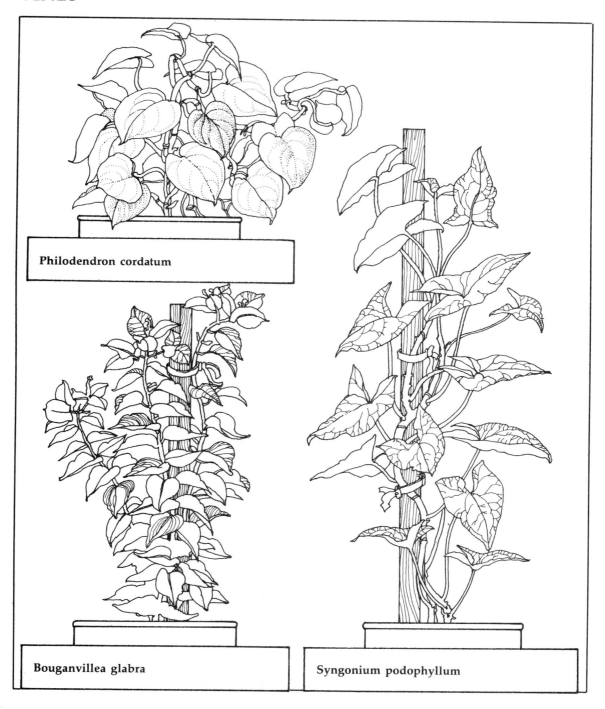

Philodendron cordatum

Bouganvillea glabra

Syngonium podophyllum

AFRICAN VIOLETS

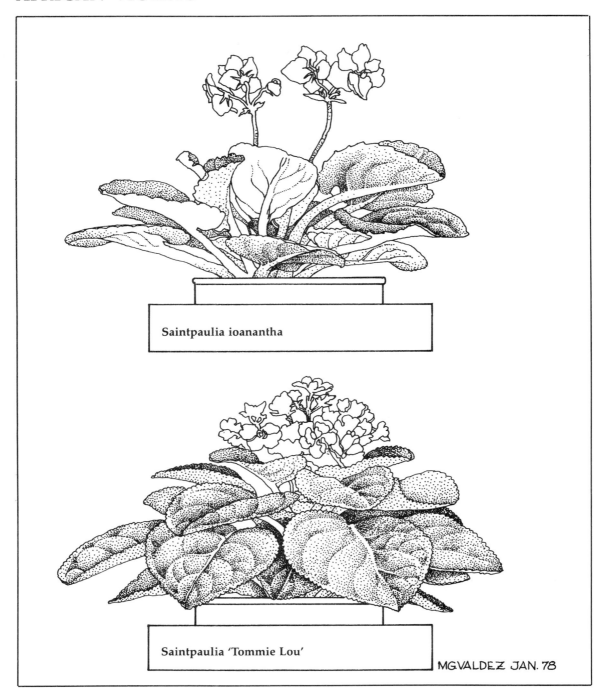

Saintpaulia ioanantha

Saintpaulia 'Tommie Lou'

MG.VALDEZ JAN. 78

INDOOR TREES

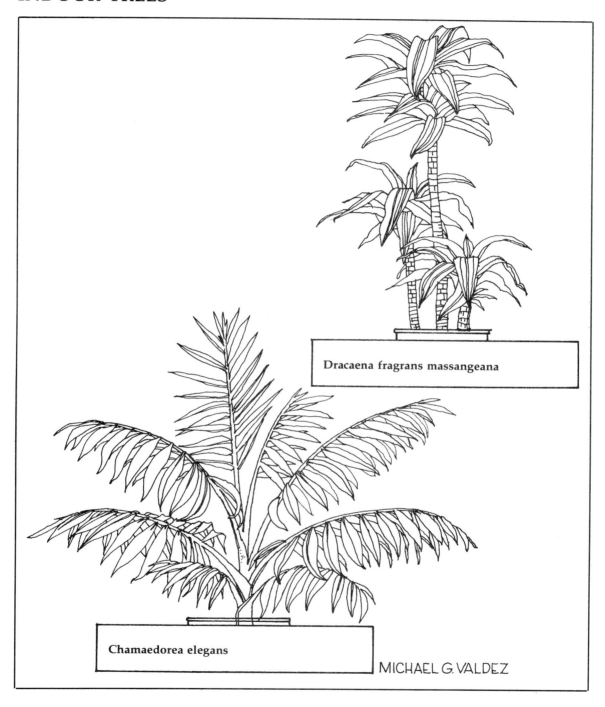

Dracaena fragrans massangeana

Chamaedorea elegans

MICHAEL G. VALDEZ

CACTI

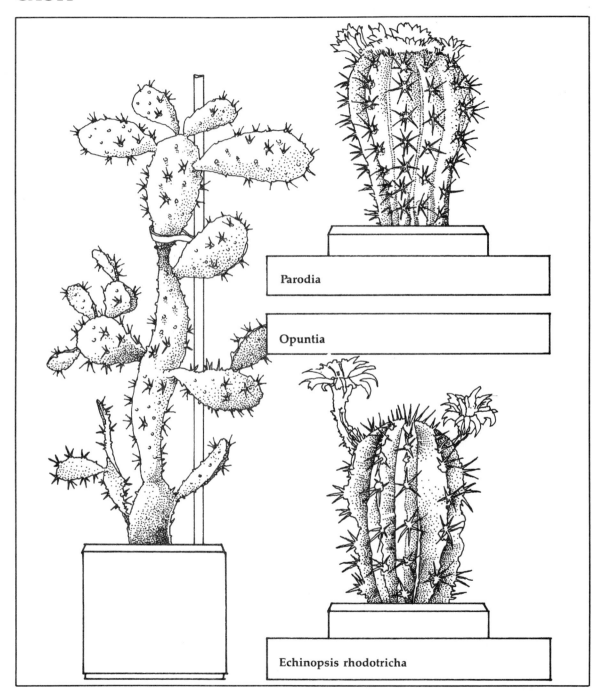

Parodia

Opuntia

Echinopsis rhodotricha

FERNS

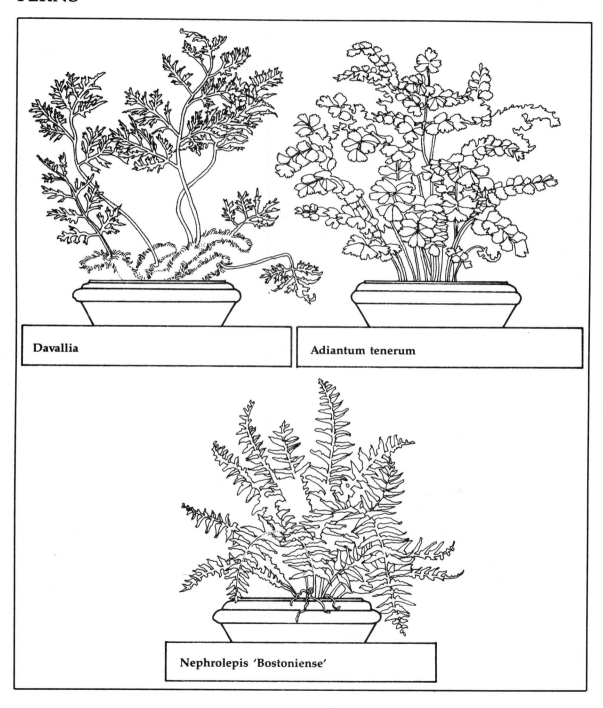

Davallia

Adiantum tenerum

Nephrolepis 'Bostoniense'

HOUSEPLANTS

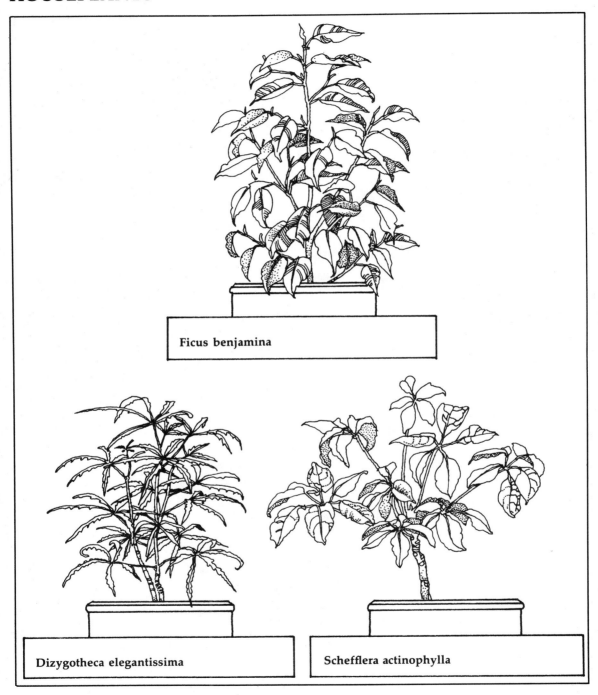

Ficus benjamina

Dizygotheca elegantissima

Schefflera actinophylla

HOUSEPLANTS

Ficus pumila

Ficus benjamina

Ficus diversifolia

HOUSEPLANTS

Kalanchoe blossfeldiana

Solanum pseudocapsicum

Aechmea racinae

Euphorbia pulcherrima

HOUSEPLANTS

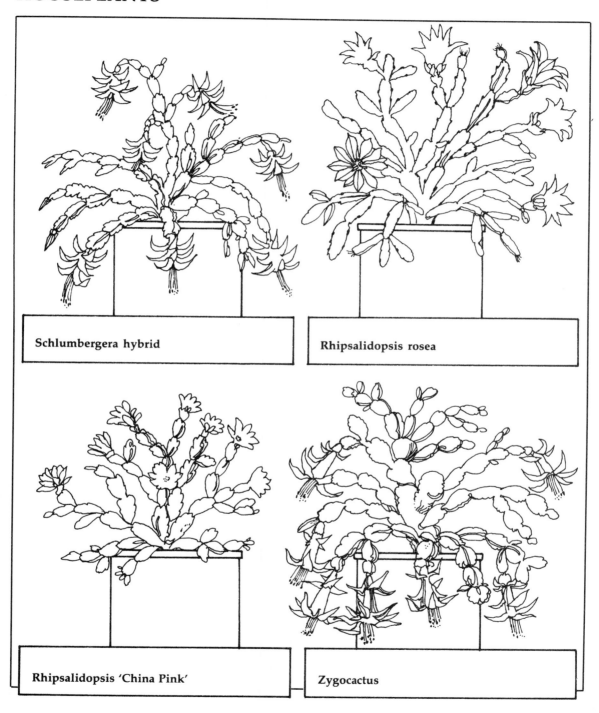

Schlumbergera hybrid

Rhipsalidopsis rosea

Rhipsalidopsis 'China Pink'

Zygocactus

PART TWO: THE GARDENING DICTIONARY

HOW TO USE THE GARDENING DICTIONARY

New varieties of annuals, perennials, and bulbs are listed under "Suggested Varieties." The different varieties of trees, shrubs, and houseplants are given in the "master" entries, because such plants are generally established. Suppliers of some of the major categories, such as water lilies, tulips, and iris, offer catalogs of just those plants, and I have noted these. But in regard to other categories, such as orchids, roses, and rhododendrons, I have made my own suggestions, based on my long experience with them.

Today, houseplants are an important part of home decoration adding beauty indoors and helping to cleanse the air. They are grown in almost all homes and apartments in America and there are countless kinds of houseplants—thousands now, where once one found only the ubiquitous philodendron and African violet. Included in the dictionary that follows are many indoor subjects (a great many of these grow outdoors in tropical climes) and they are listed as houseplants accordingly. I have included those plants I have personally grown and tried to select plants that are the easiest to cultivate under home conditions and that will afford you the greatest pleasure.

Finally, if you do not know the botanical (Latin) name of a plant, and your local nursery cannot help you, but you do know its common name, look it up in the "Common Names/Botanical Names" list beginning on page 395.

Have fun gardening!

ABELIA *shrub*

From Asia and Mexico, some abelias are deciduous; others are evergreen. They have tubular flowers—pink, white, or purple. Abelias can tolerate either shade or sun but need even moisture at the roots and good drainage. Most abelias make good hedges and provide a spot of color. Generally they are not difficult to grow and can be propagated with either softwood or hardwood cuttings. They are vulnerable to insects, so watch them carefully.

A. floribunda. Has evergreen leaves and rose-colored flowers. Tolerates temperatures down to
    −5°F.
A. grandiflora (hybrid of *A. chinensis* and *A. uniflora*). The most popular abelia. Has small pink
    flowers, attractive evergreen leaves, and colorful fall foliage. Dense growth. Tolerates
    temperatures down to 5°F.

ABELMOSCHUS MOSCHATUS *perennial/annual* **Silk flower**

Abelmoschus often are included with the hibiscus group, but they are a separate family. They need bright light and moderate water, and bloom in the summer. Their flowers are funnel shaped; their leaves are large. Abelmoschus are used as tall-growing perennials, but often the similar hibiscus take their place, as they are easier to grow. Abelmoschus can be propagated from either softwood or hardwood cuttings. They are vulnerable to insects.

ABIES *tree* **Fir**

Abies have a pyramidal shape and rigid horizontal branches, providing a definitive accent to the landscape. These evergreen firs need a cool, moist climate, or they will quickly deteriorate. Their needles last for about five years before falling; the cones do not appear every year. Abies have few insect or disease problems, but as they mature, their lower branches become unsightly, and once removed, they do not grow back. In their later years, therefore, abies may become unsymmetrical.

A. alba (European silver fir). Grows to 150 ft.; hardy to −20°F. Has dark green needles.
A. concolor (white fir). Grows, rapidly, to 120 ft.; hardy to −20°F. Has bluish green needles.
A. nordmanniana (Nordmann fir). Grows to 50 ft.; hardy to −30°F. Has glossy green needles. Susceptible to gall lice, which can kill it.

ABRONIA UMBELLATA   *annual*   Pink-sand verbena

Abronia is a trailing plant growing to 10 in. tall, with dense rose-lavender flower clusters. It needs sun and moderate water, and blooms in the spring. Grows well in sandy soil. Excellent for walkways and borders or wherever a low mass of color is needed. Provides long-lasting cut flowers.

ABUTILON   *shrub*   Flowering maple

These shrubs grow to 3 ft. tall, some bushy and others erect. They like full sun, moderate feeding, lots of water, and bloom off and on from May to August. The flowers are paper thin and bell shaped, and come in orange, yellow, red, pink, or white. The maple leaf–like foliage is either solid green or variegated.

To keep plants bushy, cut off the tops of branches in the spring. Indoors, grow in pots or hanging baskets. Outdoors, use as background in a perennial garden. Plant several, as a few tend to look sparse. Flowering maples often become leggy, so start new plants from cuttings in the spring or prune back mature plants. Abutilon is occasionally attacked by red spider mites or mealybugs. At the first sign of them, hose them off or spray with a laundry soap and water solution.

A. megapotamicum variegatum. Has green-and-yellow leaves and red-and-yellow flowers. Hardy to 40°F.
A. striatum. Provides orange flowers. Hardy to 40°F.
A. thompsonii. Has variegated leaves and yellow flowers. Hardy to 50°F.

SUGGESTED VARIETIES:
'Apricot'—orange pink flowers
'Eclipse'—pink flowers
'Golden Fleece'—yellow flowers
'Splendens'—red flowers
'Souvenir de Bonne'—orange flowers

ACACIA   *shrub/tree*

Acacia are suitable for temperate areas. They differ widely in their growing needs, but they all bloom in early spring (February–March). Some have feathery, divided leaves, and others have flat leaves. Acacias are short-lived.

A. baileyana (Bailey acacia). Grows to 30 ft.; hardy to 30°F. Has feathery, fine-cut, blue-gray leaves and clusters of light yellow flowers.

A. cyanophylla (blue leaf wattle). Grows to 30 ft.; hardy to 30°F. Has narrow bluish leaves and clusters of orange flowers.

Acalypha *houseplant* Chenille plant

From the East Indies, acalypha produces strings of red or greenish white flowers from leaf axils throughout the year, as well as green or copper-colored leaves. If it is grown as a houseplant, it should be put in a sunny window, and its soil should be kept evenly moist in a fairly humid area. Feed acalypha with a 20-10-10 fertilizer. Several plants in one container are particularly attractive. If acalypha is grown outside, it can tolerate temperatures down to 40°F. Several plants can be used either as a hedge or as bedding plants. In any case, mass them for the best effect. Take cuttings in the fall for new plants. Acalypha is rarely attacked by insects.

A. godseffiana. Grows to 20 in. Has bright green, yellow-edged leaves and greenish white flowers.

A. hispida. Grows to 30 in. Has hairy green leaves and bright red flowers.

A. macrophylla. Grows to 30 in. Has bronze and copper leaves and red flowers.

A. wilkesiana macafeana. Grows to 30 in. Has copper leaves; is mainly grown for foliage.

Acanthus *perennial* Grecian urn plant

This plant's leaves are large, bold, and ornamental, and its spring and summer flowers are white, lilac, or rose. Acanthus needs bright light and wet soil while it is actively growing. It will get as tall as 5 ft. Grecian-urn plants are good in borders if they have some shade and also as background plants with summer perennials. Let them die down after they bloom, with the soil barely moist. Propagate with seeds or divide the rhizomes in the early spring. They are occasionally attacked by mealybugs. At the first sign of infestation, spray with laundry soap and water solution.

A. mollis. Hardy to 30°F. Has broad glossy green leaves and pink and white flowers.

A. montanus. Hardy to 30°F. Has narrow dark green leaves with spines and pink flowers.

Acer *tree* Maple

The many kinds of maples are popular shade trees. Each has different growing requirements and a different size and leaf shape. Some are small and delicate, like the Japanese maple, and others are tall with round foliage, like the Norway maple. The smaller varieties are ideal for landscaping when space is limited. Although some of the maples have interesting and colorful bark, it is their autumn foliage—each variety has a different shade—that

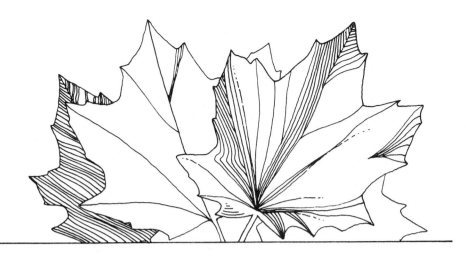

make them so popular. Maples do well in any good garden soil and generally are not bothered by insects or diseases.

A. campestre (hedge maple). Grows to 25 ft.; hardy to −5°F. Has a rounded head of foliage that turns yellow in the fall.
A. japonicum (full-moon maple). Grows to 25 ft.; hardy to −5°F. Has lobed leaves that turn bright red in the fall.
'Aconitifolium' (fern-leaf maple)—deeply lobed leaves
A. palmatum (Japanese maple). Grows to 20 ft.; hardy to −5°F. Has a rounded head of foliage that turns scarlet in the fall.
A. platanoides (Norway maple). Grows to 60 ft.; hardy to −20°F. Has broad-crowned foliage that turns yellow in the fall; also greenish yellow flowers in the spring.
A. pseudoplatanus. Similar to the Norway maple, but with a more pleasing form and more robust.
A. rubrum (red maple). Grows to 40+ ft.; hardy to −20°F. Has brilliant scarlet leaves, twigs, and buds in the fall; red flowers in the spring.
A. saccharum (sugar maple). Grows to 60+ ft.; hardy to −20°F. Has silver-gray bark and yellow-to-orange and red leaves in the fall.

ACHILLEA *perennial*   Yarrow

Achillea grow as tall as 40 in., with their white, yellow, or rosy red flowers in clusters. The leaves are fernlike. Yarrow can tolerate poor soil but needs sun and good drainage. They bloom in the spring and summer and provide good cut flowers. Yarrow also are effective in drifts. They are easily propagated by division. Hardy to −35°F.

A. filipendulina (fern-leaved yarrow). Produces bright yellow flowers.
A. millefolium (common yarrow). Produces clusters of small white flowers.
A. ptarmica (sneezewort). Produces many clusters of white flowers. The best choice for cut flowers.
A. tomentosa (woolly yarrow). Produces compact clusters of bright yellow flowers.

'Coronation Gold'—yellow flowers
'Fireking'—red flowers
'Moonshine'—white flowers

Achimenes   *houseplant*   **Rainbow flower**

These gesneriads can be grown either indoors or outdoors in temperate climates. Achimenes like sun and moist soil; if the soil becomes too dry while they are actively growing and/or blooming, they may go dormant. When the flowers fade, decrease the amount of water. In the early spring, when the danger of frost is past, plant the tubers again; they multiply rapidly. When they are a few inches high, start feeding them with a 10-20-10 fertilizer. They should bloom in six to eight weeks, with the flowers lasting for up to four months.

Rainbow flowers tend to be bushy, with cut-leaf, glossy foliage. The flowers come in all colors except green. Some are compact plants, growing to 16 in., but others can get as tall as 8 to 24 in., with those in baskets producing 20-in. cascades.

A. antiirrhina. Grows upright to 20 in.; has scarlet and yellow flowers.
A. 'Charm'. Grows compactly to 16 in.; has pink flowers.
A. flava. A basket plant with golden yellow flowers.
A. 'François cardinaux'. Grows upright to 20 in.; has lavender and white flowers.
A. grandiflora. Grows upright to 26 in.; has purple flowers with white throats.
A. 'Master Ingram'. Grows upright to 20 in.; has orange and red flowers.
A. pedunculata. Grows upright to 28 in.; has fiery orange flowers.
A. 'Purity'. Grows upright to 16 in.; has soft white flowers.
A. 'Purple King'. Grows upright to 16 in.
A. 'Vivid'. Grows upright to 18 in.; has orange and magenta flowers.

Acidanthera   *bulb*   **Abyssinian sword lily**

These lilies are somewhat similar to gladioli, with 3-in. flowers, usually scented, on stalks up to 3 ft. tall. Acidanthera need sun and moderate water, and bloom in the summer. Plant the corms in the spring. Then after the flowers have died, dig up the corms and store them in a cool dry place until the following spring. Sword lilies provide good cut flowers.

A. bicolor. Has grasslike foliage with fragrant, cream-colored flowers blotched with brown.
A. hybrida tubergenii. Produces large, very fragrant, cream-colored flowers.

Acineta   *houseplant*

This rare group of orchids has broad, pliated leaves and lots of yellow flowers. They need morning sun and a fir-bark growing medium that is kept moist but not soggy. Mist the leaves frequently when they have matured because the flowers develop at the base of the bulbs. But do not let any water stand in the buds, as it will rot them. Acineta may be divided; they are seldom attacked by insects.

A. densa. Grows to 24 in. Produces 2-in. yellow flowers spotted with red, in the spring.
A. superba. Grows to 24 in. Produces large flowers in the summer.

Aconitum *perennial*   **Monkshood**

Monkshood blooms with blue, lilac, or white flower spikes up to 60 in. tall. It is a good substitute for delphinium in light shade. Although it will not grow in wet soil, aconitum should be watered often; make sure that it has good drainage, as well as rich soil. It blooms in the summer and fall. The flowers and roots are poisonous. Monkshood are easily divided.

A. autumnale (autumn monkshood). Produces blue, lilac, or white flowers.
A. fischeri (azure monkshood). Produces violet flowers.
A. napellus (English monkshood). Produces blue, reddish purple, violet, or white flowers. The best known and most poisonous species.
A. vulparia (wolfsbane). Produces yellow flowers.

SUGGESTED VARIETIES:
'Arendsi'—blue flowers
'Bressingham Spire'—blue flowers
'Ivorine'—white flowers

Acorus *perennial*   **Miniature flag plant**

Acorus grows to about 10 in. tall, with tufted, irislike leaves and small, greenish flowers. It is a marsh flower and so needs moist soil; it thus is a good choice for water gardens and bog areas. This flag-plant blooms in the spring or summer, but its flowers are insignificant. It can be divided, preferably in the spring or fall. Acorus is rarely bothered by insects; it is truly a carefree plant. Acorus needs diffuse sun.

A. gramineus pusillus. Grows to 3 in. Has flat, waxy, dark green leaves.
A. gramineus variegatus. Grows to 10 in. Has leathery green-and-white leaves.

Actinida *vine*

Actinida grows rapidly, sometimes to 25 ft. This vine, a member of the kiwi family from East Asia, needs bright light and lots of water, and blooms in the summer or fall with small, greenish white flowers. However, the flowers are insignificant, and the leaves have no autumn color. Indeed, this vine is best for covering unsightly areas. Most need a trellis or arbor for support. They can be propagated by softwood or hardwood cuttings, planted in the fall.

A. arguta. The most commonly grown species, with alternating large green leaves.
A. chinensis. The kiwi plant, sometimes called "Chinese gooseberry." Grows rapidly and has large leaves.

ADIANTUM *houseplant*   Maidenhair fern

Maidenhair ferns are excellent for shady fern gardens in a warm, humid climate or for a greenhouse. They are fairly difficult to grow and need lots of attention. These ferns do not like much sun but do like moist, humusy soil and humid—though not soggy—surroundings. They have delicate lacy fronds and wiry black stems. The frond tips bruise easily. Propagate them by dividing clumps.

A. bellum. Grows to 12 in. Has fluffy fronds and is easier to grow than most.
A. cuneatum. Grows to 20 in.; the most popular of the maidenhairs.
A. hispidulum. Grows to 12 in. Has forked fronds.
A. tenerum 'Wrightii'. Grows to 20 in. Has pale green fronds that mature to deep green.

SUGGESTED VARIETIES:
'Elegantissium'—very ruffled fronds
'Grande'—large fronds

ADONIS *perennial/annual*

These hardy garden favorites are related to buttercups. They grow to 1 ft. tall and have showy yellow or red flowers. Adonis can tolerate full sun as well as some shade and need moderate watering. They are especially good for borders and rock gardens. Buy prestarted plants.

A. aestivalis (summer adonis). An annual, with crimson flowers in June.
A. amurensis (Amur adonis). A perennial, with yellow, white, rose, or bright red striped flowers in February.
A. autumnalis (autumn adonis). An annual, with intense red flowers with a black center.
A. vernal (spring adonis). A perennial, with yellow flowers in March.

ADROMISCHUS *houseplant*

Adromischus, succulents from Cape Province, South Africa, are mostly miniature, indoor, desert plants. They like sun and a somewhat dry soil. Although they have thick, beautifully formed, colored leaves, they seldom bloom indoors.

A. clavifolius. Grows to 6 in. Has clusters of fat, club-shaped, silver-green leaves.
A. cooperii. Grows to 12 in. Has small leaves dotted red.
A. cristatus. Grows to 10 in. Has crested leaves and red stems.
A. maculatus. Grows to 10 in. Has thick, chocolate-brown leaves.

AECHMEA *houseplant* **Living vase plant**

These plants from the bromeliad family can be small, medium, or large. They are vase shaped with brilliantly colored leaves, variegated, and deep red; some appear to be lacquered. Aechmea do well in bright light in fir-bark containers inserted in the soil. Do not fertilize them, but keep the "vase" filled with water. In a mild climate, they can be used outside as borders. These plants usually have long flower spikes, the small flowers hidden in the bracts. Most species bloom in the spring or summer, a few in the winter. When the flowers fade, suckers appear at the plant's base. Cut them off when they are 2 to 4 in. high, and plant them separately. Many bear red or blue berries in the fall and winter that last for several months. Aechmea are almost resistant to insects.

A. calyculata. Grows to 20 in. Produces vivid yellow flowers in April.
A. fasciata. Grows to 24 in. Produces tufted blue-and-pink flowers in the spring.
A. 'Maginali'. Grows to 30 in. A hybrid, with pendant red flowers that usually bloom in the winter.
A. pubescens. Grows to 12 to 20 in. Has wheat-colored flowers and white berries.
A. racinae. Grows to 14 in. Produces red, black, and yellow flowers that bloom at Christmastime.
A. ramosa. Grows to 40 in. Has a pyramidal head of yellow flowers with red bracts that blooms in the summer.
A. weilbachii var. weilbachii. Grows to 20 in. Produces lavender flowers with red bracts that usually bloom in the winter.

SUGGESTED VARIETIES:
'Burgundy'—yellow and red flowers
'Rajah'—orange and yellow flowers and bracts
'Red Wing'—straw-colored flowers
'Silver Ghost'—silvery leaves
'Silver King'—pink and blue flowers
'Spring Beauty'—rose and yellow flowers

AERIDES *houseplant*

Aerides are very fragrant orchids with pretty flowers. Most species have leathery, dark green leaves. The pendant waxy flowers, lasting for three weeks in the summer, can grow to 20 in. long. They usually are pale pink but can also be white. Plant these orchids in medium-grade fir bark, and place in your sunniest window. Mist and water them frequently; they like humidity. Buy seedlings or take offshoots from plants.

A. affine. Grows to 20 in. Produces dark rose flowers with purple spots.
A. crassifolium. Grows to 14 in. Produces amethyst flowers, usually spotted.
A. falcatum. Grows to 14 in. Produces white-and-rose flowers, usually spotted.
A. maculosum. Grows to 20 in. Produces light rose flowers with purple spots.
A. odoratum. Grows to 24 in. The best one, with large fragrant white flowers streaked magenta.

AESCHYNANTHUS   *houseplant*   Lipstick vine

These trailing indoor plants flower profusely in the summer in good bright light. They have dark, glossy green leaves and tubular orange or red flowers. Lipstick vines can grow to 10 ft. long. Do not put in the full sun; give them some shade (a north exposure is fine). In the spring and summer they need lots of water, but not so much during the rest of the year. Mist them frequently to maintain humid surroundings. Watch out for spider mites and mealybugs, and take action immediately if they appear. Propagate lipstick plants by layering or cuttings.

A. lobbianus. Produces clusters of brilliant red flowers at the tips of the branches.
A. longiflorus. Robust; produces lots of red flowers.
A. marmoratus. Produces tubular green flowers with brown spots.
A. pulcher. Produces red-and-yellow flowers.
A. speciosus. Produces spectacular orange-red flowers.

AFRICAN VIOLET   *see Saintpaulia*

AGAPANTHUS   *bulb*   Lily of the Nile

Agapanthus can be either large or dwarf; they have long narrow leaves and round blue-purple or white flowers on tall stems. They like bright light and lots of water. Feed them every two months until after they bloom. Agapanthus are good background or accent plants. It is best to grow them in the same place for several years. Divide them in the spring. They are rarely attacked by insects.

A. africanus. Grows to 36 in. The most popular one, with large umbrellas of blue flowers.
A. inapertus. Grows to 18 in. Produces compact, deep blue flower heads.
A. orientalis. Grows to 48 in. Produces blue flowers.

SUGGESTED VARIETIES:
'Dwarf White'—white flowers
'Peter Pan'—blue flowers

AGAVE   *perennial*   Century plant

Despite the name, century plants bloom after only ten years. They are large succulents with rosettes of stiff leaves in blue, gray, green, or banded white or yellow. Agaves prefer sun or bright light, moderate watering (once a week), and sandy soil. Although they grow slowly, their rosettes can extend to 5 ft. across. The smaller plants are good as houseplants. Obtain new plants from offshoots. They are susceptible to mealybugs.

A. americana marginata. No trunk; has green leaves edged with yellow that may grow to 5 ft. long.

A. attenuata. Trunk to 3 ft. tall; has soft gray-green leaves.

A. medico-picta. No trunk; has green leaves with yellow stripes in the center that may grow to 5 ft. long.

A. miradorensis. No trunk; has leaves that grow to only 3 ft. long.

A. victoriae-reginae. No trunk; has 10-in. rosettes of narrow olive-green leaves edged with white.

AGERATUM HOUSTONIANUM   *annual*   Floss flower

Ageratums grow to 2 ft. tall, like sun and moderate watering, and bloom in the summer and fall. The flowers are blue or pink. Give them loamy garden soil; they make good borders and cut flowers. Buy prestarted plants.

SUGGESTED VARIETIES:
'Blue Mink'—blue flowers
'Fairy Pink'—pink flowers
'Snow Carpet'—white flowers

AGLAONEMA   *houseplant*   Chinese evergreen

This is a tough houseplant that will tolerate almost any condition. Most species have dark green leaves—some marked with white or silver—and white flowers. They do best with bright light or semishade and constant moisture at the roots. Only root-bound plants bloom, in late summer and early fall. They are easy to propagate: Cut stems into 3-in. lengths, place them in moist sand, and barely cover. Chinese evergreens are vulnerable to spider mites and mealybugs.

A. commutatum. Grows to 2 ft. Has dark green leaves with silver markings.

A. modestum. Grows to 2 ft. The most popular one; has dark green leaves.

A. pictum. Grows to only 1 ft. Has dark green velvety leaves with silver spots.

A. 'Pseudo Bracteatum'. Grows to 2 ft. Has green leaves with yellow spots.

A. robellinii. Grows to 3 ft. Very robust; has blue-green leaves.

A. simplex. Grows to 3 ft. Grows like a weed in a jar of water.

A. treubii. Grows to 2 ft. Has lance-shaped blue-green leaves spotted with silver.

AGROSTEMMA GITHAGO   *annual*   Corn cockle

Corn cockles grow to 3 ft. high and have dainty 2-in. lilac-pink flowers. They like sun but will grow in almost any soil and, if necessary, can tolerate either dry or wet conditions. Their wildflower quality make them suitable for woodland landscapes or natural flower beds. Buy prestarted plants.

AILANTHUS ALTISSIMA   *tree*   **Tree of heaven**

This tree will grow almost anywhere. Its foliage is open, with leaves divided into leaflets. Fast growing, it becomes rounded in shape. The tree of heaven can withstand temperatures to −20°F.

AJUGA   *ground cover*   **Carpet bugle**

One of the best ground covers, ajuga is a member of the mint family. It is small leaved and low growing, spreading into mats via creeping stolons. The flowers are blue-white. Ajuga grows in almost any type of soil and in almost any type of light, provided that it has sufficient moisture. Indeed, it can be invasive. Easily propagated by division and not vulnerable to many insects.

A. *genevensis*. Hardy to −10°F. Its small blue flowers bloom in June. Spreads quickly; good for rock gardens.
A. *reptans*. Hardy to −10°F. Flat-growing mats of green.

SUGGESTED VARIETIES:
'Atropurpurea'—bronze leaves
'Metallica Crispa'—silver leaves
'Rubra'—purple leaves
'Variegata'—variegated leaves

AKEBIA QUINATA   *vine*   **Five-leaf akebia**

This graceful, open vine can grow up to 20 ft. long and provides filtered shade or a pleasing pattern on a pillar or wall. Akebia is deciduous, and it has rose-purple flowers that bloom in the spring. It does well in the sun and needs a moderate amount of water. Because it grows quickly, it requires pruning each year. It offers a lot of green for little effort. Both softwood and hardwood cuttings root easily.

ALBIZIA JULIBRISSIN *tree*   **Silk tree**

This small tree has delicate, fernlike leaves and flowers in the summer. It likes sun and sandy, loamy soil. In cold climates, silk trees die down to the ground in winter; remove the dead stems in the spring to encourage new growth. They can tolerate temperatures down to 5°F.

ALBUCA *bulb*

Albuca grows to 4 ft. tall with basal leaves and erect flower clusters in the spring and summer. They prefer sun, sandy soil, and plenty of water in the spring, less in the summer. These bulbs can be propagated by offsets from mature bulbs; they are not generally bothered by insects.

A. crinifolia. Grows to 36 in. Has waxy, white, 2-in. flowers with a green rib in the middle.
A. major. Grows to 34 in. Has pale yellow flowers.
A. nelsoni. Grows to 42 in. Has white flowers.

ALLAMANDA CATHARTICA *vine*   **Trumpet vine**

This is a vigorous, evergreen, shrubby vine that can grow up to 10 ft. tall. It has oval dark green, leaves and spectacular, large golden yellow flowers. Allamanda tolerates almost any soil, but it must have sun all day to do well. Trumpet vines need moderate watering. They are suitable only for climates mild year-round; they are easily propagated by softwood or hardwood cuttings.

SUGGESTED VARIETIES:
'Hendersonii'—maroon flowers
'Williamsii'—yellow flowers

ALLIUM *bulb*   **Flowering onion**

Flowering onions are overlooked but excellent plants for a border, growing to 60 in. They are easy to establish in deep sandy loam, with a moderate amount of water and lots of sun. Plant the bulbs in the fall, about 5 in. deep. They will multiply by themselves; just dig them up and separate the bulbs every three years. Flowering onions also provide good cut flowers.

A. azureum. Produces deep blue flowers.
A. christophii (star of Persia). Produces lavender to dark blue starlike flowers.

A. giganteum (giant onion). Produces bright lilac flowers in July.
A. moly (lily leek). Produces yellow starlike flowers in July.
A. neapolitanum (Naples onion). Produces white flowers from March to May.

SUGGESTED VARIETY:
'Sibericum'

ALLOPHYTUM MEXICANUM *annual* Mexican foxglove

This is a 10-in. plant with long, leathery, dark green leaves and fragrant, tubular, lavender flowers in the spring or summer. Mexican foxgloves like a sunny location or bright light and moderate watering. A good occasional plant, but not exceptional.

ALNUS *tree* Alder

Alnus is a fast-growing tree that thrives in moist areas, although it can tolerate almost any kind of soil conditions. It has multiple stems with coarse-toothed leaves. Good for places where little else will grow.

A. glutonusa (European alder). Grows to 75 ft.; hardy to −5°F. Has dark green leaves and can tolerate wet soil.
A. incana (speckled alder). Grows to 60 ft.; hardy to −50°F. Hardiest of the alders; rather shrubby with dense dark green leaves.

ALOCASIA *houseplant* Elephant's ear

Alocasia are showy 12- to 30-in. exotic indoor plants from tropical Asia, with velvety green heart-shaped leaves veined copper, gray, silver, or red. These plants prefer shade and high humidity. Add peat moss to the soil and keep it quite moist; dry soil hurts the plant. Make sure the drainage is good. Feed monthly with a weak fertilizer solution. Propagate from suckers. In mild climates, alocasia can be grown outside.

A. amazonica. Grows to 20 in. Has green leaves with white veins.
A. chantrieri. Grows to 20 in. Has dark green leaves with gray veins.
A. lowii-grandis. Grows to 24 in. Has metallic brownish green leaves.
A. lowii veitchi. Grows to 24 in. Has brownish green, arrow-shaped leaves.
A. watsoniana. Grows to 28 in. Has blue-green leaves with silver veins.
A. zebrina. Grows to 18 in. Has green leaves with brown bands.

ALOE *perennial*

These succulents have rosettes of long, notched, swordlike gray-green or spotted leaves. Small aloes are good for houseplants, medium aloes for patios, and the giants for the landscape. Give them sun and sandy, well-drained soil. Keep them barely moist; soggy soil will quickly kill them. Aloe bloom in the fall and winter—orange, red, or yellow tubular spikes. Obtain new plants from offshoots. These succulents are rarely bothered by insects. Note, too, that the somewhat slimy sap oozing from a broken-off leaf quickly relieves the pain of burns.

A. arborescens (candelabra aloe). Grows to 10 ft. Has thick blue-green leaves.
A. aristata (lace aloe). Rosettes grow 6 in. across. Has gray-green leaves dotted white with white teeth along the margins.
A. brevifolia. Rosettes grow 3 to 4 in. across. Has gray-green leaves, occasionally with red flowers in the fall.
A. ciliaris. Rosettes grow 6 in. across. Has soft green-white notched leaves on pencil stems. Apt to be leggy.
A. globosa (crocodile aloe). Rosettes grow to 4 to 7 in. Has gray-green leaves.
A. nobilis (fold-spined aloe). Grows to about 2 ft. Has bright green leaves edged with yellow.
A. variegata (partridge breast aloe). Grows to 12 in. Has three-cornered, dark green leaves marbled and edged with white.

ALONSOA WARSCEWICZII   *annual*   Mask flower

The mask flower gets about 20 in. tall and blooms with small red flowers in the summer. It is usually bushy. Although it likes sun, it does not do well in hot weather. Put it in a cool place in a light sandy soil, and give it a moderate amount of water. Buy prestarted plants.

ALPINIA   *houseplant*   Shell flower, Ginger lily

Shell flowers are from the South Seas and New Guinea, and can be grown indoors and, in a year-round mild climate, outdoors. There are both foliage and flowering types, growing to about 4 ft. high. These plants prefer a shady location and plenty of water. They have arrow-shaped leaves with red bracts (flower heads). Divide clumps for additional plants. Alpinia is occasionally attacked by insects; when they appear, dispatch them immediately.

A. purpurata. Grows to 3 ft. Has dense clusters of red bracts emerging from the center of the leafed stem.
A. sanderae. Grows to 16 in. Has pale green leaves edged with white. Known mainly for foliage.

ALSTROEMERIA   *bulb*   Peruvian lily

These lilies grow to about 3 ft. high, with lance-shaped leaves and 1.5-in. red, yellow, or purple flowers. They like shade, a moderate amount of water (with good drainage), and rich soil. Plant the bulbs in the early spring or early fall, setting them horizontally in holes 6 to 8 in. deep. Dig up the bulbs after they have bloomed, and separate them every three years. Peruvian lilies make good cut flowers.

A. aurantiaca. Produces bright yellow flowers with brown spots.
A. hybrid. Produces lilac or bright rosy lilac flowers striped both inside and outside.

SUGGESTED VARIETY:
Lingtu series—mixed colors

ALTERNANTHERA   *perennial*

This is a good bedding plant, small, decorative, with little white flowers and vividly colored leaves. Grow this South American plant in the sun; keep the soil slightly dry but with moderate humidity. Propagate from cuttings.

A. ramosissima. Grows to 8 to 12 in. Has broad, pointed, metallic wine-red leaves.
A. versicolor. Grows to 3 in. Has copper or red leaves.

SUGGESTED VARIETIES:
'Snowball'—predominately white markings on leaves

ALTHEA ROSEA   *annual*   Hollyhock

Some hollyhocks can grow to 30 in. tall, others to 96 in. tall. They all have furry, toothed, rough leaves and rose-on-white flowers on long spikes that bloom in the summer. Hollyhocks grow in almost any soil, need sun, but little water. Use as background, ornamental flowers. Buy prestarted plants.

AMARANTHUS   *annual*

Amaranthus are mainly grown for their brightly colored leaves. They make good background plants, growing to about 4 ft. tall. Treat them as an annual. Amaranthus need shade, with the soil kept moist. Although they are susceptible to many garden pests, these can be easily controlled with the appropriate remedies. Start from seed in the fall or buy seedlings.

A. caudatus. The popular "love-lies-bleeding" plant. Has wine-colored leaves.
A. hybridus. Has brownish red or brown leaves.
A. tricolor. Has large, variegated, oval leaves. May also be grown as a houseplant.

SUGGESTED VARIETIES:
'Joseph's Coat'—green and yellow leaves
'Molten Fire'—bronze and red leaves

Amaryllis *bulb*

Amaryllis bulbs produce flowers as large as dinner plates, usually at Christmastime. These huge blossoms come in many colors: Red, pink, and white are the most common, with striped and multicolored varieties also available. In addition, there is a dwarf amaryllis that grows only 14 in. high, with red flowers. Indoors, grow amaryllis bulbs in 5-in. pots, one to a pot, with the tip of the bulb exposed. When the leaves are 4 to 5 in. high, increase water and light; the flowers should appear in a few weeks. Outdoors, plant the bulbs at least 5 in. deep in bright light, and water often. Leave the bulbs in the ground to multiply, or if they are in pots, store the pots—bulb and all—in a shady place, watering them only occasionally. Start growing them again in three months. There are dozens of varieties available; see the source list at the back of this book.

Amaryllis Belladonna *bulb*   Belladonna lily

The belladonna lily has tall flower spikes about 28 in. tall. The strap-shaped leaves are produced in the winter, and the fragrant flowers—red, white, or rose—come in the early spring. These lilies grow in almost any kind of soil. Give them sun and a moderate amount of water. The bulbs multiply on their own. Dig them up every three years and divide them.

Amelanchier *shrub/tree*   Serviceberry

These shrubs/small trees are deciduous needing partial sun and even moisture. Their white flowers bloom in the spring; edible fruit (serviceberries) is ready in the summer; and the leaves turn in the fall.

A. bartramiana. Grows to 6 ft.; hardy to −35°F. Has flowers in May, purple berries in September.

A. canadensis (shadblow serviceberry). Grows slowly. Hardy to −20°F. A slender tree with rounded foliage; the yellow leaves turn red in the fall, and the berries are dark red.

A. humilis. (*A. spicata*) Grows to 4 ft.; hardy to −20°F. Has oval leaves.

A. intermedia (swamp juneberry). Grows to about 15 ft.; hardy to −30°F. Produces dark purple berries in the fall.

A. laevis (Allegheny serviceberry). Grows vertically to 15 ft.; hardy to −20°F. Has white flowers and bluish purple berries in July.

A. ovalis (coastal juneberry). Grows vertically to 4 ft.; hardy to −10°F. Produces purplish black berries in June.

A. sanguinea (round-leaf juneberry). Grows to 8 ft.; hardy to −10°F. A straggly shrub; produces purple berries in August.

A. spicata (running juneberry). Grows to 4 ft.; hardy to −20°F. Has oval leaves, spreading foliage.

AMMOBIUM *annual*   Winged everlasting

The winged everlasting's oblong leaves form rosettes. It grows to 3 ft. tall and produces silvery white flower heads about 1 in. across, with yellow tubular flowers. Ammobium does well in the sun, needs little water, and blooms year-round. Buy prestarted plants.

AMPELOPSIS *vine*   Porcelian vine

This alternate-leaved vine has ornamental green leaves; as it can grow very tall, it needs suitable support. Most porcelian vines have colorful berries in

the fall. They like shade and lots of water. Use stratified seeds for propagation. These vines may be vulnerable to insect attacks; watch carefully. Use ampelopsis to cover unsightly walls or to create a screen.

A. acontifolia. Has lobed leaves and colorful berries.
A. brevipendunculata. Has lobed leaves and blue, sometimes white, berries.

ANAGALLIS   *perennial/annual*   Pimpernel

Growing to 4 ft. tall, pimpernels offer showy flowers in vibrant colors, usually orange, and so they make a good accent in the garden. They bloom in the summer and fall. Anagallis like sun and moderate watering and can tolerate most soil conditions. They are slow to germinate from seed. Pimpernels are good rock garden plants.

A. arvensis. A branching plant with oval leaves and, usually, reddish pink flowers.
A. linifolia. A perennial often grown as an annual. Has narrow leaves and blue flowers.

ANANAS   *houseplant*   Pineapple

Ananas, the commercial pineapple, can also be grown as a houseplant. It is a bromeliad, with leaves that are usually striped green, cream, and pink but sometimes are just plain green. The floral bracts are pink, red, and white on tall spikes that appear in the summer. Give these plants bright light, sandy soil, and a moderate amount of water. The large species are good tub plants; the smaller ones for pots. Keep their leaves free of dust by wiping them with a damp cloth. Obtain new plants from offsets. The leaves are usually too tough for insects.

A. cosmos. Rosettes of dark green leaves grow to 30 to 36 in. across. This is the pineapple most often grown commercially.
A. nanus. Rosettes grow to 36 in. across. Has spectacular yellow-green-pink leaves.
A. variegatus. Grows to 15 in. Has green leaves; available with fruit at florists' shops.

ANAPHALIS   *perennial*

Anaphalis are erect perennials growing to 3 ft. tall with leafy stems and small, tubular flowers. They are excellent for borders. Although these plants can tolerate shade, they do better in the sun. Their soil should never be moist; water them only when they are dry. Divide them in the spring or fall. Anaphalis make good everlasting cut flowers.

A. margaritacea (pearly everlasting). Has leaves that are green on top and white underneath, with clusters of white flowers.
A. yedonis. Has clusters of silvery white, buttonlike flowers.

ANCHUSA   *perennial*   **Alkanet**

Anchusa produce lots of blue flowers. They can grow to 5 ft. tall and spread quickly. Plant alkanets in a loamy soil, give them sun, and water them regularly. They are good for borders or as a foil for other, shorter, plants. Propagate them from rooted cuttings.

A. azurea. Has shiny, lance-shaped leaves and large, blue to blue-purple flowers.
A. capensis (summer forget-me-not). Has lance-shaped leaves and blue flowers in July.
A. myosotidiflora (*Brunnera macrophylla*). Has heart-shaped leaves and blue flowers with yellow throats.

SUGGESTED VARIETY:
'Blue Angel'

ANDROMEDA   *shrub*   **Bog rosemary**

Andromeda are best for bogs or water gardens. They need much water and a bright location, as well as room to spread. These plants are ornamental, with narrow, evergreen leaves and white flowers, good for an accent. Propagation is tricky, so buy new plants. They are not usually attacked by insects.

A. glaucophylla. Hardy to −40°F. Has very narrow leaves and white flowers; strictly a bog plant.
A. polifilia. Hardy to −40°F. Low-creeping shrub with evergreen leaves and small, pinkish white flowers.

ANEMONE   *bulb*

Anemones are members of the buttercup family. They grow to 1 ft. tall and produce colorful flowers that make them good for borders. Anemones do well in a combination of sun and shade, in well-drained and neutral soil.

Plant the tubers 4 to 6 in. apart, 2 in. deep, and divide them occasionally. Greek anemones are best for cool climates, and poppy-flowered anemones are best for mild-winter climates. They bloom in the spring or fall.

A. blanda (Greek anemone). Many varieties; most have deeply cut leaves and deep blue flowers.
A. coronaria (poppy-flowered anemone). Has oblong and toothed leaves and large, solitary, red, blue, violet, or yellow flowers.
A. fulgens (flame anemone). A vining type of anemone with vermillion flowers. Needs a rich soil.
A. japonica (Japanese anemone). Has purple, red, rose, or white flowers.
A. vitifolia (grape-leaf anemone). Has white flowers.

SUGGESTED VARIETIES:
'His Excellency'—blue-violet flowers
'Robustissima'—large pink flowers
'September Charm'—red flowers
'St. Brigid'—purple flowers

Angraecum   *houseplant*   Comet orchid

These orchids come in both large and small species, with leathery leaves and white flowers. The blossoms have a long-tailed spur, sometimes up to a foot in length. Comet orchids need a bright location and a fir-bark potting mix kept moderately moist. Most bloom in the winter. Propagate by offshoots from mature plants. These orchids are seldom bothered by insects.

A. compactum. Grows to 3 in. Flowers in the winter.
A. eburneum. Grows to 36 in. Produces alternating flowers in the late fall or early winter.
A. veitchii. Grows to 24 in. Produces star-shaped flowers from January onward.

Ansellia africanus   *houseplant*   Spider orchid

There is no better orchid. Spider orchids are easy to grow, producing crowns of bright green leaves and many red-and-yellow flowers on branching stems. They can grow up to 4 ft. Put them in a sunny, humid location, planted in large-grade fir bark. To obtain new plants, divide mature orchids; the young ones do bloom. Buy mature plants. *A. africanus* is also sold as *A. gigantea* and *A. nilotica.*

Anthemis   *perennial*   Chamomille

Anthemis is easy to grow and thus a good plant for beginners. Plants like sun, almost any well-drained soil, and a moderate amount of water. Chamomilles have fernlike foliage and white, daisy-type flowers, growing to 2 ft. high. They are good bedding plants. Obtain new ones by means of division. Anthemis is resistant to most insects.

A. tinctoria (golden marguerite). A branching plant with toothed leaves; the flowers vary in color but are usually yellow.

SUGGESTED VARIETY:
'Moonlight'

ANTHENUM GRAVOELENS *herb*   Dill

This popular annual herb grows about 3 ft. high. Dill leaves are threadlike and divided. Although this is not an especially attractive plant, it does provide a desirable herb. Dill needs sun and moderate watering. Plant seeds at any time of year.

ANTHURIUM *houseplant*   Flamingo flower

From the Central and South American jungles, anthurium have striking foliage and, in the winter and spring, "lacquered" flowers. Use a potting mix of half houseplant soil and half fine-grade fir bark, so that drainage is good. Grow in a shady spot, and keep the soil moist. Be careful, though, as too-wet or too-dry soil will quickly kill plants. Keep them warm (75°F) at night and humid all the time. You can put several plants in one pot. In very warm, humid climates, anthurium can be grown outside, in the shade of a tree. Grow additional plants from seeds.

A. andraeanum. Grows to 16 in. Has green leaves and red, white, coral, or pink flowers.
A. bakeri. Grows to 15 in. Has brilliant red flowers.
A. crystallinum. Grows to 14 in. Has velvety green, silver-veined leaves, but the flowers are insignificant.
A. forgetti. Grows to 16 in. Is similar to *A. crystallinum* but with oval leaves.
A. scandens. A climbing plant, to 36 in. Has dark green leaves.
A. scherzerianum. Grows to 16 in. The most commonly grown anthurium, with red flowers.
A. warocqueanum. Grows 30-in. rosettes of long, velvety green leaves with pale green veins.

ANTIGONON LEPTOPUS *vine*   Coral vine

The coral vine is deciduous, growing to 40 in. long and doing well in almost any kind of soil. It has heart-shaped leaves and rose-pink flowers. The coral vine likes sun and summer heat but is not hardy in northern regions. It needs moderate watering and blooms in the summer and early fall. Treat it as a perennial: It dies down somewhat through the winter but revives in the early spring. Obtain new plants from division. Coral vines are good for walls and trellises.

ANTIRRHINUM *annual*   Snapdragon

Snapdragons are available in three heights: small, to 1 ft; intermediate, to 2 ft; and tall, to 5 ft. They produce many flowers in many colors, in the summer and fall. Plant them in the sun in a well-drained, loamy garden soil, and water them moderately. Pinch off the stems and tips when the plants are about 4 in. high, to produce lots of flowers. Snapdragons are good as background plants in flower beds and as cut flowers. Buy prestarted plants.

SUGGESTED VARIETIES:
'Fiesta Mix'—varied colors
'Little Darling'—varied colors
'Rocket Mix'—varied colors

APHELANDRA *houseplant*

Generally used as a gift plant, aphelandra has showy spring and summer flowers of orange or yellow, and gray-green or plain green leaves with white veins. It is occasionally planted outside in mild climates. Aphelandra grows rapidly in the sun; it needs lots of water in the spring and summer, less during the rest of the year. Outside, if it becomes leggy, cut it down to 6 in. Propagate by seed or buy new plants. Aphelandra attracts insects, so watch it carefully.

A. aurantiaca roezelii. Grows to 16 in. Has vivid orange-red flowers.
A. chamissoniana. Grows to 14 in. The most popular aphelandra; has bright yellow flowers.
A. squarrosa louisae. Grows to 20 in. Has shiny, corrugated leaves and yellow flowers.

APONOGETON   *aquatic plant*   Pond weed

This perennial herb from South Africa has long leaves and usually floats on water. Its flowers are small, white, and fragrant. Pond weed is strictly a water plant to be grown in the sun. Usually found in aquariums. It is pretty but not special. Pond weed is easily propagated by division and is not generally attacked by insects.

A. madagascariensis. An aquarium plant. Its leaves are a network of veins; its flowers are small and white on long stalks.

AQUILEGIA   *perennial*   Rocky Mountain columbine

These columbines grow to 2 ft; they belong to the buttercup family. They need sun or bright light and a moderate amount of water. The soil should drain well. The flowering ends rather early in the summer, and spent plants should be replaced with other, later-blooming ones. Rocky Mountain columbines are good border plants. Replace them with new plants every few years.

A. caerulea (Rocky Mountain columbine). Many varieties; have large lower leaves and whitish flowers tinged light blue and yellow.
A. canadensis (common American columbine). Flowers are yellowish or tinged red on back.
A. chrysantha (golden columbine). Has spreading flowers, pale yellow, tinged pink, with deep yellow petals.

SUGGESTED VARIETIES:
'Nana Alba'—dwarf, white flowers
'Mrs. Scott Elliot'—mixed colors

ARABIS   *perennial*   Rockcress

Arabis is good for rock gardens; it is low growing and produces small white flowers in the spring. These plants form mats of ground cover and can be used in borders. Most species need sun and lots of water. They are easily divided. Arabis is plagued by insects, so take precautions.

A. alpina. Has small flowers; usually called *A. albida.*
A. caucasica. A very popular species, with small flowers.

SUGGESTED VARIETIES:
'Flore Pleno'—large flowers
'Rosabella'—pink flowers

ARALIA   *see Dizygotheca*

ARALIA   *shrub/tree*   Angelica tree

Angelica trees have pinnate leaves and produce small flowers in clusters, as well as small black fruits that birds love. As a shrub, aralia is not distinctive. It grows easily in almost any light and any soil. Aralia is difficult to propagate, so buy additional plants. It is vulnerable to insects.

A. elata. Hardy to −20°F. Perhaps the most popular aralia; has large, compound leaves. This is a big tree and needs space.
A. hispida. Hardy to −20°F. A perennial shrub with handsome leaves and flowers.

ARAUCARIA   *tree*   Norfolk Island pine

This pine from Chile resembles a Christmas tree. It can grow to 25 ft. or more. Use in a landscape that needs a vertical accent. It does well in a north or bright light and requires evenly moist soil. Some araucarias are sold as large potted plants. This elegant pine grows slowly. Obtain new plants from seed or air layering. Araucaria is not generally bothered by insects.

A. excelsa. Has scalelike evergreen leaves.
A. heterophylla. The most popular araucaria.

ARCTOTIS GRANDIS   *perennial/annual*   African daisy

These 24-in. African daisies are colorful and grow well in the sun. They need moderate watering and provide pale violet flowers for a long time in the summer and fall. Some dwarf varieties grow to be only 10 in. high. Buy prestarted plants.

ARDISIA   *shrub*   Coral berry

These shrubs have hollylike leaves and white flowers followed by, or accompanied by, coral-red or white berries. Grow them in bright light and soil kept just moist. Mist them several times a week. Some coral berries are offered in containers at Christmastime. Propagate by cuttings or seeds. They are rarely bothered by insects.

A. crenata (A. crispa). Hardy to −40°F. The best coral berry; has glossy green leaves and red berries from June through December.
A. japonica. Hardy to −40°F. Not so colorful as *A. crenata* but still nice; has white berries.

ARECA CATECHU *tree*   **Betel nut**

The betel nut is a tall palm, frequently sold as *Howeia*, a different plant (and a much better indoor grower). The betel nut has long fronds and slender stems, sometimes growing to 8 ft. indoors. Its general appearance, however, is spindly and not as full as howeia's. Give areca good light (sun is fine), and keep the soil fairly moist. It is often used in tropical gardens as a vertical accent and is best grown in groups. Buy new plants, as it is nearly impossible to propagate your own. Betel nuts are rarely visited by insects.

ARGEMONE GRANDIFLORA *annual*   **Prickly poppy**

A seldom-grown, tall plant that has large, showy, satin-white flowers that bloom in the summer. Situate prickly poppies in the sun and in a sandy loam with good drainage. They need moderate watering. Buy prestarted plants.

ARISTOLOCHIA DURIOR *vine*   **Dutchman's pipe**

This vine has heart-shaped leaves and can grow 30 ft. long, forming a dense green curtain. It can tolerate both sun and shade, does well in most soils, but needs lots of water. Dutchman's pipe does not like much wind, so put it in a protected place. It grows well on an arbor or trellis. Treat it as a perennial, obtaining new plants from softwood cuttings.

ARMERIA *perennial*   **Sea pink (or thrift)**

Armeria are small plants, up to 16 in. high, with pink flowers. They do well in the sun in sandy soil with good drainage and moderate watering. These plants are ideal for borders or rock gardens and are easily divided.

A. maritima. Has somewhat hairy leaves and pink, rose-red, lilac, or white flowers.
A. plantaginea. Has tufted, slightly hairy leaves and pink flowers.

SUGGESTED VARIETIES:
'Alba'—white flowers
'Corsica'—white flowers

ARTHROPODIUM CIRRHATUM *houseplant*

This plant grows to 3 ft. tall, with grassy light green leaves and starlike white flowers in February and March. Give it sun and lots of water while is blooming. After it has flowered, decrease the amount of water, but never let the soil dry out. Divide plants after they flower.

ARUNCUS SYLVESTER   *perennial*   Goatsbeard

An unusual plant, aruncus is a member of the rose family and grows to 84 in. tall. Its flowers somewhat resemble a goat's beard; they bloom in the summer. Aruncus does well in shady areas in moist soil. Buy prestarted plants.

ARUNDO DONAX   *grass*   Reed grass

These giant reeds have grasslike plumes and look best in a corner or as a background plant in a flower bed. Reed grass prefers a sunny location and needs lots of water. Its feathery flower spire (2 ft. tall) makes a good indoor decoration. Reed grass tolerates temperatures to −5°F.

ASARINA   *vine*

Asarina grow to be 10 ft. long and produce heart-shaped leaves and distinctive trumpet flowers from November onward. Give this vine sun and keep the soil moist. It does best on a patio, but it occasionally succeeds indoors in a very sunny window. For new vines, plant seeds or take root cuttings. Asarina also may be sold as *Maurandia*.

A. antirrhinifolia. Produces 1-in. purple flowers.
A. barclaiana. Produces 1-in. white-and-purple flowers.
A. erubescens. Produces 3-in. rose-red flowers.

ASARUM   *perennial*   Wild ginger

Asarum is native to North America from Canada to South Carolina. Asarum's heart-shaped leaves make a great, thick ground cover. Some species of asarum are evergreen; others die down each fall. Wild ginger likes the shade and a moderate amount of water, and generally requires little care. The flowers are insignificant. Asarum is easily divided and is seldom attacked by insects.

A. canadense. Not evergreen; has heart-shaped leaves.
A. europaeum. The most popular asarum; is an evergreen with heart-shaped leaves and is easy to grow.

ASCLEPIA   *shrub*   Butterfly bush

The butterfly bush has narrow, lance-shaped leaves, and most species have orange flower crowns that bloom in midsummer. Asclepia grow well in a poor soil in bright light or sun. Water the bush thoroughly during the growing season. It is easily divided and also is bothered by insects; watch carefully and take action if necessary. Note that parts of asclepias are poisonous to animals, so take care if you have pets.

A. curassavica. Hardy to −20°F. Has long narrow leaves and scarlet-orange flowers.
A. mexicana. Hardy to −20°F. Produces greenish white flowers.
A. tuberosa. Hardy to −20°F. The most popular of the asclepias; has orange flowers.

Ascocentrum   *houseplant*   Carnival orchid

These small plants are called carnival orchids because of their brightly colored flowers. A healthy plant can produce as many as forty flowers in the early spring. Its leaves are leathery and straplike. Grow in the full sun in medium-grade fir bark, and provide lots of humidity. Water it often while it is actively growing, but not as much during the rest of the year. Buy new plants.

A. ampullaceum. Grows to 20 in. Produces cerise-red flowers.
A. curvifolium. Grows to 14 in. Produces red flowers.
A. miniatum. Grows to 10 in. Produces orange flowers.

Asparagus   *houseplant*   Emerald or asparagus fern

Asparagus ferns are really vines; some can grow to 6 ft. long. Their leaves are very feathery, and they produce small whitish pink, fragrant flowers, followed by red or purple berries. These ferns grow easily, even in a northern exposure. Water them often, and about once a month, give them a soaking. Asparagus ferns look good in baskets. For new ferns, divide clumps or plant seeds.

A. asparagoides. Grows to 3 ft. Has feathery, ferny foliage. Florists use this for flower arrangements.
A. plumosus. Grows to 3 ft.; a climber.
A. sprengeri. Grows to 5 ft. Has green needlelike foliage; a wonderful, easy-to-grow houseplant for beginners.

Aspidistra   *houseplant*   Cast-iron plant

These plants, with long, dark green leaves, can survive almost any abuse; hence their nickname. Sometimes they blossom with sprays of purple-brown flowers. Aspidistra are good for northern windows and other difficult growing locations. Keep the soil moist; they do not care about humidity. For a good display, put several plants in one pot. For new plants, carefully split the crown.

A. elatior. Grows to 2 ft. Has shiny green leaves.
A. elator variegata. Grows to 2 ft. Has shiny green-and-white striped leaves.

ASPLENIUM *houseplant*

Bird's nest fern

These ferns grow to 14 to 30 in. tall, and most have very thin, shiny green fronds around a center cavity. Grow them in a bright window, and keep the soil moist and the humidity high. Add chopped osmunda to the standard soil mixture. Mist often and watch out for scale infestations. Propagate by means of offsets.

A. bulbiferum. New plantlets grow on leaves, which can be used for propagation. Has wiry fronds and black stems.
A. nidus. Has broad, light green fronds.

ASTER *perennial*

Michaelmas daisy

There are over six hundred true species of asters, ranging in height from 6 in. to 6 ft. Asters need sun and a moist, loamy garden soil. Most are resistant to insects.

A. amellus (Italian aster). Has rough leaves and solitary purple flowers.
A. frikarti. Produces blue flowers.
A. tanacetifolius (Tahoka daisy). Has hairy leaves and violet-colored flowers.

SUGGESTED VARIETIES (flower form):
'Cactus'
'Duchess'
'Perfection'
'Super Giant'
'Violet Queen'
'White Heather'

ASTILBE ARENDSII *perennial* Astilbe

These well-known flowers make colorful accents in a garden. Astilbes grow to 6 ft. tall, with rosy lilac flowers blooming in the summer and rising high above most others. They are good background plants. Astilbes like shade, a loamy soil, moderate watering, and regular feeding. For new plants, divide them in the fall or spring.

SUGGESTED VARIETIES:
'Bridal Veil'—white flowers
'Pumila'—red flowers
'Sprite'—pink flowers

ASTROPHYTUM *houseplant* Star cactus

This easy-to-grow genus includes two species without prickles (that is, spineless) and with yellow flowers. Give this cactus full sun and keep the sandy soil barely moist, never wet. Propagate by means of offsets.

A. asterias. Grows 1 in. tall and 3 in. across. Has a spineless, eight-segmented dome.
A. capricorne. Grows 10 in. tall; globular with white ribs and papery prickles.
A. myriostigma (bishop's hood). Grows 2 in. tall and is star shaped, separated into five segments.

AUCUBA JAPONICA GOLDIANA *houseplant* Gold dust plant

This Japanese evergreen grows as tall as 15 ft. It has variegated leaves, insignificant flowers, but red, white, or yellow berries. Put in a semishaded location, and give it lots of water. Prune young plants into the desired shapes. These plants are good on a patio; they may work in a window. Obtain new plants from cuttings.

AZALEA *see Rhododendron*

BABIANA *bulb*   Baboon flower

These small, 12-in. bulbs from South Africa have white and blue flowers that bloom in the early spring. Baboon flowers make good edging plants and grow easily in most well-drained soils in a sunny location. Give them a moderate amount of water, and after they have bloomed, dig up the bulbs and store them through the winter. For additional plants, separate the corms.

BAMBUSA *perennial*   Bamboo

Bamboo encompass a large group of plants, over seven hundred species, ranging in size from a few feet to over a hundred and varying in appearance from impressive (in a bamboo forest) to weedy (in an undesirable place). There are clump-growing types and running types. Many people are afraid of bamboo because it is invasive and may be exceedingly difficult to eliminate once it has become established. But if you choose carefully the kind and the location, bamboo can be a fine addition to a garden. Bamboo are divided into the following groups: *Arundinaria*, which has handsome leaves; bamboo, the most popular kind, with narrow grassy leaves; *Phyllostachys*: a running type of bamboo with small leaves; and *Sasa*, a pygmy bamboo. All bamboo need a rather moist soil, and most will grow in full sun. Generally, bamboo can tolerate almost any condition; indeed, they are difficult to kill. They are not plagued by insects and propagate themselves. Cut out the centers of clumps to encourage new growth and keep the plants attractive.

Arundinaria amabilis. A small, caned bamboo with handsome leaves.
A. variegata. A variegated, ornamental bamboo.
Bambusa multiplex. The most common bamboo; forms clumps.
B. vulgaris. The most widely grown bamboo, a tree type.
Phyllostachys nigra (black bamboo). Needs lots of water; ornamental.
P. viridis. Has a graceful shape and leaves.
Sasa palmata. A pygmy bamboo; grows rapidly and can tolerate almost any condition.

BAPTISIA *perennial*   Wild indigo

Wild indigo is a member of the pea family. It has ornamental, pealike flowers on a fleshy stalk and likes a protected but bright spot and plenty of water. Baptisia's blue flowers make it a good accent plant, but when it is grown in a mass, it provides a dramatic effect. Baptisia is easily divided and is not usually bothered by insects.

B. australis. Has bluish green leaves and blue flowers.
B. tinctoria. The most commonly grown of this species; good in a meadow garden.

PLATE 1

Beds of Astilbe are graceful, elegant and create a statement in the garden.

PLATE 2

Anchusa is a brightly colored perennial that is welcome in any garden; it is especially good for vertical accent.

PLATE 3

Drifts of asters make this garden corner a demanding sight.

PLATE 4

The yellow trumpet vine adorns a fence. Its botanical name is *Allamanda*.

PLATE 5

Anemones are used as ground cover in this garden. This species is *A. blanda*.

PLATE 6

The singular beauty of *Aloe brevifolia* makes it a desirable garden plant in suitable climates.

PLATE 7

Wax begonias (*Begonia semperflorens*) are becoming more and more popular as years go by; they now bloom in profusion.

PLATE 8

This reflecting pool is lined with durable Bromeliads (against the fence) while water Cyperus accent the pond.

PLATE 9

Yesterday's favorite houseplant—the angel wing begonia is always welcome indoors where it blooms during the summer.

PLATE 10

Wax begonias, geraniums, and lobelia are a triumvirate of color at this garden entrance.

PLATE 11

Doronicum and Arabis in a colorful medley in this garden.

PLATE 12

This flower border is predominantly tulips, and borders the lawn; the splash of orange *Cherianthus* provides color contrast.

PLATE 13

Cacti and succulents have been popular through the years. This photo is the desert garden at the Berekely Botanic Gardens.

PLATE 14

The orange flowers of *Clivia* welcome spring; in the north it is grown mostly as a houseplant. In all year temperate climates, it can be used in the landscape.

PLATE 15

The beauty of orchids is tough to beat; here the popular Cattleya hybrid sports many flowers that last for weeks.

PLATE 16

Tiger lilies accent
this cottage garden.

PLATE 17

A colorful panorama
of *Cherianthus*.

BAUHINIA   *tree*   Orchid tree

Orchid trees come in both evergreen and deciduous types, and both flower in the spring. They do not grow taller than 35 ft. The flowers, not surprisingly, resemble orchids and can be white, pink, or light red-purple. Orchid trees need sun, a very mild climate, and lots of water at the roots. They are susceptible to insect attacks.

B. corymbosa. Hardy to 50°F. This is more a shrub or vine than a tree, producing small pink flowers.
B. purpurea. Hardy to 50°F. Produces purple flowers.
B. variegata. Hardy to 50°F. Produces lavender-to-purple flowers.

BEAUMONTIA   *vine*   Trumpet flower

Trumpet flowers grow well in mild climates. The vine's leaves are dark green, and its flowers are trumpet shaped, large, pinkish, and usually fragrant. It grows well in the sun and with lots of water, and it generally is not bothered by insects.

B. grandiflora. Hardy to 50°F. Has dark green leaves and big, fragrant, whitish pink flowers.
B. jerdoniana. Hardy to 50°F. Produces white, somewhat fragrant, bell-shaped flowers.

BEGONIA   *perennial*

There are many types, shapes, and sizes of begonias. They are very popular additions to the garden, and most do well without too much bother.

Semperflorens are wax begonias and bloom almost all year. They need sun and regular watering, although too much water will kill them. Prune them back after they flower, and propagate them by means of cuttings or seed. Guard against insects. Wax begonias have glossy green, dark green, or mahogany-colored leaves, and single, semidouble, or double flowers in white, pink, or red.

SUGGESTED VARIETIES:
'Andy'—grows to 6 in.; grass-green leaves, rose-colored flowers
'Apple Blossom'—grows to 12 in.; double pale pink flowers
'Ballet'—grows to 12 in.; bronze leaves and double white flowers
'Cinderella'—grows to 12 in.; pink flowers tipped red
'Green Thimbleberry'—pale green leaves and pink flowers
'Jack Horner'—grows to 12 in.; dark green leaves and pink flowers
'Little Gem'—grows to 6 in.; bronze leaves and double pink flowers
'Lucy Lockett'—grows to 14 in.; double pink flowers
'Rosa Kugel'—grows to 8 in.; rose-pink flowers
'South Pacific'—grows to 10 in.; bright orange-red flowers

Rhizomatous begonias have round or star-shaped leaves.

The gnarled growth of the rhizomes, which store water, is distinctive; they should skim the surface of the soil and should not be buried. These begonias bloom in late winter or early spring. Allow the soil to dry out thoroughly between waterings. Some varieties take a short rest; at that time, water them only a little until you see new growth in the spring. Propagate them from cuttings.

SUGGESTED VARIETIES:
B. imperialis 'Otto Forster'—grows to 14 in.; dark green leaves and white flowers
B. strigillosa—grows to 16 in.; brown-spotted green leaves and pale pink flowers

Angel wing begonias are so named because their leaves are shaped like an angel's wings. They need constantly moist soil and morning or afternoon sun. Prune these begonias quite often, as they can grow rather tall. Propagate from cuttings.

SUGGESTED VARIETIES:
'Alzasco'—grows to 36 in.; dark green leaves with silver spots, and red flowers
B. coccinea—grows to 48 in.; shiny bright green leaves and red flowers
B. maculata—grows to 40 in.; green leaves splotched with silver and pink flowers
'Elvira Swisher'—grows to 48 in.; large lobed leaves laced with silver, and pink flowers
'Grey Feather'—grows to 48 in.; shiny arrow-shaped leaves and white flowers
'Orange Rubra'—grows to 36 in.; green leaves sometimes spotted with silver, and orange flowers
'Pink Rubra'—grows to 60 in.; bright green pointed leaves and pink flowers

'Rubaiyat'—grows to 48 in.; green leaves and salmon-colored flowers
'Velma'—grows to 40 in.; green cupped leaves and red flowers

Hairy-leaved begonias have, as their name indicates, hairy leaves and even whiskery flowers. Their leaves may be round, lobed, or tapered, and their flowers may be red, pink, or white. Propagate from stem cuttings.

SUGGESTED VARIETIES:
'Alleryi'—grows to 30 in.; dark green leaves with white hairs, and pale pink flowers
B. scharffiana—grows to 30 in.; green-red plush leaves and ivory-colored flowers
'Drosti'—grows to 30 in.; very hairy leaves and pink flowers
'Prunifolia'—grows to 30 in.; cupped leaves and white flowers
'Viaudi'—grows to 36 in.; leaves green on top and red underneath, with fine white hairs, and white flowers

Tuberous begonias are the summer-flowering aristocrats of the garden. Most grow up to 20 in. tall. Situate them where they can get some sun and stay cool. They flourish in cool, humid, cloudy regions, like Seattle. Water the plants heavily on bright days but not so much on cloudy days. When they are growing well, feed them every other week. Tuberous begonias are good hanging plants for a shaded patio. After they flower, gradually cut back the water but let them continue to grow until their leaves turn yellow and dry. Then dig up the tubers, wash and dry them, and store them in a cool, dry place until the following spring.

SUGGESTED VARIETIES:
'Black Knight'—deep crimson flowers
'Flambeau'—double orange-scarlet flowers
'Flamboyante'—single scarlet flowers
'Frances Powell'—double pink flowers
'Mandarin'—double salmon-orange flowers
'Rosado'—deeply frilled and ruffled pink flowers
'Sweet Home'—double red flowers
'Tasso'—semidouble pink flowers

BELAMCANDA CHINENSIS   *bulb*   Blackberry lily

These lilies are perennials with gladioluslike leaves and rather small, reddish spotted flowers. They need lots of sun and water; they seem to be valued more for being different than for being pretty. Blackberry lilies divide easily and are resistant to most insects.

Bellis perennis   *perennial*   **English daisy**

English daisies grow to 10 in. high and bloom in the spring. They have long, toothed, and slightly hairy leaves that taper at the base. These plants like sun and lots of water and somewhat acid soil. Be sure to feed them as well. Buy prestarted plants.

SUGGESTED VARIETIES:
'Dresden China'—pink flowers
'Giant Rose'—rose-colored flowers
'Goliath'—large white flowers
'Pomponette'—pompom-shaped white flowers
'Snowball'—white flowers
'White Carpet'—white flowers

Beloperone (Justicia) Guttata   *houseplant*   **Shrimp plant**

Though officially a houseplant, shrimp plants can be grown outside in mild climates. Put them in a sunny area, and let them dry out between waterings. They should grow to be 3 to 4 ft. tall, with paper-thin bracts and tiny white flowers. Prune back leggy growth in the late summer, and propagate them from cuttings.

SUGGESTED VARIETIES:
'Red King'—red bracts
'Yellow Queen'—pink and yellow bracts

Berberis   *shrub*   **Barberry**

Barberries are dense, thorny shrubs, both deciduous and evergreen, with small flowers. They make good barriers but also can be used in a landscape because of their attractive branching. Small bright red or purple-black berries appear in the fall. Although most barberries lose their fruit soon after it ripens, the Japanese barberry retains its color through the winter. These shrubs grow in almost any kind of soil, in sun or light shade.

B. buxfolia (Magellan barberry). Grows upright to 6 ft.; hardy to −10°F. An evergreen with small leathery leaves, orange-yellow flowers, and dark purple berries.
B. julianae (wintergreen barberry). Grows to 6 ft.; hardy to 0°F. An evergreen with very leathery, spiny-toothed, dark green leaves that turn red in the fall; thorny.
B. koreana (Korean barberry). Grows to 6 ft.; hardy to −5°F. A deciduous shrub with leaves turning deep red in the fall and winter, and yellow flowers in May.
B. thunbergii (Japanese barberry). Grows to 7 ft.; hardy to −10°F. A deciduous shrub with arching stems, deep green leaves, yellow flowers, and fiery red berries.
B. verruculosa (warty barberry). Grows to about 4 ft.; hardy to −5°F. An evergreen with leathery dark green leaves and golden yellow flowers.

BERGENIA *perennial*

Bergenia is an evergreen with thick round leaves and spires of pink or whitish pink flowers that bloom in the spring. It does not do well in the sun; that is, it needs shade, as well as lots of water. Propagate bergenia by division; they are not generally bothered by insects.

B. cordifolia. Produces rose-colored flowers; makes a good ground cover.
B. crassifolia. Similar to *B. cordifolia*, but with flowers held high above the foliage.

SUGGESTED VARIETIES:
'Evening Glow'—white flowers
'Purpurea'—pink flowers
'Sunningdale'—red flowers

BESSERA ELEGANS *bulb*   Coral drops

This showy plant native to Mexico grows to 30 in. and produces scarlet or scarlet-and-white flowers in the summer. Coral drops are effective in masses. They like sun and a moderate amount of water. In cold-winter regions, dig up the bulbs and store them until spring. Propagate them by means of offsets.

BETULA *tree*   Birch

Birches are favorite deciduous trees, with the most popular having white bark flecked with black. They are somewhat short-lived and difficult to transplant unless they are balled and burlapped. Birches absolutely must not

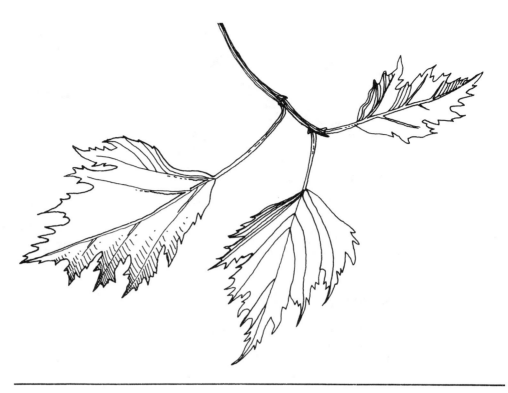

be moved except in the spring. Once established, however, birches are easy to grow and thrive in wet or dry soil. Their leaves turn bright yellow in the fall.

B. papyrifera (canoe birch). Grows to 90 ft.; hardy to −35°F. Its white bark peels off in thin sheets.

B. pendula (European white birch). Grows to 40 ft.; hardy to −50°F. White bark; pyramidal shape.

SUGGESTED VARIETY:
'Youngii' (Young's weeping birch)—pendulous branches

BIFRENARIA   *houseplant*

Bifrenarias are an uncommonly beautiful genus of orchids, with 10- to 16-in. dark green leaves and colorful flowers in the spring. Keep them in a greenhouse or a humid room. Bifrenarias will bloom readily if they are properly rested. After they flower, keep them almost dry for about two months with only an occasional misting—about once a week. Then give them bright light and lots of water throughout the summer. Buy new plants from suppliers.

B. harrisoniae. Grows to 20 in. Produces large waxy white flowers with a magenta lip.
B. tyrianthina. Grows to 20 in. Produces pink-and-red flowers on erect stems.

BIGNONIA CAPREOLATA *vine*   Trumpet vine

Trumpet vines (sometimes called *Clytosoma*) are densely growing, sometimes to 50 ft., with green leaves and large orange-red flowers. They are heavy feeders and love heat and sun. A sandy soil is best for them. Propagate by dividing.

SUGGESTED VARIETY:
'Madame Galen'

BILLBERGIA *houseplant*

Billbergia are bromeliads with varied leaves that are usually grasslike. Their flower bracts are very colorful—cerise to purple. These plants grow in a vase shape to 30 in. high. Give them sun, and keep the "vase" filled with water. Their "flowers" begin blooming in the spring and summer but last only a week or so. They can be grown outside in mild climates but rarely do well. Divide them for new plants. Billbergia are not bothered by insects.

B. amoena. Has a tubular shape growing to 40 in. Produces lavender and neon-pink bracts.
B. nutans. Has a narrow, tubular shape growing to 40 in. Produces multicolored bracts.
B. zebrina. Grows to 50 in. Has patterned leaves and lavender bracts.

SUGGESTED VARIETIES:
'Fantasia'—startling blue coloring
'Muriel Waterman'—attractive foliage

BLECHNUM *houseplant*   Tree fern

Tree ferns are seldom seen but are made to order for warm dry climates. Unlike most ferns, they will grow in low humidity with regular watering and good light. Young leaves are copper and green, maturing to dark green. Avoid overwatering; propagate by means of spores or offsets.

B. brasiliense. Grows to 48 in. Best for a plant room or for public rooms.
B. occidentale. Grows to 24 in. Best for a window.

BLETILLA *bulb*   Chinese ground orchid

These 12-in. bulbs are not easy to grow, but they are popular because they are orchids. They need to be in a shady spot and to be watered regularly. Their amethyst-purple flowers bloom in the summer. Chinese ground orchids are fragile and difficult to get started, and they require a long time to become established. In a mild climate, they may be grown, with luck, outside, in a moist, somewhat acid soil.

Boltonia *perennial*

Growing to a height of 72 in., boltonia has daisylike, white or violet flowers and grassy foliage. The plants increase rapidly and grow easily in almost any soil, watered regularly, in sun or shade. They are good for borders and are readily divided.

B. *asteroides*. Has broad, lance-shaped leaves, with white to lilac or purple flowers forming a starlike head.

B. *latiasquama* (violet boltonia). Quite small, with bluish violet flowers; more showy than B. *asteroides*.

Bougainvillea *vine*   Paper flower

Bougainvillea offer brilliant color for little effort in mild-climate gardens. Some may grow to 20 ft. or more. They have vividly colored bracts and bloom almost all summer long. In the summer they need sun and constant moisture; in the winter they are best kept somewhat dry. Cut them back whenever they grow too large. Obtain new plants from seed or buy pre-started plants, which have fragile roots and are a bit tricky to transplant. Bougainvillea are not plagued by insects.

SUGGESTED VARIETIES:
'Barbara Karst'—tall and bushy, with purplish red bracts
'Crimson Lake'—red bracts
'Harrisii'—low and bushy, with variegated leaves and white and purple bracts
'Orange Fiesta'—orange bracts
'Temple Fire'—low, compact, and bushy; red bracts

Bouvardia longifolia *perennial*

This garden flower has oval leaves in groups of two or three and bears clusters of tubular, fragrant flowers from summer to late fall. The flowers can be white, pink, or red. Bouvardia need sun and moist soil; they are good cut flowers. In addition, they can easily be divided and are not troubled by insects.

Brachycome iberidifolia *annual*   Swan River daisy

A good edging plant, these daisies grow to 12 in. and have large, slightly hairy leaves. Their blue or white flowers are fragrant and bloom in the summer and fall. These plants like sun, regular watering, and a rich soil. Buy prestarted plants.

BRASSAVOLA   *houseplant*   **Lady-of-the-night**

These epiphytic orchids have tough leathery, almost cactuslike, leaves. Their flowers are white and fragrant, blooming in the summer or fall. Grow these plants in bright light, in fir bark in small pots, and fertilize them often in the spring while they are actively growing. They can easily be divided and are not bothered by insects.

B. *digbyana* (Rhyncolaelia). A big plant with 7-in. white flowers with a fringed lip; used extensively for hybridization.

B. *nodosa*. Grows to 6 in. Produces small, very fragrant white flowers.

BRODIAEA   *bulb*

These 36-in. plants have grassy foliage and small white or purple flowers that bloom in the spring. Plant the corms in a sunny spot, 3 to 5 in. apart and 5 in. deep, in poor garden soil with good drainage. They need little water and can be propagated from offsets; a good addition to a rock garden.

B. *elegans* (harvest brodiaea). Has glossy leaves and purple flowers.

B. *hyacinthina*. Produces white-to-purple flowers.

BROMELIA   *houseplant*   **Volcano plant**

The volcano plant's flowers are a fiery, spectacular red. Its leaves are dark green and heavily spined; so wear gloves when handling them. Pot this plant in equal parts of soil mix and fir bark, and give it sun and regular watering all year-round. The volcano plant is not fussy about humidity. Obtain new plants from offshoots; remove them when they have several leaves and pot separately. These are good tub plants, suitable for public rooms.

B. *balansae*. Leaf rosettes grow to 24 to 36 in. across, the smallest available.

B. *humilis*. Leaf rosettes grow to 36 to 50 in. across, a giant.

BROMELIAD   *houseplant*

Bromeliads are becoming more popular each day; they are almost care-free plants with colorful bracts and decorative foliage. They can even survive in shade for many months. There are small, medium, and giant species. Most form rosettes of leaves; some have vases of leaves. Plant them in a mixture of osmunda and potting soil. Keep the center of the plant filled with water and the soil barely moist. Sun makes the plants even more lovely. Bromeliads' bracts are the real drawing card: They stay colorful for months and come in cerise, violet, scarlet, chartreuse, and even black. The flowers are small and hidden in the bracts. Do not feed bromeliads, and throw away your insecticides; the leaves are too tough for bugs.

For specific descriptions, see the following:

Aechmea	Guzmania
Ananas	Hohenbergia
Billbergia	Neoregelia
Bromelia	Nidularium
Catopsis	Portea
Cryptanthus	Tillandsia
Dyckia	Vriesea

Broughtonia sanguinea   *houseplant*

This 4- to 6-in. orchid bears cerise-colored flowers all winter long; its leaves are dark green and leathery. Grow it in a 4-in. pot of fir bark; give it sun and water, and it will take care of itself. Its flowers look like miniature versions of the popular cattleya orchid. Buy seedlings from suppliers.

Browallia   *annual*   **Bush violet**

Bush violets grow to 2 ft. and produce lots of blue flowers. They do well in most soils in bright light and even, if necessary, in shade. Browallias need a moderate amount of water. They are most effective in groups. Buy prestarted plants.

B. speocisa major. Produces flowers that are dark purple on top and lilac underneath.
B. americana. Has oval leaves and dark blue flowers with white centers.

SUGGESTED VARIETIES:
'Marine Bells'—blue flowers
'Sapphire'—purple-blue flowers
'Silver Bells'—white flowers

Brunfelsia   *shrub*

Brunfelsia are really groups of shrubs up to 7 ft. tall. They bear white or blue flowers off and on during the warm months. Although they are not frequently grown, they are good in temperate climates to fill in corners and the like. Grow them in bright light with ample moisture and drainage. Brunfelsia can be easily propagated from seed and are generally not susceptible to insect attack.

B. americana. Hardy to 40°F. Produces small white flowers that are fragrant after dark.
B. latifolia. Hardy to 40°F. Produces many small blue flowers.

Buddleia   *shrub*   **Butterfly bush**

Butterfly bushes bring beautiful flowers during the summer. Even though they are classified as hardy, they usually die down to the ground in the winter but revive in the spring. These shrubs need sun and a loamy garden soil. Keep the soil moist. They do not live long but are worthwhile while they do.

B. alternifolia. Grows to 12 ft.; hardy to −20°F. A deciduous shrub bearing large spikes of light purple flower clusters.

B. colvillei. Grows to 30 ft.; hardy to −20°F. Produces small rose-colored flower clusters in June.

B. davidii (orange-eye butterfly bush). Grows to 15 ft.; hardy to −5°F. Produces white, pink, or red flowers.

B. farquhari. Grows to 5 ft.; hardy to −10°F. Produces pendant clusters of fragrant lavender florets in July.

B. weyeriana. Grows to 6 ft.; hardy to −10°F. Produces clusters of golden orange florets.

Bulbocodium vernum   *bulb*   Spring meadow saffron

This bulb grows to 12 in. and blooms in the spring. It is similar to a crocus, with funnel-shaped, pink flowers. The flowers appear before the leaves. Plant these bulbs in the early fall 4 in. apart and 3 in. deep. Give them sun and water them regularly. They are good under trees or in rock gardens. Propagate by means of offsets.

Buxus   *shrub*   Boxwood

These evergreen shrubs are ideal for hedges and as edging. All varieties grow in full sun or shade. During the summer they need extra watering and feeding, and less water in winter months. Boxwood becomes soft and billowy if not pruned regularly.

B. *microphylla* (little-leaf box). Grows to 5 ft.; hardy to −5°F. Has evergreen leaves about 1 in. long.

B. *sempervirens* (common box). Grows to about 20 ft.; hardy to −5°F. Has dark, lustrous leaves.

Cactus   *perennial*

The cactus family is huge, and although all cacti are succulents, not all succulents are cacti. Cacti can be grown outdoors in warm dry areas and indoors everywhere. They offer both unusual shapes and interesting flowers. Cacti grow slowly, and so small ones stay small. But there are large cacti as well, if you have room for them. Most cacti have spines (prickles) to reduce evaporation of stored moisture. Many cacti are from the desert and rest in the winter and grow in the summer. These need a porous, sandy soil in well-drained containers just big enough to hold them; do not put cacti in a too-large pot. Repot them every two or three years. Water infrequently, keeping the soil just this side of dry. Give cacti as much sun as possible.

Orchid cactus (*Epiphyllum*), mistletoe cactus (*Rhipsalis*), Thanksgiving and Christmas cactus (*Zygocactus*), and Easter cactus (*Schlumbergera*) are not from the desert. Accordingly, they need to be potted in a leaf-mold, sand, and loam mixture with some shredded osmunda. Be sure that the pot drains well, and do not pack the soil around the plant very firmly. Keep the soil wet in the summer and almost dry the rest of the year. In the winter, give these plants full sun, but in the spring, summer, and fall, keep them in a shaded place. A temperature of 50°F at night is ideal. Cacti that make good plant companions are the following:

Ariocarpus
Astrophytum
Cephalocereus
Echinocactus

Echinocereus
Echinopsis
Epiphyllum
Epiphylopsis
Gymnocalcium
Hylocereus
Mammilaria
Notocactus
Opuntia
Pereskia
Rebutia
Rhipsalis
Schlumbergera
Selenicereus
Zygocactus

CALADIUM   *houseplant*

These 20- to 30-in. plants have unusually attractive foliage. Their paper-thin, heart-shaped leaves can be white, pink, red, olive-green, and more, in bands or splotches. Give caladium shade and warmth; water well while actively growing, even keeping the soil wet; and provide a humid atmosphere. The growing season is from April to October. In the fall, when the leaves begin to die, gradually reduce the watering. When the plant has stopped growing, dig up the tubers, dry them out, and store them in heavy paper bags at 60°F for two to three months. When you replant them, allow one tuber per 5-in. pot. Although you can buy mature plants at nurseries, it is easy and fun to start your own.

SUGGESTED VARIETIES:
'Ace of Hearts'—crimson-and-moss-green leaves
'Ace of Spades'—leaves with red veins, red-and-white marbling, and green edges
'Ann Greer'—large red-bronze leaves with emerald-green tracing
'Edith Meade'—dark green-and-white leaves with red veins
'Gray Ghost'—creamy white-and-green leaves
'Pinkie'—delicate pink leaves with red veins
'Red Chief'—scarlet leaves
'Stacy'—large white-and-pink leaves

CALANDRINIA UMBELLATA   *annual*   Rock purslane

Rock purslane grows to 20 in. tall and has crimson-magenta flowers that bloom in the summer. It is good in borders or rock gardens. Give it sun and heat and a moderate amount of water, but do not feed it. Propagate from cuttings.

CALATHEA *houseplant*

These foliage plants from Brazil have decorative green leaves marked with other colors, sometimes in stripes. They need good light and heat, and lots of water and humidity. Although calathea is not easy to grow, its beautiful leaves are worth the extra care. Divide the plants when you repot them.

C. bachemiana. Grows to 16 in. Has gray-green leaves marked with dark green.
C. concinna. Grows to 20 in. Has leaves with a dark green feather design running into a deeper green, on top, and purple underneath.
C. leopardina. Grows to 12 in. Has waxy green leaves marked with a darker green.
C. lietzei. Grows to 24 in. Has light green leaves, on top, and purple underneath.
C. makoyana. Grows to 48 in. Has olive-green and pink leaves marked with silver.
C. roseo-picta. Grows to 12 in. Has dark green and red leaves.
C. vandenheckei. Grows to 30 in. Has white and dark green leaves.
C. veitchiana. Grows to 48 in. Has leaves with a peacock-feather design in brown, chartreuse, green, and red.
C. zebrina. Grows to 36 in. Has dark green velvety leaves with a chartreuse background.

SUGGESTED VARIETIES:
'Burle Marx'—gray leaves
'Roseo-Lineata'—rose-colored leaves

CALCEOLARIA *annual*   **Pocketbook plant**

These funny little plants have dark green leaves and puffy flowers. Because they are annuals, after they have flowered, you must discard them, but they are desirable anyway, especially as seasonal color. If they are kept cool and shaded with even moisture at the roots, they will remain fresh for two to three weeks. Plant seeds in April or August for new plants.

C. herbeohybrida. Grows to 24 in. A bushy compact ball of color, generally yellow or red with spots.
C. multiflora. Grows to 16 in. Produces clusters of yellow flowers.
C. multiflora nana. Grows to 10 in. A popular dwarf sold as a gift plant.

SUGGESTED VARIETY:
Monarch series—mixed colors

CALENDULA *annual*   **Pot marigold**

These easy-to-grow, 24-in. plants produce lots of flowers over a long season. These flowers come in yellow or orange or shades in between; they are most effective used in masses. Pot marigolds can grow in almost any soil as long as they have plenty of sun and water. Buy prestarted plants.

C. officinalis (pot marigold). Produces orange flowers, one after another, for many weeks.

CALLA PALUSTRIS *aquatic plant* **Water arum**

This plant is often confused with the calla lily (*Zantedeschia*), but the plants are quite different. The true water arum or calla is a water plant used in bog gardens or areas where the soil is wet. It has arrow-shaped leaves and a spathe flower head, green on the outside and white on the inside, that blooms in May or June. These plants can be propagated from their root stalk in the spring. They are not bothered by insects, and they can tolerate temperatures down to −20°F.

CALLIRHOE INVOLUCRATA *perennial* **Poppy mallow**

The best place in the garden for poppy mallows is a sunny spot. They grow to 36 in. and bloom profusely during the summer. The flowers are red-purple. The type of soil they are in is not important as long as they are watered regularly and are well drained. Obtain new plants by dividing them.

CALLISTEMON LANCEOLATUS *shrub/tree* **Bottle brush**

This evergreen shrub or tree has frilly leaves and long red flowers that look like bottlebrushes. It usually grows no taller than 25 ft. and likes almost any soil and any moisture condition—even months of drought does not harm it. Bottlebrushes are propagated from hardwood cuttings. They may be vulnerable to insects and are hardy to 40°F.

CALLISTEPHUS *annual* **China aster**

This is a difficult plant to grow and requires a rich, well-drained, loamy soil. China asters can reach 24 in., and their flowers are deep violet, flaming red, or brilliant yellow and are spectacular in a flower bed in the summer. They need sun and moderate watering. They are, however, prone to fungus diseases, and so use a fungicide if necessary. Buy prestarted plants.

CALLUNA VULGARIS   *shrub*   Heather

Heather, with its evergreen foliage and tiny pink and red flowers, makes it a valuable member of any garden. It can be used as a ground cover, an accent plant, or a background plant. Heather likes an acid soil, not rich but somewhat poor in condition. Keep the soil evenly watered, neither too dry nor too moist. Heather does best in the sun. Some types bloom in the summer; others in the fall. Some have purple flowers; others, pink. Divide them for new plants. Heather is not usually troubled by insects, and it is hardy down to −20°F. Do not confuse heather with heath (*Erica*), which blooms only in the fall.

SUGGESTED VARIETIES:
'Aurea'—purple flowers
'Cuprea'—purple flowers
'H. E. Beale'—pink flowers
'J. H. Hamilton'—pink flowers
'Nana Compacta'—pink flowers
'Tomentosa'—lavender flowers

CALOCHORTUS   *bulb*   Mariposa lily

Mariposa lilies, growing to 24 in., prefer a somewhat dry and sandy garden soil and produce small flowers in the spring and summer. In the fall, plant the bulbs in a sunny spot, 4 to 6 in. apart and 2 in. deep. In the summer, when the foliage has died, dig up the bulbs and store them in a cool dry place. These lilies are good in rock gardens and also as border plants. Propagate them from offsets.

C. albus. Produces delicately fringed, snow-white flowers.
C. pulchellus (golden lantern). Produces golden yellow pendant flowers.
C. venustus (white mariposa). Produces pale lilac flowers, though the colors may vary.

CALONYCTION (IPOMOEA) ACULEATUM   *vine*   Moonflower

Moonflowers grow to 20 ft. long, are large and white, and although each flower lasts for only a day or so during the summer, it is quickly followed by another. This vine grows rapidly in the sun and with lots of water. Plant it in a loamy soil. Moonflowers make an excellent screen when one is needed quickly. Because they are difficult to propagate, it is best to buy new plants.

CALTHA PALUSTRIS   *perennial*   Marsh marigold

The marsh marigold is a sought-after plant, with its heart-shaped leaves and yellow buttercuplike flowers. It is ideal for wet areas and blooms in the early spring. Marsh marigolds do best in sunny locations. They can be divided for new plants and are not usually troubled by insects.

SUGGESTED VARIETIES:
'Alba'—white flowers
'Montrosa-plena'—double flowers

CALYCANTHUS FLORIDUS   *shrub*

These deciduous shrubs have fragrant flowers with ribbonlike petals. They are best for hedges or wherever you need mass in a garden. Calycanthus grow to about 10 ft. tall. They need sun, a fertile soil, and plenty of water at the roots. Obtain new plants by division. These shrubs are occasionally attacked by insects; they can withstand temperatures down to $-30°F$.

CAMASSIA   *bulb*   **Camass**

These spring-flowering bulbs belong to the lily family. They have grassy leaves and blue flowers. Grow them in a bright light, and keep them moist at the roots. Plant the bulbs about 4 in. deep; they multiply themselves. Camassia are not bothered by insects.

C. cusickii. Produces blue flowers.
C. scilloides. The bulb most commonly grown.

CAMELLIA   *shrub*

Camellias are evergreen shrubs that bear beautiful flowers from October to May. The flowers come in many shapes, sizes, and colors—shades of white, pink, and red, solid or striped or mottled. The *Japonica* hybrids are perhaps the most popular; the *Sasanqua* hybrids' flowers are smaller and generally single and bloom earlier than do the *Japonicas*.

Both kinds of camellias need a well-drained, rich soil and coolness at the roots. They should be kept moist but not wet and should be fed a commercial acid food. Camellias should never be planted with their trunk base below the soil. Their roots are very delicate and should not be disturbed, for example, when fertilizing them. Prune camellias immediately after they bloom or in the fall. Watch for aphids, scale, and mites, and take action if you find them. Scorched or yellowed areas on the leaves indicate sunburn; yellow leaves with green veins reveal a lack of iron. In this case, give the camellia iron chelate (available at nurseries). If the flower buds drop off, it is probably a result of overwatering or just camellias' natural tendency to shed some of their buds.

C. japonica (common camellia). Grows to 45 ft.; hardy to 5°F. Has evergreen leaves and is available in many flower shades.

SUGGESTED VARIETIES:
'Adolphe Audusson'—semidouble dark red to rose-colored flowers
'Alba Simplex'—single white flowers
'Brian'—large pink flowers
'Buddha' (reticulata)—ruffled rose-pink flowers
'Drama Girl'—huge semidouble deep salmon to rose-pink flowers
'Guest of Honor'—double pink flowers
'Inspiration'—semidouble pink flowers with darker veins
'Lady Clare'—semidouble carmine-rose flowers
'Magnoliaeflora'—semidouble shell-pink flowers
'Mary Williams'—semidouble deep pink flowers
'Mrs. Tingely'—small pink flowers
'Yours Truly'—pale pink flowers

C. sasanqua (sasanqua camellia). Grows to 20 ft.; hardy to 5°F. Varies from upright and dense to vinelike and spreading. Has shiny dark green leaves, and its flowers bloom in the fall.
C. williamsii. Grows to 10 ft.; hardy to 10°F.

CAMPANULA   *perennial/annual*   Bellflower

There are over one thousand species of bellflowers. They grow to 20 in., some perennials and others annuals and even a few biennials. Bellflowers are easy to grow if you give them a somewhat shady spot (not totally without sun) where it is moist and the soil drains quickly. Some of the plants' flowers are large; others are small, with blue the predominant color, although some varieties have white flowers. Buy prestarted plants every year.

C. carpatica (tussock bellflower). Produces big, bell-shaped blue flowers.
C. medium (Canterbury bellflower). Produces violet-blue flowers.

SUGGESTED VARIETIES:
'Alba'—white flowers
'Joan Elliot'—blue flowers
'Superba'—large flowers

CAMPSIS TAGLIABUANA   *vine*   Trumpet creeper

This popular vine bears a multitude of funnel-shaped orange flowers during the summer. It likes a bright, somewhat sunny location, regular watering but not too much, and support such as a trellis. Obtain new plants from cuttings; this vine survives temperatures down to −20°F. Do not confuse this plant with *C. radicans*, which is similar in appearance.

CANNA HYBRIDA   *bulb*

These bulbs grow into 8- or 9-ft. spikes of leaves and flowers, although now there are dwarf varieties available. Cannas need moist soil and a sunny spot. They grow like gladioli and so can be used in masses for color or against a wall or fence. They bloom in the summer. For new plants, divide them and also watch for insect attacks.

SUGGESTED VARIETIES:
'Apricot'—apricot-colored flowers
'City of Portland'—pink flowers
'Eureka'—white flowers
'Orange Humbert'—orange flowers
'President'—red flowers
'Rosamund'—red flowers

CAPSICUM FRUTESCENS   *houseplant*   Red pepper plant

This is a colorful and compact pot plant with white flowers followed by purple or red berries. Give it full sun but a cool spot and moist soil. Although it lasts only one season, this plant is still worthwhile. Propagate by means of seeds planted in the spring.

'Piccolo'—grows to 26 in., with variegated leaves, lavender flowers, and blackish purple berries

'Robert Craig'—grows to 30 in., with green leaves and red berries

'Weatherhillii'—grows to 30 in., with shiny green leaves, white flowers, and yellow-to-red berries

CARDIOSPERMUM HALICACABUM   *annual*   **Balloon vine**

Although it is often classified as a perennial, this 10-ft. vine is usually grown as an annual. It is fast growing, with heart-shaped leaves and small white flowers in the summer—a decorative screen plant. Balloon vines like sun, lots of water, and almost any soil as long it is well drained. They are generally grown from seed.

CARICA PAPAYA   *tree*   **Papaya**

The papaya tree grows to 20 ft. in mild climates and produces delicious fruit. Its leaves are long and lobed, and its flowers are yellow. Unless you live in an area such as Hawaii or Mexico where you can harvest the fruit, this tree is generally used only as a "spot" tree that must be replaced every few years. Papayas can tolerate temperatures down to 40°F.

CARISSA GRANDIFLORA NANA COMPACTA   *houseplant*

This fast-growing, vinelike shrub grows to 3 ft. indoors, with glossy green leaves and fragrant white flowers followed by red berries. It needs full sun, moist soil, and frequent misting to maintain humid surroundings and to set its flower buds. Water it sparingly, however, when it rests over the winter. Propagate from cuttings.

CARPENTERIA CALIFORNICA   *shrubs*   **Mock-orange**

These showy green shrubs have satiny green leaves and clusters of very fragrant white flowers. They grow to about 10 ft. and will tolerate almost any kind of soil but need moisture and good drainage. Mock-oranges are usually not bothered by insects and can withstand temperatures down to −5°F.

CARYOTA   *houseplant*   **Fishtail palm**

These 36-in. palms from tropical Asia and Australia have scalloped glossy green fronds on tall stems. Although the leaf edges turn brown with age, the plant is decorative and grows slowly. Give this palm bright light and moist soil. Obtain new plants from offsets or division.

C. *mitis.* Has clusters of green, fan-shaped fronds.
C. *plumosa.* Has leathery bright green fronds.

CASSIA   *shrub*   Senna

Cassia is an annual, evergreen shrub, a member of the pea family, with large leaves and golden yellow flowers in the summer. It does well in a somewhat dry soil and needs sun and warmth. Cassia is best as a vertical accent plant. Obtain new plants from cuttings; they are not usually troubled by insects.

C. *alata.* Grows to 15 ft.; hardy to 15°F. Produces yellow flowers in the winter.
C. *corymbosa.* Hardy to 15°F. A good southern plant with yellow flowers.
C. *fasiculata.* Hardy to 15°F. A fast-growing vine, with yellow flowers from summer into fall.

CATALPA   *tree*   Western catalpa

Catalpas can withstand hot summers, dry soil and full sun; their pyramidal foliage is handsome, and they produce white flowers in June. These trees are easy to grow, and there now are varieties of *C. bignoniodes* that are smaller than the original.

C. *bignoniodes* (southern catalpa). Grows to 45 ft.; hardy to −10°F. Has large leaves and long, beanlike pods in the fall.
C. *speciosa* (common catalpa). Grows to 90 ft.; hardy to −10°F. Not as attractive as *C. bignoniodes.*

CATANANCHE CAERULEA   *perennial/annual*   Cupid's dart

This flower has narrow, somewhat toothed leaves and blue flowers in the summer that are prized for dried arrangements. Cupid's dart can be easily grown in sun and in a slightly dry, well-drained soil. Buy prestarted plants.

CATHARANTHUS (VINCA) ROSEUS   *perennial*   Madagascar
                                                         periwinkle

Vincas are useful garden plants, with pointed leaves and flat white or rose-colored flowers that bloom over a long period of time during the warm months. These periwinkles do well in sun and with a moderate amount of water. They are best used in borders, as edging, or in a mass for color. Because they cannot survive freezing temperatures, in some parts of the country they are grown as annuals. Vinca are easily grown from seed and are not vulnerable to insect attacks.

CATOPSIS *houseplant*

These easy-to-grow bromeliads have a bottle shape and spikes of white or yellow flowers. Pot them in equal parts of fir bark and soil, and place them in your sunniest window. In the summer, flood them with water; during the rest of the year, let them become somewhat dry, but still with some humidity. Obtain new plants from offsets.

C. *berteroniana*. Grows to 20 in. Has vase-shaped, apple-green leaves and yellow flowers.
C. *floribunda*. Grows to 14 in. Has dark green leaves and white-and-yellow flowers.

CATTLEYA *houseplant*

This is the grand-daddy of the orchid family and the famous corsage orchid. The flowers can be as big as 9 in. across and come in lavender or white. Because they have been extensively hybridized, there are now thousands of varieties, in colors from white to yellow to chartreuse to purple and on and on. The flowers last for about six weeks on the plant. Cattleya need bright light and even moisture. They should be potted in fir bark and fed monthly with a 10-30-20 fertilizer. These orchids can easily be divided and are rarely bothered by insects. I have grown the following varieties and have found them to be exceptional:

ORANGE:
Naomi Kerns 'Fireball'
Orient Amber 'Orchidglade'
Harlequin Peak 'Orange Princess'

YELLOW:
Melinda Wheeler 'Halcyon'
Bouton d'Or
Lorraine Malworth 'Orlando'

RED:
Rebecca Merkel 'Denise Trowbridge'
Jewel Box 'Dark Waters'
Riffe 'Burlingame'

LAVENDER-PURPLE:
Susan Pigors
Irene Finney
Stephen Oliver 'Elmhurst'

WHITE:
Marjorie Hausermann 'York'
Bob Betts 'White Lightning'
Mount Hood

CEANOTHUS *shrub*   **Wild lilac**

These evergreen shrubs have blue or white flowers, and there is a variety for almost every temperature zone. They need good soil and even moisture and sunlight. Use them as accent or background plants, and propagate them by means of softwood or hardwood cuttings in the late summer. They are prone to insect invasions, so watch them carefully.

C. *americanus.* Hardy to −20°F. Likes poor, dry soil. Its leaves were once used to brew tea, hence its nickname, New Jersey tea.
C. *ovatus.* Hardy to 10°F. Produces white flowers.

CEDRUS *tree*   **Cedar**

These big evergreen trees need lots of space, but their sculptured shapes are a desirable addition to the landscape. Cedars must have a somewhat rich soil; they are relatively resistant to insects and disease.

C. *atlantica* 'Glauca' (blue atlas cedar). Has silvery blue needles.
C. *deodora* (deodar cedar). Grows to 150 ft.; hardy to 5°F. Has a narrow, pyramidal shape and dense needles.
C. *libani* (cedar of Lebanon). Grows to 120 ft.; hardy to −5°F. Has stiff horizontal branches.

CELASTRUS SCANDENS *vine*   **Climbing (American) bittersweet**

This 20-ft. vine has 2-to-4-in.-long, sharply pointed and finely toothed, oval leaves, yellow flowers, and colorful berries in the fall. (Note that the leaves are poisonous.) Bittersweet needs sun, moderate watering, and support such as a trellis or wall. It is, however, invasive, so do not put it near shrubs or trees. New plants can be obtained from softwood or hardwood cuttings.

CELTIS AUSTRALIS *tree*   **Hackberry**

Although hackberry leaves do not change color in the fall, these trees are easy to grow in most conditions. They usually are very tall trees, some reaching 100 ft., probably not suitable for a small garden. In addition, hackberries are inviting to both insects and diseases. These trees are hardy to −10°F.

CENTAUREA *perennial/annual*   **Basket flower**

Basket flowers grow to 30 in. high, like sun, a moderate amount of water, and a well-drained location. They have lobed leaves and yellow or blue flower heads that appear in the summer. Basket flowers are very versatile, as they can be used as border plants or for dried or cut flowers. It is best to buy new plants each year.

C. *cyanus* (bachelor's button cornflower). This annual produces flower heads in all shades from white to blue to deep rose.
C. *dealbata* (Persian centaurea). This perennial produces deeply fringed, rose-purple or pink flower heads.
C. *macrocephala* (golden centaurea). This perennial produces large yellow flower heads.
C. *moschata*. This annual produces fragrant white, yellow, or purple flower heads.
C. *rutifolia* (dusty miller). Has silvery white leaves.

SUGGESTED VARIETY:
'Snow Ball'—white flower heads

CEPHALOCEREUS   *houseplant*   Old-man cactus

These 12- to 30-in. cacti have long white hairs and a barrel shape. They seem to thrive with almost no care at all. But they are happiest in a sandy soil, barely moist, and lots of sun. They grow very slowly and last almost forever. Propagate them by means of seeds.

C. *chrysacanthus*. Has blue-ribbed stems with yellow spines.
C. *palmeri*. A white, hairy plant with purplish flowers.
C. *senilis*. Has long white hairs; a curiosity.

CERASTIUM TOMENTOSUM   *perennial*   Snow-in-summer

Snow-in-summer is a 12-in. plant with many underground creeping stems. It is covered with white and, later, greenish white hairs (in poor soil the plant often looks all white). Snow-in-summer is valued for its grayish woolly foliage and is often used as a ground cover or with other low-growing perennials. It needs sun and moderate watering, but it will grow in any soil as long as the drainage is good. Obtain new plants from division.

CERATOSTIGMA PLUMBAGINOIDES   *perennial*   Leadwort

Used primarily as a ground cover, leadwort grows only about 10 in. high. It has oval leaves and purplish blue flowers in the summer and fall. Give it sun, a moderate amount of water, and a well-drained soil. It can be divided.

CERCIS   *tree*   Redbud

Redbuds are small deciduous trees with heart-shaped leaves and clusters of small magenta-pink flowers in the spring. The blossoms are long lasting, and the leaves turn bright yellow in the fall. Redbuds can tolerate either full sun or light shade and are not particular about their soil conditions.

C. *canadensis* (eastern redbud). Grows to 36 ft.; hardy to −10°F. A flat-topped tree with small purplish pink flowers and yellow autumn leaves.
C. *chinensis* (Chinese redbud). Grows to 40 ft.; hardy to −5°F. Often shrublike; has dense, pealike, rosy purple flowers and yellow autumn leaves.
C. *siliquastrum* (Judas tree). Grows to 30 ft.; hardy to −5°F. A flat-topped tree with lots of purplish rose flowers.

CEROPEGIA   *houseplant*   Rosary vine

These indoor vines grow to 6 ft. and have heart-shaped leaves; some produce tiny tubular flowers on the end of pendant stems. They grow best in an airy place, with full sun and soil that can dry out between waterings. Rosary vines are more bizarre than beautiful. Obtain new plants from cuttings.

C. *barklyi*. Grows to 18 in. Has fleshy dark green leaves and purple-brown flowers.
C. *cafforum*. Grows to 20 in. Has fleshy green leaves and green-and-purple flowers.
C. *sandersonii*. Grows to 20 in. Has small green leaves and green flowers.
C. *stapeliaeformis*. Grows to 26 in. Has dark green leaves and white flowers marked with purple.
C. *woodii*. Grows to 20 in. Has pink or purple flowers.

CESTRUM   *houseplant*   Night jasmine

These shrubs are grown mainly for their fragrance; they also produce red or white flowers off and on throughout the year. Their leaves are bright green. Grow night jessamine in a humid, sunny window, and keep the soil evenly moist. Because these plants can be large—some to 12 ft.—prune them drastically; even the small ones bloom. Propagate in the spring by means of cuttings.

C. *nocturnum*. Grows to 12 ft. Has glossy green leaves and fragrant, star-shaped white flowers.
C. *parqui*. Grows to 6 ft. Has willowlike leaves and greenish white flowers.
C. *purpureum*. Grows to 10 ft. Produces an abundance of red flowers.

CHAENOMELES   *shrub*   Flowering quince

With brightly colored flowers appearing before the leaves, the flowering quince is a source of color in the early spring. There are many varieties in a wide range of colors: white and shades of pink, red, and orange. Some flowering quinces have single flowers, and others have semidouble or double blossoms. The fruits turn yellow when they are ripe. Several of the varieties have thorns; most grow to be 6 ft. tall. Flowering quinces need lots of sun and even moisture.

C. japonica (Japanese quince). Grows to 3 ft.; hardy to −10°F. A deciduous shrub with red flowers in early May.

C. lagenaria (flowering quince). Grows to 6 ft.; hardy to −10°F. Has glossy dark green leaves and red, pink, or white flowers.

SUGGESTED VARIETIES:
'Crimson Beauty'—single red flowers
'Nivalis'—single white flowers
'Yaegaki'—pink flowers

CHAMAECYPARIS   *tree*   False cypress

These evergreens come in many colors and varieties. The Japanese species withstand drier conditions than do the others. Generally dense and pyramidal in shape, false cypresses are relatively resistant to insects and disease. They need little care.

C. lawsoniana (Lawson false cypress). Grows to 120 ft.; hardy to −5°F. A slender tree, it usually has blue-green foliage and shredding bark.

C. obtusa (hinoki false cypress). Grows to 120 ft.; hardy to −10°F. Has a broad pyramid shape, with glossy green, dense, scalelike foliage.

C. pisifera—to 30 ft., variable species. Hardy to −5°F.

C. pisifera (sawara false cypress). Grows to 150 ft.; hardy to −20°F. Has a pyramidal shape, with horizontal branches.

SUGGESTED VARIETIES:
'Allumii' (scarab Lawson cypress)—grows to 30 ft., with steel-blue foliage

'Filifera' (thread cypress)—grows to 8 ft., with dark green foliage
'Fletcheri'—grows to 20 ft., with blue-gray foliage that turns purplish or brown in the winter
'Stewartii'—grows to 30 ft., with golden yellow foliage that turns green
'Squarrosa Minima'—dwarf; comes in several shapes under this name; gray-green to dark green foliage

CHAMAEDOREA   *houseplant*   **Bamboo palm**

Chamaedorea are rather showy, shade-loving palms from Central and northern South America, with single or multiple trunks. They are good for the porch, patio, or indoors. Give these palms bright light, and keep the soil moist and the atmosphere humid. Grow new plants from seed.

C. cataractarum. Grows to 30 in. A compact palm with dark green fronds.
C. elegans (parlor palm). Grows from 2 to 6 ft. A fast grower with dark green fronds.
C. erumpen (bamboo palm). Grows from 20 to 30 in.
C. graminifolia. Grows to 5 ft. Has slender green fronds.

CHEIRANTHUS   *perennial/annual*   **Siberian wallflower**

These 12-in. plants need a well-drained soil and cool, moist conditions. Siberian wallflowers come in yellow, gold, or red and bloom in the spring and summer. Pinch off the stem tips when the plants are 4 in. high, in order to encourage branching. These wallflowers are good cut flowers and are easily grown from seed.

C. allionii. Has erect, slightly coarse, toothed leaves, about 2 to 3 in. long, and bright orange flowers. Best treated as a biennial, as it is apt to flower so freely as to kill itself.
C. cheiri (English wallflower). Grows to 2 ft. A perennial, its fragrant flowers vary in size and color, from white, yellow, a brown that is nearly red, and purple.

SUGGESTED VARIETIES:
'Fireking'—red flowers
'Moonlight'—whitish yellow flowers
'Rose Queen'—rose-colored flowers

CHIONANTHUS   *tree*   **Fringe tree**

This ornamental tree has white flowers in June and dark blue berries in the fall when the leaves turn golden yellow to complement them. The fringe tree thrives in full sun and even moisture, and it tolerates temperatures down to −10°F.

CHIONODOXA SARDENSIS   *bulb*   **Glory-of-the-Snow**

These small 12-in. bulbs have blue flowers with white centers that bloom in the spring; they can sometimes be grown outside. They like sun but cool conditions, moderate watering, and a well-drained soil. Plant the bulbs in the fall, 3 to 6 in. apart and 3 in. deep. Leave them in the ground to multiply. They are good for rock gardens.

SUGGESTED VARIETY:
'Pink Giant'—large pink flowers

CHLIDANTHUS FRAGRANS *bulb*   Delicate lily

This lily from South America grows to 12 in., its leaves at the base, and fragrant yellow flowers in clusters that bloom in the summer. It needs full sun and a moderate amount of water. Plant the bulbs 6 to 8 in. apart and 2 in. deep, and in cold climates dig them up in the fall and store them. Propagate the lilies by means of offsets.

CHLOROPHYTUM *houseplant*   Spider plant

Spider plants can be neglected and survive. They have grassy green leaves on runners, making them excellent basket plants. Large pots are best, as the roots will quickly fill the containers. Mature plants produce tiny white flowers in the winter. Give spider plants light, and let the soil dry out between waterings. Their strong, ropelike roots store water if you forget to water them. Obtain new plants by cutting off and potting the runners or by dividing them.

C. bichetii. Grows to 36 in. Has green and white striped leaves.
C. comosum picturatum. Grows to 36 in. Has yellow and green leaves.
C. variegatum. Grows to 36 in. Has green leaves with white margins.
C. elatum. Grows to 36 in. The most popular spider plant; has glossy green leaves.

CHRYSANTHEMUM *perennial/annual*

Chrysanthemums encompass a large group of popular plants of varying heights. They produce an abundance of flowers in the summer and fall, in many shapes, sizes, and colors. The annual types are very easy to grow; the perennial types, which include the painted daisy, require a bit more care. Most chrysanthemums tolerate any good garden soil but need sunlight, adequate water, and excellent drainage.

C. carinatum. An annual with fleshy leaves and 2-in. flowers with a yellow base and dark purple splotches.
C. coccineum (painted daisy). A perennial with white or red flowers that are sometimes tipped yellow.
C. frutescens (marguerite). A perennial with white or pale yellow flowers.
C. maximum (Shasta daisy). A perennial with solitary flowers in a wide range of colors.
C. parthenium (feverfew). A perennial with small white flowers with yellow centers.

CHYSIS   *houseplant*

This is a small genus of unusual orchids, generally deciduous, with large white or orange flowers. When they are not blooming, they are not attractive. These orchids should be put in a bright spot with good air circulation. Water them often while they are blooming (in the spring), but not so much the rest of the year. They are difficult to propagate, so buy new plants. They are not bothered by insects.

C. bracteatum. Produces many large white flowers.
C. laevis. Produces large orange-brown flowers.

CIBOTIUM SCHIEDEI   *houseplant*   Mexican tree fern

This fern is graceful and appealing only for about three years, after which it becomes too large for inside. Large tree ferns can be grown outside in mild climates, where they may reach 10 ft. They need lots of water and humidity and a shady location and can withstand temperatures down to 50°F.

CIMICIFUGA   *perennial*   Bugbane

These tall 8-ft. plants prefer the shade; their flowers are white and showy but small, blooming in the summer. Bugbane can grow in almost any kind of soil but prefers an acid loam and moderate water. These are good plants for the beginner, and they provide good cut flowers. Divide them for new plants.

C. racemosa (black snakeroot). A leafy plant with fragrant greenish white flowers.
C. simplex. Produces greenish yellow or white flowers.

CINERARIA (SENECIO)   *annual*

Cineraria have brightly colored flowers in deep shades of blue and magenta, drawing one's attention to them immediately. They are difficult to grow, however, needing cool conditions and an evenly moist soil. The flowers fade in a month or so, and the constant threat of the cineraria mite make these plants difficult to recommend.

CITRUS   *tree*   Virgin's bower

Lemons, oranges, grapefruit, tangerines, limes, and the like are members of the citrus family. They come in regular, semidwarf, and dwarf sizes and are good ornamental as well as good fruit trees. Usually they grow well in mild climates without freezing temperatures (hardy down to 40°F) and without an overabundance of water. Citrus also have become popular indoor container plants. Give them sun and regular watering and fertilizing.

CLEMATIS *vine*   **Virgin's bower**

These 20-ft. deciduous vines have large flowers in rose, blue, purple, or white. Clematis need a rich, loose, fast-draining soil with some lime added. They look wonderful on arbors and trellises. Plant them deep and feed them heavily. The summer-blooming types should be pruned in the late fall, and the spring-blooming ones need a light pruning after they flower. Buy new plants yearly.

C. armandii. Has glossy dark green leaves and clusters of white flowers.
C. heracleifolia. Has dark green leaves and clusters of fragrant blue flowers.
C. patens. Fine blue to white flowers.

SUGGESTED VARIETIES:
'Crimson Star'—red flowers
'Duchess of Edinburgh'—white flowers
'Jackmanii'—purple flowers
'Nelly Moser'—pink flowers
'Ramona'—pale blue flowers

CLEOME SPINOSA *annual*   **Spider flower**

Spider flowers grow to 40 in. in almost any soil but prefer hot dry locations (but with moderate watering). Their leaves are spiny and their flowers are fragrant—white or rose—and bloom in the summer and fall. These are good background plants. Buy prestarted plants every year.

SUGGESTED VARIETY:
'Pink Queen'

CLERODENRUM   *houseplant*   Glory bower

This is a good houseplant or even a good garden shrub plant in mild climates. Its flowers are exotic, white and red in hanging clusters, and its leaves are wide and big. Glory bowers tend to become bushy and can grow quite large indoors, so are best put into tubs. Outside they do well in a bright, somewhat sunny place with even moisture at the roots. Propagate by seed or cuttings. Aphids like clerodenrum, and so watch for them and dispatch them if necessary.

C. *fragrans*. A smallish plant with dramatic flowers.
C. *thompsoniae*. A twining evergreen vine.

CLETHRA   *shrub/tree*

Clethras are well known for their dense growth and showy flowers. They need a somewhat acid soil, good light, and even moisture, but not necessarily full sun.

C. *alnifolia* (summer sweet). Grows to 15 ft.; hardy to 20°F. Leaves appear in May and flowers in late summer.
C. *arborea* (lily-of-the-valley tree). Grows to 20 ft.; hardy to 20°F. Has bronzy green leaves, and its flowers resemble lilies of the valley.

CLIVIA MINIATA   *bulb*   Kaffir lily

Clivia have dark green leaves and erect flower clusters of bright scarlet or orange with a yellow throat. They grow in almost any soil but need a moist shady place to do well. Let them dry out between waterings. The Belgian hybrids are more robust and have more flowers, but all varieties bloom reliably. Kaffir lilies are best used in masses. Divide them for new plants.

SUGGESTED VARIETY:
Belgian hybrids

COBEA SCANDENS   *vine*   Cup-and-saucer vine

An ornamental plant for gardens in mild climates, this vine produces purple cup-shaped flowers in the summer that last for almost five months. It requires lots of water and sun. As it usually is an annual plant, you must replace it every year. It can tolerate temperatures down to 40°F and may be attacked by insects; watch carefully.

CODIAEUM *houseplant*   Croton

The croton's multicolored foliage makes it a good accent plant that can grow to 3 ft. or more. The leaf shapes vary, and the colors can be pale yellow, pink, orange, red, brown, or many shades of green. Crotons do need attention. Give them good air circulation and two to three hours of sun. Keep the soil evenly moist except in December and January; then decrease the watering somewhat. Maintain high humidity, and be on the alert for red spider mites. Obtain new plants from cuttings.

SUGGESTED VARIETIES:
'America'—maroon, oak-leaf shape
'Cameo'—delicate pink leaves
'Gloriosa'—large, broad red-and-purple leaves
'Harvest Moon'—broad yellow and green leaves
'Monarch'—brilliant red leaves
'Spotlight'—narrow green-yellow and red leaves
'Sunday'—orange, yellow, and red leaves

COELOGYNE *houseplant*

These cool-growing orchids have pendant white, beige, or green flowers. Some of them grow all year-round, and others need a rest for a month with only occasional watering before and then again after blooming. Grow these orchids in fir bark kept evenly moist except as just noted. Give them bright light and humidity but no sun. Some specimens bloom twice a year. Buy new plants from suppliers.

C. cristata. Grows to 20 in. Produces white flowers in January and February. Needs rest.
C. flaccida. Grows to 16 in. Produces beige flowers in the winter or early spring. Needs rest.
C. massangeana. Grows to 36 in. Produces an abundance of beige flowers in the spring and sometimes again in the fall. Does not need rest.
C. ocellata. Grows to 10 in. Produces white and orange flowers. Needs rest.
C. speciosa. Grows to 14 in. Produces beige flowers, usually in the winter. Does not need rest.

COIX LACRYMA-JOBI *grass*   Job's tears

This ornamental grass is an annual, growing to 24 in., and its decorative hard-shelled white, gray, or brown seeds are often used in dried arrangements. It is easy to grow in ordinary garden soil. Buy new plants yearly.

COLCHICUM   *bulb*   **Autumn crocus**

These bulbs grow to 10 in. and bloom in the fall. In August, plant them in masses 6 to 8 in. apart and 4 in. deep. Leave them undisturbed for years and in time you will have a colorful display. Propagate them from offsets.

C. autumnale. Has spatula-shaped leaves and pale rose or white flowers, one to six on a stem.
C. speciosum (meadow saffron). Has oblong leaves and rose, purple, or white flowers.

SUGGESTED VARIETIES:
'Lilac Wonder'—lilac-colored flowers
'The Giant'—large flowers

COLEUS   *houseplant*   **Painted-leaf plant**

Coleus can grow to 16 in. without much attention, and they are known for their colorful leaves—plum, red, pink, green, or yellow. Put them in a bright place, and water them every second or third day. If you put them outside in the summer, they will produce blue flowers. Obtain new plants from seeds. Watch out for mealybugs, and be ready to take action.

SUGGESTED VARIETIES OF *C. blumei*:
'Brilliancy'—large red and gold leaves
'Candidum'—large, broad, wavy yellow-green and white leaves
'Christmas Cheer'—wine-red leaves edged with yellow green
'Firebrand'—all-red leaves
'Forest Park'—red and light green leaves
'Pink Rainbow'—red and moss-green leaves with red veins
'Sunset'—salmon-rose leaves splotched with moss green
'The Chief'—ruffled bright red leaves

COLLINIA   *see Chamaedorea*

COLOCASIA   *houseplant*   **Elephant ear**

An elegant plant with large green velvety leaves on tall stems, the elephant's ear does best in a bright spot with lots of water while actively growing. In the winter when it is dormant, it should be kept almost dry but fairly warm. Obtain new plants from tubers.

C. antiquorum. Grows to 48 in. Has green leaves with purple spots.
C. esculenta. Grows to 40 in. Has quilted, satiny green leaves.

COLUMNEA *houseplant*

These are beautiful trailers or climbers—sometimes upright plants to 36 inches—from the Gesneriad tribe. Foliage varies; some have buttonlike leaves, others have elliptical foliage up to 6 inches. Tubular flowers are borne in leaf axils and may be orange, yellow, red, or pink. Grow the plants in equal parts fine-grade fir bark and soil. Give them partial sunlight and keep the potting medium evenly moist. Propagate by tip cuttings. Not usually bothered by insects.

C. arguta. Trailing plant, pointed leaves, and salmon-red flowers.
C. microphylla. Red and yellow flowers, small leaves. Trailing plant to 36 inches.

SUGGESTED VARIETIES:
'Butterball'—upright grower, yellow flowers
'Early Bird'—orange-red flowers; a trailer
'Yellow Gold'—sulphur yellow flowers; a trailer

CONSOLIDA AMBIGUA *annual*   Larkspur

Larkspur often goes by the name *Delphinium ajacis* and has tall spikes of feathery blue or salmon-colored flowers in the summer and lacy green leaves. Both tall and dwarf varieties are available. Larkspur is good for masses of color. Plant it in the shade, and give it a moderate amount of water in a fertile, well-drained soil.

CONVALLARIA MAJALIS *bulb*   Lily of the valley

These lilies' very fragrant flowers bloom in June. They grow to only 12 in. high and look best in large groups. Once established, lilies of the valley require little care, and they like to be crowded. Lilies of the valley are happiest in shady moist areas that are not too hot. In the winter the leaves die down. These bulbs are rarely troubled by insects and can be divided.

SUGGESTED VARIETY:
'Flore Pleno'—large flowers

CONVOLVULUS   *perennial/annual*   Morning glory

Morning glories are fast-growing plants that bloom abundantly in the summer and fall in hot dry places. Some are perennials, and others are annuals. Most species can grow in any soil that is well drained and regularly watered. Some morning glories are trailing, vinelike plants that need a trellis or fence; others are smaller and more upright. They are susceptible to insects. Grow new plants yearly.

C. mauritanicus (ground morning glory). Has oval leaves and blue flowers with white throats.
C. tricolor (dwarf morning glory). A semiupright plant with small pale blue flowers.

SUGGESTED VARIETIES:
'Blue Flash'—blue flowers
'Heavenly Blue'—blue flowers

CORDYLINE   *houseplant*   Ti plant

The ti plant, often known as *Dracaena*, has palmlike leaves. It prefers a small pot in a bright airy place. The soil should be moderately moist except in the winter, when it should be kept drier and cooler. Check for aphids in the leaf axils, and grow new plants from stem cuttings.

C. banksii. Grows to 10 ft. Has strap-shaped, dark green leaves with a pale yellow midrib.
C. terminalis. Grows to 10 ft. This is the most popular ti plant and comes in many bright colors.

SUGGESTED VARIETIES:
'Bicolor'—metallic green leaves edged pink
'Firebrand'—red leaves
'Margaret Storey'—copper leaves splashed red and pink

COREOPSIS   *perennial/annual*   Tickseed

Coreopsis grows to be 18 in. high, and its flowers, usually yellow and daisylike, have a long season. These plants do well in any soil in the sun. Keep them evenly moist. Because they are vulnerable to insect attack, watch them carefully. Buy prestarted plants each year except in mild climates, where they may be pruned back to encourage new and bushier growth.

C. drummondii. Produces orange-yellow flowers.
C. grandiflora. Grows to 24 in. Has narrow dark green leaves and large yellow flowers.
C. verticillata (thread-leaf coreopsis). Produces deep yellow flowers.

SUGGESTED VARIETIES:
'Badengold'—dark yellow flowers
'Goldfink'—buttercup yellow flowers
'Moonbeam'—whitish yellow flowers
'Zagreb'—yellow flowers

CORNUS *shrub/tree* Dogwood

Dogwood shrubs and trees are ideal garden plants: They grow quickly and have beautiful spring flowers and colorful autumn foliage. There is a dogwood for almost every part of the United States. Some are wide and spreading with horizontal branches, and others are narrow and upright.

C. alba (Tatarian dogwood). Grows upright to 9 ft.; hardy to −35°F. Dense foliage and red twigs in the winter.
C. a. sibirica (Siberian dogwood). Grows to 10 ft. Red branches.

C. florida (flowering dogwood). Grows to 40 ft. with horizontal branches; hardy to −10°F. Has scarlet leaves in the fall.
'Rubra'—pink or rose-colored flower bracts
C. kousa (Japanese dogwood). Grows to 21 ft. with horizontal branches; hardy to −5°F. Has scarlet leaves in the fall.
C. k. chinensis. Similar to *C. kousa.*
C. mas (cornelian cherry). Grows to 24 ft.; hardy to −10°F. A round, dense, shrublike tree. Has red leaves in the fall.
C. nuttallii (Pacific dogwood). Grows to 75 ft.; hardy to 5°F. Has dense foliage, a pyramidal shape, large white flowers, and scarlet and yellow leaves in the fall.
C. stolonifera (red-twig dogwood). Grows to 15 ft. Has deep green oval leaves and small white flowers.

CORTADERIA SELLOANA *perennial*   Pampas grass

Pampas grass is tall, to 15 in., and has silvery plumes on green stalks. It is excellent for dried arrangements and ornamental in the garden. Pampas grass needs ample water. It grows in almost any soil in the sun; indeed, it can become invasive. It is not bothered by insects and can be divided.

COSMOS *perennial/annual*

Cosmos is a valuable background plant, growing rapidly to 5 ft. Cosmos flowers bloom freely in dry soil. Do not feed them, but water them regularly and keep them in the sun. Red spider mites may be a problem; be vigilant. Buy prestarted plants every year.

C. bipinnatus. Produces solitary rose or purple flowers with a yellow center.
C. sulphureus (yellow cosmos). Produces golden yellow flowers.

SUGGESTED VARIETIES:
'Candy Stripe'—red-and-white flowers
'Crimson Scarlet'—red flowers
'Pinky'—pink flowers
'Sensation'—gold flowers
'Sunny Gold'—gold flowers
'Sunny Red'—red flowers
'Sunset'—dark purple flowers

COSTUS *houseplant*   Spiral ginger

From Central and South America, costus have succulent stems and large, paper-thin, and open-face flowers. They need sun, evenly moist soil, and humidity. Divide clumps in the spring.

C. igneus. Grows to 36 in. Has shiny green leaves and orange flowers.
C. malortieanus. Grows to 36 in. Has green-banded leaves and orange-and-red flowers.
C. speciosus. Grows to 10 ft. Produces white flowers with yellow centers.

COTONEASTER *shrub*

Although cotoneaster cannot tolerate full shade, it can grow under almost any other conditions. It has white or pink flowers and bright red berries. Cotoneasters can be deciduous, semideciduous, or evergreen. In hot dry weather, they are vulnerable to red spider mites or lacebugs.

C. apiculata (cranberry cotoneaster). Grows to 3 ft.; hardy to −10°F. A deciduous shrub, it has bright green leaves, pinkish white flowers, and red berries.

C. dammeri (bearberry cotoneaster). Hardy to −5°F. An evergreen, trailing shrub (to 1 ft.), it has bright green oval leaves, white flowers, and red berries.

C. dielsianus. Grows to 6 ft.; hardy to −5°F. A deciduous shrub, it has pink flowers and red berries.

C. divaricata (spreading cotoneaster). Grows to 6 ft.; hardy to −5°F. A deciduous shrub, it has dark green leaves, pink flowers, and red berries.

C. franchetti. Grows to 10 ft.; hardy to −5°F. A semievergreen shrub, it has pink flowers and orang-red berries.

C. horizontalis (rock-spray cotoneaster). Low growing to 3 ft.; hardy to −5°F. A deciduous shrub, it has stiff, spreading branches, small glossy bright green leaves, pink flowers, and red berries.

C. microphylla (small-leaved cotoneaster). Grows to 3 ft.; hardy to −5°F. An evergreen, trailing shrub, it has small green leaves, white flowers, and large scarlet berries. A good ground cover.

C. multiflora (large flowering cotoneaster). Grows to 8 ft.; hardy to −5°F. A deciduous, spreading shrub, it has round gray-green leaves, white flowers, and light red to pink berries.

C. racemiflorus . Grows to 8 ft.; hardy to −20°F. A deciduous shrub, it is the best and hardiest cotoneaster. Has gray-green leaves, white flowers, and pink berries.

C. salicifolia floccosus (hardy willow-leaf cotoneaster). Grows to 15 ft.; hardy to −15°F. A semievergreen shrub, it has narrow pointed leaves, white flowers, and red berries.

COTYLEDON *houseplant*

These South African succulents have sculptured shapes and brightly colored leaves and flowers. (Small species are listed under *Adromischus*.) Give these plants full sun, evenly moist soil, and good air circulation. Do not water them from overhead, as any water on the leaves coupled with dark days will rot them. Obtain new plants from leaf or stem cuttings in the spring.

C. orbiculata. Grows to 36 in. Has frosty red leaves and red flowers.
C. teretifolia. Has 10-in. clusters of hairy dark green leaves and yellow flowers.
C. undulata. Grows to 36 in. Has waxy snowy leaves and orange-and-red flowers.

CRATAEGUS *tree*   Hawthorn

Hawthorns are deciduous trees, dense, twiggy, dependable, and produce white flowers in May and bright red fruit in the fall. They are slow growing and beautifully shaped. They can survive in any soil, and some keep their fruit all winter.

C. *monogyna* (single-seed hawthorn). Grows to 30 ft.; hardy to −10°F. Round headed with pendulous branches and red leaves in the fall.

C. *oxyacantha* (English hawthorn). Grows to 15 ft.; hardy to −10°F. Round headed and densely branching.

C. *prunifolia*. Grows to 20 ft.; hardy to −10°F. Has dark green leaves that turn crimson in the fall.

CREPIS RUBRA *annual*   Hawk's beard

Hawk's beard grows to 12 in. and is considered a weed in some areas. Nonetheless, it has red flowers in the summer and is good for borders or rock gardens. It thrives even in poor soil, but it prefers sun and little water.

CRINUM *bulb*

This bulb belongs to the amaryllis family and can be grown either indoors or out. The flowers are large and white, pink, or red, blooming in the late summer. Crinums need heavy watering in a well-drained soil (but little water after the growing season) and sun for most of the day. In cold climates, dig up the bulbs before winter. They can be easily multiplied by offsets in the spring.

C. *asiaticum*. The largest species, with slender, cylindrical white flowers.

C. *longifolium*. Produces large white or pink flowers.

CROCOSMIA CROCOSMIIFLORA *bulb*   Montbretia

These bulbs from South Africa have showy orange flowers on tall stems about 36 in. tall. They provide good color in an ornamental garden in the summer and fall and also make good cut flowers. Plant the bulbs 3 in. apart and 2 in. deep in well-drained soil in a partially shady spot. Water them regularly. In cold climates, after the foliage turns brown, dig up the bulbs and store them in a cool dry place. Montbretia are not bothered by insects. Propagate them by means of offsets.

SUGGESTED VARIETIES:
'Aurora'—orange flowers
'His Majesty'—large red flowers
'Lord Nelson'—scarlet flowers

CROCUS *bulb*   Scotch crocus

Early spring-flowering bulbs that can grow to 20 in., crocus do best in cold-winter regions. Plant them 3 to 4 in. apart and 2 in. deep where they will get

both sun and shade; water but do not feed them. Crocus are not attacked by insects and can be divided. They can be used in borders, rock gardens, and woodland landscapes. Grow different varieties to lengthen the blooming season.

C. chrysanthus (golden crocus). Produces bright orange-red flowers.
C. sieberii (sieber crocus). Produces orange-throated flowers.
C. vernus (common crocus). Produces white or lilac-colored flowers.

SUGGESTED VARIETIES:
'Dutch Yellow'—yellow flowers
'Blue Pearl'—blue flowers
'Bowle's White'—white flowers

CROSSANDRA INDUNDIBULIFORMIS   *houseplant*

This shiny green-leaved plant bears orange flowers off and on throughout the year. Give it sun and an airy place at the window, and keep it well watered in the spring, less during the rest of the year. Obtain new plants from seed.

CRYPTANTHUS   *houseplant*   Star plant

These are small plants with waxy white flowers, but it is the leaves that make them unusual. They are vibrantly colored in shades of copper, gold, silver, or bronze. Undemanding, star plants need only bright light and 3- to 4-in. pots of osmunda kept evenly moist. They are a good addition to terrariums and dish gardens and even can endure drought for months. Offsets provide new plants.

C. acualis. Grows to 10 in. Has apple-green leaves.
C. bivittatus. Grows to 8 in. Has salmon-rose, olive-green leaves.
C. bromelioides tricolor. Grows to 14 in. A rainbow plant, it has white, rose, and olive-green leaves.
C. fosterianus. Grows to 14 in. Has dark brown and silver leaves.
C. zonatus. Grows to 12 in. Has wavy brown-green leaves with silver markings.

SUGGESTED VARIETIES (all with brightly colored leaves):
'Aloha'
'It'
'Koko'
'Minibel'

CRYPTOMERIA JAPONICA   *tree*   Japanese cedar

These evergreens can grow to over 100 ft. tall and are widely used as vertical accents in large gardens. Cryptomeria like a standard soil—not too rich or poor—and even moisture. The cones are often used in Christmas decorations. They can withstand temperatures down to −10°F. Because they are so popular, there are many varieties.

C. japonica 'Elegans'. Grows to only 25 ft.
C. j. 'Globosa Nan'. A dwarf, round in shape, grows to only 36 in.
C. j. 'Lobbii'. Very compact and hardy.
C. j. 'Spiralis'. Leaves are twisted around branches.

CUPHEA IGNEA   *annual*   Cigar plant

The cigar plant grows to about 24 in. and is rarely used in gardens, which is unfortunate, because it is easy to grow. It has lots of white flowers splotched with red and flourishes in almost any kind of soil. Cigar plants need bright light and abundant water; they bloom in the summer.

Cyanotis *perennial*   **Pussyears**

Small, to 10 in., with gray-green leaves, these are not spectacular plants but
are desirable for their purple flowers in the spring. Give them full sun, and
keep them evenly moist. Propagate from cuttings at any time.

C. kewensis. Has velvety brown, hairy leaves.
C. somaliensis. Has triangular green leaves with white hairs.

Cycas *tree*   **Sago palm**

Tough, slow-growing trees, sago palms look like a cross between a palm and
a fern with dark green, leathery foliage. Grow them in bright light in sandy
soil kept evenly moist except in the winter when the plants are not actively
growing. Divide to obtain new plants.

C. circinalis. Grows to 12 ft. Has shiny dark green leaves.
C. revoluta. Grows to 10 ft. Has leaves that are rolled on the edges.

Cyclamen *bulb*

Most gardeners find cyclamens difficult to grow, but they make good garden
plants, with their heart-shaped leaves and white, pink, or red flowers.
Outside, they should placed in bright light but in the shade of a tree or
whatever. Cyclamens need a moderate amount of water and bloom in the

summer and fall. They may be troubled by insects, so watch them and take action if necessary. Buy new plants yearly.

C. coum. Produces purple flowers with deep carmine spots.
C. neapolitanum (Neapolitan cyclamen). Produces red or white flowers.
C. persicum (florist's cyclamen). Produces large white or rose flowers.

Cynoglossum amabile *annual* Chinese forget-me-not

These 24-in. plants have bell-shaped flowers in blue, pink, or white, and they prosper in almost any conditions. They bloom in dry or wet soil and in heat or cold, and they are not usually plagued by insects. Buy prestarted plants annually.

SUGGESTED VARIETIES:
'Firmammi'—blue flowers
'Snow Bird'—white flowers

Cyperus *aquatic* Umbrella plant

The stems of these water-growing plants have a crown of leaves, and in the late summer, little green flowers appear in the crowns. Umbrella plants do best in the shade in quite-wet soil. They can be divided.

C. alternifolius. Grows to 4 ft., the familiar umbrella plant, with tall stems and green crowns.
C. elegans. Grows to 36 in. Has stiff narrow leaves.
C. papyrus (Egyptian paper plant). Grows to 8 ft. Has flamboyant foliage.

Cypripedium *houseplant* Lady's slipper orchid

Lady's slippers are an endangered species and are valuable wildflowers. Their leaves are straplike, and their flowers are shaped like a lady's slipper in yellow and brown. They are difficult to transplant and should never, never be picked. They are, however, available from suppliers and sometimes succeed in a meadow garden. Lady's slippers like shade and wet feet. They are difficult to propagate but are seldom bothered by insects.

C. acaule. Has grassy foliage and yellow-and-brown flowers.
C. calceolus pubescens. Produces large, predominately yellow flowers.

Daffodil *see Narcissus*

Dahlia *bulb*

This huge group of very popular plants grows from 2 to 8 ft. tall and bears flowers from 2 to 12 in. wide. There are dozens of flower shapes and colors available. Dahlias bloom in the late summer and early fall and need full sun. Plant the tubers 6 in. deep and keep the soil moist. Dahlias are troubled by insects, so be vigilant and take action if necessary. The tubers multiply naturally, so in the spring separate them to obtain new plants.

SUGGESTED FLOWER FORMS:
Cactus
Collarette
Miniature
Pompom
Semicactus
Single

Daphne *shrub*

These shrubs have many uses in the garden. Daphne produce fragrant flowers in the summer and fall; some species grow to 6 in. and others to 6 ft.

All daphne need bright light but not necessarily sun. Give them ample water, and use them as a background or as a hedge.

D. burkwoodii. Hardy to 10°F. Easy to grow and free flowering, with fragrant white or pink flowers.
D. cneorum. Grows to 10 in.; hardy to −10°F. Very popular, many varieties. Produces large clusters of white flowers.
D. genkwa. Grows to 30 in.; hardy to 10°F. White flowers appear before leaves.
D. mezereum. Grows to 40 in.; hardy to 10°F. Produces purple flowers followed by red berries.

Datura *houseplant* Angel's trumpet

These large, showy shrubs grow to 60 in. with green leaves and 3- to 5-in. pendant pink or white trumpetlike flowers. Grow them in the sun and some humidity, and let the soil dry out between waterings. Cuttings provide new plants.

D. mollis. Produces salmon-pink flowers.
D. suaveolens. Has large green leaves and huge fragrant white flowers.

Datura metel *annual* Trumpet flower

The trumpet flower, from Peru, grows to 5 ft. tall, with hairy hearted-shaped leaves and immense flowers in the summer. Despite its spectacular flowers, this plant's sprawling growth can make it a nuisance. It likes heat and sun and regular watering, and it can be invaded by insects. Buy new plants when needed. Note that some of the flower parts are poisonous.

SUGGESTED VARIETIES:
'Alba'—white flowers
'Caerulea'—blue flowers
'Cornucopia'—purple flowers
'Ivory King'—creamy yellow flowers

Davallia *houseplant* Squirrel's foot fern

Davallia are ferns with lacy fronds and hairy brown or gray rhizomes growing across the surface of the soil. Grow them in bright light, and keep the soil consistently moist. Mist the plants as well. For new plants, divide the rhizomes by cutting them into sections and partially burying them in sand until they root.

D. bullata mariesii. Has 10-in. fronds and brown rhizomes.
D. fejeenis plumosa (rabbit's foot fern). Has dainty, fluffy, 15-in. fronds and brown rhizomes.
D. griffithiana. Similar to *D. fejeenis* but with gray-white rhizomes.
D. pentaphylla. Grows to 20 in. Has broad leaves and roots covered with black fuzz. An unusual plant.

D. solida. Grows to 24 in. Has stiff bright green fronds and brown rhizomes.
D. tenufolia (carrot fern). Grows to 24 in. Has leathery fronds and brown rhizomes.

Delphinium   *perennial/annual*   Larkspur

Delphiniums are tall, growing to 6 ft., and produce blue flowers in the summer and fall. The annual variety is known as larkspur. Delphiniums are not easy to grow but are valuable background plants and worth the effort; they also provide good cut flowers. They need lots of sun and a well-drained, loamy garden soil. Watch out for insect invasions. Buy new plants each year.

D. belladonna. Produces blue flowers.
D. elatum (candle larkspur). Produces blue flowers with a yellow beard.
D. grandiflorum (Chinese larkspur). Produces large blue or whitish flowers.

SUGGESTED VARIETIES:
Giant Pacific hybrid—mixed colors
'Blue Dawn'—blue flowers
'Butterball'—yellow flowers
'Fanfare'—pale blue flowers

Dendrobium   *houseplant*

These orchids have 2- to 10 in. cane growth, leathery leaves, and large white, pink, or yellow flowers. Pot them in fir bark and water them heavily when the plants are actively growing. Then rest them with very little water in late October for about four to six weeks at 45° to 50°F to encourage buds. After they bloom, rest the plants again for about six weeks, and then return them to warmth. Repot only if the fir bark has deteriorated. Buy new plants from specialists.

D. dalhousieanum. Grows to 36 in. An evergreen with tawny yellow flowers with crimson markings in spring or early summer.
D. jenkinsii. Grows to 2 in. An evergreen with golden yellow flowers in summer and fall.
D. loddigesii. Grows to 6 in. An evergreen with lavender-pink flowers in late winter or early spring.
D. moschatum. Grows to 36 in. A deciduous plant with large, musk-scented, yellow-rose flowers from spring to August.
D. nobile. Grows to 8 in. An evergreen with fragrant white flowers. All hybrids created by Dr. Jirō Yamamoto.
D. pierardii. Grows to 36 in. A deciduous plant with pink flowers in March or April. Easy to grow.
D. thyrsiflorum. Grows to 36 in. An evergreen with white-and-gold flowers in April or May.

SUGGESTED VARIETIES:
White:
  Den. White Pony 'Akematsu'
  Den. Yuzuki 'Royal'

Purple:
   Den. Hickham Deb Walcrest
   Den. Jacqueline Concert
Red-Lavender:
   Den. Malones 'Saitomi'
   Den. Utopia 'Luster'
Yellow:
   Den. Golden Blossom 'Kogane'
   Den. Golden Blossom 'Lemon Heart'

Deutzia *shrub*

Most species of deutzia are dense growing, from 3 to 8 ft. It is their spring flowers that make them especially desirable. Deutzias grow in any soil and prefer full sun but can withstand light shade. Prune the plants each year in the very early spring, and select species for their bloom times: Some flower in May, others later. The flowers bloom on wood made the previous year. Deutzias are usually free from insect or disease problems; they are easily propagated from softwood or hardwood cuttings.

D. gracilis (slender deutzia). Grows to 3 ft.; hardy to −10°F. Has bright green leaves and white
   flowers.
D. lemoines (lemoine deutzia). Grows to 7 ft.; hardy to −10°F. Has toothed leaves and clusters
   of white flowers.
D. scabra. Grows to 10 ft.; hardy to −10°F. Has dull green leaves and clusters of white flowers.

Dianthus *perennial/annual*   Pink

Dianthus encompasses a large group of plants that vary in height from 8 to 48 in. and in flower color from white to purplish pink. Dianthus need even

sun and moisture and a loamy garden soil. They bloom for a long time, from summer until fall. Spider mites are a problem. Buy new plants each year.

D. barbatus (sweet William). A perennial with clusters of almost flat flowers with reddish striped petals dotted white and red at the base.
D. caryophyllus (carnation). An annual with clusters of red flowers.
D. chinensis (China pink). A perennial with bright to dull red or white flowers.
D. plumarius (border pink). A perennial with pink flowers.

SUGGESTED VARIETIES:
'Allwoods Pink'—pink flowers
'Doris'—pink flowers
'Orchid Love'—orchid-colored flowers
'Robin'—pink flowers

DIASCIA BARBERAE   *annual*   Twinspur

Diascia grow to 18 in. and have bluntly toothed leaves and clusters of rosy pink flowers with yellow-green dotted throats. If they are in the sun, they will grow in any soil. With a moderate amount of water, they will bloom in the summer. Pinch the terminal tips to encourage bushiness. They are not usually troubled by insects. Buy these good border plants prestarted.

DICENTRA   *perennial*   Bleeding heart

These 24- to 30-in. plants bloom from spring to frost. They do best in a loamy, well-drained soil in a shady location and are usually easy to grow once they are established. Bleeding hearts need a moderate amount of water, and they are not bothered by insects. Propagate by division.

D. eximia. Produces reddish purple flowers.
D. spectabilis (bleeding heart). The most popular species, with rosy red flowers.

SUGGESTED VARIETY:
'Alba'—white flowers

DICHORISANDRA   *houseplant*

Dichorisandra from South America grow to a height of 12 to 20 in. and bear blue flowers in the spring and summer. These are houseplants that prefer a north exposure. Give them plenty of water while they are actively growing, but in the winter, when they are dormant, water them only sparingly. Grow new plants from seed.

D. reginae. Has small leaves with purple and silver markings.
D. warscewicziana. Has silver-streaked leaves.

DICTAMNUS ALBUS *perennial*   Gas plant

Gas plants grow to 36 in., with heart-shaped leaves and white and pale purple flowers in the summer. They thrive in almost any kind of soil and are best used in borders or in clumps by themselves. Give them sun and water them regularly. They are not generally troubled by insects, and new plants are most commonly grown from seed.

SUGGESTED VARIETY:
'Rubra'—pink flowers

DIEFFENBACHIA *houseplant*   Dumb cane

Dieffenbachia are easy houseplants, growing to 40 in. They have large ornamental leaves marked with yellow, blue, or white. These plants need light shade and lots of water in the summer, not so much the rest of the year. As they can become quite large, they do best in tubs. Obtain new plants from cane cuttings in the spring or by air layering.

D. amoena. Grows to 36 in. Robust; has heavy green-and-white leaves.
D. bowmannii. Grows to 36 in. Has mottled chartreuse-green leaves.
D. picta barraquiniana. Grows to 48 in. Has bright green leaves with white spots.
D. splendens. Grows to 36 in. Has velvety green leaves with small white dots.

SUGGESTED VARIETIES:
'Bausei'
'Camille'
'Millie White'
'Silver'

DIGITALIS *perennial/biennial*   Foxglove

Growing as tall as 6 ft., foxgloves provide masses of color in the summer. They need only moist soil—not too dry or wet—and can tolerate shade if necessary. Digitalis looks good in woodland landscapes. Watch out for insect invasions. Divide foxgloves for new plants.

D. aurea. A leafy plant with clusters of rusty red flowers.
D. grandiflora (yellow foxglove). Produces yellowish flowers marked with brown.
D. purpurea (common foxglove). Flowers vary in color but are usually purple.

SUGGESTED VARIETIES:
'Alba'—white flowers
'Foxy Miss'—pink flowers

DIMORPHOTHECA   *perennial/annual*   Cape marigold

Cape marigolds grow to 26 in., and their red or yellow flowers bloom in the summer. The leaves are lobed and dull green. Cape marigolds like sun, heat, a moderate amount of water, and a well-drained soil. They make a good color accent or even a good ground cover. Insects are not a problem; obtain new plants from cuttings.

SUGGESTED VARIETY:
'Starshine'—yellow flowers

DIONAEA MUSCIPULA   *houseplant*   Venus flytrap

This is a novelty plant, particularly appreciated by children. It reaches a height of 10 in. and has apple-green leaves, edged with toothlike claws. This perennial plant has the unusual feature of being carnivorous, and it sometimes catches flies. Flytraps need humidity and are best grown under a glass jar. Use a rich soil and keep the plant moist. You do not, however, need to feed it raw meat or even flies. Buy new plants from a nursery.

DIOSPYROS VIRGINIANA   *tree*   Persimmon

The persimmon is a dense foliage tree with orange flowers in the spring and orange-red fruit and orange leaves in the fall. It is generally slow growing, to about 30 ft. This tree may be attacked by borers, so watch for them and use the appropriate measures. Usually, however, it needs little attention. It can tolerate temperatures down to $-20°F$. Obtain new trees from budding or grafting.

DIPLADENIA   *houseplant*   Mexican love vine

These climbing plants, usually to 7 ft., have leathery leaves and large pale pink flowers in the spring and summer and sometimes even into the fall. They require a sunny window and moist soil except after they have flowered, when they should be kept somewhat dry for about six weeks. The surrounding atmosphere should be fairly humid. Get new plants from cuttings.

D. amòena. Has oblong dark green leaves and pink flowers.
D. suaveolens (Chilean jasmine). Has long light green leaves and fragrant white flowers.

DIZYGOTHECA   *houseplant*   False aralia

Dizygotheca are treelike plants with dark green-brown, palmlike leaves. They will grow to 72 in. but can be kept cut back. Keep them moist but do not overwater them. Place them in bright light. For new plants, take cuttings in the spring.

D. elegantissima. Has leathery, notched-riibon-like, metallic-toned leaves.
D. veitchii. Has coppery green leaves with light red veins.

Doronicum Caucasicum *perennial* Leopard's bane

With their kidney-shaped, deeply toothed leaves and yellow flowers in the spring, doronicum make fine garden plants. They are easy to grow and bloom from May to July. Give them partial sun, and be sure that the soil drains easily. The foliage fades in the summer, so plant them where a bare spot will not be noticed. They are not usually troubled by insects and can be divided.

SUGGESTED VARIETIES:
'Miss Mark'—yellow flowers
'Spring Beauty'—yellow flowers

Doxantha (Macfadyena) Unguis-Cati *vine* Trumpet vine

Doxantha is a partly deciduous vine from the West Indies that has glossy green leaves and yellow trumpet-shaped flowers in the spring. It climbs high—to 20 ft.—and quickly, and so it is good for screening and to cover almost any surface. This vine needs sun or bright light and heavy watering. After it blooms, prune it back. The trumpet vine is seldom troubled by insects. Obtain new plants from cuttings.

Draba *perennial/annual*

Draba are a group of plants related to the mustard family; they are generally grown in rock gardens. Their flowers are small but many. Draba do best in bright light or sun and need a moderate amount of water and good drainage. Used in masses, they create a colorful display. Divide for new plants.

D. aspera. A 6-in. perennial with yellow flowers.
D. sibirica. A fast-growing, trailing plant with yellow flowers.

Dracaena *houseplant* Corn plant

This genus of African plants can tolerate poor conditions. However, they like good light—though little sun—and constantly moist soil, but no water on the leaves, as it can cause spotting. Dracaena's lance-shaped or oval leaves are usually dark green banded with white or yellow. Most are large plants; some reach 72 in. Cuttings provide new plants.

D. deremensis. Grows to 30 in. Has green-and-white, lance-shaped leaves.

D. dermensis 'Janet Craig'. Grows to 36 in. Has dark green, strap-shaped leaves with wavy edges.

D. deremensis 'Roehrs Gold'. Grows to 36 in. Has long canary-yellow leaves bordered with white and green.

D. deremensis warneckei. Grows to 24 in. Has white leaves with a green center stripe.

D. draco (dragon tree). Grows to 60 in. or more. Has sword-shaped green leaves outlined in red.

D. fragrans. Grows to 60 in. Has green leaves with creamy yellow margins that measure up to 36 in.

D. fragrans 'General Pershing'. Has creamy pink, almost red, leaves that measure up to 24 in.

D. fragrans 'Lindenii'. Has pendant green-yellow leaves.

D. fragrans massangeana (corn plant). Has arching yellow-and-green leaves that measure up to 24 in.

D. godseffiana (gold-dust dracaena). Grows to 36 in. Has oval yellow-and-green leaves that measure up to 6 in.

D. goldiana. Grows to 16 in. Has wide gray-and-green leaves with crossbands of darker green.

D. marginata. Grows to 60 in. or more. Has dark green leaves edged with red that measure up to 18 in.

D. sanderiana. Grows to 50 in. Has green leaves banded with white that measure up to 9 in.

DROSANTHEMUM FLORIBUNDUM   *perennial*

This is a group of succulent plants from South Africa with typically succulent leaves and vividly colored, daisy-shaped flowers in the summer and fall. They can quickly create a ground cover with masses of pink, red, or orange flowers and are rarely bothered by insects. Give them sun and little water. These plants can be easily divided.

DUCHESNEA INDICA   *perennial*   Indian mock strawberry

This group of strawberrylike plants can be used as a ground cover. Its leaves are toothed, and its flowers are small and yellow, blooming in the summer. Mock strawberry grows well in bright light but will tolerate some shade. It needs lots of water. Use its runners to obtain new plants.

DYCKIA   *houseplant*   Earth star

Earth stars are bromeliads with 12- to 16-in. rosettes of thick, often spiny, multicolored leaves. In good light, mature plants produce erect spikes of orange flowers. Pot dyckia in sphagnum and soil, keep it barely moist, and put it in bright light. New plants can be started from offsets in the spring.

D. brevifolia Has dark glossy green rosettes of leaves. Grows for years with little attention.

D. fosteriana. Has narrow, arching silver leaves. A good accent plant.

D. frigida. Has large frosted-green leaves.

ECHEVERIA   *houseplant*

From Central and northern South America, echeverias have handsome rosettes of leaves, with red, orange, or yellow tubular flowers on tall spikes appearing in the spring and summer. These plants grow to 14 to 30 in. and do best in a mix of half sand and half ordinary potting soil. Give them sun and keep the soil somewhat dry. Echeverias are easily propagated from seed or offsets.

E. affinis. Has a dark greenish black rosette of leaves and red flowers.
E. amoena. Has a small rosette of leaves and pink flowers.
E. derenbergii. Has a pale green rosette of leaves and orange flowers.
E. elegans. Has a pale blue-white rosette of leaves and coral pink flowers.
E. glauca pumila. Has a bluish gray rosette of leaves and pinkish yellow flowers.
E. multicaulis. Has a copper-colored rosette of leaves and orange flowers.
E. pilosa. Has a hairy, red-tipped rosette of leaves and orange flowers.

ECHINACEA PURPUREA   *perennial*   Coneflower

Coneflowers grow to 48 in. tall, have slightly toothed oval leaves, and are somewhat weedy looking. But they also have attractive 4-in. reddish purple cone flowers, gray-green at the tips, that bloom in the summer. These plants grow well in the sun but also tolerate some shade. They do not like too much water at the roots. Coneflowers are effective used in masses.

SUGGESTED VARIETIES:
'Bright Star'—magenta flowers
'White Luster'—white flowers

ECHINOCACTUS   *houseplant*   Barrel cactus

Echinocactus is a group of prickly desert plants with a cylindrical shape that are good in a sunny window. They need fresh air and cool surroundings in the winter when they rest, and their soil should be allowed to dry out between waterings. The optimal size for these cacti is 16 in. Grow new ones from offsets or cuttings rooted in damp sand.

E. grusonii (golden barrel cactus). Grows to 48 in. Has yellow flowers.
E. horizonthalonus (eagle-claw cactus). Grows to 10 in. Has silvery gray and pink leaves with red spines and pink flowers.
E. ingens. Grows to 60 in. Has a barrel-shaped, brownish blue body and yellow flowers.

ECHINOCEREUS   *houseplant*   Hedgehog cactus, rainbow cactus

These small desert cacti rarely grow higher than 12 in., and they have ribbed, cylindrical, or globular stems and white or pink flowers. Besides giving them sun and keeping their soil somewhat dry, they require little attention.

E. baileyi. Grows to 4 in. Has a cylindrical body and pink flowers.
E. dasyacanthus. Grows from 4 to 12 in. Has small, dense spines and yellow flowers.
E. delaetii (lesser old-man cactus). Grows to 8 in. Has long white spines and pink flowers.
E. luteus. Grows to 6 in. Has a globular body and yellowish green flowers in the summer.
E. pantalophus. Grows to 5 in. Has a cylindrical body, fingerlike stems, and violet-red flowers.
E. reichenbachii. Grows to 8 in. Has a globular body, close ribs, and whitish to reddish brown flowers.
E. rigidissimus. Grows to 8 in. Has a cylindrical body and multicolored spines colored pink, white, red, and brown.

ECHINOPS   *perennial/biennial*   Blue globe thistle

These thistles are unusual plants that grow to 48 in., with spiny, lobed leaves and globes of tiny blue flowers in the summer and fall. They like sun and moderate to little water. For new plants, divide them in the spring or root cuttings.

SUGGESTED VARIETY:
'Taplow Blue'

ECHINOPSIS   *houseplant*   Sea urchin cactus

These globe-shaped cacti grow from 4 to 16 in. high and bear trumpet-shaped flowers. Keep them in a sunny window, with the soil moderately moist except in the winter, when they should be drier. The flowers on these cacti open in the evening and last through the next day. Propagate sea urchin cacti from offsets.

E. calochlora. Has a yellow and brown body and white flowers.
E. campylacantha (lencantha). Has a dark grayish green body, stiff spines, and purple-white flowers.
E. eyriesii. Has brown spines and lilylike white flowers.
E. ferox. Has a spiny gray-green body that grows to only 3 in. high, and brilliant red flowers.
E. globosa. Has an unusual contorted body that grows to only 3 in., and greenish white flowers.
E. rhodotricha. Has a barrel-shaped dark green body with brown spines and rose-colored flowers.

ECHIUM   *perennial/biennial*   Bugloss

Bugloss grows to 18 in. and has rough, tongue-shaped leaves and, in summer, bell-shaped flowers that are usually blue but sometimes rose or white. This is a long-flowering plant ideal for a dry, sunny location and soil that is not too rich. When it is watered, it should be soaked. Bugloss is good in masses. Buy new plants.

ELAEAGNUS   *shrub/tree*

Elaeagnus come in both evergreen and deciduous varieties and make good screens. They have colorful foliage, and the deciduous types bear fruit. All species are dense, full, and tough and need little attention. The evergreens have dotted leaves, and the deciduous varieties have silvery gray leaves. Use softwood or hardwood cuttings for new plants. Elaeagnus plants are generally not troubled by insects.

E. angustifolia (Russian olive). Grows to 20 ft.; hardy to −35°F. A deciduous tree, it has gray-green leaves and yellow olives.

E. multiflora (cherry elaeagnus). Grows to 9 ft.; hardy to −10°F. A deciduous shrub, it has red, cherrylike fruits.

E. umbellata (autumn elaeagnus). Grows to 20 ft.; hardy to −20°F. A deciduous tree/shrub, it has silvery leaves and fragrant flowers.

EMILIA FLAMMEA   *annual*   Tassel flower

Growing to 24 in., the tassel flower has oblong and slightly hairy leaves and scarlet flowers in terminal clusters. It will tolerate a dry soil if necessary but prefers a moderate amount of water, sun, and generally hot conditions. The blooms make good cut flowers. Obtain new plants from seed.

ENKIANTHUS   *shrub*

Enkianthus are members of the heath family, growing to about 30 ft. tall. They like an acid soil and a somewhat shady place. In the fall these shrubs' leaves turn orange or red; in the summer they have heathlike flowers. Enkianthus can be used as hedges, as borders for paths, or just as seasonal accents. Take softwood or hardwood cuttings for new plants. These shrubs are usually not vulnerable to insects.

E. campanulatus. Grows to 30 ft. Produces pinkish white flowers that appear before the leaves.

E. deflexus. Similar to *E. campanulatus* but grows to only about 20 ft. Produces large flowers.

EPIDENDRUM   *houseplant*

Some of these orchids are cane stemmed; others grow from pseudobulbs. Their flowers come in shades of pink, red, yellow, or white and last for six weeks. Grow epidendrums in fir bark and give them full sun. Keep the cane-stemmed ones moist all year, and rest the others for six weeks both before and after they bloom. All of these plants require high humidity. Buy new plants.

E. atropurpureum. Grows to 30 in. from pseudobulbs. Produces brown-and-purple flowers in the early spring.

E. cochleatum. Grows to 30 in. from pseudobulbs. Produces dark maroon and chartreuse flowers on and off throughout the year; should rest in November.

E. fragrans. Grows to 24 in. from pseudobulbs. Produces fragrant red-and-white flowers in the late summer.

E. lindleyanum. Grows to 30 in. from cane stems. Produces white-lipped rose-purple flowers in the fall.

E. nemorale. Grows to 24 in. from pseudobulbs. Produces rose-mauve flowers in the summer.

E. obrienianum. Grows to 7 ft. from cane stems. Produces tiny flowers in various colors.

E. pentotis. Grows to 20 in. from pseudobulbs. Produces fragrant white flowers striped with purple in the summer.

E. polybulbon. Grows to 4 in. from pseudobulbs. Produces tiny yellow-and-brown flowers in the summer.

E. porpax. Grows to 2 in. Produces reddish brown flowers in the fall.

Epigaea *perennial*

This trailing plant grows close to the ground and has evergreen leaves and white to pink flowers. Epigaea likes moist, shady places; it can survive in poor soil if necessary. Although it is used mainly as a ground cover, it can also act as a trailing plant in a suitable spot. Obtain new plants from division. Epigaea is not usually bothered by insects.

E. repens. Has 3-in. long leaves and white to pink flowers. Usually grown as a ground cover.

Epilobium *perennial*   **Fireweed**

With showy flowers in loose clusters, this fireweed is seldom grown but is useful as a border or in a rock garden. Although it can tolerate poor soil, it does need full sun. It blooms in June or July, and the few species available rarely grow taller than 5 ft. It can be divided for new plants.

E. angustifolium. Grows to 5 ft. The species most commonly seen, with rose-pink flowers.

E. hirsutum. Grows to 4 ft. A branching plant with purple flowers.

Epimedium *perennial*   **Bishop's hat**

Epimedium is a garden plant valued as a ground cover. It blooms in the spring and has heart-shaped leaves that turn reddish bronze in the fall. Bishop's hat likes a moist soil and either sun or shade. Divide the plants in the spring or fall.

E. grandiflorum. Has heart-shaped leaves with spiny edges and violet-colored flowers.
E. pinnatum. Yellow and red flowers.
E. sulphureum. A yellow species.

SUGGESTED VARIETIES:
'Niveum'—white flowers
'Rubrum'—rose-colored flowers

EPIPHYLLUM HYBRIDS   *houseplant*   Orchid cactus

Orchid cacti either hang, to 48 in., or grow upright if staked. Their flowers
are huge and red, pink, purple, or white, peaking in July and August. There
are many varieties. Keep these plants root bound in a bright window. Water
them heavily in the spring and summer—not so much the rest of the year—
but never let them dry out. They are fine in hanging baskets. Take cuttings in
the spring for new plants.

SUGGESTED VARIETIES:
'Conway Giant'—red flowers
'Eden'—pink flowers
'Nocturne'—white flowers
'Royal Rose'—rose-colored flowers

EPIPHYLOPSIS (RHIPSALIDOPSIS)   *houseplant*

Appearing somewhat similar to, but technically different from, the *Schlumbergera* varieties, these 12- to 20-in. plants bloom when very small, with red, pink, or orange-pink flowers. Grow them in the sun in the fall and winter in a cool room and in uninterrupted darkness for twelve hours each night. In the spring and summer, regularly water them a fair amount. They also need high humidity. Propagate new plants from cuttings.

E. gaertnerii (formerly *Schlumbergera gaertnerii*). The true Easter cactus. Produces bright red flowers in the spring.
E. rosea. A short plant, with soft pink flowers in the spring.

SUGGESTED VARIETY:
'Orange Spring Beauty'—Produces delicately colored, early spring flowers.

EPISCIA   *houseplant*   Peacock plant

These 14- to 20-in. gesneriads from South America have exotic foliage and brightly colored flowers in the spring and summer. Mostly trailers, they need bright light, lots of water, and high humidity. If conditions are good, they will bloom through the winter without going dormant. Keep water off their leaves to avoid spotting them, and grow new plants from seeds, cuttings, or offsets.

E. 'Acajou'. Has bright silver leaves and red flowers.
E. 'Cameo'. Has metallic rose-red leaves and orange-red flowers.
E. 'Chocolate Soldier'. Has dark brown and silver leaves and red flowers.
E. cupreata. Has copper-colored leaves with white hairs, and scarlet flower.
E. cupreata 'Cygnat'. Has furry leaves and fringed, pale yellow flowers.
E. dianthiflora. Has velvety green leaves and tufted white flowers.
E. 'Emerald Queen'. Has green leaves and red flowers.
E. 'Frosty'. Has white leaves and red flowers.
E. lilacina. Has copper-colored leaves and lavender flowers.
E. punctata. Has toothed green leaves and white flowers spotted purple.
E. 'Silver Streak'. Has bronzy green and silver leaves and red flowers.

EQUISETUM HYEMALE   *perennial*   Horsetail

This rushlike plant with a hollow stem is seldom used in gardens but should be considered in moist or marshy areas where an unusual vertical accent is needed. Horsetails are best grown in small groups. They require sun and lots of water, have no problem with insects, and can be divided. Note that some parts of this plant are poisonous.

ERANTHEMUM   *houseplant*   **Blue sage**

One of the truest-blue flowering plants, eranthemums need full sun, soil kept moist, and a fairly humid atmosphere. Overwatering, however, causes the leaves to drop off. Small plants bloom as readily as do large ones. Obtain new blue sage plants from cuttings in the spring and summer.

E.nervosum. Grows to 36 in. Has pointed green leaves and deep blue flowers.
E. wattii. Grows to 24 in. Has green leaves with a metallic sheen, and violet-blue flowers.

ERANTHIS   *bulb*   **Aconite**

These early spring-blooming plants are members of the buttercup family and grow to 12 in. They are not true aconites, which are summer perennials. These aconites' flowers are yellow, and the plants are low growing, making them excellent for rock gardens and woodland landscapes. Plant the tubers 2 to 3 in. apart and 2 in. deep.

E. cilicicia. Has bronze-green leaves and scented bright yellow flowers.
E. hyemalis. Similar to *E. cilicicia.*

EREMURUS   *bulb*   **Himalayan foxtail lily**

This group of spectacular, tall (to 96 in.) flowering plants has small but many flowers. These lilies grow well in a sandy garden soil with lots of water and good drainage and full sun. After they bloom, let them dry out somewhat as the leaves die; the plants will come back the following year. They are good as background plants or planted in a mass.

E. robustus. Has tall plumes of white flowers.

SUGGESTED VARIETY:
Shelford hybrids

ERICA   *shrub*   **Heath**

The heaths have small evergreen, needlelike leaves and also flowers. Although most prefer an acid soil in a somewhat bright but not sunny place, some kinds do well with some sun and a standard soil. Heaths can be used for ground cover or as background or accent plants. They can easily be divided.

E. carnea. Grows to only 1 ft. or so; hardy to −5°F. This plant is a relative of the true heathers (*Calluna*) and produces rosy red or white flowers. There are many varieties.

E. cinerea. Grows to 2 ft.; hardy to −5°F. Produces purple flowers.
E. vagans. Grows to 1 ft.; hardy to −5°F.

ERIGERON   *perennial/annual*   Fleabane

Fleabane is bushy plant that grows to 26 in. and has pink or purple flowers with a yellow eye that bloom in the summer and fall. It needs sun and little water but a well-drained soil that is not too rich. For new plants, divide them or take cuttings.

SUGGESTED VARIETIES:
'Pink Jewel'—pink flowers
'Profusion'—lots of flowers

ERIOBOTYRA JAPONICA   *tree*   Loquat

This evergreen tree has large spatula-shaped leaves, white flowers, and orange fruit. Loquats like a sunny location and a well-drained soil. They make a nice accent in the garden where a small tree is needed and can withstand temperatures down to −5°F.

ERODIUM   *perennial*   Cranesbill, geranium

Cranesbills have lobed leaves and white or pink flowers in the summer, and they rarely grow above 1 ft. They do well in almost any kind of soil as long as it is in a sunny area and is watered regularly. These plants can be used in flower beds or rock gardens, or in masses, for their color. Either plant seeds or buy prestarted plants.

E. chamaedryoides. A low grower with pink-veined white flowers. Good in rock gardens.
E. guttatum. Grows to 9 in. Produces pink flowers. Somewhat delicate.

ERTHRONIUM   *bulb*   Adder's tongue, dog-tooth violet

These woodland bulbs grow to 10 in. and have lance-shaped leaves and dainty flowers that bloom in the spring. They need shade and a moist soil. Plant the bulbs in the summer or fall, 3 in. apart and 2 in. deep. For new plants, use offsets.

E. albidum Has plain or mottled leaves and white, pink, or purple flowers.
E. americanum. Produces yellow flowers.
E. oregonum. Produces creamy white flowers.

ERYNGIUM   *perennial*   **Sea holly**

These perennials grow to about 3 ft. and have fleshy leaves and blue flowers; their spiny teeth give them a rather surreal look. Sea holly can grow in any soil but prefers a poor one, and it likes sun. It blooms in the summer and fall. Use sea holly as either an accent or a background. Divide it for new plants.

E. amethystinum. Grows to 1 ft. Has small round heads of bluish purple flowers and spiny bracts.
E. oliverianum. Grows to 3 ft. Has heart-shaped leaves and big flower heads.

ERYTHRINA HERBACEA   *shrub/tree*   **Coral bean**

Coral beans are shrubs or sometimes small trees with scarlet flowers, used as ornamentals in large gardens. Some species reach 25 ft., but most are smaller. They need sun and even moisture. Coral beans survive temperatures down to 40°F. Propagate by means of softwood cuttings.

ESCALLONIA RUBRA   *shrub*

Escallonia is an evergreen shrub from Brazil, with lance-shaped leaves and red flowers that grows about 10 ft. tall and makes a nice background. It requires sun, lots of water, and temperatures no lower than 20°F. This shrub is a bit different, and it is not bothered by insects. Obtain new plants from cuttings.

ESCHSCHOLZIA CALIFORNICA   *perennial*   **California poppy**

California poppies grow to 24 in. and have bright golden yellow flowers (in the spring) and finely cut, silver-green foliage. Now poppies are also available with pink or white flowers. Give them sun, regular watering, and start new seeds in March through September. California poppies look especially good in flower beds or drifts.

EUCALYPTUS   *tree*   **Gum tree**

Eucalyptus encompass a large group of evergreen trees and shrubs from Australia that do particularly well in California and Arizona. They are shallow rooted, and most are fast growing. Many eucalyptus bear flowers that are as striking as roses or rhododendrons. Others have fragrant leaves that are often used in flower arrangements. All gum trees are free of insect problems. Many grow as much as 10 to 15 ft. a year and can live for one hundred years or more. Propagate them by seed.

E. *ficifolia* (scarlet flowering gum). Grows to 30 ft.; hardy to 30°F. Has succulent leaves and white or pink flowers.
E. *globulus* (blue gum). Grows to 200 ft.; hardy to 30°F.
E. *lehmannii*. Grows to 30 ft.; hardy to 30°F. Has oval leaves and flowers in dense heads.
E. *leucoxylon* (white ironbark). Grows to 60 ft.; hardy to 30°F. Has grayish green leaves and small flowers.
E. *preissiana*. Grows to 10 ft.; hardy to 30°F. A shrublike tree with yellow flowers.

EUCHARIS GRANDIFLORA   *bulb*   Amazon lily

The Amazon lily is spectacular, with 2-in. scented white flowers on 2-ft. stems in the spring, summer, and fall. It blooms, rests, and then blooms again. This bulb prefers its roots to be crowded. Put it in a bright light; water it heavily while it is actively growing and blooming; and let it dry out while it is resting. Amazon lilies cannot tolerate cold temperatures (lower than 60°F). Take offsets in the spring for new plants.

EUCOMIS PUNCTATA   *bulb*   Pineapple lily

A rosette of leaves surrounding a 2-ft. stalk topped with hundreds of greenish white flowers, the pineapple lily needs sun, lots of water, and a well-drained soil. It blooms in the summer, so plant the bulbs in the early fall, about 10 in. apart and 5 in. deep, and give them protection in the winter.

EUGENIA   *tree*

Eugenia are small trees that can be grown indoors or out. In the fall they have red berries. Place them in the full sun, and keep the soil moist. Grow new plants from cuttings.

E. *jambos* (rose apple). Has smooth, pointed leaves and greenish yellow flowers.
E. *uniflora* (Surinam cherry). Has glossy green leaves and white flowers.

EUONYMUS   *shrub*

Athough the euonymus's flowers are insignificant, the autumn leaves are special. The euonymus may be deciduous or evergreen. Most grow in any good garden soil, but they are susceptible to scale and so must be sprayed regularly. These shrubs are easily propagated from cuttings and grow rapidly.

E. *alatus* (winged euonymus). Grows to 9 ft.; hardy to −20°F. Branches out horizontally. A deciduous shrub with dark green leaves that turn scarlet in the fall.
E. *fortunei*. Grows to 4 ft.; hardy to −5°F. An evergreen vine or shrub with dark green leaves.
E. *sachalinensis*. Grows to 7 ft.; hardy to −20°F. Produces bright red hanging fruits.

SUGGESTED VARIETIES:
'Compacta'—grows to 4 ft., a dwarf.
'Sarcoxie'—grows upright to 4 ft.
'Vegetus' (big-leaf wintercreeper)

Eupatorium coelestinum   *perennial*   **Mist flower**

Mist flowers grow to 36 in. and have heart-shaped leaves and crowns of blue flowers in the summer. Give them a moderate amount of water in a well-drained soil in the sun, and they will spread rapidly. These perennials provide good cut flowers. Divide the plants in the spring.

Euphorbia   *houseplant*   **Spurge**

A large group of plants for indoors or out, most of them are easy to grow. They generally have small leaves and develop contorted forms. The poinsetta (*E. pulcherrima*), however, has large leaves. They all need full sun and sandy soil kept moist but never soggy. Propagate them from cuttings.

E. globosa. Has a ridged, globular body growing to 8 in. and unusual yellow-green flowers.
E. keysii (a hybrid). Grows to 30 in. Has succulent leaves and coral pink flowers in the winter and spring.
E. lactea cristata. Grows to 24 in. A crested, cactuslike species.
E. splendens (crown of thorns). Grows to 24 in. Has spiny green leaves and red flowers.
E. s. 'Bojeri'. A dwarf form, with pale green leaves.
E. s. 'Pixie Red'. Grows to 30 in. Produces red flowers. An improved form, with flowers.

Euphorbia pulcherrima *houseplant* Poinsettia

The "flowers" of this familiar Christmas plant are actually its highly colored bracts—red, pink, or white—the tiny real flowers being hidden in the center of the bracts. Poinsettas grow to 48 in. tall. Water them every other day until the leaves start to fall. Then reduce the water until the soil is almost dry, and move the plants to a semishaded place. Water them about once a month. In late March or early April, cut them back to about 6 in. high. Water them well, and place them in a sunny place (outside if it is not cold) and keep the soil moist. In September bring them back indoors, and give them more water and sun. From late September on, these plants must have six weeks of uninterrupted darkness—twelve to fourteen hours a day—to initiate the production of flower buds.

SUGGESTED VARIETIES:
'Mikkeldawn'—variegated pink-and-cream bracts
'Mikkelpink'—clear-colored bracts
'Mikkelwhite'—not so strong as the other varieties
'Paul Mikkelsen'—brilliant red bracts

Exacum affine *houseplant* German violet

Used as a houseplant and sometimes as a ground cover, exacum has fragrant blue flowers and small green leaves. It grows to 24 in. The plant starts blooming in September and reaches its peak in January. Give it full sun and keep the soil moist. Cut it back in August to ensure future bloom. Obtain new plants from seed in the spring.

SUGGESTED VARIETY:
'Rosendale Rose'—rose-red flowers

Fagus *tree* Beech

These elegant ornamental shade trees are beautiful all year, but especially in the fall when their leaves turn gold. Beeches are large trees with thick trunks and smooth bark. Note that little else can grow beneath a beech because of the shade they provide. The American beech has sharply toothed leaves, and the European beech has less toothed leaves. Beeches are difficult to propagate.

F. sylvatica (European beech). Grows to 90 ft.; hardy to −10°F. Has a pyramidal shape with glossy, dense, dark green leaves that turn bronze in the fall.
F. s. heterophylla (fern-leaved beech). Attractive foliage.
F. s. purpurea (purple beech).
F. s. 'Tricolor' (tricolor beech). Has green leaves marked with white or pink.

PLATE 18

Convallaria majalis, old-fashioned lily-of-the-valley makes a handsome ground cover in shady areas.

PLATE 19

Appearing almost artificial, this waxy lady slipper orchid is known both as Paphiopedilum and Cypripedium in catalogs.

PLATE 20

Crocosmia, a bulb bears long stalks of bright orange-red flowers—a fine vertical accent in gardens.

PLATE 21

A popular gift plant and houseplant, Cinerarias are good for seasonal color.

PLATE 22

A lovely perennial *Centaurea macrocephala* is stately and colorful in garden.

PLATE 23

Dictamus, the gas plant, is a mass of color and makes a vertical statement in the garden.

PLATE 24

***Doronicum caucasicum* in mass is always a dependable garden accent.**

PLATE 25

A fine stand of airy Dianthus; many varieties are available.

PLATE 26

The crown-of-thorns (*Euphorbia splendens*) is rarely grown today and yet it was once a favorite houseplant. This specimen grown in a warm climate is a houseplant in Northern climates, and blooms at Christmastime.

PLATE 27

Dianthus blaze with color in any garden. Use them in masses.

PLATE 28

Fuchsias can create a waterfall of color.

PLATE 29

Geraniums are admired for their layered petals and charming hanging buds.

PLATE 30

A bulb garden with Hyacinths and Daffodils—early spring harbingers.

PLATE 31

Iris and Lupine combine to create a panorama of color in this well tended garden.

PLATE 32

Even a single iris roars with color and in masses the plants provide a stunning sight.

PLATE 33

Dutch Iris.

PLATE 34

Iris blooms have unusual coloring and dramatic impact in the garden.

PLATE 35

A bed of Kniphofia (Tritoma) are excellent perennials for yearly bloom; even when flowers fade the foliage makes a good ground cover.

Fatshedera *houseplant*

These shrubby plants have green or variegated leaves on a central stem that must be staked. Fatshedera are accidental hybrids—a cross between an English ivy and a fatsia—and are good for a vertical accent. The foliage develops its best color without sun. Soak these plants and allow them to dry out before watering them again. Grow new plants from cuttings or by air layering.

F. lizei. Grows to 36 in. Has leathery dark green leaves.
F. l. variegata. Grows to 36 in. Has green leaves edged with white.

Fatsia *houseplant*

Fatsia are decorative plants with green, ivylike leaves. They can withstand almost any conditions and survive for many years. Give them shade, and keep their soil wet but not sodden. Indeed, fatsias will grow in shady places where most plants would die. Obtain new plants from seed.

F. japonica. Grows to 60 in. Has leathery, shiny, dark green leaves.
F. variegata. Grows to 60 in. Has medium-green leaves edged with white.

Felicia *annual*   **Blue daisy**

Blue daisies are fine plants for full sun and are used as annuals in cold climates. They grow to 24 in., with blue daisylike flowers in the summer and fall. When they become straggly, cut them back to 6 in. Felicias like a lot of water. In the spring, divide them.

F. amelloides (blue daisy). Also known as *Agathaea coelestis.* Has oval leaves and sky-blue flowers.
F. bergeriana. Easy to grow, with lots of flowers.

Fern *houseplant*

Ferns can be grown both inside and outside. Indoors, they do best in a cool, light window rather than a sunny one (although some winter sun is acceptable) and in moist humusy soil (one part loam to one part each of sand, peat moss, and leaf mold). Once a week give the plants a shower in the sink or tub, and at least once a month give them a deep soaking so that all the roots get wet. Take care that they do not stand in water, however, as this will harm their roots. In the summer, put the ferns outside. Although some gardeners feed their ferns, they seem to do well without any fertilizer. Try not to break or even brush against the fronds, for if they are bruised at the tips, they will turn brown. Trim away any dead leaves. Many ferns can be propagated from their spores (seeds). These appear, usually in a pattern, on the underside of the fronds and should not be confused with scale, which they resemble. Do check your ferns regularly for scale. A strong spray of water will sometimes chase them away; if not, use the appropriate preventatives. For descriptions of some of the species and their culture, see the following:

Adiantum
Asplenium
Blechnum
Davallia
Lygodium
Nephrolepsis
Pellaea
Phyllitis
Platycerium
Polypodium
Polystichum
Pteris
Woodwardia

Ferocactus   *houseplant*

This spiny desert genus is probably not often grown because of its formidable curved spines. Generally ferocactus are medium sized, dark green globes with handsome flowers; they are very slow growing. Pot them in a sandy soil that drains readily, and keep them just barely moist, except in the winter, when they can be a bit more moist and cool (like the desert). Start new plants from offsets.

F. acanthoides. Grows to 14 in. A globular green body, fearsome prickles, and orange-yellow flowers.
F. fordii. Grows to 6 in. A globular gray-green body, stiff spines. and yellow-to-red flowers.
F. latispinus (fishhook cactus). Grows to 20 in. A depressed, globular body, with rose-colored flowers.
F. orcutti. Grows to 8 in. Has a barrel-shaped body and brownish flowers.

Ficus   *houseplant*   Fig

Ficus are good houseplants or outdoor plants in mild climates, with diversified foliage and growth. Some, like *F. elastica decora*, are erect, with broad, leathery, 12-in. leaves. *F. pumila* is a creeping plant with 1-in. leaves, and *F. benjamina* forms a small tree with 2-in. oval leaves. Grow all ficus varieties in bright light and keep the soil consistently moist except in winter, when they need less water. Occasionally wipe off the leaves with a damp cloth to keep them shiny, but avoid clogging the leaves' pores with oil or any special leaf-polishing preparations. Obtain new plants from leaf cuttings or by air layering.

F. benjamina (weeping fig). Grows to 60 in. Has a dense head of drooping branches.
F.b. exotica. Grows to 60 in. Has arching branches and pendulous glossy green leaves twisted at the tip.
F.b. variegata. Grows to 36 in. Has small, elliptical, glossy green leaves with white margins.
F. carica (common fig). Grows to 48 in. Has big green leaves that drop off in the winter.
F. diversifolia (mistletoe fig). Grows to 36 in. Produces small, round yellowish fruit.
F. elastica decora (rubber plant). Grows to 36 in. Has thick glossy green leaves.
F. elastica 'Doescheri'. Grows to 60 in. Has variegated leaves colored green, gray, white, and yellow.
F. lyrata (or *F. pandurata*) (fiddle-leafed fig). Grows to 60 in. Has enormous leaves. Do not put this plant in drafts, which cause the leaves to drop off.
F. nitida. Grows to 60 in. Has graceful branches and small glossy green leaves. Easier to grow than *F. benjamina.*
F. pumila (or *F. repens*) (creeping fig). Vinelike growth and 1-in. leaves. Often used as a soil cover for big pot plants.
F. retusa (Chinese banyan). Grows to 60 in. Has dark green scalloped leaves.

Fittonia *houseplant*

Fittonias are low, dense creepers growing to 24 in. and having bright green leaves with red or white veins. They need shade and humidity, and the soil should be allowed to dry out between waterings. Stem cuttings root easily.

F. argyroneura. Leaves have white veins.
F. verschaffeltii. Leaves have red veins.

Forsythia *shrub*

The bright yellow flowers of forsythia signal the arrival of spring. In northern regions, the blossoms appear on leafless stems in March or April. Even after the flowers have gone, forsythias are a good addition, as they grow quickly and gracefully. Give these plants space, and trim them regularly. Because forsythias bloom on previous years' wood, always prune them after they flower, never before. There are several types of forsythias: dwarf and compact, or upright and spreading. They can survive in almost any kind of soil and are nearly trouble free. Obtain new plants from softwood or hardwood cuttings.

F. intermedia (border forsythia). Grows to 9 ft.; hardy to −5°F. Has long, arching branches and pale to deep yellow flowers.

SUGGESTED VARIETIES:
'Arnold Giant'—large yellow flowers
'Beatrix Farrand'—vivid yellow flowers

'Densiflora'—upright growth and pale yellow flowers
'Lynwood Gold'—upright growth and golden yellow flowers
'Nana'—small
'Spectabilis'—yellow flowers; the most floriferous
'Spring Glory'—pale yellow flowers

FOTHERGILLA   *shrub*

These shrubs are noted most for their fall color; they also produce small white flowers in midsummer. The fruits are dried capsules. Fothergillas need a somewhat shady location and a rich loamy soil. They are not bothered by insects.

F. gardenii (dwarf fothergilla). Grows to about 3 ft.; hardy to −20°F. A low, rounded shrub, with red leaves in the fall.
F. major (large fothergilla). Grows to 10 ft.; hardy to −20°F. Has bright orange-red leaves in the fall.
F. monticola (Alabama fothergilla). Grows to 5 ft.; hardy to −20°F. Has large flower clusters and crimson leaves in the fall.

FRAGARIA VESCA   *perennial*   American strawberry

These low, creeping plants extending about 8 in. have triangular leaves, white flowers, and red strawberries from June to September. Strawberries need moderate watering in a well-drained soil and bright light, but they also can tolerate some shade. They make a fine ground cover; use runners for new plants.

FRANKLINIA ALATAHAMA   *tree*

This tree (or shrub) has single white flowers and is especially noteworthy in the fall. It can grow to 25 ft. If it has a western exposure, its foliage can be colorful in the fall. Franklinia is sometimes used as an ornamental tree in large gardens. It is generally easy to grow and is not troubled by insects. Propagate new trees from softwood or hardwood cuttings.

FRAXINUS   *tree*   Ash

The deciduous ash, a fast-growing shade tree, has brilliant yellow leaves in the fall. Some ash trees grow to 100 ft. or more. They will do well in any reasonably good soil if they have adequate moisture. Ash trees are, however, sometimes bothered by insects—especially ash whitefly in California—and are difficult to propagate, so buy new trees.

F. americana (white ash). Grows to 120 ft.; hardy to −20°F. Has dense foliage, oval crown, and straight trunk.

F. excelsior (European ash). Grows to 120 ft.; hardy to −20°F. Round headed with open branches.

F. ornus (flowering ash). Grows to 60 ft.; hardy to −5°F. Has a broad, rounded crown and lavender-and-yellow leaves in the fall.

F. pennsylvania (green ash). Grows to 60 ft.; hardy to −35°F. Dense, round headed, with yellow leaves in the fall.

Freesia hybrids   *bulb*

Native to South Africa, freesias are so beautiful and so sweetly scented that it is a shame that it is difficult to grow them in the garden. They grow to 12 in., require bright light, even moisture, a well-drained soil, and a cool location. The flowers come in many shades of white, yellow, orange, or red. Obtain new freesias by means of offsets.

SUGGESTED VARIETIES:
'Blue Banner'—blue flowers
'Gold Coast'—yellow flowers
'Stockholm'—pink flowers

Fremontia mexicana   *tree*

This is a small tree growing to 15 ft., with evergreen leaves and orange-yellow flowers. It is sometimes used as an accent tree in temperate gardens. Fremontia needs sun, a moderate amount of water, and a well-drained soil. Insects are not usually a problem. Use softwood cuttings for new trees.

Fritillaria   *bulb*   Crown imperial

Fritillaria are members of the lily family and produce unusual but pretty flowers in the spring, with types for all regions. The plants grow to 36 in. and can be left undisturbed for years. Plant the bulbs in the summer or fall, 3 in. apart and 3 to 4 in. deep, in a loamy, easily draining soil. Propagate new plants from offsets. Fritillaria are good in borders or in groups.

F. imperalis (crown imperial). Produces purple, brick-red, or yellow-red flowers.
F. meleagris (snake's head). Produces flowers with purple or maroon veins.

SUGGESTED VARIETIES:
'Lutea'—yellow flowers
'Rubra Maxima'—pink flowers

Fuchsia   *perennial*

Lady's eardrops

Some fuchsias are trailing plants; others are upright to 36 in. They all have small dark green leaves and dangling red, white, pink, or purple (or combinations of these colors) flowers. There are dozens of varieties. Grow fuchsias in rich soil, out of the sun but in bright light, and in temperatures below 70° but above 45° F. In these conditions, they should set their flower buds in the spring and summer. Give them a lot of water while they are actively growing, and pinch them at early stages to encourage branching. While they are dormant in the winter, keep them almost dry. Take cuttings in January or February for new plants.

F. 'Brigadoon'. A trailer, with double purple and pink flowers.
F. 'Carmel Blue'. A trailer, with single bluish purple flowers with white sepals.
F. 'Cascade'. A trailer, with single rose-red flowers with white sepals.
F. 'Dark Eyes'. A trailer, with double violet-blue flowers.
F. 'Marenga'. A trailer, with variegated leaves and double red flowers.
F. 'Mrs. Marshall'. Upright growth, with single soft pink flowers with white sepals.
F. 'Sleigh Bells'. Upright growth, with large, single white flowers.
F. 'Swingtime'. A trailer, with double white flowers with red sepals.
F. 'Tiffany'. A trailer, with double white flowers.

GAILLARDIA ARISTATA *perennial/annual* **Blanket flower**

Also called *G. grandiflora*, blanket flowers grow to 24 in. and, in the summer, bear 3-in. yellow or red flowers on slender stems. These plants like a loamy garden soil and almost perfect drainage. Although they will survive heat and drought, they do best with a moderate amount of water and sun. Blanket flowers are a nice addition to a cutting or an ornamental garden. For new plants, either start from seed or buy prestarted flowers.

SUGGESTED VARIETIES:
'Burgundy'—red flowers
'Dazzler'—orange-yellow flowers
'Goblin'—yellow-orange flowers
'Sundance'—yellow flowers

GALANTHUS *bulb*   **Snowdrop**

Growing to 10 in. high, snowdrops bloom in the very early spring. Their flowers are, not surprisingly, white, and their foliage is grassy. Give snowdrops shade and regular waterings. Plant the bulbs in the early fall 2 in. apart and 2 in. deep. They can be left undisturbed for years. Propagate them by means of offsets. Snowdrops are often found in rock gardens.

SUGGESTED VARIETIES:
'Flore Pleno'—double flowers
'Lutescens'—white flowers

GALAX APHYLLA *perennial*

Galax is a good ground cover for moist shady areas. The plants grow to about 1 ft. and produce white flowers. Usually easy to grow, they do well in a slightly acid soil and are a good choice for shady moist spots where a ground cover is needed. Obtain new plants from runners. Galax is rarely bothered by insects.

GALIUM VERUM *perennial/annual*   **Bedstraw**

A seldom-used garden plant sometimes grown as a ground cover or as part of a rock garden, bedstraw reaches about 1 ft. in height. Its leaves are leathery, and its flowers, blooming in the spring and summer, are tiny and yellow. Galium prefers full sun, a moderate amount of water, and almost any soil. Use runners for new plants.

GALTONIA CANDICANS *bulb*   **Giant summer hyacinth**

Galtonia of the lily family has strap-shaped leaves and, in the summer, fragrant, bell-shaped, white flowers. It grows to 48 in. tall. Plant the bulbs—preferably in groups—1 ft. apart and 8 in. deep. Provide sun, even moisture, and protect them from frost; propagate them from offsets.

GAMOLEPIS TAGETES *annual*   **Sunshine daisy**

These daisies grow only 12 in. high, but in the summer they bear an abundance of either bright yellow or orange flowers. Plant them in the summer, and give them a moderate amount of water; however, they can, if necessary, tolerate dry soil. Sunshine daisies are easy to grow and are nice for a spot of bright color. Buy prestarted plants yearly.

GARDENIA *perennial* Cape jasmine

Unless you live in a mild climate, you must grow gardenias in the house. They are evergreen shrubs with shiny, dark green leaves and very fragrant white flowers. Grow gardenias in an acid soil, made up of equal parts of loam, sand, and peat moss; do not let the soil dry out too much. Give them bright light in the summer and sun in the winter. From spring to fall, feed gardenias once a month with an acid fertilizer or a solution of 1 oz. of ammonium sulfate to 2 gals. of water. (A vinegar-and-water solution will acidify the soil but not feed the plant.) Mist the foliage daily to discourage spider mites. Gardenia buds may drop off or fail to open if the surrounding temperature fluctuates too much, if there are drafts, if the surrounding humidity falls below 50 percent, or if the night temperature rises above 70°F or falls below 60°F. If your gardenia does not grow or seems to be ailing, try the "plastic bag treatment" for a few weeks: Put the plant in a plastic bag, holding it over the foliage by means of stakes, and tie the bag, gently, around the base of the plant. In the spring, obtain new gardenias from cuttings.

G. jasminoides. Grows to 48 in. Produces double flowers.
G.j. stricta nana. Grows to 30 in. Free flowering; the one best for the home.
G.j. veitchii. Grows to 48 in. Has smaller flowers but is easier to grow.

SUGGESTED VARIETIES:
'Fortuniana'—formerly *G. veitchii*
'Prostrata'—dwarf

GARRYA ELLIPTICA *shrub* Silktassel

The silktassel is an interesting shrublike plant with yellow ornamental tassels and silky berries. It grows to 6 ft. tall and thrives in rocky or sandy soils without much care. Give it more water in the summer than during the rest of the year. Silktassels tolerate temperatures down to 5°F and can be divided.

GASTERIA *houseplant* Ox-tongue plant

These South American succulents are perfect for a sunny windowsill. Their long, flat leaves are usually smooth but sometimes are "warty." Long sprays of scarlet flowers appear in the spring and summer. Water these plants lightly, and propagate them from offsets.

G. carinata. Triangular, fleshy leaves growing to 5 or 6 in.; flower spikes to 36 in.
G. lingulata. Dark green, white-spotted leaves growing to 10 in.; flower spikes to 36 in.
G. maculata. Glossy green leaves growing to 8 in.; flower spikes to 48 in.
G. verrucosa. Pink-and-purple leaves growing to 6 to 9 in.; flower spikes to 24 in.

Gaultheria   *shrub*   **Wintergreen**

Wintergreen is a member of the heath family, and it has evergreen leaves and bell-shaped flowers. These plants can be either low growers (to 3 in.) or medium growers (to 1 ft.). They do best in the shade with regular watering but in a well-drained soil. Wintergreen can tolerate wet soil if necessary. It is generally used as a ground cover or an accent plant. Some species produce red berries, which are a nice touch of color in the fall or winter. Obtain new plants from division.

G. procumbens. The most popular species. Produces waxy white flowers and red berries.
G. veitchiana. Produces pink flowers and purple berries.

Gaura Lindheimeri   *perennial*

This small plant grows to only 2 ft. high, with pinkish white flowers all summer. Its lance-shaped leaves are evergreen. Gaura needs full sun and regular watering in a well-drained soil. It is easily propagated by division.

Gaylussacia Brachycera   *shrub*   **Box huckleberry**

Box huckleberry grows to about 2 ft. tall and looks especially good in the fall when its leaves turn bronze-red. Place this shrub in the sun, and give it a moderate amount of water in a loose, well-drained soil. Divide box huckleberry for new plants. It is seldom troubled by insects.

Gazania   *perennial*

These popular, colorful plants grow to 16 in. and have long, narrow, woolly, gray-green leaves. They produce large, black-eyed, yellow-to-orange, daisylike flowers in the late spring and summer, although in mild climates, they bloom intermittently throughout the year. There are dozens of varieties, some clumping and others trailing. The flowers open in the sunlight and close at night. Gazanias need lots of water. Grow new ones from seed or cuttings.

G. rigens. Produces golden yellow flowers with brown-black centers.
G. splendens. Produces orange flowers.

SUGGESTED VARIETIES:
'Aztec Orange'—orange flowers
'Aztec Queen'—yellow-orange flowers
'Copper King'—white flowers
'Pinata'—white and yellow flowers
'Silver Burgundy'—white flowers

GELSEMIUM SEMPERVIRENS   *vine*   Carolina jessamine

This evergreen vine grows to 20 ft. long, with shiny light green leaves and fragrant, tubular yellow flowers in the summer. It prospers in the sun, in any soil and with lots of water. Try planting this vine on a trellis or a fence; it will cover it quickly. New plants can be had from cuttings.

GENTIANA ASCLEPIADEA   *perennial*   Gentian

If you have an area with an acid soil in the shade, by all means grow some gentians there, as they bear vivid blue flowers, a color that is always welcome in any garden. Gentians grow to 12 in. in large clumps and need an evenly moist soil. Propagate them by seed or buy prestarted plants.

GERANIUM   *see Pelargonium*

GERANIUM GRANDIFLORUM   *perennial*   Cranesbill

The cranesbill, growing to 20 in., produces lilac-colored flowers in the summer that last for a long time. Put these plants in a sunny place, and water them regularly. They will thrive in almost any garden soil and are a good choice for borders. Obtain new plants from cuttings. Note that the genus geranium does not include the common garden variety (*Pelargonium*).

SUGGESTED VARIETY:
'Johnson's Blue'

GERBERA JAMESONII   *perennial*   Transvaal daisy

Growing to 16 in., Transvaal daisies have hairy foliage and flowers that are 4 to 5 in. in diameter. The flowers can be any shade of white, pink, red, or violet, and they bloom for several months, beginning in the spring. Give these plants full sun, regular watering, good drainage, and a somewhat acid soil. Obtain new plants by division.

SUGGESTED VARIETIES:
'Happipot'—varied colors
'Tempo Scarlet'—brilliant red flowers

GESNERIAD   *houseplant*

Gesneriads offer bright color indoors. In baskets, *Achimenes, Aeschynanthuses, Columneas, Episcias,* and *Hypocyrtas* provide cascades of blossoms. *Rechsteinerias, Sinningias, Smithianthas,* and *Streptocarpuses* grow upright and so are best for ordinary pots and planters. The main requirement for all gesneriads is high humidity: Some need as much as 60 percent. Although some gesneriads do well at 70°F, others must have a cooler temperature (58°F). Most of these plants do not require much sun but, rather, bright light and good air circulation. Plant them in a loose soil that holds moisture yet drains readily. For descriptions of some of the species, see the following:

Achimenes
Aeschynanthus
Columnea
Episcia
Hypocyrta
Kohleria
Rechsteineria
Saintpaulia
Sinningia
Smithiantha
Streptocarpus

GEUM BORISII   *perennial*

A relative of the rose family, this perennial grows to 24 in. and produces bright yellow or orange flowers in the summer and clumps of dark green leaves. These plants are good additions to any garden. They need a moderate amount of water, good drainage, and bright light, but they will tolerate shade if necessary. Remove the dead blossoms before they set seed, for a longer bloom period. Divide the plants for new ones.

GILIA CAPITATA   *annual*

Gilias, members of the phlox family, grow to 30 in., have feathery leaves, and produce globes of tiny light blue flowers. They like sun and lots of water, and do well in almost any soil. Gilias' flowers last a long time in the summer. Grow new plants from seed.

GINGKO BILOSA   *tree*   Gingko

This tree's lineage can be traced to prehistoric times, but it is generally considered native to China. Its leaves are fan shaped, and as an ornamental, it is often used as a street tree. Gingko nuts, which come in the fall, are eaten in some countries, but they smell bad when crushed. The flowers are insignificant. Gingkos can tolerate most soils in most regions, which is why they are so popular. Although they can become very tall, most reach only 35 to 40 ft. Gingkos tolerate temperatures down to −10°F and lower. They are difficult to propagate but are not bothered by insects.

GLADIOLUS   *bulb*

This popular group of standard (to 48 in.) and dwarf (to 24 in.) plants has handsome flowers that come in many colors. Glads grow easily in most areas if dug up each year and replanted. They should be placed 4 to 6 in. apart and 4 to 6 in. deep. Give them sun, lots of water, and a well-drained soil. Most types need to be staked. The flowers, which are excellent cut, bloom in the summer. Obtain new gladioli from offsets.

G. *blandus.* Grows to 2 ft. Produces pink flowers.
G. *hybridus.* The popular florists' gladiolus most often used for cut flowers, coming in an array of colors and flower sizes.

GLAUCIUM   *perennial/annual*   Sea poppy

Both the perennial and the annual species of sea poppies have showy orange flowers in the summer. They do well in a sandy soil and in the full sun.

Glauciums need regular watering. Use them either in borders or as background plants. Buy new ones each year, or plant seeds.

G. corniculatum. An annual. Produces red flowers with black spots.
G. flavum. A perennial. Produces orange flowers.

GLEDITSIA TRICANTHOS   *tree*

This is a fast-growing tree with spreading, upright branches; its leaves turn golden in the early fall. The trunks and branches of the sweet locust are thorny, and the pods make a mess, but thornless varieties have been developed. These are good lawn trees, growing well in almost any soil and in most areas. Sweet locusts can withstand temperatures down to −10°F, are resistant to most insects, and can be propagated by root cuttings in the spring.

GLOBULARIA   *perennial*

Globularias are small, cushionlike plants with mounds of evergreen leaves and light blue flowers at variable times, from spring to fall. They grow to about 8 in. and are fine for a spot of color in the garden or rock garden. Put them in the sun and give them regular waterings in a well-drained soil. For new plants, division is the means.

G. cordifolia. A woody, prostrate plant, sometimes used as a ground cover.
G. repens. A small, creeping plant, with blue flowers.

GLORIOSA   *houseplant*   Glory lily

These vining plants grow to 40 in. and have narrow green leaves and lilylike orange-and-yellow flowers in the spring and summer. They can be relied on to bloom and require little attention. All glory lilies need is sun, plenty of water, and a fairly humid spot. After they bloom, store them dry in their pots in a paper bag, in a dry cool place. Revive them when they have rested for six to nine weeks. For new plants, either start them from seed or divide the tubers in the spring.

G. rothschildiana. Grows to 72 in. Produces 3-in. orange-and-yellow flowers edged with crimson.
G. simplex (or *G. virescens*). Grows to 48 in. Produces 2-in., broad-petaled, orange-and-yellow flowers.
G. superba. Grows to about 48 in. Has dark green oval leaves and red flowers with wavy petals.

GNAPHALIUM SYLVATICUM   *perennial*   **Cudweed**

This group of 24-in. plants has woolly leaves and small white flowers in the summer and fall. They like a sandy, somewhat dry soil—but regular watering—and a sunny spot. Because of their weedy habits, these perennials are seldom grown in gardens but are good for an area where most plants will not succeed. Division is the best way to get new plants.

GODETIA   *annual*   **Satin flower**

Satin flowers (or *Clarkia*) prefer cool conditions, bright light or some sun, and a moderate amount of water. They have narrow leaves and lots of clumps of flowers in the spring and summer. A sandy loam is the best soil for them. Plant seeds for new plants.

G. *amoena* (farewell-to-spring). Produces 2-in. pink or lavender, cup-shaped flowers.
G. *grandiflora*. Produces lots of 2- to 4-in. red flowers.

GOMPHRENA GLOBOSA   *annual*   **Globe amaranth**

Available in tall (to 28 in.) and short (to 10 in.) varieties, globe amaranths have small round flower heads, usually white or purple. They are good in borders or in dried flower arrangements. These plants can tolerate hot weather, need sun and an abundance of water, and bloom in the summer and fall. In short, they are easy to grow, and new plants can be had from seed.

GONGORA   *houseplant*   Punch-and-Judy orchid

These large, curious epiphytes have pairs of 20-in. green leaves and hanging, tawny yellow flowers. They should have diffused sun and be kept moist except in the winter, when they can be allowed almost to dry out. Try growing these orchids under glass, where they can have a humid atmophere. For more orchids, divide the plant clumps.

G. bufonia. Has broad pale green leaves and dozens of 1-in. flowers in the summer.
G. galata. Produces 1-in. flowers from June to September.

GORDONIA LASIANTHUS   *tree*   Loblolly tree

The loblolly tree is a tall (to 60 ft.) tree, with leathery evergreen leaves and white flowers in the spring. It is a good choice for a large garden and grows well in almost any soil. Give it a fair amount of water, and its flowers will last for months. It can withstand temperatures down to 10°F. In appearance, the loblolly tree is similar to *Franklinia alatamaha.*

GUNNERA MANICATA   *perennial*

With large leaves measuring up to 7 ft. across, these plants have a striking effect near the water, where they do best. Accordingly, they need very moist soil—lots of water—and will grow in either sun or shade. Plan carefully where you will put them, as they take up lots of space. Divide them for new plants.

GUZMANIA   *houseplant*

Guzmanias are bromeliads, with rosettes of leaves and small flowers hidden in bracts that stay vividly colored for about four months. They are happiest in bright light, potted in fir bark and soil, and kept wet but never soggy. The "vase" formed by the leaves should always be filled with water. Buy new plants from specialists.

G. berteroniana. Has a 20-in. rosette of wine red leaves and yellow flowers in the spring.
G. lingulata. Has a 26-in. rosette of apple green leaves and orange, star-shaped flowers all summer.
G. minor. Has a 16-in. rosette of bright green leaves and brilliant orange-red bracts.
G. monostachia. Has a 26-in. rosette of leaves and white flowers in the fall.
G. musaica. Has a 20-in. rosette of dark green and reddish brown leaves and white flowers in the fall.
G. zahnii. Has a 20-in. rosette of green leaves and red-and-white flowers in the summer.

'Magnifica'—white bracts
'Orangeade'—orange bracts
'Symphonie'—yellow, pink, green foliage

GYMNOCALYCIUM *houseplant*   **Chin cactus**

Chin cacti grow to only 12 in. high, with white, yellow, or chartreuse flowers that usually open in the spring and summer. Place these plants in the sun, in a sandy soil, moist in the summer and dry in the winter, and propagate them from offsets.

G. fleisherianum. A 4-in., spiny globe with many large pink flowers.
G. mihanovichii (plaid cactus). A 2-in., dark green globe with brown markings, and yellowish white flowers.
G. quehlianum. A 6-in. globe with white-and-red flowers.
G. schickendantzii. A 4-in. globe with white or pinkish flowers.
G. venturii. A 4-in., bright green globe with red flowers.

GYPSOPHILA *perennial*   **Baby's breath**

Gypsophila is a fine, lacy plant that likes to branch and has tiny white-to-pink flowers in the spring and summer. It is often used in borders and does well in the full sun and in a neutral soil. Give it plenty of water. Obtain new plants from seed.

G. elegans. Has feathery leaves and lots of white or rose-colored flowers.
G. paniculata (baby's breath). Produces more flowers than does *G. elegans.*

SUGGESTED VARIETIES:
'Bristol Fairy'—white flowers
'Early Snowball'—early white flowers
'Flamingo'—pink flowers
'Snowflake'—snowy white flowers

HAEMANTHUS *bulb*   **Blood lily**

Blood lilies come from South Africa, grow to 36 in., and, in the summer, produce clusters of flowers on tall stems. They should have bright light and regular watering. Pot them in the spring with the tip of the bulb just above the soil line. Then let them rest in the fall and winter, keeping the soil just barely moist. Use offsets to get new plants.

H. coccineus. Produces coral red flowers in the early fall.
H. multiflorus. Produces blood red flowers in the summer.

Hakea laurina   *shrub*

This small evergreen tree (or large shrub) from Australia can withstand drought and poor soil, but it does need full sun. It has narrow, long, gray-green leaves, often with red margins, and blooms in the late fall or winter—round red flowers that look like pincushions. It tolerates temperatures down to 40°F. The pincushion tree is a good patio tree; be sure to stake it.

Halesia carolina   *tree*   **Silverbells**

The silver bell tree is deciduous and can grow to 30 ft. or more. Its white bell-shaped flowers bloom in May. Give it a cool location and a rich, humusy soil. An easy-to-grow tree, it makes a good vertical accent. Larger species, growing to 80 or more ft., also are available. Silver bells can tolerate temperatures down to −5°F.

Hamamelis   *shrub*   **Witch hazel**

Witch hazel is a tall-growing shrub with fragrant yellow flowers in the (sometimes early) spring and yellow leaves in the fall. It needs sun or light shade, a moderate amount of water, and a loamy, somewhat acid soil. These shrubs look best in groups rather than alone; they are not troubled by insects. Grow new plants from softwood cuttings.

H. mollis (Chinese witch hazel). Grows to 30 ft.; hardy to −5°F. Produces very fragrant yellow flowers.
H. virginiana (common witch hazel). Grows to 10 ft.; hardy to −10°F. Produces small fragrant yellow flowers sometimes as early as February.

Haworthia   *houseplant*

These small succulents native to South Africa measure 16 in. high and resemble aloes. Haworthias have rosettes of stiff brown, green, or purple-brown leaves. Some grow upright, and others are low to the ground. They need little water in the summer and even less the rest of the year. Full sun and a sandy soil are best. Plant seeds for more haworthias.

H. fasciata. Has a small, erect rosette of 1.5-in., upcurved, dark green leaves banded with white.
H. margaritifera. Has a low-growing rosette 6 in. in diameter, with 3-in., sharply pointed leaves with raised white dots and 24-in. sprays of greenish white flowers.
H. retusa. Has a stemless, clustered rosette of flat, pale green, 1.5-in. leaves.
H. viscosa. Has an erect rosette 8 in. in diameter, with 3-in., rough, dull green leaves.

Hebe *shrub/tree*

Some of these evergreen shrubs/trees are short (to 4 ft.), and others are taller, growing to 15 ft. or more. Hebes are generally used in hedges; they are easy to grow, needing sun or partial shade and plenty of water and good drainage. White-to-pink flowers come in the summer. Grow new hebes from cuttings.

H. buxifolia. A low-growing, spreading shrub with white flowers. Hardy to −5°F.
H. decumbens. Can grow to 15 ft. and can tolerate cold weather to −5°F. Needs full sun to survive.

Hechtia argentea *houseplant*

This is a thorny, not-too-attractive bromeliad, with treacherous prickles and silvery foliage. However, it is different and grown by some intrepid indoor gardeners. This is strictly a pot plant and easy to grow: Give it sun and keep it somewhat dry.

Hedera *perennial* Ivy

These trailing or climbing evergreen foliage plants have many leaf forms. Outdoors, ivy is good on a fence or trellis or used as a ground cover and, indoors, in a basket or perhaps climbing up a wall. A cool temperature and humidity are the keys to success. Ivy also prefers bright light to sun. Soak the soil, let it dry out, and then soak it again. Grow new plants from cuttings at any time.

H. canariensis (Algerian ivy). Has large, leathery, slightly curved, fresh green leaves.
H. helix (English ivy). Has dark green leaves.
H. h. 'Goldheart'. Has gold-centered leaves with green edges.
H. h. 'Green Ripples'. Has pleated leaves.
H. h. 'Itsy Bitsy'. Has tiny, pointed leaves.
H. h. 'Jubilee'. Has green-and-white leaves.
H. h. 'Manda's Crested'. Has wavy, five-pointed leaves.
H. h. 'Shamrock'. Has small, compact leaves.
H. h. 'Star'. Small, good for a dish garden or terrarium.

Hedychium *houseplant* Ginger lily

These large tropical plants, growing to 72 in., have canes of pale or glossy green leaves and fragrant white or yellow flowers in the summer. Ginger lilies are perfect for tubs in a sunny corner or outdoors on a terrace. Give them lots of water and up to 50 percent humidity, and then reduce the water after they have bloomed. Divide the rootstock in the spring to get more plants.

H. coronarium (garland flower). Produces fragrant, white flowers.
H. flavum (yellow ginger). Has pointed green leaves and yellow flowers.
H. gardnerianum (Kahili ginger). Has 18-in. leaves and yellow flowers with red stamens.

HELENIUM AUTUMNALE   *perennial*   Helen's flower

This is a fine garden flower that nonetheless is somewhat weedy in appearance. The Helen flower grows to 40 in. tall and, in the summer and fall, bears great clusters of bright orange or yellow daisylike flowers, 2 in. across. These perennials grow in almost any kind of soil, and they like sun and an abundance of water. Pinch off the tips of the stalks in the early summer to prolong the bloom; divide them for new plants. Helen flowers are often used as background plants.

SUGGESTED VARIETIES:
'Bressingham Gold'—yellow flowers
'Bruno'—red flowers
'Butterpat'—brilliant yellow flowers
'Chippersfield Orange'—orange flowers
'Riverton Gem'—lemon yellow flowers

HELIANTHEMUM NUMMULARIUM *shrub* **Moss rose**

These trailing evergreen shrubs grow to about 1 ft. tall, and their flowers resemble small pink, red, or yellow roses. This member of the rose family can be used as a ground cover or simply as a spot of color in the garden. The moss rose does best in a somewhat dry soil and thrives in the sun. Prune it down to about 6 in. high after it has bloomed, and propagate it from runners. It can tolerate temperatures down to −5°F.

SUGGESTED VARIETIES:
'Fire Dragon'—red flowers
'Raspberry Ripple'—pink flowers
'Wisley Pink'—pink flowers

HELIANTHUS *perennial/annual* **Sunflower**

Sunflowers are excellent as tall (to 60 in.) background plants. They are easy to grow, needing sun (naturally) and much water. Their very large flowers—and the source of sunflower seeds—bloom in the summer. Because these plants spread rapidly, it is good to dig them up every second year, in the spring or fall, and divide them. Dwarf varieties also are now available.

H. annuus. An annual and a favorite. Produces large flowers.
H. multiflorus. A perennial. Has thinner leaves than those of *H. annuus*, and yellow flowers.

SUGGESTED VARIETIES:
'Italian White'—white flowers
'London Gold'—yellow flowers
'Sunburst'—yellow flowers
'Sunrose'—brilliant yellow flowers
'Teddy Bear'—a dwarf, with yellow flowers

HELICHRYSUM BRACTEATUM *annual* **Strawflower**

Strawflowers grow to be 30 in. tall and bear red or orange daisylike flowers in the summer. In fact, however, the so-called flower petals are really stiff modified leaves; the true flowers are in the center. Strawflowers require sun and lots of water, and almost any soil will do. They often are used as cut flowers and also are dried for winter arrangements. Start new plants from seed, or buy prestarted plants.

SUGGESTED VARIETIES:
'Diamond Head'—yellow flowers
'Golden Star'—yellow flowers
'Moe's Gold'—brilliant yellow flowers

HELICONIA *houseplant*

This member of the banana family is a large plant, growing to 48 in., with leathery leaves and orange flowers on tall stalks in the spring and summer. It is a good patio or mild-climate outdoor plant. Give heliconia sun, rich soil kept moist, and humidity. In the winter when it is dormant, give it less water, and in the spring when it begins growing again, divide the rootstock for new plants.

H. anustifolia. Grows to 36 in. Has 24-in. leathery leaves and orange-red bracts.

H. aurantiaca. Grows to 30 in. Has smooth leaves and orange-and-green bracts.

H. psittacorum (parrot flower). Grows to 24 in. Has rich green leaves, orange bracts, and greenish yellow flowers. The best choice to put in a window.

HELIOCEREUS *houseplant*   Sun cactus

This popular sun cactus blooms during the day; its sister genus, *Selinicereus*, flowers during the night. The sun cactus can sprawl out to 8 ft., and its "leaves" are really elongated stems, generally with spines. Its flowers are spectacular and appear in the late summer. These plants need large tubs and full sun to bloom. Use a sandy soil that drains readily. Once established, these cacti can grow for years in the same container. Grow new plants from stem cuttings.

H. schrankii. Grows to 6 ft. Has elongated leaves and vivid red flowers.

H. speciosus. Grows to 7 ft. Has elongated gray-green leaves and red flowers.

HELIOPSIS SCABRA *perennial*

Heliopsis grows to 36 in. and has a long blooming season, with a profusion of bright yellow flowers in the summer and fall. It does well in almost any soil, with sun and lots of water. Heliopsis is a fine addition to any garden. Buy prestarted plants yearly.

HELIOTROPUM *perennial*   Heliotrope

The fragrant and popular heliotrope reaches a height of 40 in. and can tolerate shade if necessary. Indeed, it is easy to grow if it is not overwatered. The flowers come in the summer, and they are good bedding plants for a color accent. Propagate new plants from cuttings.

H. manglessi. Produces many and large clusters of purple flowers.

H. peruvianum. Produces fragrant, dark violet flowers.

HELLEBORUS   *perennial*   Hellebore

These plants can bloom anytime from late winter to early spring, and they
grow to be only 12 to 16 in. high. Hellebores need a shady, moist place in the
garden—under trees or shrubs, perhaps—and an alkaline soil. They are
good rock garden flowers. For additional plants, divide them in the fall.
Plants are poisonous.

H. niger (Christmas rose). Has scalloped green leaves and large white flowers.
H. orientalis (Lenten rose). Produces large (4-in.) flowers.

HELXINE SOLEIROLII   *ground cover*   Baby's tears

A popular ground cover, baby's tears has tiny, almost mosslike leaves, and it
spreads rapidly. For the best and quickest results, give this plant warmth,
bright light, and plenty of moisture. Use baby's tears to cover ugly areas;
obtain new plants anytime by placing stems in the ground.

HEMEROCALLIS HYBRID   *perennial*   Daylily

There are many kinds of daylilies, both evergreen and deciduous, some
short (to 20 in.) and others tall (to 40 in.), in an array of colors, but mainly

orange or yellow. For a dramatic effect, plant daylilies in bunches. They need bright light (too much sun tends to fade the flowers), a moderate amount of water, and almost perfect drainage. Daylilies take time to become established, but when they are, they bloom from spring through to fall. New plants come from offsets. There are innumerable species and hybrids of daylilies; check the catalog lists at the back of this book.

Hesperis Matronalis *perennial* Sweet rocket

Sweet rocket's clusters of fragrant white or purple flowers in the summer grow to 30 in., making a good color accent in the garden. This plant thrives in either bright light or shade, in any type of well-drained soil, and with regular watering. Remove faded flowers to prolong the blooming season. Buy prestarted plants.

Heuchera Sanguinea *perennial* Coral bell

Coral bells grow to 36 in. and bloom even in the shade. Their many flowers, which come in the summer and fall, are pink, on wiry stems. Coral bells require a fair amount of water in a rich, rapidly draining soil, and they are best planted in clumps—in borders, in rock gardens, on paths—in short, in those shady places where little else will grow. Divide them for new plants.

SUGGESTED VARIETIES:
'Chartreuse'—green flowers
'Coral Cloud'—coral red flowers
'Firebird'—red flowers
'Pearl Drops'—white flowers
'Raspberry Regal'—pink-red flowers

Hibiscus *shrub*

Hibiscus are densely growing, evergreen or deciduous shrubs that produce large, showy flowers. They are easy to care for: Give them sun—to make better flowers—regular watering and feeding, and a well-drained soil. Note that dwarf varieties also are available. Hibiscus are generally not bothered by insects. Root cuttings for new plants.

H. mutabilis. A deciduous shrub. Produces 4- to 6-in. flowers that first are pink and then change to red.
H. rosa-sinensis (Chinese hibiscus). A fast-growing evergreen, to 15 ft.; best in mild climates. Produces large flowers.

SUGGESTED VARIETIES:
'Agnes Gault'—pink flowers
'D. L. O'Brian'—orange flowers

'Blue Bird'—blue flowers
'Lavender Lady'—pink flowers
'Woodbridge'—magenta flowers

HIPPEASTRUM *bulb*   **Amaryllis**

Amaryllis have straplike leaves and spectacular, mammoth flowers in white, pink, red, rose, or violet—with their throats sometimes lighter or darker and the petals sometimes banded, striped, or bordered in a contrasting color. The flower stalks grow to 26 in. Buy quality bulbs in the late fall, and plant them anytime between January and March. Allow one bulb to a 6- or 7-in. pot, always with 1 in. of space between the sides of the pot and the bulb. Bury only the bottom two thirds of the bulb, letting the top third rise above the soil. Moisten the soil and set the pots in a cool dark place, letting them grow almost dry until the flower buds are up at least 6 in. Then move them into the sun, and water them heavily. Three or more weeks will elapse between planting and blooming. After the amaryllis bloom, keep them growing so that the leaves can manufacture food for next year's flowers. When the foliage turns brown, let the soil remain almost dry for about three months or until you see a new flower bud emerging. At that time, replant the bulbs in fresh soil but, if possible, in the same containers.

If you have a garden, set out the plants only when the danger of frost has passed. Then, when the temperature drops below 55°F in the fall, bring them inside, to a cool place and water them lightly—only enough to keep the leaves from wilting—until you begin a new cycle of growth. For additional amaryllis, either start them from seed, or plant separately the little bulbs that grow next to the mature one.

There are dozens of varieties and colors of amaryllis.

H. unemannia fumariaefolia. This species has smaller flowers.

SUGGESTED VARIETIES:
'Appleblossom'—pink flowers
'Fire Dance'—red flowers
'Scarlet Admiral'—red flowers

HOFFMANNIA *houseplant*

Hoffmannia is a splendid foliage plant from Mexico, growing to 30 in. It has velvety leaves in various shades of green and dark red or brown. This is one of few houseplants that do well in a north window. Keep the soil consistently moist, and obtain new plants from cuttings. Hoffmannia is good wherever a bright color is needed.

H. ghiesbreghtii. Grows to 48 in. Has brown-green leaves.
H. refulgens. Grows to 15 in. Has almost iridescent, crinkled leaves edged with magenta and rose.
H. roezlii. Grows to 30 in. Has copper-and-bronze leaves.

Hohenbergia *houseplant*

These large bromeliads are striking plants that need space, as their rosettes of broad, golden green leaves measure 48 in. across and their spikes of vivid lavender-blue flowers reach 40 in. high. Place these plants in the full sun, and keep the bromeliad "vase" filled with water. Hohenbergias make good terrace plants in temperate climates. But they are prickly, and so wear gloves when handling them. Buy new ones from specialists.

H. ridleyii. Has a golden yellow rosette of leaves and a lavender flower head.
H. stellata. Has a golden green rosette of leaves and a violet-colored flower head.

Hosta *perennial*   Plantain lily

Hosta form a large group of useful garden plants. Growing to 2 ft., they are good for a ground cover or in a border or simply massed by themselves for a rich green accent. Most species of hosta have large, 7- to 8-in. leaves, and all bear flowers on tall spikes in the summer and fall. Hosta do well in either poor or rich soil and like a light/shady location and a moderate amount of water. Divide them to get more plants.

H. fortunei. Has pale green leaves and tall flower spikes. Many varieties are available.
H. plantaginea. Probably the most widely grown hosta. Produces scented flowers.
H. sieboldiana. Has very large, bluish leaves.
H. undulata. Has large, wavy leaves; different.

HOUSTONIA LONGIFOLIA   *perennial*   **Bluet**

Bluets grow to about 1 ft. in wet soil. They have rosettes of leaves and, not surprisingly, blue (or white) flowers that bloom in the summer. Plant them in a bright light, in trouble areas of very moist soil. Bluets can be divided for new plants.

HOWEA (KENTIA)   *houseplant*

These feathery palms are indestructible plants with graceful fronds that grow to 60 in. Put them in a semishady spot, and keep the soil consistently moist (even though this may not seem right for a palm). Outdoors, group them in a mass for a dramatic effect. Use offsets for new plants. Tender.

H. *belmoreana* (sentry palm). Has very sharply pointed fronds bending slightly away from the main stems.
H. *forsteriana* (paradise palm). Has dark green fronds drooping more noticeably away from the main stems.

HOYA   *houseplant*   **Wax plant**

The vines in this genus grow to 48 in. or more, with leathery, glossy leaves and clusters of very fragrant flowers. Only mature plants, those four or five years old, are likely to bloom; young hoyas rarely produce flowers. Hoyas need full sun and will not bud at all in the shade. Let them become root bound, and give them lots of water in the spring, summer, and fall. In the winter, let the soil become almost dry. Do not remove the stem or spur on which the flowers have been produced, as this is the source of next season's bloom. Mist the leaves frequently, and check for mealybugs. Hoyas can be grown on a trellis or other support, although they also look handsome hanging from a basket. Propagate them in the spring from cuttings.

H. *australis*. The most popular species. Grows to 60 in. Has waxy green leaves and clusters of fragrant white flowers.
H. *bandaensis*. Grows to 72 in. Has large glossy green leaves with dark green veins, and greenish white flowers with scarlet centers.
H. *bella* (miniature wax plant). Bushy; grows to 20 in. Has tiny leaves and purple-centered white flowers.
H. *carnosa*. Grows to 48 in. Produces white flowers with pink centers.
H. 'Compacta'. Short; grows to only 12 in. Produces white flowers.
H. *engleriana*. Grows to 36 in. Has thick, round, hairy leaves and tiny, fragrant white flowers.
H. *keysii*. Grows to 30 in. Has gray-green leaves and white flowers.
H. 'Minibel'. Strong; grows to 72 in. Has green leaves and clusters of scented, waxy pink flowers.
H. *motoskei*. Grows to 48 in. Has oval leaves with silver spots and pink flowers.

HUERNIA *houseplant* Star flower

Resembling stapelias, these 24-in., bizarre-looking succulents from South Africa have somewhat gnarled growth (leaves) and gigantic flowers that are more weird than beautiful. Star flowers require equal parts of sand, gravel, and soil, with an additional thin layer of gravel on top of the mix. Water the plants carefully, as too much moisture will kill them. Give them ample sun and somewhat cool conditions. Some of the flowers smell terrible. Grow new plants from offsets.

H. barbata. Grows to 20 in. Has erect, angled stems with long green teeth and pale yellow flowers with red spots.

H. pillansi. Grows to 20 in. Has cylindrical stems covered with raised dots and long spines. Produces pale yellow flowers with crimson spots.

H. primulina. Grows to 20 in. Has short, fat, toothed, angled stems and pale yellow or pinkish yellow flowers.

HYACINTHUS *bulb* Hyacinth

Fragrant hyacinths growing to 24 in. can be used both in the garden and as an indoor plant. Their flowers and scent are welcome signs of spring. In most areas, plant the bulbs in the fall, 5 in. apart and 3 in. deep. Spread mulch over them for winter protection in freezing climates. Hyacinths

should be planted in a sunny place and be given a moderate amount of water. They are spectacular in drifts. Propagate them from offsets.

H. orientalis. The most popular hyacinth. Produces large blue flowers.
H. o. albulus. An improved variety of *H. orientalis*, more robust, with blue, pink, or white flowers.
H. romanus. Produces blue or white flowers.

SUGGESTED VARIETIES:
'Delft Blue'—blue flowers
'Innocence'—white flowers
'Pink Pearl'—pink flowers
'Snow Princess'—white flowers

HYDRANGEA *bulb*

Hydrangeas are native to both Asia and North America, and they make excellent garden plants with their large green leaves and clusters of white, blue, or pink flowers in the summer and fall. Hydrangeas prefer a sandy, loamy soil with good drainage. In bright sun they are at their best; in shade they will grow but will not be as colorful. Some species can be easily divided; others are better started from cuttings. Hydrangeas are not generally troubled by insects, although minor pests may attack.

H. macrophylla. Grows to 10 ft.; hardy to −5°F. Has bright green leaves and blue or pink flowers.
H. paniculata 'Grandiflora' (peegee hydrangea). Grows to 25 ft.; hardy to −10°F. Produces white flowers.
H. quercifolia (oak-leafed hydrangea). Grows to 6 ft.; hardy to −5°F. Produces white flowers that later turn purple.

SUGGESTED VARIETIES:
'Heinrich Seidel'—large purple or purple-red flowers
'Mariesii'—rosy pink flowers
'Nikko Blue'—lots and lots of blue flowers

HYLOCEREUS UNDATUS *houseplant* Night-blooming cactus

These huge, vining, jungle plants can extend 7 ft. and produce mammoth white flowers once a year on a summer night—an occasion for a party because the blossoms last only a half-day or a day. Nonetheless, to some people, a night-blooming cactus is hardly worth the care it needs for the other 364 days. It needs a sandy soil, sun, warmth to 78°F by day, and lots of water in the summer, and bright light in the winter, with less moisture and a cooler location (about 50°F). Established plants need ample space for growing and their yearly blossoming is truly exciting. Grow new plants from cuttings in the spring.

HYMENOCALLIS NARCISSIFOLIA   *bulb*   Spider lily

Its large, fragrant flowers make the spider lily a desirable addition to the temperate garden. The blossoms appear in the summer on tall (30-in.) leafless stalks; the straplike leaves, which come later, may be evergreen or deciduous. Give these bulbs sun and lots of water (but allow the soil to dry out before watering them again), and dig them up and store them in the fall. When you plant the bulbs, space them 1 ft. apart and 5 in. deep. Spider lilies are easily propagated by offsets.

SUGGESTED VARIETY:
'Daphne'

HYPERICUM MOSERIANUM   *perennial*   Saint Johnswort

This perennial has cup-shaped, golden yellow flowers in the summer and fall. It grows to 24 in., needs sun or bright light and regular watering, and does well in almost any soil. The stems should be cut to the ground each year to encourage new growth. St. Johnswort can be used as a ground cover or massed in flower beds. Buy prestarted plants.

HYPOCYRTA   *houseplant*   Goldfish plant

Goldfish plants originated in Central America, and they have tiny leaves and brilliant orange-and-red pouchlike flowers. The best soil mix for them is equal parts of shredded fir bark and soil. In the winter they like sun; in the summer, shade. Grow goldfish plants in hanging baskets, as they may trail as much as 24 in. After the flowers fade, prune back the plants to encourage branching. New blossoms will appear on the new growth in the following fall and winter. Obtain more goldfish plants from stem-tip cuttings of new growth.

H. 'Emile'. Grows to 24 in. Has leathery dark green leaves and bright orange flowers shaped like—what else?—goldfish.
H. nummularia. A creeper with vermilion-yellow-violet flowers. May become dormant in the summer but leafs out again in the fall.
H. strigillosa. Spreading, semierect growth. Produces reddish orange flowers.
H. wettsteinii. A pendant grower with orange-yellow flowers on and off throughout the year.

IBERIS   *perennial/annual*   Candytuft

Candytuft, which grows to 12 in., has dark green leaves and clusters of flowers in shades of white, red, purple, or pink. This plant needs sun or bright light and regular watering. Almost any soil will do, as long as it is well drained. One selling point for candytuft is that it blooms from the spring through the fall: Cut off old flower stems as soon as the flowers begin to fade, to encourage new ones. Cuttings provide additional plants. Candytuft is a good edging plant.

I. amara coronaria. An annual, with clusters of fragrant white flowers.
I. sempervirens (evergreen candytuft). A perennial, with evergreen, dark green leaves and 2-in. clusters of tiny white flowers.
I. umbellata (globe candytuft). An annual, with bushy foliage and small pink flowers.

SUGGESTED VARIETIES:
'Autumn Snow'—white flowers
'Purity'—white flowers

ILEX   *shrub*   Holly

Holly can be either evergreen or deciduous; there are hundreds of varieties. All kinds prefer sun, even though they will tolerate shade, as well as ample water and a rich, slightly acid soil. Their leaves may be tiny or large, smooth or toothed, and green or variegated. Their berries range in color from red to orange to yellow to black. Because holly plants are either male or female, both must be present in an area to ensure fertilization of the flowers. (Chinese holly, however, can produce fruit without the pollen of other hollies.) Although holly is not susceptible to disease, scale and mealybugs may be a problem. Be vigilant, and take the appropriate measures. In all, holly is a very desirable shrub for the garden. It is easily propagated from cuttings.

I. aquifolium (English holly). An evergreen. Grows to 15 ft.; hardy to −5°F. Many varieties, with different leaves, shapes, and colors.
I. cornuta (Chinese holly). An evergreen. Grows, either dense or open, to 9 ft.; hardy to 5°F. Has glossy, leathery leaves and bright red berries.
I. crenata (Japanese holly). An evergreen. Grows, dense and erect, to as much as 20 ft.; hardy to −5°F. Has finely toothed leaves and black berries.
I. glabra (inkberry). An evergreen. Grows to 9 ft.; hardy to −20°F. Produces black berries.
I. opaca (American holly). An evergreen. Grows to 50 ft.; hardy to −35°F. Has spiny leaves and bright red berries. The holly most often used as a Christmas decoration.
I. pernyi. An evergreen. Grows to 30 ft.; hardy to −5°F. Has glossy green leaves and very large red berries.
I. serrata (Japanese winterberry). An evergreen. Grows to 7 ft.; hardy to −20°F. Has saw-toothed leaves and red berries.
I. verticillata (winterberry). An evergreen. Grows to 10 ft.; hardy to −35°F. Produces bright red berries.

IMPATIENS *annual*   Patience plant

Small varieties of impatiens grow to only 10 in. at most, but others can reach 3 ft. Impatiens also come in a wide range of colors, whether solid or striped or mottled: white, red, pink, orange, or purple. They do well in either sun or shade, in a sandy soil, and with lots of water. Use impatiens in flower beds, in borders, and in hanging pots. Buy new plants each year.

I. balsamina. Produces pink flowers on tall plants.
I. sultanii. One of the oldest species. Produces pink flowers.
I. walleriana. Produces bright red flowers on bushy plants.

SUGGESTED VARIETY:
'Shady Lady'—red flowers

INCARVILLEA *perennial*

These perennials grow to 26 in. and bear pink, trumpet-shaped flowers in the summer. Incarvillea requires sun, a moderate amount of water, and a rich loamy soil that has excellent drainage. Remove the flowers when they fade, to extend the blooming season, and divide the plants to obtain new ones. Incarvillea makes a good color accent.

I. delawayi. Produces an abundance of pink flowers.
I. grandiflora. Produces larger flowers and is more robust than *I. delawayi.*

INDIGOFERA *shrub*   Indigo

Indigo is a 2-ft. shrub with small pink flowers that is occasionally seen in gardens. It likes a sunny location and a fair amount of water in a well-drained soil. Indigo makes either a good color accent or a background shrub. Cuttings provide new plants.

I. amblyantha. Grows tall, to about 5 ft. Produces tiny flowers.
I. tinctoria. Occasionally grown in specialty gardens, this is the indigo plant from which the blue dye is made.

INULA ORIENTALIS *perennial*

This perennial is easy to grow: Give it sun, lots of water, and almost any soil. Inula grow to 24 in. and, in the summer, produce large yellow flowers. Use them in groups in flower beds for a spot of bright color, or as edging plants. Buy new ones yearly.

IPOMOEA PURPUREA *vine* Morning glory

Morning glories are annual vines that can extend to 15 ft. They have decorative leaves and short-lived, usually blue, funnel-shaped flowers in the summer. Morning glories are happiest in the sun, with little water. They

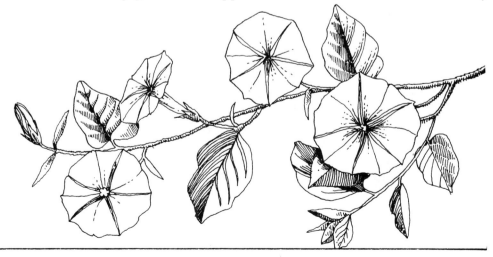

grow quickly in any soil and need support such as a trellis. Do not feed them. Start new plants each year; there are many varieties from which to choose.

SUGGESTED VARIETIES:
'Candy Pink'—pink flowers
'Early Call'—blue flowers
'Heavenly Blue'—violet-blue flowers
'Pearly Gates'—white flowers
'Scarlet O'Hara'—red flowers

IRESINE HERBSTII *annual*   Blood leaf

This plant grows to 24 in. and is valued mainly for its unusual multicolored leaves (generally red and yellow). The so-called bloodleaf needs sun and heavy watering but will tolerate bad soils. The leaves are at their most colorful in the summer and fall; the flowers are insignificant. Obtain new plants from cuttings.

IRIS *bulb*   Iris

The nearly 200 species of iris come in many shapes, sizes, and flower colors; better flowers would be hard to find. Most grow to about 2 ft., but medium-sized and dwarf irises also are available. There are bearded, beardless, and crested types. All irises like a somewhat shaded to bright location, with lots of water at the roots. They bloom in the spring and summer.

I. hybrids (Dutch iris). Many varieties in many colors.
I. reticulata. Several species, with violet-scented, violet-colored flowers edged with gold.
I. xiphiodes (English iris). Produces white through shades of blue to purple flowers.
I. xiphium (Spanish iris). Produces white, yellow, orange, or blue flowers.

IXIA VIRIDIFLORA *bulb*   African corn lily

These bulbs are hybrids of South African flowering plants, growing to 24 in., with 2-in. flowers on wiry stems. The corn lily's foliage is both grassy and swordlike. Its flowers range from red to pink to orange to yellow, with dark centers, and they bloom in the spring and summer. Plant the bulbs in the fall, 3 to 6 in. apart and 3 in. deep. Give them sun and water them regularly. Corn lilies make fine cut flowers and also are effective planted in masses. Dig up and store the bulbs each year; divide them if you want more plants.

IXORA   *houseplant*   Flame-of-the-woods

Ixoras can be grown outside in mild climates; elsewhere they must be grown inside as houseplants. They have ornamental leaves and clusters of brightly colored flowers. Ixoras grow to 36 in., and outside they can be used as hedges. Some plants bloom twice, in the early spring and again in the summer. To make these plants happy, give them sun and a moist soil, except in the winter when they should be kept somewhat dry. Even young plants bloom! Grow new plants from cuttings.

I. chinensis. Has 4-in. leaves and red-to-white flowers.
I. 'Gillette's Yellow'. Produces lots of yellow flowers.
I. javanica. Has 7-in. leaves, willowy branches, and orange-red flowers.
I. 'Super King'. A compact plant. Produces many, twice-blooming, 6-in., ball-shaped flower
   clusters.

JACARANDA ACUTIFOLIA   *shrub/tree*

In mild climates, jacarandas are magnificent tall trees with often sparse foliage but spectacular dark lavender flowers in the late spring; when they fall, it is like purple snow. As a houseplant, jacarandas grow to only shrub size, 72 in. Put them in a bright location, and keep the soil consistently moist. Indoors, however, jacarandas rarely flower. They are easily grown from seed.

JACOBINIA   *houseplant*   King's crown

From Brazil, these 30-in. plants have downy green leaves and plumes of pink or orange flowers in the summer. Grow them in a sunny window with good air circulation, and keep the soil wet: Insufficient moisture causes the leaves to drop. Take stem cuttings in the spring for new plants, and discard the old ones.

J. carnea. Grows upright. Has dark green leaves and pink flowers.
J. ghiesbreghtiana. Has light green leaves and orange flowers.
J. suberecta. Has spreading growth, hairy leaves, and orange flowers.

JASMINUM   *vine*   Jasmine

Mostly climbing or sprawling plants, jasmine is associated with fragrance, even though not all jasmines are scented. Indeed, the so-called star jasmine, which is well known for its spicy perfume, is not a true jasmine at all. In any case, however, most species of real jasmine thrive in regular garden soil and

will tolerate shady spots but prefer some sun. Jasmine can be used to cover trellises, fences, or walls; the shrubby types can even be made into hedges.

J. azorium. An evergreen. Grows to 15 ft.; hardy to 5°F. Has broad green leaves and white flowers.

J. mesnyi (primrose jasmine). An evergreen. Grows to 10 ft.; hardy to 5°F. Produces unscented lemon yellow flowers.

J. nudiflorum (winter jasmine). A deciduous climber. Grows to 15 ft.; hardy to 5°F. Produces unscented yellow flowers.

J. officinale (common white jasmine). A semievergreen-to-deciduous climber. Grows to 15 ft. Produces small, fragrant, white flowers.

J. rex. A deciduous climber. Grows to 15 ft.; hardy to 10°F. Produces large white flowers.

Jatropha *shrub*

These tropical evergreen shrubs grow to 48 in. and have broad green leaves and brilliant red flowers. They bloom throughout the year in mild climates and make excellent hedges. Place them in the sun, and keep the soil consistently moist. Grow new jatrophas from seed.

J. hastatum. Grows to 30 in. Has bright green leaves and clusters of vivid red flowers.

J. pandurifolia 'Dwarf'. A small variety, growing to only 14 in.

J. pandurifolia 'Holly Leaf'. Produces scarlet flowers.

JUGLANS REGIA *tree* **Walnut**

Walnut trees are seldom grown in gardens; rather, they are usually grown commercially for their walnuts. In any event, they are big trees, growing to 60 ft., and have coarse leaves. Walnut trees often are hosts to aphids, and they also exude a sticky substance that is difficult to remove from any unlucky cars parked under them. They can withstand temperatures down to −10°F but really are best grown by specialists.

JUNIPERUS *shrub/tree* **Juniper**

Junipers are evergreens best known for their colorful berries in the fall and winter. Dozens of varieties are available, both tall treelike kinds and low-growing shrub types. Note that both male and female junipers must be grown near each other to ensure their fruiting. Most will tolerate hot dry conditions if they are in a somewhat alkaline soil, making them a good choice for drought-striken areas. However, junipers are also vulnerable to many insects, especially spider mites, aphids, and twig borers. Watch them carefully, and try to head off the bugs at the pass. Junipers are difficult to propagate.

J. chinensis (Chinese juniper). Grows to 60 ft.; hardy to −10°F. Has a pyramidal shape and scalelike leaves.
J. excelsa (Greek juniper). Grows to 60 ft.; hardy to 10°F. Has a pyramidal shape and dense, scalelike leaves.
J. sabina. Grows to 10 ft.; hardy to −10°F. Has needlelike leaves.
J. squamata. Grows to 36 ft.; hardy to −20°F. Has oval-shaped leaves.
J. virginiana (eastern red cedar). Grows to 90 ft.; hardy to −35°F. Has a dense, pyramidal shape and usually scalelike leaves.

SUGGESTED VARIETIES:
'Canaertii'—conical shape and dark green leaves
'Glauca' (silver red cedar)—grows to 20 ft., silvery blue leaves

KADSURA JAPONICA *vine*

This evergreen vine can grow to 12 ft. Its whitish yellow flowers are small, and its berries are scarlet, a nice complement to its green leaves. Water this plant often, and place it in a sunny spot. The flowers bloom in the summer. Kadsura is a good cover for unsightly areas; for new plants, take cuttings.

KAEMPFERIA ROSCOEANA *houseplant* **Peacock plant**

The peacock plant grows to 12 in. and has lavender flowers—a few each day—all summer long. What is more, its leaves are almost iridescent, making it indeed a treasured addition to any house's decor. Grow the peacock plant in bright light, and keep the soil fairly moist but not soaked. Let it die down in the winter, and store the rootstock in a paper bag in a cold place. Then repot it in March or April in a 6-in. container. Divide the rootstock if you want more plants.

KALANCHOE   *houseplant*

Kalanchoes are succulents that include both small and large plants. They can be grown outdoors in mild climates; otherwise, they make good houseplants. *K. blossfeldiana* is the most popular kalanchoe, with fleshy green leaves and red, orange, or yellow flowers. Those plants in bloom at Christmastime will continue to flower for a month or more. Others are prized for their colorful foliage. Place kalanchoes in a bright light, and let the soil dry out well between waterings. To avoid mildew, take care not to overwater them. If the leaves develop a white coating, dust them lightly with powdered charcoal. New plants can be started by planting seeds in the spring or by separately potting the naturally forming plantlets.

K. blossfeldiana. Grows to 20 in. Has waxy leaves and sometimes blooms twice, in the winter and again in the spring.
K.b. 'Tom Thumb'. A dwarf hybrid sold in florists' shops at Christmastime.
K. pumila. Grows to 16 in. Has leathery dark green leaves and vivid pink flowers.
K. tomentosa (panda plant). Grows to 20 in. Has fuzzy, brown-spotted, gray-green leaves. Raised primarily for its foliage.
K. uniflora. Grows to 14 in. Produces pink-to-orange, bell-shaped flowers in the late winter and sometimes again in the spring.

KALMIA   *shrub*   Laurel

Laurel is related to the rhododendrons, and like them, laurel also bears beautiful flowers. An evergreen shrub, it prefers an acid soil but will also thrive in partial shade. Laurel is a good ornamental shrub as well as a good background plant. It is easy to grow and does not usually have a problem with insects.

K. latifolia (mountain laurel). Grows to 10 ft.; hardy to −35°F. Has long leaves and, in May or June, rose-colored flowers marked with purple.
K. polifolia (bog kalmia). Grows to 2 ft.; hardy to −35°F. Has whitish leaves and rose-purple flowers.

KERRIA   *shrub*

This thick-growing deciduous shrub needs to be pruned often. But it produces bright yellow flowers in May, and its twigs stay green all winter. Kerria grows to about 6 ft., with arching branches. Give it partial shade—although it will take sun in cooler areas—and a fair amount of water until it is established; then it can tolerate drought. This shrub is not bothered by insects, and its softwood and hardwood cuttings root easily.

K. japonica. Grows to 6 ft. or more; hardy to −35°F. Has toothed green leaves and yellow flowers.
'Picta'—green leaves edged with white
'Pleniflora'—double flowers

KNIPHOFIA ALOIDES *perennial*   Red-hot poker

This popular garden plant, native to South Africa, grows to 9 ft. and has long gray-green leaves. In the summer and fall, its flowers first are coral red, then turn orange, and finally become greenish yellow. Red-hot pokers are ideal as background plants or as vertical accents. They require sun and lots of water and are almost impervious to insects. Buy prestarted plants.

SUGGESTED VARIETIES:
'Maid of Orleans'
'Springtime'

KOCHIA SCOPARIA TRICHOPHYLLA *annual* Mexican fire bush

The Mexican fire bush is raised mainly for its foliage. It grows to 36 in., and its very narrow light green leaves turn red after the first frost. This plant needs good sun and will tolerate heat. It also should have a moderate amount of water, but it is not fussy about soil. Note that it can reseed itself profusely enough to become invasive. Each year, however, buy prestarted plants.

KOELREUTERIA PANICULATA *tree*   Goldenrain tree

This beautiful tree grows to about 30 ft. and produces yellow flower clusters in May. If it must, it can withstand drought, wind, cold (to −10°F), or heat, and it can grow in almost any soil—truly a valuable member of any garden or yard. Goldenrain trees do need some pruning, however, to remain shapely. They are generally not bothered by insects and can be propagated from root cuttings.

KOHLERIA *houseplant*

This tropical gesneriad grows to 20 to 30 in.; some are trailers, and others grow upright. They all have attractive foliage and colorful tubular flowers. Put kohlerias in a bright light rather than sun, and water them heavily while they are actively growing. They need much less water the rest of the time, but never let them dry out completely. Do not mist the plants, but do give them a fairly humid atmosphere. Either take stem-tip cuttings for new plants, or divide large rhizomes and pot them separately.

K. amabilis. Grows to 16 in. Has green leaves and pink flowers in the spring and summer. A
    good basket plant.
K. bogotensis Grows upright (staked) to 24 in. Produces brilliant red-and-yellow flowers in the
    summer.
K. eriantha. Grows upright to 24 in. Produces bright red flowers from summer to fall.
K. lindeniana. Grows upright to 10 in. Produces fragrant, violet-and-white flowers in the late
    fall.
K. 'Longwood'. Grows upright to 24 in. Produces large, spotted, pink flowers.

KOLWITZIA AMABILIS   *shrub*   Beauty bush

This handsome deciduous shrub has spreading branches, gray-green leaves, and small, pink, yellow-throated flowers in the late spring or early summer. The flowers are followed by pinkish brown, bristly fruit. The beauty bush grows about 10 ft. tall and can withstand temperatures down to −20°F. Place it in a sunny location in a well-drained soil.

LABURNUM   *shrub/tree*   Goldenchain tree

The deciduous goldenchain tree is usually kept pruned, as a small (30 ft.) tree, for it can become rather shrubby if the basal suckers are allowed to grow up. In the spring, it produces hanging, wisterialike clusters of yellow flowers. This branching tree should not have too much sun; it needs regular watering; and it does well in most well-drained soils. Cuttings supply new trees.

L. anagyroides (common goldenchain tree). Many varieties. Hardy to −10°F.
L. watereri. Has denser foliage and larger flowers than the other species. Can be espaliered.
    Hardy to −10°F.

LACHENALIA   *bulb*   Cape cowslip

From South Africa and growing to only 12 in. high, the Cape cowslip is a fine bulb for spot color. Its straplike, succulent leaves often have brown spots, and its flowers are white, red, or yellow and bloom in the spring. To do its best, this plant should have sun and a moderate amount of water while it is actively growing, but less light and little water at other times. Cape cowslips grow easily if they are in a readily draining soil. Divide them for new plants.

L. bulbifera. Has erect dark green, sometimes spotted, leaves and large, deep purple, red, or
    yellow flowers.

L. tricolor (Cape cowslip). Has dark green leaves with dull purple spots, and red and yellow flowers.

LAELIA   *houseplant*

These showy orchids resemble cattleyas. Laelias grow to 30 in., with leathery leaves and pink flowers in the fall. Plant them in fir bark; soak it; and then allow the soil to dry out before watering it again. Be sure to put these orchids in the sun, in a place where the humidity is 50 percent. Buy young plants from specialists.

L. anceps. Grows to 30 in. Produces clusters of 4-in. pink flowers.
L. gouldiana. Grows to 30 in. Produces an abundance of rose-magenta flowers.
L. pumila. A dwarf, growing to only 8 in. Produces 4-in. pale rose-colored flowers.
L. purpurata. Grows to 36 in. Has narrow, leathery leaves and large white flowers with magenta throats.

LAGERSTROEMERIA INDICA   *shrub/tree*   Crape myrtle

This is almost the perfect shrub/tree. (In mild climates, such as southern California, crape myrtles are relatively small trees; in cooler regions, such as Washington, D.C., they are shrubs.) Crape myrtles have nice shapes, rather twisted but smooth trunks, dainty little green leaves that turn orange or yellow in the fall, and beautiful shocking pink or white (or sometimes purplish pink) flowers in the summer. They do best in the sun and in a well-drained soil. Crape myrtles can survive temperatures down to 5°F and can be propagated by means of cuttings.

LAMIUM MACULATUM   *perennial*   Dead nettle

This somewhat weedy-looking plant has small, crinkled, oval, dark green leaves splotched with silver, and lavender flowers that bloom in the summer. As it grows to only about 1 ft., dead nettle can be used as a ground cover or simply as a background plant. Give it bright light and regular waterings in a well-drained soil. Divide this perennial for additional plants.

SUGGESTED VARIETIES:
'Alba'—white flowers
'White'—white flowers

LANTANA   *shrub*

Lantana is a woody shrub that grows about 3 ft. high. It needs lots of sun, deep but infrequent watering, and a rich loamy soil. Varieties come in a multitude of flower colors—white, purple, red, orange, yellow—and some have multicolored flowers. Lantana blooms in the summer and fall. Take cuttings for new plants.

L. *camara*. A prickly stemmed shrub, with flowers that open as pink or yellow and then change to red or orange. In warm climates, it is a perennial.
L. *montevidensis*. A trailing plant, with rosy lilac flowers.

SUGGESTED VARIETY:
'Christmas Red'—red flowers

LAPAGERIA ROSEA   *vine*   Chilean bellflower

A noteworthy evergreen vine—growing to 10 ft.—for a fence or trellis, the Chilean bellflower has leathery dark green leaves and bell-shaped, rose-colored flowers that bloom in the summer and fall. This vine likes the shade or bright light (but not sun) and moist soil. Buy new plants each year.

LAPEIROUSIA CRUENTA   *bulb*

These little plants, growing to only 12 in., look good in borders or in clumps by themselves, for a bit of color. The leaves are narrow and dark green, and the flowers—blooming in the summer and fall—are carmine red. Put these bulbs in the sun, and give them a fair amount of water. In freezing climates, dig up and store the bulbs over the winter.

LARIX   *tree*

Larches are very tall, deciduous conifers, some reaching over 100 ft. They are noted for their pyramidal shape and beautiful gold and orange leaves in the fall. Most species of larch prefer a well-drained soil and grow readily under most conditions. Larches, however, are more often used as street trees than as garden trees.

L. *decidua* (European larch). Mature trees have wide spreading branches; younger ones have a pyramidal shape. Hardy to −50°F.
L. *laricina* (American larch). Sometimes called a tamarack. Hardy to −50°F.

LATHYRUS   *perennial/annual*   Sweet pea

Sweet peas can be tall vines or short plants. They provide a welcome spot of color, and sometimes fragrance, in any garden. Sweet peas are happiest in the sun, with a moderate amount of water and a rich loamy soil. They do need time to get established and generally require a support of some sort, such as a trellis or a fence. Buy new plants, or grow them from seed.

L. laetiflorus. A climber, with large rose-colored flowers.
L. odoratus (sweet pea). An annual and a climber, with fragrant flowers in various colors. Excellent for window boxes or planters. Cutting it back stimulates new growth.

SUGGESTED VARIETIES:
'Bijou'—pink, red flowers
'Knee-hi'—mixed colors
'Red Ensign'—red flowers
'Xenia Field'—pink flowers

LAURUS NOBILIS   *shrub/tree*   Sweet bay

This tree, or shrub, is where we get bay leaves for cooking. It grows slowly (so it is a shrub at first), needs filtered shade, only little water when it is established, and any soil that is well drained. Bay leaves are oval, rather long and stiff, and aromatic, and its small yellow flowers give way to black or dark purple berries in the fall. This tree can survive temperatures down to 5°F, and it can easily be propagated from cuttings.

LAVANDULA ANGUSTIFOLIA   *perennial*   English lavender

Lavender, which grows to 30 in., produces in the summer and fall the familiar, fragrant, pale gray-blue lavender flowers that are often dried. The lavender plant can easily be grown in a rich soil that, when watered regularly, drains readily, and it should be situated in the sun. Cuttings provide new plants.

SUGGESTED VARIETIES:
'Jean Davis'—pale blue flowers
'Munstead Dwarf'—blue flowers
'Twicket Purple'—blue-purple flowers

LAVATERA TRIMESTRIS   *annual*   Tree mallow

From the mallow family, these annuals look like single hollyhocks, growing to 72 in. and having roundish leaves and rose-colored flowers in the summer and fall. Tree mallows prefer sun and a moderate amount of water in a well-drained soil. They are, however, vulnerable to hollyhock rust. Grow new plants from seed.

LAYIA CAMPESTRIS   *annual*   **Tidytips**

Tidytips is a member of the sunflower family that grows 16 in. high, has narrow leaves, and, in the spring, bears yellow flowers tipped with white. It does best in the sun, with regular watering of the roots. Grow new plants from seed.

LEONOTIS LEONURUS   *perennial*   **Lion's ear**

Lion's tails are tall perennials, to 6 ft., with elliptical leaves and furry, red-orange flowers on long spikes. When massed several to a group, they are effective as a color accent in the garden. This plant blooms in the summer, prefers bright light or shade, and needs regular watering in a well-drained soil. Cuttings provide new tails.

LEONTOPODIUM ALPINUM   *perennial*   **Edelweiss**

These small white woolly plants are the famous wildflowers of the Swiss Alps. They are short-lived, only 4 to 12 in. high, and produce star-shaped flowers blooming in midsummer on the tips of their woolly stems. Edelweiss need sun and lots of water in a well-drained sandy soil. Divide them for additional plants.

LEPTOSPERUM SCOPARIUM   *tree*   **Australian tea tree**

Growing to 20 ft. or more, the tea tree is decorative, with small evergreen leaves and white flowers in the spring and summer. It does best in a readily draining sandy soil and can be propagated from cuttings.

LEUCHTENBERGIA PRINCIPIS   *houseplant*

This is the only species of this genus that is cultivated, but it appears frequently in collections, and although it cannot be called pretty, it does have some admirers. Leuchtenbergia is a desert cactus having a fleshy, elongated stem with star-shaped spines and yellow flowers. It likes the sun and a sandy soil kept barely moist. Plant seeds to obtain more of these curious cacti.

LEUCODENDRON   *tree*

Occasionally seen in southern gardens, silver trees—which are native to South Africa—grow to about 40 ft. and have silky-haired leaves and a rounded shape. They do well in most soils and can be propagated by cuttings.

Leucojum   *bulb*

Defying their name, snowflakes bloom in the spring and summer, white flowers on 12-in. plants. Plant these bulbs in the fall, 4 in. apart and 2 in. deep, in a sunny location, perhaps under deciduous trees or anywhere you need a bit of green and white. Give snowflakes lots of water. They can be left undisturbed for years.

L. aestivum. Produces white drooping flowers in clusters of four to eight.
L. vernum (snowflake). Produces solitary, drooping, fragrant white flowers.

Levisticum officinale   *perennial*   Lovage

Lovage is an herb and a member of the carrot family. It grows 6 in. tall and is often used as a flavoring in salads and the like. But it also is decorative when planted in borders, for it has glossy dark green leaves and small greenish yellow flowers that bloom in the summer and fall. Put it in a bright light, water it regularly, and divide it for new plants.

Lewisia rediviva   *perennial*

Lewisia grows only 6 in. high, with strap-shaped leaves and rose-colored or white flowers that look like waterlilies and appear in the spring. This plant is mainly used in rock gardens, where it requires shade and very little water in a well-drained soil; indeed, too much water can hurt it. Divide it for new plants.

Liatris   *perennial*   Gay feather

This perennial is tall, to 60 in., with narrow grassy leaves and spires of lavender or white flowers that bloom in the summer and fall. It makes a good background plant. Give the gayfeather sun but little water in a well-drained loamy soil. Divide it for new plants.

L. pycnostachya. Produces pale purple flowers.
L. scariosa. Taller than *L. pycnostachya*, with purple flowers.
L. spicata. Produces purple or white flowers.

LICUALA GRANDIS   *perennial*

This 30-in.-diameter palm grows slowly to 72 in. tall, with wide fans of fronds. It thrives in either sun or shade as long as it is kept moist. Although it can withstand temperatures down to 40°F, it is grown outside only in warm climates.

LIGULARIA   *houseplant*   **Leopard plant**

The leopard plant comes from Japan, grows to 24 in. tall, and has round, variegated leaves. It does best in the shade in moist soil. To obtain new plants, divide the roots.

L. kaempferi argentea. Has green leaves with creamy white margins.
L.k. aureo-maculata (leopard plant). Has green leaves spotted with gold.

LIGUSTRUM   *shrub/tree*   **Privet**

Privet can be evergreen or deciduous, and it is commonly used as a hedge plant. Fast growing, it bears small white flowers followed by blue or black berries. Most privets are remarkably free of problems and can thrive in almost any kind of soil in either sun or shade. The many kinds of privets are not easily differentiated until they are mature, so be sure to consult with your nursery before buying any. Both softwood and hardwood cuttings root easily.

L. ibolium (ibolium privet). Grows to 12 ft.; hardy to −10°F. Produces white flowers and black berries.
L. japonicum (Japanese privet). Grows densely to 18 ft.; hardy to 5°F. Produces clusters of small white flowers.
'Lusterleaf' (texanum)—very large leaves
L. vicaryi (golden privet). A hybrid. Grows to 12 ft.; hardy to −10°F. Has golden yellow leaves and blue-black berries.
L. vulgare (common privet). Grows to 15 ft.; hardy to −10°F. Produces clusters of white flowers and black berries.

LILIUM   *bulb*   **Lily**

This popular group of plants has lilies for almost all regions of the United States. They all require sun or filtered shade at the tops of the plants where the flowers form, coolness and shade at the roots, and lots of water in a loose, well-drained soil. Lilies look especially good in clumps in the garden. They bloom in the summer. There are innumerable varieties, so check the source list at the back of this book for the type(s) you want.

L. candidum (Madonna lily). Produces 2- to 3-in.-long, pearl-white flowers tinged purple.
L. regale (regal lily). Produces fragrant white flowers.

SUGGESTED VARIETIES:
American hybrids
Asian hybrids
Aurelian hybrids
Candidum hybrids
Longiflorum hybrids
Martagon hybrids
Oriental hybrids

LIMONIUM (STATICE)   *perennial*   Sea lavender

Some species of these popular garden plants are low growers, to 8 in., but others can reach 2 ft. In the summer they have colorful heads of flowers that are often dried. Sea lavender likes sun and a moderate amount of water in a well-drained soil. Plant seeds for new plants.

L. bonduelii. Grows to about 2 ft., compact, with yellow flowers.
L. latifolium. Produces bright purplish flowers on tall stems.
L. perezii. Grows to 3 ft., somewhat shrubby, with yellow flowers.
L. sinuatum. Many varieties available, with white, blue, or red flowers.

LINUM   *perennial/annual*   Flax

Flax is frequently used in flower borders and rock gardens. It grows to about 2 ft. and has narrow leaves and blue or yellow flowers that appear in the summer. Most kinds of flax do well in a sunny spot in most soils and with regular watering. It can easily be divided for new plants.

L. grandiflorum. An annual. Grows to 2 ft., with many varieties.
L. perenne. A perennial. Grows to 2 ft., with blue flowers.

LIQUIDAMBAR STYRACIFLUA   *tree*   American sweet gum

This is a good ornamental tree because it has a fine form, is easy to grow, and has purple, yellow, or red leaves in the fall. (Its flowers are insignificant.) The sweet gum does well in ordinary garden soil and grows quickly once it becomes established, reaching about 60 ft. It can tolerate temperatures down to −5°F. Softwood cuttings provide new plants. Sweet gums are occasionally attacked by tent caterpillars.

LIRIODENDRON TULIPIFERA   *tree*   Tulip tree

True to its name, the tulip tree bears tulip-shaped flowers in the late spring; they are greenish yellow and orange at the base. In the fall, this tree's leaves turn bright yellow. Mature tulip trees need space, as they can reach 150 ft. They also need a rich, well-drained soil. Their disadvantages are that they are difficult to propagate, so you must buy young plants, and they can be troubled by insects, particularly scale and aphids. Tulip trees tolerate temperatures down to −10°F.

LIRIOPE MUSCARI   *perennial*   Lily turf

A good "filler" plant or ground cover, lily turf grows to only about 1 ft. tall, with grassy foliage. It thrives in almost any condition but prefers ample water in a well-drained soil, and sun if the air is cool but some shade if it is hot. Lily turf is fine as an edging plant or can be used in lieu of a lawn. It is hardy down to −5°F and is easily divided. Liriope is similar in appearance to *Ophiopogon*.

SUGGESTED VARIETIES:
'Evergreen Giant'—robust
'Monroe White'—white variation in leaves
'Royal Purple'—brilliant purple sheen in leaves

LITHODORA DIFFUSA   *shrub*

This shrub (also called *Lithosperum*) is a prostrate grower, to about 1 ft. tall, and produces bright blue flowers in the late spring and summer. It needs a somewhat shaded spot, regular watering, and a well-drained soil. Lithodora is often used as a ground cover, tolerates temperatures down to 5°F, and can be divided for new plants.

SUGGESTED VARIETIES:
'Grace Ward'—purple flowers
'Heavenly Blue'—blue flowers

LITHOPS HYBRIDS *houseplant*   Living rock

An oddity in the plant world, this succulent from South Africa resembles a small stone with a fissure across the middle. From this fissure come new "leaves" and yellow or white flowers. The living rock needs sun but only little water in the summer and even less in the winter. Plant seeds if you want to add to your rock collection.

LIVISTONA CHINENSIS *houseplant*   Chinese fountain palm

This robust palm from China has a solitary trunk and big, fan-shaped leaves. It grows to 6 ft. Unless you live in a warm climate (temperatures no lower than 22°F), this palm is best grown indoors. Give it bright light and a consistently moist soil. Buy new plants.

LOBELIA *perennial/annual*

These small plants grow to only 12 in. high and can be used in many ways, in borders, in beds, in pots with other flowers, and so on. Lobelia prefers a bright-to-shady cool spot, lots of water, and a loamy garden soil. Propagate them from stem cuttings or seed.

L. cardinalis. Produces red flowers.
L. erinus (blue lobelia). A perennial in mild climates. Produces blue flowers.
L. laxiflora. Has hairy leaves and red and yellow flowers.

SUGGESTED VARIETIES:
'Blue Cascade'—blue flowers
'Cambridge Blue'—dark blue flowers
'Crystal Palace'—purple-blue flowers
'Rosamond'—carmine red flowers with a white eye

LOBIVIA *houseplant*   Cob cactus

This small group of desert cacti bear paper-thin flowers in the summer and early fall. They need sun and sandy, readily draining soil. Water them moderately all year except in the winter, when they should be kept somewhat dry. Use offsets for new plants.

L. bruchii. A depressed cylindrical globe growing to 16 in., with small spines and red flowers.

L. cylindrica. A deep green, cylindrical plant growing to 14 in., with brown, needlelike spines and canary yellow flowers.

L. famatimensis. An oval globe growing to 10 in., with short yellow spines and orange flowers.

L. rubriflora. A columnar plant growing to 10 in., with small spines and red-to-orange flowers.

LOBULARIA MARITIMA   *annual*   Sweet alyssum

Sweet alyssum grows to only 8 in. and blooms with tiny, scented flowers, from late spring to early fall. Some varieties have white flowers, others pink, blue, or purple. All are welcome additions as edging plants in rock gardens

or to provide color after the spring bulbs have faded. Sweet alyssum needs sun and a moderate amount of water, and does well in almost any soil. Obtain new plants from seed.

SUGGESTED VARIETIES:
'Little Dorrit'—white flowers
'Wonderland'—pink flowers
'Carpet of Snow'—whit flowers

LONICERA   *shrub/vine*   Honeysuckle

Honeysuckles are vigorous shrubs or vines that can be grown almost all over the United States. There are both evergreen and deciduous types, but the leaves of the latter do not change color in the fall, though some do turn brown. Honeysuckle flowers, however, range from white to pink to yellow to red, and their berries may be blue-black, red, or yellow. Most honeysuckles are trailing plants; only a few grow upright. All of them prefer a

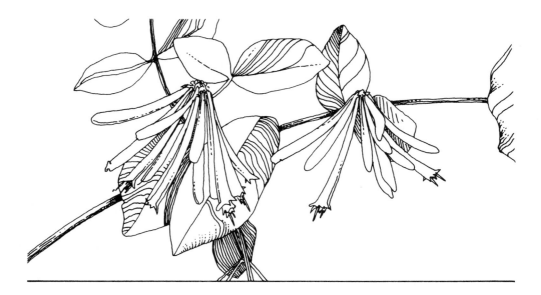

moderate amount of water and full sun, although some will tolerate light shade. New plants can be grown from either softwood or hardwood cuttings. And birds love honeysuckle berries.

L. brownii (scarlet trumpet honeysuckle). A deciduous plant. Grows to 4 ft.; hardy to 10°F. Produces glowing red flowers.

L. fragrantissima (winter honeysuckle). Usually a deciduous plant, but evergreen in mild climates. Grows to 6 ft.; hardy to −5°F. Has stiff, leathery leaves and fragrant white flowers.

L. henryii. Either an evergreen or a semideciduous vine. Hardy to −35°F. Has dark green leaves, yellow to purple flowers, and black berries.

L. hildebrandiana (giant Burmese honeysuckle). Fast-growing,evergreen vine. Hardy to 30°F. Produces fragrant white flowers.

L. japonica (Japanese honeysuckle). An evergreen vine, though wholly or partly deciduous in very cold regions. Has dark green oval leaves and fragrant white flowers tinged with purple.

L. maackii (Amur honeysuckle). A deciduous plant. Grows to 15 ft.; hardy to 35°F. Produces fragrant white flowers and dark red berries.

L. syringantha (lilac honeysuckle). A deciduous plant. Grows to 9 ft.; hardy to −10°F. Produces fragrant, rosy lilac-colored flowers and red-to-orange berries.

L. tatarica (Tatarian honeysuckle). A deciduous plant. Grows to 9 ft., with twiggy branches; hardy to −20°F. Has oval blue-green leaves and pink-to-white flowers.

LOPHORPHORA WILLIAMSII *houseplant*

This slow-growing, blue-gray, globular cactus has no spines. Despite this shortcoming (for a cactus), it grows well in the sun and in a potting medium of equal parts of sand and soil. Water the cactus only when the potting mix is dry. In the spring, plant seeds for more cacti.

LUNARIA ANNUA   *annual*   **Money plant**

This annual grows to 24 in., with violetlike flowers that bloom in the spring and pods that unfortunately only look like silver dollars. The pods are, however, good in dried arrangements. Although the money plant prefers sun, it will tolerate light shade. Water it regularly, and use seed for more plants.

LUPINUS   *perennial/annual*   **Lupine**

Although best known for their purply blue flower spikes, lupine also come in reds, pinks, and even yellows. This is a tall flower, making a good background plant. Lupine likes sun, regular watering, and a loamy soil. It blooms in the summer and fall. New plants are most easily had from seed, although once established, some kinds of lupine seem to spread readily.

L. hartwegii. Produces yellow flowers.
L. subcarnosus (Texas bluebonnet). Produces bright blue flowers.

SUGGESTED VARIETY:
Russell hybrids

LYCASTE   *houseplant*

Lycaste is an orchid that grows about 14 in. high, with broad, pleated leaves and flowers in white, green, pink, or yellow, several to a plant. It does best if potted in fir bark and given sun and plenty of water while it is actively growing. Then, to encourage budding, let it dry out somewhat for about a month after the leaves have matured. After it has bloomed, keep it completely, absolutely dry for about six to eight weeks. Buy new plants from specialists.

L. aromatica. Produces three to ten fragrant yellow flowers in the spring.
L. deppei. Produces pale green, red-spotted flowers in the winter.
L. skinneri. Produces bluish white flowers in the winter.

LYCHNIS   *perennial/annual*

Lychnis produces an abundance of flowers in the summer that provide a mass of color in the garden. It must have full sun, lots of water, and excellent drainage. Either division or seeds bring new plants.

L. chalcedonica (Maltese cross). Produces brilliant scarlet flowers on a stiff, erect, hairy stem. A good plant for wet areas.

L. coronaria (rose campion or mullein pink). Produces purple, flesh-colored, or white bell-shaped flowers.

L. viscaria (catchfly). Produces large rose-colored or white flowers. Perfect for a rock garden.

LYCOPODIUM CLAVATUM   *ground cover*

This ground cover is an evergreen, mosslike herb that either grows only a few inches high or creeps along the ground. It needs both shade and a moist location. Lycopodium prefers an acid soil. Note that it is an endangered species.

LYCORIS   *bulb*   Spider lily

The spider lily is native to China and Japan, grows to 30 in., and has grassy foliage and large flowers that bloom in the fall or winter if grown indoors. Plant these bulbs in April or May, with their tops just above the soil and only one to each 6- or 7-in. pot, and put them in a somewhat dark place. Water them moderately until the end of summer, and then flood the plants and give them sun. In the late fall, when the leaves develop, the flowers will also appear. Then, in the spring, the leaves will turn yellow and die. At this time, let the plants dry out for a few months before starting them growing again. Use offsets for more plants.

L. radiata (nerine). Grows to 20 in. The best known and easiest to grow of the spider lilies. Produces 4-in., bright coral red flowers.

L. squamigera (hardy amaryllis). Grows to 24 in. Produces 4-in., fragrant, lilac-colored flowers.

LYGODIUM JAPONICUM   *perennial*   Climbing fern

Originating in Southeast Asia, these vinelike ferns grow to 40 in. long, with lacy, blue-green fronds that can survive almost any conditions. Nonetheless, climbing ferns prefer shade, but with some sun in the winter, and a loose, moist, well-drained, acid soil. Start new plants from spores.

L. palmatum (Hartford fern). Has 4- to 7-in. lobed fronds.

L. scandens. Has 2-in., feathery, blue-green fronds.

LYSIMACHIA   *perennial*   Loosestrife

This erect, somewhat branching plant grows to 24 in. even in poor conditions, and it produces many yellow flowers in the summer. If it had a choice, however, it would be planted in bright light or shade and given lots of water. Loosestrife provides a spot of color in the garden and offers good cut flowers. Be aware, however, that loosestrife spreads rapidly—that is, it can easily become invasive—and so you may want to think twice before dividing it.

Lythrum salicaria   *perennial*   Purple loosestrife

This plant is similar to *Lythrum virgatum*. It is tall, growing to 60 in., and bears magenta flowers in the summer—a good plant for both borders or just a mass of color. Purple loosestrife thrives in the sun and with lots of water. Divide it for new plants.

SUGGESTED VARIETIES:
'Fire Candle'—red flowers
'Rose Queen'—pink flowers
'The Rocket'—red flowers

Macleaya cordata   *perennial*   Plume poppy

The plume poppy grows to 2 ft. and can be used as a background plant or in a perennial border. It has figlike leaves and pink flowers in the summer and fall. Give it sun and a moderate amount of water in a well-drained soil. Plume poppies are easily divided for more plants.

Magnolia   *shrub/tree*

Magnolias can be either evergreen or deciduous, generally depending on the temperature of the region in which they are grown. They bloom in either the early spring or the summer. The dozens of varieties of magnolias offer white, pink, red, or reddish purple flowers, and they are spectacular. Magnolia trees grow to 90 ft. and have wide-spreading branches. The shrubs should be pruned after they bloom. All magnolias do well in a well-drained soil, with

lots of water in the summer. Because they are difficult to propagate, buy young plants. Magnolias also are susceptible to scale, so be vigilant.

M. denudata (yulan magnolia). A deciduous tree. Grows to 45 ft.; hardy to −5°F. A round shape, with white, fragrant, tulip-shaped flowers.

M. grandiflora (southern magnolia). An evergreen tree. Grows to 90 ft.; hardy to 5°F. Usually a dense, pyramidal shape, with fragrant white flowers.

M. liliflora (lily magnolia). A deciduous shrub. Grows to 12 ft.; hardy to −35°F. Produces purple flowers that bloom throughout the summer.

M. sieboldii. A deciduous shrub. Grows to 10 ft.; hardy to −5°F. Produces white flowers with crimson stamens that bloom for a long time.

M. soulangiana (saucer magnolia). A deciduous hybrid that is often, but erroneously, called a tulip tree. Grows to 25 ft.; hardy to −5°F. A variable form, with white-to-pink or purplish red flowers.

M. stellata (star magnolia). A deciduous shrub. Grows to 10 ft.; hardy to −5°F. Produces very early white flowers.

M. veitchii (Veitch magnolia). A deciduous, hybrid shrub. Grows to 10 ft.; hardy to 5°F. Produces pink flowers.

M. virginiana (sweet bay). An evergreen tree. Grows to 60 ft.; hardy to −5°F. A round shape, with creamy white flowers.

MAHERNIA VERTICILLATA   *perennial*   Honey bells

These 30-in., sprawling plants bear fragrant yellow flowers in the spring. Honey bells grow best in the sun. When watering them, soak the soil and then let it dry out before watering it again. Use these perennials as background plants, and propagate them from cuttings.

MALCOLMIA MARITIMA   *annual*   Virginian stock

Virginian stock, an erect, branched plant, grows to 12 in. and produces clusters of lilac, rose, red, or white flowers in the spring. It does well in either sun or shade and with regular watering. Virginian stock makes a good edging or border plant. For new plants, sow seeds or buy prestarted plants.

MALOPE TRIFIDA   *annual*   Mallow-wort

A bushy plant growing to 36 in., the mallow wort offers large purple or white flowers in the summer. It requires a sunny location, a fair amount of water, and good drainage. This annual is best in beds or borders, and makes excellent cut flowers. Obtain new plants from seed or buy prestarted ones.

Malpighia coccigera   *houseplant*   Miniature holly

This dwarf evergreen grows only 20 in. high and has small, spiny leaves and pale pink flowers that pop out in the spring and summer and last for months. Miniature holly also can be planted outside (in warm areas) or in cold climates moved outside in the summer. Put it in a sunny spot, and keep the soil consistently moist. In the spring, grow new plants from cuttings.

Malus   *tree*   Crabapple

Crabapples are deciduous trees that bear beautiful flowers in the spring and little red crabapples (sour but good for jelly) in the fall. Some varieties have single blossoms, and others have semidouble or double blossoms in colors ranging from pure white to shades of pink to purple-red; and some of the trees produce scented flowers. Most crabapple trees are relatively small, to about 30 ft., although a few may reach 50 ft. Several have hanging branches, but the shapes also may be columnar or round. Crabapples should have sun and, when young, extra feeding. Regularly spray crabapple trees, as they are prey to the same problems—fire blight, scale, and borers—that ordinary apple trees have.

M. arnoldiana (Arnold crabapple). Grows to 20 ft.; hardy to −10°F. Broad and spreading shape, with fragrant pink flowers.
M. baccata mandshurica. Grows to 50 ft.; hardy to −35°F. Has bushy, dense foliage and fragrant white flowers.
M. halliana. Grows to 15 ft.; hardy to −5°F. Has dense foliage and rose-colored flowers.
M. purpurea. Grows to 25 ft.; hardy to −10°F. Has dense foliage and deep rose-colored flowers.
M. sargentii (Sargent crabapple). Grows to 8 ft.; hardy to −10°F. Rounded and low branching, with fragrant white flowers.
M. spectabilis. Grows to 24 ft.; hardy to −10°F. Produces double pink flowers.

Malva alcea   *perennial*

With palm-shaped leaves and growing to 36 in., malva looks much like a hollyhock, with red flowers at the tops of tall stems, which bloom in the summer and fall. These plants grow well in almost any soil, in the sun or bright light, and with lots of water. Use them where you need color. They are easily divided.

Mammillaria   *houseplant*   Pincushion cactus

This group includes a number of 12- to 20-in. cylindrical or globe-shaped cacti, with white, red, black, or gray spines and crowns of tiny flowers, usually blooming in the late summer and early winter. These desert plants are happiest in the sun, in a sandy soil, and with water every other day in the summer and about once a week in the winter. Use offsets for new plants.

M. applanata. A dark green plant with creamy white flowers.
M. bocasana. Clustered, round, dark green stems growing to 2 in. high and covered with white hairs and yellow spines, and yellow flowers.
M. fragilis (powderpuff cactus). A globe covered with white spines and producing cream-colored flowers.
M. haageana. A spiny globe growing to 3 in. high, with a circle of small cerise flowers.
M. hahniana. A flattened globe growing to 3 in. high, with curly white hairs and white spines, and red flowers.
M. meyeranii. A spiny globe growing to 4 in., with many small pink flowers.

MANDEVILLA SUAVEOLENS   *vine*   Chilean jasmine

This vine is really from Argentina. It grows to 20 in. long and, in the summer, produces an abundance of fragrant, creamy white, pink-tinged flowers. A deciduous climber, it needs support on a trellis or a fence. Give the Chilean (Argentine) jasmine heat and sun, plenty of water, and a loamy garden soil. Cuttings provide new plants.

SUGGESTED VARIETY:
'Alice du Pont'—pink flowers

MANETTIA INFLATA   *perennial*   Mexican firecracker

A climbing plant that grows to 24 in., the Mexican firecracker brings yellow-tipped red flowers, usually in the late summer or early fall. It likes a sunny exposure and moderate moisture, and it also can be grown inside as a houseplant. Obtain new plants from cuttings.

MANGIFERA INDICA   *tree*   Mango

An evergreen tree that grows to about 70 ft., the mango is a tropical plant, sometimes grown in gardens in very warm regions but more often grown commercially for its fruit. It needs consistent moisture but is not fussy about soil. Although it may produce large yellow flowers, it is unlikely to bear fruit, except with great care in the warmest climates. Mangoes are susceptible to insects.

MARANTA   *houseplant*

Their ornamental foliage have made marantas popular. Plant them in 4- to 5-in. pots, with the soil moist and good air circulation and out of the direct sun. When they rest in the late fall, cut away the old foliage (leaving the more recent), and keep the soil barely moist. In January and February, resume watering the plants regularly, and divide them for new ones.

M. arundinacea (arrowroot). Grows to 48 in. Has alternating, arrow-shaped, gray-green leaves.
M. bicolor. Grows to 12 in. Has dark gray-green leaves.
M. leuconeura kerchoveana (prayer plant). Grows to 15 in. Has 6-in., oval, gray-green leaves with rows of brown spots on them. The leaves fold up at night to funnel dew down to the roots; hence the nickname.
M. leuconeura massangeana. Grows to 15 in. Has smaller gray-green leaves with silver markings.

Masdevallia   *houseplant*   Kite orchid

Masdevallias are 5- to 15-in. orchids with leathery, spatulate leaves and curious triangular flowers that appear in the winter. These plants like cool temperatures (55°F) and should be potted in fir bark and kept moist all year, with the surrounding humidity high. Buy new plants from specialists.

M. bella. Produces large yellow-and-red flowers.
M. coccinea. The most popular kite orchid. Produces pink-to-magenta flowers.
M. ignea. Produces large cinnabar red flowers.
M. tovarensis. Produces pure white flowers.

Matricaria recutita   *annual*   Chamomile

This is the chamomile of the fragrant chamomile tea, made from the dried flowers. Growing to only 2 ft., this plant looks best when massed—a good "filler" plant. Its white, daisylike flowers bloom in the summer. Chamomile thrives in a sunny place and needs lots of water. Plant seed for new plants.

Matthiola incana   *annual*   Stock

Stock grows to be 36 in. tall, with single or double flowers in various colors—white, pink, red, purple, lavender, or cream. Stock is an excellent vertical garden plant, and its flowers, fragrant in the evenings, last a long time when cut. Put these plants in the sun, and give them lots of water; they bloom in the summer. Obtain new stock from seed, or buy prestarted plants.

SUGGESTED VARIETIES:
Brompton series—varied colors
'Excelsior Red'—red flowers
'Rose Midget'—pale rose-colored flowers
Trysomic mix—varied colors

MAURANDIA ERUBESCENS (SCANDENS) *vine*

With triangular leaves and trumpet-shaped, rosy pink flowers, this vine grows 12 ft. long and blooms in the summer and fall. If it is given plenty of sun and a moderate amount of water, it is easy to grow. Besides being used to cover fences and walls, maurandia can be grown in a pot. Seeds are the best way to get new plants.

MAXILLARIA PICTA *houseplant*

These small orchids' flowers generally are red and appear in the autumn. The plants grow to about 1 ft. high, and many have a coconut scent. Pot them in fir bark, and put them in a shady place. These orchids need lots of water in the summer but not so much the rest of the year. Divide them for additional plants.

MECONOPSIS BETONICIFOLIA *perennial*   **Blue poppy**

Little known, short-lived, but beautiful, these 60-in. poppies bear sky blue to rosy lavender flowers in the summer. They like a cool location, some shade, plenty of water and good drainage, and an acid soil. Buy prestarted plants.

MEDINILLA MAGNIFICA *houseplant*

A plant with blue-green foliage and carmine red flowers in pink bracts in summer, medinillas grow to 40 in. tall. They do best in bright light and need copious water. Medinillas can also be grown in the garden in warm climates. Propagate these plants from seed or buy them.

MENTHA *perennial*

Mentha is mint, and there are several varieties and several flavors. Mainly grown as an herb, mint grows to about 2 ft. high, with small flowers and fairly small leaves. It prefers a cool moist location, in partial shade, and it reproduces itself by means of underground stems.

M. arvensis (common field mint). Very easy to grow.
M. piperita (peppermint). Produces purple flowers. Grows quickly and so should be cut back occasionally.
M. spicata (spearmint). Grows quickly in shady, moist places.

MENTZELIA LINDLEYI   *annual*   **Blazing star**

The flowers of the blazing star are bright yellow with an orange or reddish center ring and yellow stamens. And they are fragrant. Blooming in the summer, the flowers open in the evening and last until the next morning. These are good border plants. Give them sun, moderate water until they begin blooming and then little or none, and good drainage. Start new plants from seed, or buy prestarted plants.

MESEMBRYANTHEMUM CORDIFOLIUM   *ground cover*   **Fig marigold**

Fig marigolds are succulents that grow to 12 in. high and have creamy white, variegated leaves and purple or red flowers that bloom in the summer and fall. They are oddities, as they resemble small rocks. Fig marigolds can grow in almost any soil and need sun and little water. They are mainly used as houseplants except in regions such as Arizona or New Mexico.

MILTONIA   *houseplant*   **Pansy orchid**

Miltonias are 12- to 20-in. orchids with large, open-faced flowers that last on the plant (they are not good cut flowers) for a month. Pot them in fir bark, keep it moist but not wet, and provide a humid atmosphere.

M. candida. Produces chestnut brown flowers tipped with yellow, in the fall.
M. flavescens. Produces yellow flowers with yellow sepals and a yellow lip marked with purple, in the summer.
M. roezlii. Produces white flowers stained with purple, in the summer.
M. vexillaria. Produces lilac-rose flowers with a yellow lip, in the spring.

SUGGESTED VARIETIES:
Hanover 'Red Bird'—red flowers
Bert Field 'Crimson Glow'—red flowers
Evergreen Joy Carmen 'Cole'—pink flowers

MIMULUS GUTTATA   *annual*   **Monkey flower**

The monkey flower is native to Chile, grows to 12 in. high, and has bright green leaves and variously colored flowers that bloom in the summer. Although this plant does best in bright light or partial shade and with lots of water, it can tolerate poor conditions and still prosper. Get new plants from seed.

SUGGESTED VARIETIES:
'Malibu Orange'—orange flowers
'Malibu Yellow'—yellow flowers

MIRABILIS JALAPA   *annual*   Four o'clock

This 24-in. bushy plant bears fragrant, funnel-shaped, white, yellow, or crimson flowers in the summer. They open in the afternoon—hence their nickname—and close in the morning. Four o'clocks require sun and a moderate amount of water in a well-drained soil. They are especially good in borders; divide them for additional plants.

MITCHELLA REPENS   *ground cover*   Partridgeberry

This widely grown ground cover is popular as a Christmas decoration. It does well in a moist, acid soil in partial shade. The red partridge berries come in the fall, and the plant can be divided.

MONARDA DIDYMA   *perennial*   Bee balm

Bee balm is a 36-in., hairy-leafed plant with bright scarlet flowers in the summer and fall—a welcome spot of color in a garden border. To prolong the blooming period, remove the faded flowers before they produce seed. In addition, give bee balm sun and lots of water, and divide it for new plants.

SUGGESTED VARIETY:
'Croftway Pink'—pink flowers

MONSTERA   *houseplant*   Swiss cheese plant

Monstera is a favorite houseplant, actually a vine, growing to 72 in. or more, with 24-in. perforated (Swiss cheese) green leaves. Put it in a bright light, and keep the soil consistently moist. The plant will adjust to either warmth or coolness, but it does not like drafts. Wash off or wipe the foliage with a wet cloth about once a month. Aerial roots grow from stem nodes, and they can be cut off without harming the plant. The best way to get new plants is by means of stem cuttings or air layering.

M. acuminata. Has 14-in. leaves.
M. deliciosa. Has 36-in., slitted leaves.
M. schleichtleinii. Has 20-in., filigreed leaves.

MONTBRETIA (CROCOSMIA)   *bulb*

This South African bulb grows to about 3 ft. tall and has grassy leaves and yellow to orange to red flowers in the summer. It requires sun, regular watering (but it can handle drought), good drainage, and a porous soil. New plants come from offsets. There are many varieties.

Moraea   *bulb*   Yellow moraea

The yellow moraea is an irislike plant that grows to 24 in. It blooms for a long time in the summer, one flower after another. Yellow moraeas are particularly effective in clumps by themselves. They need sun and a moderate amount of water and can be divided. There are many varieties.

M. bicolor. Produces scented yellow flowers with a black-brown blotch at the base of the outer segments.
M. iridioides (butterfly iris). Has fanlike leaves and pale yellow or white flowers with yellow or brown spots on the outer segments.

Muehlenbeckia   *vine*

This small, round-leafed vine is effective in a basket or in the garden. It grows rapidly into a tight mat of foliage about 12 in. across. The flowers are insignificant. This plant likes the sun, or partial shade, and dislikes too much water, so keep the soil barely moist. Grow new plants from stem-tip cuttings.

M. complexa (wire plant). Has small round green leaves and tiny terminal flowers.
M. platyclados (centipede plant). Has soft-jointed green stems and red flowers.

Murraya   *shrub*   Orange jasmine

The orange jessamine is an evergreen, with glossy green, ferny foliage and clusters of very fragrant white flowers in the summer and fall, followed by red berries. Growing from 6 to 15 ft. tall, it makes a good background plant. This shrub needs sun and lots of water while it is actively growing, less in the winter. Use cuttings for new plants.

M. exotica (orange jasmine). Hardy to 20°F. The flowers smell like orange blossoms.
M. paniculata (satinwood). Slow growing to 20 in.; hardy to 20°F. The flowers also smell like orange blossoms.

Musa nana   *perennial*   Banana

The banana is a good accent plant in tropical climates. It has a solitary trunk, and shiny green, spatulalike leaves. If not grown outside, bananas can be potted in tubs and put on a patio in the summer. They can withstand temperatures down to 40°F. Give them lots of sun and water—a constantly moist soil—and divide them for new plants.

Muscari *bulb*   Grape hyacinth

These popular bulbs are easy to grow and reach 16 in. high. Grape hyacinths look especially good in clumps under trees or wherever some blue color is needed in the spring. Be sure that they get sun and a fair amount of water. Plant them in early September, covering the bulbs with about 2 in. of soil. Propagate them by means of offsets; do not dig them up. Indeed, they can be left undisturbed for years.

M. armeniacum. Has long dark green leaves and azure-to-purplish blue flowers.
M. botryoides (grape hyacinth). Produces deep sky blue flowers in the shape of little bells near the top of the stem.

Myosotis *perennial*   Forget-me-not

Forget-me-nots are small, dainty plants growing to 12 in. high, with small, usually light blue flowers in the spring. They look best in beds or in small islands. Forget-me-nots require sun, regular watering, and a rich loamy soil. They seed themselves.

M. alpestris. Produces azure blue flowers with a small yellow eye.
M. sylvatica (woodland forget-me-not). Produces blue flowers with a yellow eye.

SUGGESTED VARIETIES:
'Bluebird'—blue flowers
'Carmine King'—red flowers
'White Ball'—white flowers

Myrica pennsylvanica *shrub*   Bayberry

This evergreen shrub has long, narrow, glossy green, aromatic leaves and purple fruit. It grows to 9 ft. tall and has a dense and compact shape. A great advantage of bayberries is that they do well in either sun or shade, good or poor soil, or moist or dry conditions. They can tolerate temperatures down to 10°F and are not generally bothered by insects or diseases. Softwood cuttings provide new plants.

NANDINA DOMESTICA *shrub*　　　　　　　　　　　Heavenly bamboo

This is not really bamboo but, rather, an evergreen or semideciduous shrub that makes a good background plant. Heavenly bamboo grows to about 8 ft. tall and has pointed oval green leaves, clusters of tiny white flowers in the summer, and red berries in the fall. It does well in the sun and does not need much water. Divide it for more plants.

NARCISSUS *bulb*　　　　　　　　　　　　　　Daffodil

Everybody welcomes the arrival of daffodils in the spring. They come in standard sizes (to 24 in.) and dwarf sizes (to 12 in.), with strap-shaped leaves and single or double flowers in dozens of color combinations and shapes. Daffodils are wonderful in drifts or in smaller clumps. They do well in bright light—the flowers face the sun—or partial shade and with a moderate amount of water with good drainage in a loamy garden soil with lots of compost. Offsets provide new plants.

SUGGESTED VARIETIES:
Flower forms:
Cyclamineus
Jonquil
Large cupped
Poeticus
Small cupped
Tazetta
Triandrus
Trumpet

NASTURTIUM *see Tropaeolum*

NEMESIA STRUMOSA *annual*

From South Africa, nemesias are striking plants, growing to 16 in., with lance-shaped, toothed leaves and white, pale yellow, orange, or rosy purple flowers in the summer. They thrive in sunny, though cool, conditions and need a moderate amount of water and a compost-rich soil. Nemesias make excellent bedding or edging plants. Either plant seeds or buy new plants.

NEMOPHILA MENZIESII *annual*　　　　　　　Baby blue eyes

This 10-in. annual is a spreading, hairy plant with round lobed leaves and, in the spring, cup-shaped blue flowers with a whitish center. Baby blue eyes

PLATE 36

Marantas are available in a galaxy of leaf colors and provide fine indoor color in warm areas.

PLATE 37

Masdevallia coccinea is a collector's orchid which thrives in cool nights (55F). Makes a handsome houseplant.

PLATE 38

Called the pansy orchid, the flat-faced flowers of Miltonia 'Carmen Cole' is a study in soft pink color.

PLATE 39

One of the most popular Bromeliads is *Neoregelia carolinae* tricolor, an open rosette of color used mainly as a houseplant.

PLATE 40

Neoregelia carolinae leaf rosette holds color for months.

PLATE 41

A mass of Cattleya orchids; there are now many hybrids in the yellow color family.

PLATE 42

Oncidium forbesi is one of the popular "dancing lady" orchids—the flowers moving in the wind.

PLATE 43

Known as the tiger orchid this popular houseplant is officially *Odontoglossum grande* and has become a good houseplant for lovers of the exotic.

PLATE 44

Peonies are always splendid in a garden; this white single form is reminiscent of yesterday.

PLATE 45

A roof garden with the popular and colorful Petunias.

PLATE 46

Lantana in a colorful array of beauty.

PLATE 47

The typical flower from
Hawaii, Plumeria comes in
pink or yellow colors.

PLATE 48

Orchids are exotic and this
Paphiopedilum curtisi proves
the point. A fine houseplant.

PLATE 49

There is little more beautiful in a garden than a sprawling profusion of Phlox.

PLATE 50

Romney coulteri is the California tree poppy that graces many fences in that state with its large white flowers.

PLATE 51

Rudbeckia plants are now offered in many varieties and have become a very popular garden subject.

need sun or bright light and regular watering in a well-drained soil. They are especially good in a rock garden or as edging plants. Obtain new plants from seed or buy new ones.

Neomarica   *houseplant*   Apostle plant

The apostle plant has straplike leaves and fragrant winter flowers on tall stalks. Pot it in sandy soil in shallow, 4- or 5-in. containers, and give it full sun and plenty of water. After it has bloomed, let it rest for about a month, watering it only infrequently. For more plants, either split the rhizomes or pot the small plantlets that form at the tops of the flower stems.

N. caerulea. The best neomarica. Grows to 30 in. Produces blue-and-white flowers.
N. gracilis. Grows to 18 in.; similar to *N. caerulea.*
N. northiana. Grows to 36 in. Produces larger, fragrant, white-and-violet flowers.

Neoregelia   *houseplant*   Living-vase plant

The living vase plant is a bromeliad with a 30- to 40-in. rosette of leaves that provide color for months. The center of the plant turns red at blooming time, but the flowers themselves are insignificant. Give this bromeliad good light, and keep the "vase" formed by the leaves filled with water and the soil just damp. Wipe the leaves with a damp cloth about once a month. Create more living vases from the offset suckers.

N. carolinae. The perfect houseplant. Has dark green and copper-colored leaves and blooms in the winter.
N.c. 'Tricolor'. Has leaves striped white, pink, and green.
N. cruenta. Has a smaller, upright, straw-colored rosette of leaves.
N. marmorata. Has a 20-in.-diameter rosette of pale green leaves with reddish brown blotches, and violet-petaled flowers.
N. spectabilis (painted fingernail plant). Has pale green leaves tipped with brilliant red and blooms in the summer.
N. zonata. Has a 16-in.-diameter rosette of stiff, olive green leaves marked and banded with wine red, and pale blue-petaled flowers.

Nepeta hederacea   *perennial*   Ground ivy

Ground ivy is, true to its name, a good ground cover. It is a trailing plant, with prostrate stems and small round leaves bordered with white. Occasionally it bears minute mauve flowers in the summer. Grow it in semishade, and in the summer, keep the soil moist; in the winter, keep it cool and give it less water. Get new plants from dividing the roots or planting the runners.

NEPETA MUSSINII *perennial* **Catmint**

Catmint is indeed a member of the mint family—not of the cat family—and grows to 16 in. It has silvery gray leaves and pale lavender flowers in the summer. Catmint is an invaluable edging plant, needs full sun, a moderate amount of water, and almost any well-drained soil. And yes, cats love it. Divide it for new plants.

NEPHROLEPIS *houseplant*

Sword ferns, native to the American tropics and subtropics, are popular houseplants that grow rapidly to 36 in. in diameter. They need sun in the winter and shade in the summer. Keep the soil moist, but avoid overwatering it. When the temperature outside is above 50°F and it is raining, let your ferns have a shower. They are easily propagated from the runners at the base of mature plants.

N. exaltata (sword fern, but often called a Boston fern). Has bushy, stiff fronds up to 60 in. long.
N.e. bostoniensis (the true Boston fern). Has 36-in., arching fronds.
N. e. bostoniensis 'Fluffy Ruffles'. Has 12-in., lacy fronds.
N. e. bostoniensis 'Verona'. An 8-in. dwarf with lacy fronds.
N. e. bostoniensis 'Whitmannii'. Has 18-in. fronds.

NERINE BOWDENII *bulb*

This bulb comes from South Africa and has 12-in., glossy green leaves and, in the summer and fall, large, pale pink, lilylike flowers. Nerine should have sun, and a lot of water while it is actively growing. In very warm climates it can be grown outside. Get new plants from offsets.

SUGGESTED VARIETIES:
'Baghdad'—red flowers
'Margaret Rose'—rose-colored flowers

NERIUM OLEANDER *shrub* **Oleander**

Oleanders must be among the world's strongest and most tolerant shrubs, because they often are planted along the freeways in several states. They can grow to 6 ft. and more, and the many varieties produce flowers in the summer in various colors: red, pink, salmon, and white. Oleander flowers have a faint vanilla fragrance. Despite their willingness to prosper in any conditions, oleanders do best in the full sun and with plenty of water. They need less water after they have bloomed. New plants can be had from seed or cuttings from the stem tip in the spring. Keep them pruned (in the fall) to maintain a pleasing shape. Note that all parts of this plant are poisonous.

SUGGESTED VARIETIES:
'Comte Barthelemy'—hardy to 30°F; double red flowers
'Mrs. Roeding'—hardy to 30°F; double salmon pink flowers
'Peachblossom'—hardy to 30°F; double apricot-colored flowers

NICOTIANA ALATA   *annual*   Flowering tobacco

This annual grows to 30 in., with greenish yellow foliage and scarlet, yellow, or white flowers that bloom in the summer and are very fragrant at night. Flowering tobacco can be a perennial in areas with mild winters. It is good in borders or by itself. Either plant seeds or buy new plants yearly.

SUGGESTED VARIETIES:
'Domino'—white flowers
'Lime Green'—pale green flowers
'Niki Pink'—pink flowers
'Niki Red'—red flowers
'White Domino'—white flowers

NIDULARIUM   *houseplant*

These easy-to-grow bromeliads have colorful leaves in 20- to 30-in. rosettes and dense clusters of tiny white or pink flowers. They are especially suitable for planters and north windows. Plant them in a standard potting soil, and put them in a bright light. Keep the "vase" formed by the leaves filled with water, and wipe the leaves with a damp cloth about once a week. Propagate these bromeliads from offset suckers.

N. billbergioides. Grows to 20 in. Has spiny dark green leaves and orange bracts, and a flower spike rising high above the center of the plant.
N. fulgens. Has yellow green leaves spotted with dark green.
N. innocentii. Has purple leaves.
N. procerum. Has a 30-in. rosette of broad, leathery, light green leaves tinged with copper, and brilliant red bracts.
N. regelioides. Has a 20-in. rosette of leathery green leaves mottled with dark green, and deep orange bracts.

NIEREMBERGIA   *perennial*   Cup flower

This stiff, erect plant grows to 30 in., with thin, white-haired stems. The 1-in. cup-shaped flowers, blue-violet with darker lines and yellow in the throat, bloom in the summer. Cup flowers like bright light or shade, cool conditions, and lots of water. Divide them for new plants.

SUGGESTED VARIETY:
'Purple Robe'—violet-blue flowers

NIGELLA DAMASCENA   *annual*   Love-in-a-mist

A member of the buttercup family, nigellas grow to 30 in., have feathery foliage, and, in the spring, produce large blue flowers. They dry up in the summer. Love-in-a-mist needs a sunny location and regular watering; almost any soil will do. It reseeds itself.

SUGGESTED VARIETY:
'Miss Jekyll'—blue flowers

NOLANA PARADOXA   *annual*

An unusual plant from Chile, nolana looks like a trailing petunia. It grows to be about 1 ft. long, has hairy leaves, and blue, bell-shaped flowers with a yellowish spot on their throat. Nolana blooms in the summer and is happiest in the sun, with a moderate amount of water and in a well-drained soil. Divide it for new plants.

NOTOCACTUS   *houseplant*   Ball cactus

These round South American desert cacti offer large yellow flowers in the spring and summer and look good in dish gardens. Pot them in a sandy soil that drains readily, and give them sun and a small amount of water all year long. Propagate these cacti from offsets.

N. apricus. A 2-in. globe covered with bristly spines.
N. arachnites. A 6-in. ridged globe with yellowish green flowers.
N. leninghausi. A 4-in. spiny globe.
N. ottonis. A 2-in. ribbed globe.
N. rutilans. A 5-in. dark green globe with bright pink flowers.
N. scopa. An 8-in. globe covered with white hairs.
N. submammulosus. A 3-in. shiny green globe.

NYMPHAEA   *water plant*   Water lily

The water lily's round lily pads float on the surface of the water, a perfect diving board for frogs. The water lilies themselves, which appear in the summer, are large and, depending on the variety, can be white, pink, yellow, red, or even blue. There also are night-blooming (tropical varieties) and day-blooming types. Besides needing to be in water at all times, water lilies should have full sun. For the many varieties of water lilies, see the sources at the back of this book.

N. odorata. Produces fragrant waxy white flowers.
N. tetragona. A dwarf water lily, with smaller leaves (to 3 in.) and smaller flowers (to 5 in.) than those of the ordinary water lilies.

ODONTOGLOSSUM *houseplant*

From the cool regions of Colombia and Peru, these orchids are best kept in an unheated, (about 55°F.) but not freezing, room. They have leathery leaves and, usually, yellow-and-brown flowers that stay in bloom for over a month—sometimes even for three months—with one flower opening as another fades. Grow these orchids in fir bark, and give them sun in the winter and bright light in the summer. They should have lots of water except during their four-week rest both before and then again after they flower. Buy seedlings from specialists.

O. bictoniense.. Has 15-in. leaves and 24-in. flower spikes, with 20 to 30 yellowish green and chestnut brown flowers in the fall.
O. citrosmum Has 10-in. leaves and 24- to 36-in. flower spikes, with 15 to 30 round, fragrant, pink flowers in the spring or early summer.
O. grande (tiger orchid). Has 12-in. leaves and 10-in. flower spikes, with yellow-and-brown flowers in the fall.
O. krameri. Grows to 8 in., with violet flowers.
O. pulchellum. Grows to 10 in., with small, fragrant white flowers in the spring.
O. rossii. Grows to 8 in., with pink-and-dark brown flowers with wavy, rose-colored lips, in the winter.
O. uro-skinneri. Has 14-in. leaves and 24- to 36-in. flower spikes, with 10 to 15 fairly small, greenish flowers marked with brown, in the early spring.

SUGGESTED VARIETIES:
Chignik—red-and-pink flowers
Jelly Roll—white-and-red flowers
Tiger Hamburhen—yellow-and-brown flowers
Anneliese Rothenberger—yellow-and-brown flowers
Golden Ransom 'Pride of Vashon'—yellow flowers
Ocean Falls—white flowers

OENOTHERA *perennial/annual* **Evening primrose**

Evening primroses grow to 24 in. high and produce lots of flowers in the summer. They are particularly good in borders and rock gardens. Give evening primroses sun, regular watering, and a well-drained, sandy soil. Buy prestarted "six packs" from a nursery.

O. deltoides. Produces 1.5- to 3-in. fragrant white flowers that later turn pink and last for one to two days.
O. missourensis. Has 5-in.-long velvety leaves and 3- to 5-in. yellow flowers that open in the evening.
O. tetragona (sundrop). Sometimes a biennial plant. Produces 1- to 1.5-in. yellow flowers.

OLEA EUROPAEA   *tree*   **Olive**

The olive tree grows slowly to about 25 or 30 ft., a relatively small, pretty tree. It has small gray-green leaves and purplish black olives that, however, drop all over and stain the pavement, besides making a general mess. Olive trees should have sun and prefer a rich soil, although they will grow in poor soils. They thrive in hot, dry areas and can tolerate temperatures down to 10°F. Note that their branches have a tendency to break off suddenly (in a not-so-severe wind, for instance), and are unusually heavy.

OLEANDER   *see Nerium oleander*

ONCIDIUM   *houseplant*   **Dancing lady orchid**

This is a large genus of orchids with leathery leaves and either pseudobulbs or cane stems. They produce large, solitary flowers or clusters of small flowers. Grow these orchids in fir bark, in the sun, and provide good air circulation. The pseudobulbs need to rest, with almost no water, for four weeks both before and after they bloom. The cane-stemmed types require constantly moist soil.

O. ampliatum. A pseudobulb. Grows to 28 in. Has leathery leaves and 1-in. yellow-and-brown flowers in the early spring.

O. ceboletta. A pseudobulb. Grows to 20 in. Has leathery, dark green (almost black) leaves and tiny yellow-and-brown flowers in the spring.

O. lanceanum. A cane stem. Has spatulate, speckled leaves and fragrant yellow-green flowers in the summer.

O. macranthum. A pseudobulb. Grows to 30 in. Has leathery leaves and wands of yellow flowers.

O. papilio (butterfly orchid). A cane stem. Grows to 18 in. Produces large chestnut brown-and-yellow flowers in either the summer or the fall.

O. splendidum. A pseudobulb. Grows to 24 in. Has hard, leathery leaves and small yellow-and-brown flowers in the winter.

O. triquetrum. A cane stem. Grows to 15 in. Produces 1-in. purple-green-and-white flowers in the fall.

O. wentworthianum. A pseudobulb. Grows to 30 in. Has leathery leaves and yellow-and-reddish brown flowers in the summer.

SUGGESTED VARIETIES:
Copper Falls—brown-and-yellow flowers
Maui Gold 'July'—brown-and-yellow flowers
Waimaio Gold x Ellen 'Flambeau'—yellow-and-brown flowers

OPHIOPOGON JAPONICUS   *ground cover*   **Lily turf**

This is the dwarf lily turf, which makes a wonderful ground cover, with grassy leaves and similar to *Liriope*, with which it is sometimes confused. The dwarf lily turf is not so hardy as *Liriope*. Its white to purple flowers hide deep in the foliage. Lily turf is evergreen, needs sun if it is cool and shade if it is hot, and a moderate amount of water. It is hardy to 5°F and can be divided for new plants.

Opuntia *houseplant*   Prickly pear

Some of these desert cacti are handsome and decorative, but others are unsightly and so should be avoided. Most opuntias have flat, broad joints, or pads, which, in some species, are edible. But other opuntias are erect cylinders. All of them should have sun but little or no water once established. In the winter, move them to a relatively cold place (50°F). Opuntias rarely bloom when grown indoors. Propagate them from offsets.

O. brasiliensis. Grows to 48 in., with spineless pads shaped like a beaver's tail, and yellow flowers.

O. erinacea. An erect cylinder growing to 12 in., with white spines and pink flowers.

O. linguiformis. A fleshy green cylinder growing to 36 in., with yellow flowers.

O. microdasys (bunny ears). Grows to 24 in., with spineless pads covered with white hairs, and yellow flowers.

O. strobiliformis. An erect cylinder resembling a pinecone, growing to 15 in., with yellow flowers.

O. vestita. A white, woolly cylinder growing to 20 in., with red flowers.

Orchid *houseplant*

Many orchids make splendid houseplants, as most of them are easier to tend than even some of the familiar foliage plants are. The majority of orchids have water-storage vessels (pseudobulbs), and so if they are not watered for a few days, or even a few weeks, they will survive. And few other plants besides orchids bear such dramatic flowers. Most thrive in average home temperatures of 60° to 72°F with 30 to 50 percent humidity. Although some need sun in order to bloom, others do well in only bright light. Orchids generally must rest, with the potting mixture kept somewhat dry, for a month both before and after they bloom. Those that grow all year should be kept constantly moist. Orchids are rarely bothered by insects. For descriptions of some of the species, see the following:

Acineta
Aerides
Angraecum
Ansellia
Ascocentrum
Bifrenaria
Brassavola
Broughtonia
Cattleya

Coelogyne
Dendrobium
Epidendrum
Gongora
Laelia
Lycaste
Masdevallia
Miltonia
Odontoglossum
Oncidium
Paphiopedilum
Phalaenopsis
Pleione
Rhynchostylis
Stanhopea
Vanda

ORNITHOGALUM *bulb*

These small bulbs grow to 20 in. high and have either narrow or broad, mostly floppy, leaves and star-shaped flowers in the summer, which last for weeks when they are cut. Give the bulbs sun and regular watering in a well-drained soil. Propagate by means of offsets.

O. arabicum (star of Bethlehem). Produces large fragrant flowers with a black center.
O. thyrsoides (chincherinchee). Produces long-lasting, dense, white to golden yellow flowers.
O. umbellatum (common star of Bethlehem). Produces satiny white flowers that have green stripes on the outside.

OSMANTHUS *shrub/tree* **Sweet olive**

Sweet olives have leathery, evergreen foliage and small but fragrant flowers in the spring. They have many uses in the garden, as foundation plants or as background plants. Although sweet olives prefer sun, they will tolerate some shade, and they do well in almost any soil. And once they are established, they do not need much water. Prune them into the desired shape, and obtain new plants from softwood cuttings. Sweet olives are not usually troubled by insects.

O. fragrans (sweet olive). Grows to 20 ft.; hardy to −5°F.
O. heterophyllus (holly-leaf osmanthus). Grows to 12 ft.; hardy to −5°F. Has dark green leaves.

OXALIS   *bulb*

The shamrock is a member of the oxalis family, a group of small (to 12 in.) plants that like moisture and both sun and shade. The flowers bloom in the summer and, depending on the species, may be pink, white, rose, or yellow. In most areas, oxalis is considered a weed, but if you do not share this judgment, put it in a rock garden or wherever you want some color. It spreads quickly, and new plants can also be had from offsets.

O. bowieana. A nearly stemless plant with large, purple, bell-shaped flowers.
O. cernua (Bermuda buttercup). A stemless plant, with yellow, bell-shaped flowers nearly 1 in. long. In mild climates, this is known as a weed.

OXYDENDRUM ARBOREUM   *tree*   Sourwood

A small deciduous tree, sourwood is very popular in gardens. In the summer it produces clusters of white, bell-shaped flowers at the tip ends, and in the fall its narrow leaves turn scarlet. Sourwood grows slowly, to 15 to 25 ft. and eventually to 50 ft. It likes lots of water and an acid soil with good drainage. It is hardy to −10°F and is not bothered by insects. Softwood cuttings root easily.

PACHYPODIUM BARONI WINDSOR   *houseplant*

This genus from South Africa and Madagascar has fifteen species, and this particular plant has thick, fleshy roots and a single trunk. Although it is not a palm, it looks somewhat palmlike, growing from 2 to 4 ft. tall and having long, shiny green leaves as well as orange flowers. Plant it in equal parts of sand, gravel, and soil, and water it only when it becomes dry; too much water can harm the plant. Give it bright light and good drainage, and grow new plants from cuttings in the spring.

PACHYSANDRA TERMINALIS   *ground cover*   Japanese spurge

An evergreen ground cover, Japanese spurge may grow to 10 in. in deep shade, but to only 6 in. in partial shade. Likewise, its leaves are dark green in the shade, but yellowish green if it gets any sun. It also has fragrant white flowers in the summer, followed by white fruit. Be sure this ground cover gets lots of water and is in a rich, acid soil. It is seldom attacked by insects and can be divided.

PAEONIA *perennial* **Peony**

There are two types of peonies: herbaceous and tree. The latter are taller (to 6 ft. rather than 2 to 4 ft.) and less dependent on winter cold for a good bloom in the early summer. Indeed, peonies need a cold winter and do not like hot dry weather. But they do like full sun, and plenty of water. Peony flowers come in many varieties—single or double—and in various colors, and they all have a wonderful fragrance. Plant them in beds by themselves where their roots will not be disturbed; get new plants from cuttings. For the many varieties, see the source list at the end of this book.

P. lactiflora. Produces fragrant white flowers 3 to 4 in. in diameter.
P. officinalis (common peony). Produces solitary red flowers to 5 in. in diameter.

PALM *tree/houseplant*

Palms comprise a huge family of plants, from trees to "shrubs" to houseplants, the category depending mainly on the climate in which they are grown. Though a few are from colder regions, most palms come from subtropical or tropical areas and so cannot withstand cold temperatures. But aside from that requirement, there are dozens of varieties, with single or multiple trunks, fan-shaped or feathery foliage, and in many sizes. They look good alone or in groups, need little care, and live a long time. Palms should be planted in a rich soil containing some peat moss and sand, in containers fairly small for the size of the plant. Their peak growth is in the spring and the summer, and thus they need a lot of water then, but not so much at other times, although the soil should never be permitted to dry out. Put palms in a bright light, and wipe their leaves, or fronds, with a damp cloth once a week. Occasionally feed them—but not more than once a month in the spring and summer and not at all the rest of the year. Palms like to be outside in the rain on a warm day, and they are rarely bothered by insects. For descriptions of particular palms, see the following:

Caryota
Chamaedorea
Howeia (kentia)
Licuala
Livistona
Phoenix
Rhapis

PANAX QUINQUEFOLIUS *perennial* **Ginseng**

Ginseng is an herb whose roots—supposedly in the shape of a man—have been used for centuries in Asia for medicinal purposes. Its leaves are actually five leaflets, and it produces greenish-white flowers in the summer and red fruits in the fall. Ginseng is occasionally grown in gardens for nonmedicinal purposes. Give it sun, and water it regularly. Insects seldom are interested in ginseng, and it can be divided for more plants.

PANDANUS   *houseplant*   Screw pine

The screw pine's spiny, lance-shaped leaves are arranged in a spiral—hence its nickname. Some plants grow to 60 in., although the ones mentioned here rarely exceed 40 in. They do best in a bright light and a warm location and in soil that is kept somewhat dry. They do not like fluctuating temperatures. Propagate screw pines from offsets.

P. baptistii. Has stiff, bluish green-and-yellow leaves.
P. utilis. Has long, curving, olive green leaves.
P. veitchii. The best one for indoors. Has curved, variegated leaves.

PAPAVER   *perennial/annual*   Poppy

Poppies vary in height from 20 to 48 in., with brightly colored flowers in the summer. By themselves, they provide a mass of color. Although poppies thrive in almost any soil, they do need sun and a moderate amount of water with almost perfect drainage. Divide poppies for more plants.

P. nudicaule (Iceland poppy). An annual (except in warm climates). Produces fragrant solitary flowers in a variety of colors. Good as a border or show plant.
P. orientale (oriental poppy). A perennial. Produces solitary, 4- to 5-in. scarlet flowers with black centers, though not until the second year.
P. rhoeas (Shirley poppy). An annual. Produces 2- to 3-in. white to scarlet flowers.

SUGGESTED VARIETIES:
'Barr's White'—white flowers
'Harvest Moon'—yellow flowers
'Surprise'—varied colors
'Watermelon'—pale pink flowers

PAPHIOPEDILUM   *houseplant*   Lady slipper orchid

These 10- to 16-in. orchids produce colorful flowers. Some like warmth (60° to 80°F), and others like coolness (50° to 70°F). Give all of them a shaded place, and keep the potting mixture (equal parts of soil and fir bark) moist. Buy new plants from suppliers. Lady's slipper orchids are good as cut flowers or for corsages; there are hundreds of varieties.

P. callosum. Needs coolness. Has marbled leaves and 2-in. pale green to rose-colored flowers, from winter to summer.
P. concolor. Needs warmth. Produces 2-in. yellow flowers spotted with red, in early summer.

P. fairieanum. Needs coolness. Has soft green leaves and 1-in. yellow-and-purple flowers, in late summer and winter.

P. hirsutissimum. Needs warmth. Produces 2- to 3-in. apple green flowers spotted with rose, in the spring.

P. sedeni. Needs warmth. Has dark green leaves and lady slipper-shaped, red flowers with a tinge of white in the center, in the summer.

P. spicerianum. Needs coolness. Has pale green leaves and purple-and-white flowers, in the winter.

P. venustum. Needs coolness. Has mottled leaves and 2-in. purple-and-green flowers, in the spring.

SUGGESTED VARIETIES:
Green and yellow:
Bell O'Ireland
Diversion 'Green Glory' x Prime Time 'Clear Day'
Divisidero Val x Van Ness
Meadow Mist 'Tricolor' x Fall Tones 'Goldenrod'
Merce-Lou Audino
Mahogany:
Milionette 'Red Flame' x Everett Wilcox 'Hastings'
Omdurman Morocco x Florence Wilks 'Supreme'
Pittsburg Banner x Yeat's Country 'Open Spaces'
Portovan 'Princely' x Florence Wilks 'Supreme'
Red-burgundy:
Carl Keyes 'Bion' x Valwin
Redvale 'Sunspot' x Futura 'Silver Lining'
Yellow:
Divisidero 'Val' x Bantry Bay
Liz Greenlees 'Betty's Sister' x Bantry Bay

Parodia *houseplant*   Ball cactus

Most of this large group of desert cacti are small globes that bear large, colorful flowers in the summer. And most of them will bloom readily indoors if they are given sufficient sun. Ball cacti need a soil of equal parts of sand and potting mix, with a thin layer of fine gravel on top of the soil. Keep the soil just barely moist, never wet. In the winter, allow them to rest, at 55°F. Propagate them from offsets.

P. mutabilis. An olive green globe to 9 in. across, with golden yellow flowers.
P. rubriflora. A spiny globe to 3 in. across, with large scarlet flowers.
P. sanguiniflora. A soft green globe to 3 in. across, with red flowers.

Parthenocissus *vine*

This deciduous vine grows to 15 ft., and its leaves turn brilliant red in the fall. Its flowers are insignificant. Parthenocissus does well in either sun or shade but requires a lot of water. Use it to cover fences or walls; it grows quickly. Obtain new plants from cuttings.

P. quinquefolia (Virginia creeper). One of the best garden vines.
P. tricuspidata (Boston ivy). A well-known garden vine.

Passiflora *vine* Passion flower

These evergreen, semievergreen, or deciduous Brazilian vines can grow to 72 in. and offer large beautiful flowers in the summer and fall. Train them on a trellis or wall, and give them lots of sun, water, and fertilizer while they are actively growing. Then let them rest for about three months after they have bloomed, and after that, prune them. Cuttings taken in the summer root readily for spring plants. There are many species and varieties.

P. alata. Has lobed leaves and blue-and-white flowers.
P. caerulea. Produces dark blue-and-pink flowers.
P. coriacea. Produces yellowish green flowers.
P. racemosa. Produces red flowers.
P. trifasciata. Has purple-and-green leaves and blue flowers.

Pelargonium *perennial* Geranium

In mild climates, geraniums can be grown outdoors all year-round; in freezing climates, they can be used as summer bedding plants; and in all climates, they can be enjoyed as houseplants. There are many, many kinds of geraniums, mainly classified into three types: Martha Washington, common, and ivy. In addition, there are scented geraniums, raised just for the fragrance of their leaves (when crushed). In any case, most geraniums need a soil mixture of three parts loam to one part sand, plus a little peat moss to increase the acidity. After watering geraniums, let them dry out a bit before watering them again. They bloom best when crowded in the pot. The Martha Washington and ivy-leafed types need to rest in the winter, during which time you should not water them too much and should not feed them. While geraniums are actively growing, however, they should be fed every other week. Avoid overwatering them and putting them into humid surroundings, and do not mist them. Geraniums sometimes are troubled by edema: Water-soaked spots appear on the leaves when moisture collects in the plants faster than it can be transpired, and thus the leaf cells burst. Some geraniums are best grown from seed; others can be propagated from cuttings taken either in the spring for winter bloom or in August or early September for spring and summer flowering.

Zonal geraniums (*P. hortorum*) are the most familiar ones, with scalloped leaves and brightly colored flowers.

STANDARD:
'Apple Blossom Rosebud'—single, rose-edged, white flowers
'Better Times'—single red flowers
'Dreams'—double salmon pink flowers

'Flare'—single salmon pink flowers
'Harvest Moon'—single orange flowers
'Holiday'—single red flowers with white centers
'Patricia Andrea'—single rose-colored flowers
'Princess Fiat'—double shrimp pink flowers
'Salmon Irene'—double flowers (there are five 'Irenes')
'Snowball'—double white flowers
'Starlight'—single white flowers
'Summer Cloud'—double white flowers

DWARF:
'Capella'—forest green leaves and double salmon pink flowers
'Epsilon'—soft pink flowers
'Goblin'—large, double scarlet flowers
'Lyric'—double orchid pink flowers with white centers
'Minx'—double crimson purple flowers
'Perky'—single bright red flowers with white centers
'Pigmy'—scalloped leaves and semidouble bright red flowers

MINIATURE:
'Black Vesuvius'—dark green leaves and single orange-scarlet flowers
'Fairytale'—white flowers with lavender centers
'Imp'—dark green leaves and single pink flowers
'Saturn'—dark green leaves and red flowers
'Venus'—double light pink flowers

Carefree geraniums grow true to type and color from seed. Do not pinch them back to make them bushy, as they are naturally thick. Seeds planted in mid February will produce blooming plants in early July (in the Midwest).

FANCY LEAFED:
'Crystal Palace Gem'—yellow and bright green leaves
'Filigree'—tricolored silver leaves and single dark salmon pink flowers
'Jubilee'—yellow-green and red-brown leaves
'Skies of Italy'—tricolored golden leaves and red flowers

Free blooming, large dwarf (good window plants for 4-in. pots because of their small size and almost constant bloom):

'Brooks Barnes'—dark green leaves and single pink flowers
'Dancer'—single salmon-colored flowers (one of the largest dwarfs)
'Emma Hosler'—double rose pink flowers with white centers
'Mr. Evaarts'—double pink flowers

Scented-leafed geraniums are not grown for their flowers but, rather, for their variously scented leaves. Some have leaves resembling maple leaves, others like gooseberry's, and still others like ferns.

P. crispum—lemon scented
P. graveolens—rose scented
P. odoratissimum—apple scented
P. tomentosum—peppermint scented

Ivy-leafed geraniums (*P. peltatum*) have trailing stems and glossy, ivylike leaves, perfect for hanging baskets. They also have lots of flowers in the summer. Pinch back these plants in the late winter or early spring to encourage growth.

'Charles Turner'—double pink flowers
'Comtesse de Grey'—single light pink flowers
'New Dawn'—double rose-cerise flowers
'Santa Paula'—double lavender-purple flowers
'Victorville'—double dark red flowers

Martha Washington geraniums (*P. domesticum*) bloom in the spring. The flowers have blotches of other colors or of darker shades of the main color. There are also small, pansy types. Cut back these geraniums after they have bloomed, and always keep them cool (45° to 55°F).

'Dubonnet'—ruffled wine red flowers
'Easter Greetings'—cerise flowers
'Gardener's Joy'—blush-white flowers with rose markings and stripes
'Holiday'—ruffled white flowers with crimson markings
'Lavender Grand Slam'—lavender flowers
'Madame Layal'—pansy type, purple-and-white flowers
'Springtime'—ruffled white flowers with rose-colored throats

PELLAEA   *houseplant*   **Cliff-brake fern**

These ferns, native to New Zealand and the West Indies, have fronds with heart-shaped segments that bear little resemblance to most other ferns. The plants grow to 30 in., and their fronds are either erect or low and spreading—good accents in a woodland or fern garden. In their natural settings these ferns prefer limestone. Whatever soil you choose, keep it moist but never wet, and give the ferns some shade. Watch out for scale on both sides of the leaves, but do not mistake the spores on the undersides of the fronds for scale. Use the spores to obtain more ferns.

P. rotundifolia. Low and spreading growth. Has small, round dark leaves. Nice for baskets.
P. viridis. Has larger green leaflets. Will climb if supported.

PENNISETUM   *perennial*   **Fountain grass**

This ornamental grass grows to 4 ft. and has narrow blades and, in the summer, fuzzy coppery pink or purplish flower spikes. It needs sun but not much water. Any soil is fine, as long as it is well drained. This grass can be divided, but it is apt to become invasive.

PENSTEMON *shrub*   Beardtongue

These evergreen shrubs grow to 30 ft. and produce large, brightly colored, red, violet, blue, or white flowers in the summer. They require full sun and a moderate amount of water in a well-drained soil. Protect them over the winter in freezing climates. Cuttings provide new plants; there are many species.

SUGGESTED VARIETIES:
'Firebird'—red flowers
'Huntington Pink'—pink flowers
'Pink Endurance'—pink flowers
'Ruby King'—rosy pink flowers
'True Blue'—blue flowers

PENTAS LANCEOLATA *perennial*   Egyptian star flower

The Egyptian star flower grows to 30 in. and almost continuously produces showy flowers in lavender, pink, rose, or white. Put these plants in a sunny spot and give them plenty of water while they are actively growing. Older plants tend to become leggy, so it is best to start new ones every year, from seed or stem cuttings. The cut flowers last a long time.

SUGGESTED VARIETIES:
'California Lavender'—lavender flowers
'Orchid Star'—lilac-colored flowers

PEPEROMIA *houseplant*

Peperomias are good foliage plants for windows, tables, planters, or terrariums. They have smooth-edged leaves and insignificant flowers. Whereas some are vining types, others are upright bushes. Peperomias do best in a bright light, in a sandy soil, and with very little water. Propagate them from stem cuttings.

P. cubensis. Grows upright to 12 in. Has waxy, fresh green leaves.
P. gardneriana. Grows to 12 in. Has bushy, glossy green, crinkled leaves.
P. glabella variegata. Grows to 12 in. Has vining, yellow-and-pale green leaves.
P. gracilis. Grows to 10 in. Has crinkled green leaves, red underneath and with silver veins.
P. hederaefolia. Grows to 14 in. Has vining, bright silvery purple leaves.
P. maculosa. Grows upright to 12 in. Has narrow gray-green leaves.
P. metallica. Grows upright to 12 in. Has small waxy brown leaves with pale green stripes.
P. nivalis. Grows to 14 in. Has unusual keel-shaped, succulent leaves.
P. obtusifolia. Grows to 16 in. Has vining, large, fleshy, oval leaves.
P. ornata. Grows upright to 12 in. Has dark green leaves with maroon stripes.
P. pericattii. Grows to 12 in. Has thick green leaves with red edges.
P. prostrata. Unusual, creeping stems growing to 18 in. Has gray-green succulent leaves.
P. resediflora. Grows to 8 in. Has a rosette of green leaves.

PERESKIA *houseplant*   **Lemon vine**

These unusual desert cacti hardly look like cacti. Lemon vines have long, narrow leaves and spiny stems, and occasionally bear greenish white or pink flowers in the late summer. They need full sun and good air circulation. Give them a moderate amount of water all year long. Offsets or cuttings provide new plants.

P. aculeata. Grows to 8 ft. Has thick, oval leaves and white, yellow, or pink flowers.
P. godseffiana. Similar to *P. aculeata,* but with somewhat smaller green leaves marked with
    crimson and yellow.

PETREA VOLUBILIS *vine*   **Queen's wreath**

True-blue flowers open in the spring and summer on this 6- to 8-ft. vine, which also has brittle, dark green leaves. Queen's wreath is a big plant that grows quickly. Give it full sun, and let it dry out between waterings. These vines must be three or four years old before they will flower, so be patient. Obtain new plants from cuttings.

PETUNIA *annual*

One of the most widely grown annuals, petunias grow to be 6 to 12 in. high and bear large, funnel-shaped, fragrant flowers in a variety of colors, blooming continuously throughout the summer. Petunias need lots of water and

sun. Some are cascading, others upright; some are small, others large. Pinch off flowers to ensure a second flowering in the early fall. Plant seed or buy prestarted plants.

SUGGESTED VARIETIES:
'Cherry Blossom'—pink flowers
'Cherry Tart'—dark pink flowers
'Comanche'—red flowers
'Pale Face'—pale pink flowers
'Pink Cascade'—pink flowers
'Sugar Plum'—plum pink flowers

PEURARIA LOBATA   *vine*   Kudzu

This is an extremely fast growing vine that can easily and quickly reach 50 ft., with dense foliage and beanlike, purple flowers. Kudzu can easily and rapidly get out of hand, so be warned if you plant it. It likes lots of sun and water, so do not be too generous. Cuttings provide new plants, something you will probably never need or want.

PHACELIA CAMPANULARIA   *annual*   Desert bluebell

Desert bluebells are native to the California deserts, which means that they can tolerate drought, like lots of sun, and thrive in poor soil. These plants grow to 12 in. tall and, in the summer, bear deep blue, bell-shaped flowers with a white spot at the base. Desert bluebells look best planted in masses. Obtain new plants from seed, or buy prestarted ones.

PHALAENOPSIS   *houseplant*   Moth orchid

This popular group of orchids have large, paper-thin, white or pink flowers, dozens to a stem. Moth orchids' leaves are leathery and spatulate. Pot these plants in medium-grade fir bark, in an area with good air circulation and relatively high humidity, and keep the soil moist all year-round, making sure that the water does not accumulate in the plants' crowns. Moth orchids bloom in the fall or winter. Buy new plants from specialists.

P. amabilis. Used extensively for hybrids. Has leaves to 26 in. long and large white flowers.
P. leuddemmanniana. Has leaves to 26 in. long and pale pink flowers.

SUGGESTED VARIETIES:
Pink/lavender/purple:
    Arlene Andrews
    Zada's Best x Zauberrose 'Dark'
    Zauberrose x Diana
    Zauberrose x Lippstadt x Monticello

Red:
     Carnival 'Bonsall'
     Coral Isles 'York' x Golden Buddha 'Carriage Hill'
     P. Winter Dawn x P. Luedde-Violacea
     Sophie Hausermann x Vitrail 'Bon Bon'
White:
     Carl Hausermann x Winter Maiden
     Cherryvale
     Portola 'Mt. Madonna' x Grace Palm
     Winter Beauty 'York'
     Winter Maiden
Yellow:
     Gold Cup 'Everlasting'
     Golden Amboine
     Desert Wind
     Sun Prairie 'Yellow Star'
Striped:
     Autumn Symphony
     Class President 'Willowbrook'
     Painted Cave 'York'

Phaseolus   *vine*   **Scarlet runner bean**

Scarlet runner beans grow to 8 ft. long, quickly covering trellises and fences. They need sun and a moderate amount of water in a well-drained soil. Blooming in the summer, they are a good addition if a colorful vine is needed in the garden. Buy new plants yearly.

P. coccineus. A tall twiner. Produces usually scarlet, though sometimes white or scarlet-and-white, flowers.

P. c. albus (Dutch runner bean). Produces white flowers.

Philadelphus   *shrub*   **Sweet mock orange**

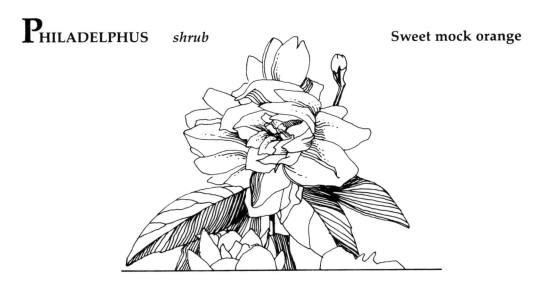

Grown mainly for their white flowers with an orange blossom fragrance, mock orange also has attractive bright green leaves. There are both low and tall growers, and most can take heavy pruning. Mock orange grows in almost any soil and likes full sun, except in the hottest areas, and regular watering. It blooms in the late spring, is seldom attacked by insects, and can be propagated by means of softwood or hardwood cuttings.

P. coronarius (sweet mock orange). Grows to 9 ft.; hardy to −10°F. Has oval leaves and very fragrant white flowers.
    'Flore Pleno'—double-flower form of *P. coronarius*
    'Silberregen'—upright, narrow grower with fragrant flowers
P. lemoninei. A hybrid. Grows to 8 ft.; hardy to −5°F. Produces single or double white flowers.
    'Belle Etoile'—single flowers
P. virginalis. A hybrid. Grows to 9 ft.; hardy to −5°F. Produces single or double white flowers.

SUGGESTED VARIETIES:
'Glacier'—double flowers
'Minnesota Snowflake'—double, fragrant flowers
'Virginal'—a fast grower, best for cut flowers

PHILODENDRON   *houseplant*

The many varieties of philodendron are perhaps the most widely grown and most tolerant houseplants; they will endure almost any abuse or neglect and seem none the worse for the experience. This is the plant for beginners and for those whose thumbs are truly purple. Philodendrons do like sun, with some shade, but if you have a dark apartment, these are the plants of choice. Try to keep the soil moist, and mist the leaves occasionally. Some species of philodendron have medium-sized leaves, others have large ones; many are vining plants, others have rosettes of leaves. For additional plants, take stem or cane cuttings.

P. andreanum. Grows to 36 in. Has vining, 10-in., dark green leaves.
P. bipinnatifidum. Grows to 30 in. Has vining, 8-in., scalloped, dark green leaves.
P. cordatum. Has a 20-in.-wide rosette of lance-shaped leaves on short stems.
P. cruentum. Grows to 20 in. Has vining, 8-in. leaves.
P. erubescens. Grows to 24 in. Has vining, 10-in., dark green leaves.
P. 'Hastatum'. Grows to 36 in. Has vining, 10-in., arrow-shaped leaves.
P. imbe. Grows to 24 in. Has vining, 10-in., leathery maroon leaves.
P. 'Multicolor'. Grows to 36 in. Has lance-shaped, green-yellow leaves.
P. oxycardium. Grows to 36 in. Has vining, 10-in. leaves.
P. selloum. Grows to 30 in. Has a rosette of 15-in., notched leaves.
P. verrucosum. Grows to 24 in. Has vining, 8-in., multicolored, heart-shaped leaves.
P. wendlandii. Has a 36-in.-diameter rosette of 15-in. green leaves.

PHLOX   *perennial/annual*

Phlox, whose varieties can grow from 10 to 36 in. high, provides a mass of color in the garden for very little investment. These plants are happiest in the sun, with an average amount of water and an average, well-drained soil. Their flowers bloom in the spring and summer. Among the many species and varieties available, there are certain to be some suitable for your garden.

P. divaricata (sweet William). Has thin green leaves and lilac-colored, sometimes white, flowers.
P. drummondii (annual phlox). Produces flowers in various colors, except blue and orange, some with a contrasting center.
P. paniculata (summer phlox). Produces fragrant flowers in white and shades of lavender, pink, rose, or red, some with a contrasting center.
P. subulata (moss phlox). A small (to 10 in.) plant, with flowers in purple, rose, lilac, or lavender, with a darker center.

SUGGESTED VARIETIES:
'Amethyst'—violet-blue flowers
'Bright Eyes'—blue flowers
'Emerald Pink'—pink flowers
'Fountain Pink'—bright pink flowers
'Fuller's White'—white flowers
'Pink Petticoat'—pink flowers
'Twinkle Mix'—various colors

PHOENIX *tree* Date palm

Date palms, with crowns of feathery fronds, grow wild in Africa and the Middle East, where they may reach 100 ft. Here, however, they seldom grow taller than 8 ft. Date palms can survive temperatures down to only about 20°F, so they can be grown only in mild climates. And of course, date palms are the source of dates, which in this country come from the desert areas of southern California. Put date palms in bright light, soak the soil, and then let it dry out before watering it again. Buy prestarted plants.

P. canariensis. Has shiny green, feathery fronds.
P. dactylifera (date palm). Has blue-green fronds.
P. roebelenii (pygmy date palm). A dwarf, growing to about 40 in., with a thick crown of dark green fronds.

PHORMIUM *perennial* New Zealand flax

These evergreen perennials grow to be quite tall, with long lance-shaped leaves and tall flower (dull red or yellow) spikes. They are best used alone, as a background, or against a fence or wall. Except for needing full sun to light shade, New Zealand flax can get along with a lot or a little water, in heat or cold. Ideally, let the soil dry out a bit between waterings. Grow new plants from offsets.

P. atropurpureum. Has green leaves delicately marked with bronze.
P. tenax. The most popular kind. Has dark brownish green leaves edged with red.

PHOTINIA VILLOSA   *shrub/tree*   Photinia

Classed as either a shrub or a small tree, photinia grows to about 15 ft. tall and has pale gold leaves that turn scarlet in the fall. In the spring it has white flowers that later become red fruit, which remain on the tree (shrub) from fall through early winter; photinia is hardy down to −20°F. Give this plant sun and regular watering. It is not usually bothered by insects, and softwood and hardwood cuttings root easily.

PHYLLITIS SCOLOPENDRIUM   *houseplant*   Hart's tongue fern

This 20-in. fern has dark green, crinkly fronds and thrives indoors if kept cool. In addition, it likes a shady location and plenty of water—it will even tolerate, for many months, the dim light of a hall. For more hart's tongue ferns, divide the roots.

PHYSALIS ALKEKENGI   *perennial*   Chinese lantern

This is an unusual plant sometimes found in gardens as a spot accent. The Chinese lantern plant grows to about 2 ft. high and has long light green leaves, white flowers, and, in the fall, orange-red, cherrylike fruit that looks rather like a Chinese lantern. These plants require sun and lots of water but do well in almost any soil. Divide them for additional plants.

PHYSOSTEGIA VIRGINIANA   *perennial*   False dragonhead

This strangely named plant is easy to grow—it reaches 48 in.—and has dark green, willowlike leaves. In the summer and fall, it produces flesh-colored or purple flowers. Situate this perennial in either sun or shade, in an acid soil, and water it regularly. Divide it for new plants.

SUGGESTED VARIETY:
'Vivid'—deep pink flowers

PICEA   *tree*   Spruce

Although young spruce trees are indeed a pretty sight, the older ones lose their lower branches and often their good looks. Most of these evergreens grow to around 100 ft. or even more, and so they are not good candidates for a small garden. Spruce need cool conditions and ample water, but they are not particular about their soil. However, many insects like these trees, especially aphids, scale, spider mites, and tussock moths. Be vigilant and prepared to do battle. Obtain new plants from softwood or hardwood cuttings.

P. abies (Norway spruce). Pyramidal growth to 150 ft.; hardy to − 35°F. Has dark green needles.
P. amorika (Serbian spruce). Pyramidal growth to 90 ft.; hardy to − 10°F. Has bluish green needles.
P. glauca (white spruce). Pyramidal growth to 90 ft.; hardy to − 35°F. Has bluish green needles.
P. orientalis (oriental spruce). Pyramidal growth to 150 ft.; hardy to − 10°F. Has glossy dark green needles, the smallest of all the species.
P. pungens (Colorado spruce). Pyramidal growth to 100 ft.; hardy to − 35°F.
    'Moerheimii'—very blue needles
P. sitchensis (Sitka spruce). Pyramidal growth to 140 ft.; hardy to − 5°F. Has wide, spreading branches and bright green-and-silver needles.

PIERIS   *shrub*

These shrubs are related to the rhododendrons and have evergreen, leathery leaves and, in the spring, waxy white flowers. They do best in a somewhat shady spot, in an acid soil with excellent drainage, and protected from the wind. Most—but not all—species can be propagated from softwood or hardwood cuttings. Because lacebugs can sometimes be a problem, be forearmed.

P. floribunda. Grows to 6 ft.; hardy to − 10°F. Has dull gray-green leaves and clusters of white flowers.
P. forrestii (Chinese pieris). Grows to 8 ft.; hardy to − 10°F. Denser than *P. floribunda*.
P. japonica (lily-of-the-valley shrub). Grows to 7 ft.; hardy to − 20°F. Produces drooping clusters of fragrant, creamy white flowers.
    'Chandleri'—colorful leaves turning from pink to green
P. phillyreifolia. Grows to 15 ft.; hardy to 10°F. A vinelike shrub, with white, vase-shaped flowers in the early spring.

PILEA   *houseplant*

These small foliage plants have plain green or variegated leaves and clusters of tiny flowers. Pileas make a good ground cover for planters or large pots or are nice just as small plants on their own merits. Bright light or light shade is best, and keep the soil moist. Take cuttings for new plants.

P. cadierei (aluminum plant). Grows to 12 in. or more. Has silver-and-green leaves and rose red flowers.
P. grandis. Grows to 16 in. Has glossy green leaves, deeply serrated along the edges and copper colored underneath.
P. involucrata. Grows to 12 in. or more. Has bushy brown leaves and rose red flowers.
P. microphylla (artillery plant). Grows to 18 in. Has tiny bright green leaves, somewhat ferny; its flowers shoot out their pollen, hence the nickname.
P. nummulariifolia (creeping Charlie). Grows to 8 in. Has green leaves and rose red flowers.
P. repens. Grows to 8 in. Has quilted, round, coppery brown leaves and greenish white flowers.

Pinus *tree*   Pine

Pines come in many shapes, colors, and sizes, and the various species respond differently to sun, soil, and wind. Generally, pines need full sun, any soil that is well drained, and not too much water. Their particular evergreen needles indicate the various species. Pines also can be prey to a number of diseases and pests, so watch them carefully and take action if necessary. Because pines are difficult to propagate, it is best to buy new ones.

P. cembra (Swiss stone pine). Slow, dense, pyramidal growth to 60 ft.; hardy to −35°F. Has dark green needles.

P. contorta (beach pine). Rounded top, dense growth to 30 ft.; hardy to 10°F. Has dark green needles.

P. densiflora (Japanese red pine). Horizontal-branching growth to 100 ft.; hardy to −10°F. Has bright bluish green needles.

P. halepensis (Aleppo pine). Rounded top, open growth to 60 ft.; hardy to 20°F. Has light green needles.

P. mugo (Swiss mountain pine). Pyramidal growth to 15 ft.; hardy to 10°F. Has fat, dark green needles.

P. nigra (Austrian pine). Dense, full, pyramidal growth to 90 ft.; hardy to −10°F. Has very dark green needles.

P. parviflora (Japanese white pine). Dense, pyramidal growth to 90 ft.; hardy to −5°F. Has wide-spreading branches and bluish green to gray needles.

P. peuce (Macedonian pine). Dense, pyramidal growth to 60 ft.; hardy to −10°F. Has long blue-green needles.

P. pinea (Italian stone pine). Broad, flat-topped growth to 80 ft.; hardy to 20°F. Has stiff, gray-green needles.

P. resimosa (red pine). Spreading growth to 75 ft.; hardy to −35°F. Has dark green needles.

P. strobus (eastern white pine). Rounded or pyramidal growth to 150 ft.; hardy to −20°F. Has soft, blue-green needles.

P. sylvestris (Scotch pine). Pyramidal when young, round-topped growth when mature, to 75 ft.; hardy to −35°F. Has stiff, bluish green needles.

P. thunbergiana (Japanese black pine). Dense, spreading growth to 90 ft.; hardy to −5°F. Has stiff, dark green needles.

Pittosporum *shrub/tree*

Pittosporum is known for its ornamental foliage and form. It does best in full sun to half-shade, and although it can withstand drought if necessary, it prefers regular watering. This shrub has clusters of long, rounded oval, fairly thick leaves, either plain green or variegated, with small, waxy yellowish white flowers in the spring that smell like orange blossoms. In the fall they produce hard white berries. In areas like southern California, pittosporum is commonly used as a hedge or a background plant.

P. crassifolium. Dense growth to 8 ft.; hardy to 30°F. Has gray-green leaves.
    'Variegatum'—variegated leaves
P. tobira. Branching growth to 15 ft.; hardy to 30°F. Has shiny green leaves.

P. undulatum. Dome-shaped growth to 30 ft.; hardy to 30°F. Has dark green leaves with wavy edges.

PLATANUS *tree*

Sycamores have maplelike leaves and smooth bark; they are deciduous. Although they grow quickly, most of those used in gardens do not exceed 50 ft., and although sycamores will tolerate drought, they do better with regular watering. They do, however, have problems with diseases (blight) and insects (spider mites and scale). Watch them and use natural sprays if necessary. Take softwood or hardwood cuttings for new trees.

P. acerifolia (London plane tree). Spreading growth to 100 ft.; hardy to −10°F.
P. hispanica. Branching growth to 100 ft.; hardy to −20°F.
P. orientalis (oriental plane tree). Rounded growth to 80 ft.; hardy to −5°F.

PLATYCERIUM *houseplant* Staghorn fern

These ferns can, of course, be grown indoors, and also outdoors in warm climates. But they must be grown on slabs of wood (cedar or cork) and soaked daily. These plants have two kinds of fronds: The fertile fronds are hanging and forked (that is, staghorns), and the sterile ones are flat—not forked—and rest against the wood. Staghorn ferns need bright light or semishade. For additional ferns, pot the little plants that grow between the sterile fronds.

P. bifurcatum. Has 36-in.-long, grayish green fronds.
P. grande. Has 72-in.-long, spreading, glossy green fronds.
P. stemmaria. A curious plant. Has 36-in.-long, thick, gray-green fronds.
P. veitchii. Has 24-in.-long, rounded, basal fronds.
P. wilhelminae-reginae. Has 36-in.-long, glossy, silvery green fronds.

PLATYCODON *perennial* Balloon flower

These 36-in. plants, with light olive green leaves, produce balloon-shaped buds that open in the summer into 2-in.-wide, star-shaped flowers in shades of blue-violet, white, or light pink. Balloon flowers also make good cut flowers. Give them sun and a moderate amount of water, and divide them for new plants.

P. grandiflorum (Chinese bellflower). Produces bell-shaped, blue, pink, or white flowers on tall stems.
P. mariesii. A small (to 18 in.) version of *P. grandiflorum,* with blue flowers.

SUGGESTED VARIETIES:
'Baby Blue'—blue flowers
'Blue'—blue flowers
'Shell Pink'—pink flowers

PLECTRANTHUS   *houseplant*   Swedish ivy

Swedish ivy is a dependable houseplant—good for beginners or those unsure of their gardening skills—that has waxy, scalloped green leaves on
trailing stems and little flowers on and off throughout the year. It is the plant
often seen when the president of the United States is talking to dignitaries in
front of the fireplace in the Oval Office; it has survived many administra-
tions. Grow Swedish ivy in either light or shade, and keep the soil consistently moist. Plant seed or cuttings at any time.

P. australis. Grows to 20 in. Has waxy, saw-toothed leaves and pink flowers. Good for a basket.
P. a. variegatum. Has irregular, white-edged leaves.
P. behril. Grows to 30 in. Has slightly hairy leaves that are green on top and rose pink
    underneath.
P. coleoides. Grows to 20 in. Has small, crinkled leaves and white-and-purple flowers.
P. oertendahlii. Grows to 20 in. Has apple green leaves with silver veins, and pale pink flowers.
P. saccatus. Grows to 20 in. Has matted, dark green leaves and spreading branches.

PLEIONE   *houseplant*   Indian crocus

This group of mostly deciduous orchids is from China, Taiwan, and Southeast Asia. The flowers are large and solitary, but there are many to a plant.
Pleiones have compressed, cormlike pseudobulbs tipped with a few light
green leaves that generally fall off after the bulb matures. The flowers grow
from the base of the bulb either before or along with the new growth. Most
species bear their flowers in the fall, and they last for more than a week on
the plant. Grow these orchids in a potting mix of equal parts of fine-grade fir
bark and soil. Keep them in bright light, and keep the soil consistently moist,
except in the late summer when it should be somewhat dry, to encourage
bloom. Buy new plants from suppliers.

P. hookeriana. Grows to 5 in. Has paper-thin leaves and rose-colored flowers with a purple
    splotch on the lip.
P. maculata. Grows to about 12 in. Produces 4-in. white flowers with the lip streaked purple.
P. pricei. Grows to about 5 in. Produces pale rose-colored flowers with a white, fringed lip.

PLEOMELE   *houseplant*

Similar to dracaenas, pleomeles have a denser, bushier shape, with narrow,
leathery leaves edged with pale yellow stripes. These plants are good for the
difficult north exposure, although they prefer a brighter light. Use a readily
draining houseplant potting mix, and keep it consistently moist all year-
round. Wipe the foliage occasionally with a damp cloth. Disturb the plants
only when absolutely necessary; for instance, instead of repotting them, put
new soil on the top. Pleomeles can tolerate coolness (55°F) if necessary. In the
spring, take cuttings for new plants.

P. angustifolia. Has willowy stems to 30 in. and leathery green leaves with yellow borders.
P. reflexa. Grows to 40 in. Has sword-shaped green leaves lined with yellow.
P. r. variegata. Grows to 40 in. Has a richer leaf color than that of *P. reflexa.*

Plumbago *shrub/vine*

From South Africa, these 8-ft. climbers have pale blue flowers that bloom for a long time from the spring to the fall, and throughout the year in frost-free climates. Although plumbago likes sun, the hot summer sun can bleach the flowers. Water it a lot until it is established; after that it does not need much.

P. capensis. Produces small, pale blue flowers.
P. scandens (Cerastostigma plumbaginoides). Has oval leaves and lots of small white flowers.

Plumeria emarginata *tree* Frangipani

This is a popular tropical tree that can be grown only in the warmest climates (it can withstand temperatures down to only 40°F). Its flowers—white, waxy, and very fragrant—are perhaps best known for making beautiful Hawaiian leis. This small (to 20 ft.) tree likes sun and some shade, and more water in the summer than in the winter. Take cuttings for additional plants.

Podocarpus *shrub/tree* Southern yew

In warm climates, podocarpus is frequently used as a hedge. It is long-lived, with narrow evergreen leaves. Grow it in the shade, and let the soil dry out between waterings. Plant seed for more shrubs.

P. macrophyllus maki. Branching growth to 72 in. Has waxy black-and-green leaves.
P. nagi. Spreading growth to 20 ft. Has shiny green leaves.

Podophyllum peltatum *perennial* May apple

The may apple is a popular wildflower in the eastern United States, with green leaves and white flowers in the spring. Plant it in a moist, shady place, such as a rock garden, where it can spread naturally. Underground stems bring new plants.

Polemonium *perennial*

One of the first perennials to start growing in the spring, these plants reach about 30 in. They bloom in the summer, require sun and lots of water, and need a rich soil that drains readily. Divide for additional plants.

P. caeruleum (Jacob's ladder). Has erect, hollow stems with bell-shaped blue or white flowers.
P. reptans (creeping Jacob's ladder). A creeping plant with drooping blue or white flowers.

POLIANTHES TUBEROSA   *bulb*   Tuberose

Tuberoses came from Mexico and now are favorite garden plants. They have long, narrow, grasslike leaves and pure white, very fragrant flowers that bloom in the summer. But if you plant bulbs every two weeks, you can have flowers throughout most of the summer. Tuberoses are excellent for borders and also as cut flowers. When you plant them, space the bulbs about 6 to 8 in. apart and 4 in. deep. Each fall, dig them up and store them until the weather turns warm in the spring, when they can be replanted. New plants can be had from offsets.

SUGGESTED VARIETY:
'Pacific Giant'

POLYGALA   *shrub*

Polygalas are small shrubs, most growing to only 1 ft. tall. They have boxwoodlike leaves and flowers that bloom in the spring and then irregularly from then on. These shrublets like sun and regular watering in a well-drained soil. They can be used as bona fide shrubs or as border plants. Polygalas tolerate temperatures down to −5°F; get new plants from seed.

P. chamaebuxus. A small shrub, likes an acid soil.
P. lutea. A low-growing annual with yellow flowers.
P. polygama. A perennial with purple flowers, likes a sandy soil.

POLYGONATUM   *perennial*   Solomon's seal

Solomon's seal is a member of the lily family; it grows to about 2 ft. and has bright green leaves and greenish white, bell-shaped flowers in the summer. Give this plant shade and ample water, and divide it for more plants.

POLYPODIUM   *houseplant*

These tropical ferns are easy to grow indoors, or outdoors in mild climates. They grow to 30 in. and have bold-textured, blue-gray fronds and colorful, usually orange-brown or white, scaly rhizomes. Grow these ferns in a mixture of humus, sphagnum moss, and sand. Keep them moist and mist them often. In the winter give them sun, and in the summer, shade. Divide the rhizomes in the spring for new ferns.

P. aureum glaucum (hare's foot fern). Has 24-in., wavy-edged, blue-gray fronds.

P. a. 'Mandaianum'. Similar to *P. aureum glaucum,* but with crested or fringed fronds.
P. formosum. Grows to 24 in. Has creeping, bright green rhizomes and lacy fronds.
P. lepidopteris. Grows to 30 in. Has deeply pinnate, silver-green fronds.
P. polycarpon. Has yellow-green fronds.
P. subauriculatum. Has long, hanging fronds. Good for baskets.

Polyscias *houseplant*

Treelike plants, polyscias have either finely cut, somewhat fernlike leaves or simple, shiny dark green leaves. Both kinds need bright light and little water in a quickly draining and drying soil. Let the soil dry out before watering it again, and provide good air circulation. If you live in a warm climate, you can use polyscias outside as a hedge. Propagate them by means of stem cuttings or air layering.

P. balfouriana. Grows to 40 in. Has round, shiny dark green leaves.
P. b. marginata. Has dark green leaves edged with white.
P. b. variegata. Grows to 48 in. Has green leaves with white stripes.
P. fruticosa. Grows to 40 in. Has finely cut, fernlike leaves.
P. guilfoylei. Grows to 40 in. Has saw-toothed leaflets.

Polystichum *houseplant*   Holly fern

Among this group of ferns are some large and some small plants. Many have stiff fronds; others have feathery ones. The fronds of both kinds of ferns grow from a dark, partly underground, scale-covered crown. Put holly ferns in a bright light, and keep the soil moist and slightly acid. In warm weather, when it is raining, set the plants outside in a protected place. And in the spring, divide the roots for more ferns.

P. acrostichoides (Christmas fern). Has 24-in., feathery fronds.
P. aculeatum (hedge fern). Has heavy, 24-in. fronds.
P. adiantiforme (leather fern). Has 24-in., bright green fronds.
P. tsus-simense. Low and compact growth. Has 12-in., triangular fronds with a bright metallic sheen. Good for terrariums.

Populus *tree*   Poplar

Poplars are popular because they grow quickly, so quickly in fact that their roots can push up sidewalks and block sewer lines. They also offer little in the way of flowers or interesting foliage. But they are easy to maintain and, again, are fast growing if that is a desired quality. In addition, most can tolerate drought, as well as hot summers, if necessary. They are not generally bothered by insects. Use root cuttings in the spring for new trees.

P. alba (white poplar). Grows to 90 ft.; hardy to −35°F. Has grayish green leaves that are white and woolly underneath and—an exception—turn yellow in the fall.

P. berlinensis (Berlin poplar). Grows to 150 ft.; hardy to −50°F. Has glossy coarse leaves and highly invasive roots. Plant only where there is more space than necessary to accommodate the roots.

P. caescens (gray poplar). Grows to 90 ft.; hardy to −20°F. Has small leaves.

P. lasiocarpa (Chinese poplar). Grows to 60 ft.; hardy to −5°F. Round headed, with large, bright green leaves.

P. nigra 'Italica' (Lombardy poplar). Grows to 80 ft.; hardy to −35°F. Dense foliage, columnar shape; short-lived.

PORTEA PETROPOLITANA EXTENSA   *houseplant*

This bromeliad has a 36-in. rosette of dark green leaves and spectacular green-and-pink flower heads in the summer or fall. It will grow in the shade but does best in the sun, potted in soil that is kept moist. Grow new plants from offsets.

PORTULACA GRANDIFLORA   *annual*   Moss rose

These summer plants offer brightly colored flowers from early summer until the first frost. Moss rose grows to 16 in., and its leaves are small and succulent. Its flowers come one to four in a cluster and are red, yellow, or purple, opening in direct sunshine and closing in the shade. The plant prospers in a hot dry location, with sun, very little water, and a sandy soil. It is a good choice for places where other plants may not grow. Seed is the best way to get more moss rose.

POTENTILLA   *shrub*   Cinquefoil

Cinquefoil is either an evergreen or a deciduous shrub belonging to the rose family. Most of those grown are varieties of *P. fruticosa*, with flowers in several colors, white to pale yellow to orange. The leaves are either bright green or gray-green, divided into small leaflets. Most potentillas are low growing, bloom a long time—from the early summer through the fall—and can withstand poor soil if necessary. All need a sunny location, and most can easily be divided. They are not usually troubled by insects.

P. arbuscula (bush cinquefoil). Grows to 4 ft.; hardy to −35°F. Produces 1-in. yellow or white flowers.

P. fruticosa (cinquefoil). Grows to 4 ft.; hardy to −50°F. A popular species with many varieties. 'Jackman's Variety'—bright yellow flowers

P. f. mandshurica. A dwarf form. Grows to 2 ft.; hardy to −35°F. Produces white flowers.

P. tridentata. Grows to 3 ft.; hardy to −20°F. Produces yellow flowers.

PRIMULA *perennial* **Primrose**

Primroses make up a large group of flowering, small and medium-sized plants. They bloom in the spring, in a choice of several different colors and color combinations. Primroses are happiest in partial shade, in an acid soil, and with plenty of water. Buy prestarted plants yearly.

P. auricula. Produces fragrant yellow flowers.
P. denticulata (Himalayan primrose). Produces pale purple flowers with a yellow eye. Especially good for rock or wildflower gardens.
P. japonica (Japanese primrose). Produces white, rose, or purple flowers.
P. obconica. Produces funnel-shaped, pale lilac or purple flowers with a yellow eye.
P. officinalis (*P. veris*) (cowslip). Produces very fragrant, deep yellow flowers.
P. vulgaris (true primula). Produces sulfur yellow flowers blotched with dark yellow near the eye.

PRUNUS *shrub/tree*

Prunus comprises both evergreen and deciduous trees and shrubs, including the "stone" fruit trees, evergreen ornamentals, and deciduous flowering fruit trees. Among the stone fruits are cherry, plum, peach, apricot, and almond. If you live in a mild climate, you may well want to grow some of the fruit trees expressly for their fruit, or the flowering fruit trees for their beautiful flowers in the spring, but be forewarned that these trees do have problems with diseases and insects. So be forearmed with natural sprays and preventatives. The evergreen ornamentals are used for hedges, screens, and shade, but given their susceptibility to insects and diseases, you may want to select something else. All of the plants in this group like sun and a moderate amount of water.

P. americana. Grows to 20 ft.; hardy to −10°F. Has long leaves, white flowers, and red plums.

P. besseyi (western sand cherry). Grows to 7 ft.; hardy to −20°F. Produces very sweet black cherries.

P. cistena (purpleleaf sand cherry). Grows to 7 ft.; hardy to −35°F. Produces reddish flowers and blackish purple cherries.

P. glandulosa (dwarf flowering cherry). Grows to 7 ft.; hardy to −35°F. Produces white or pink flowers and red cherries.

P. maritima (beach plum). Grows to 10 ft.; hardy to −20°F. Has oval leaves, white flowers, and red plums.

P. nigra. A flowering fruit tree. Grows to 40 ft.; hardy to −10°F. Produces white flowers.

P. subhirtella (rosebud cherry). A flowering fruit tree. Grows to 30 ft.; hardy to −5°F. Produces an abundance of single light pink flowers. One of the earliest to bloom.

P. susquehanae (sand cherry). A flowering fruit tree. Grows to 4 ft.; hardy to −20°F. Has short oval leaves and white flowers.

P. tomentosa (Nanking cherry). Grows to 9 ft.; hardy to −35°F. Produces white flowers and scarlet cherries.

P. triloba (flowering almond). Not really an almond. Grows to 12 ft.; hardy to −10°F. Produces pink-white flowers and red fruit.

P. virginiana (chokecherry). Grows to 12 ft.; hardy to −5°F. Has smooth, shiny green leaves, white flowers, and dark red, harsh-tasting fruit.

PSIDIUM GUAJAVA   *shrub/tree*   Guava

The guava is a dense shrub that reaches 20 ft. It has oval leaves, white flowers, and small, lemonlike, purplish brown fruits. Put the guava in a rich, moist soil, in the sun, and in the heat. It can tolerate temperatures down to 40°F. Take cuttings for new plants.

PTERIS   *houseplant*   Brake fern

These are mostly small, tropical ferns, with feathery fronds, that are perfect for a window garden or for a table decoration. Give them sun in the winter and shade in the summer. Keep the soil consistently moist and the humidity at 50 percent. Mist the foliage frequently. These crowns of these ferns can be easily divided for more ferns.

P. cretica wilsonii. Has slender, 12-in. fronds.

P. ensiformis victoriae (sword brake fern). Has variegated, 12-in. fronds.

P. quadriaurita. Has 24-in., white-and-green fronds.

P. tremula (Australian bracken). Has fast-growing, 24-in., yellow-green fronds.

PULMONARIA ANGUSTIFOLIA   *perennial*   Cowslip lungwort

A plant with a rather curious name, it grows to 26 in. and has narrow dark green leaves and dark blue flowers that bloom for a long time beginning in the spring. This perennial is good for spot color; it likes bright light and some shade and a fairly moist soil. Divide the plants if you want more of them.

'Aurea'—white flowers
'Salmon Glory'—pink flowers
'Sissinghurst White'—white flowers

PUNICA GRANATUM   *shrub/tree*   Pomegranate

Pomegranates are deciduous shrublike trees—or treelike shrubs—that have shiny green leaves, orange-red flowers in the spring, and the familiar red pomegranates and yellow leaves in the fall. Put pomegranate trees in the full sun, and let the soil dry out between waterings. For more trees, either plant seed or buy new plants.

Punica. g. 'Chico'. A dwarf. Produces orange, carnationlike flowers but no fruit.
P. g. 'Nana'. A dwarf growing to 3 ft., with orange-red flowers and small, dry red fruit.

PUSCHKINIA SCILLOIDES   *bulb*   Striped quill

These small bulbs grow to only 12 in. The leaves are broad and strap shaped, pointing upward, and a bit shorter than the stem. The flowers are quite small and blue or whitish, with a blue stripe, and they bloom in the summer. Striped quills like sun, a moderate amount of water, and cool conditions. Plant the bulbs in the fall, 2 to 3 in. apart and 3 in. deep. They can grow undisturbed for years. Get new plants from offsets.

PYRACANTHA   *shrub*   Firethorn

Pyracanthas are grown primarily for their evergreen foliage and brightly colored berries in the fall. The flowers are small, fragrant, and cream colored. Pyracanthas grow rapidly and easily. All of the species have glossy green leaves, and most have thorns. These shrubs do best in the sun and in soil that is allowed to dry out between waterings. They can be trained into almost any shape, and birds love their berries—when they become fermented, they like them even more and sometimes eat enough to become tipsy. Insects do not bother pyracanthas, and both softwood and hardwood cuttings root easily.

P. angustifolia. Grows to 12 ft.; hardy to −10°F. Has prostrate branches and orange berries.
P. atlantioides. Grows to 15 ft.; hardy to −5°F. Has small, bright red berries.
        'Aurea'—somewhat taller and more robust
P. coccinea 'Lulandi'. Grows to 10 ft.; hardy to −20°F. Has red-orange berries.
P. rogersiana 'Flava'. Grows to 10 ft.; hardy to 5°F. Has bright green leaves and orange-red berries.

Pyrethrum Roseum *perennial*

Also called *Chrysanthemum coccineum*, this garden favorite produces daisylike flowers in the summer in red, pink, or white. It has long stems and bright green leaves. These perennials grow to about 2 ft. and do best in the sun, with regular watering, and in a well-drained soil. Divide them for new plants. A source of natural preventative.

Quamoclit (Ipomoea) *vine* Star glory

This long—to 20 ft.—vine grows quickly and bears handsome red flowers on and off during the summer. Give star glories sun, lots of water, and a sandy, loamy soil. They also will need a support such as a trellis, fence, or wall. Buy new plants.

Q. coccinea. A twiner. Produces fragrant scarlet flowers with a yellow throat.
Q. pennata. Has fernlike foliage and small bright red flowers.
Q. sloteri. Has lobed leaves and large red flowers.

Quercus *tree* Oak

Oaks have always been popular, for their sturdiness, longevity, and yellow fall leaves. Although there are many kinds of oaks, most are large, with strong wood that does not split easily. But only the North American oaks have autumn color; the European ones do not. Oak trees are fine shade trees for large areas, each type having a different leaf shape. But oaks are susceptible to diseases and insects, so watch them carefully and use natural sprays if necessary.

Q. alba (white oak). A deciduous tree. Broad, open-crowned growth to 90 ft.; hardy to −35°F. Has bright green leaves turning purplish brown in the fall.
Q. coccinea (scarlet oak). A deciduous tree. Open-branching growth to 75 ft.; hardy to −10°F. Has bright green leaves that turn brilliant red in the fall.
Q. ilex (holly oak). An evergreen tree. Round-headed growth to 60 ft.; hardy to 20°F. Has dark green leaves that are yellow underneath.
Q. laurifolia (laurel oak). A semievergreen tree. Dense, round-topped growth to 60 ft.; hardy to 5°F. Has dark green leaves.
Q. palustris (pin oak). A deciduous tree. Pyramidal growth, with drooping branches, to 75 ft.; hardy to −20°F. Has glossy dark green leaves that turn yellow, then red, and finally brown in the fall.
Q. robur (English oak). A deciduous tree. Broad-headed, open growth to 150 ft.; hardy to −5°F. No fall color.
Q. virginiana (live oak). An evergreen tree. Wide-spreading growth to 60 ft.; hardy to 5°F. Has small, narrow leaves.

Radermachera   *houseplant*

This is an indoor (usually) small evergreen tree, with small, shiny green leaves and yellow, trumpet-shaped flowers. It is happiest in a bright spot in evenly moist soil. This little tree is rarely bothered by insects and can be propagated from cuttings.

R. pentandra. Grows to 15 ft. Has dense foliage.
R. sinica. Grows to 10 ft.

Ranunculus asiaticus   *bulb*

Ranunculus grow to be about 12 in. high and have rather fernlike foliage and brightly colored semidouble to double flowers, slightly resembling roses, in many colors—yellow, white, pink, red, or orange. There are several varieties. Ranunculus bloom in the spring and need sun, a moderate amount of water, and excellent drainage. Dig up the bulbs and store them over the winter; use offsets for new plants. These flowers make good border or bedding plants.

Raphiolepis indica   *shrub*   Indian hawthorn

A shrub growing to about 4 ft. tall, raphiolepis has several uses in the garden—from a hedge to a background to even just a spot of color—for they also bloom in the spring, with pink or sometimes white flowers. The pointed leaves are dense. These shrubs like sun but will tolerate some shade, and like regular watering but can withstand some dryness. Put them in well-drained soil, and divide them for new plants. They are hardy to 5°F and should be pruned into compact shape.

Rebutia   *houseplant*   Crown cactus

These small—1- to 5-in.—barrel-shaped cacti produce brightly colored flowers in the spring. Like most desert plants, the crown cactus does best in the sun but needs more water than do other cacti, except in the winter when it can be kept somewhat dry and cool (55°F). For more plants, divide the clumps.

R. calliantha. A gray-green globe with showy red flowers.
R. cristata. A small globe with white spines and carmine rose flowers.
R. deminuta. A cluster of small globes with rigid spines and orange flowers.
R. kupperiana. A tiny globe with scarlet flowers.
R. minuscula. A flattened globe with white spines and scarlet flowers.
R. pseudodeminuta. A little globe with golden yellow flowers.
R. violaciflora. A depressed olive green globe with purple flowers.

Rechsteineria   *houseplant*   Cardinal flower

These handsome South American gesneriads have velvety green leaves and, in the summer, red, pink, or orange-red tubular flowers. Cardinal flowers need light but not strong sun—a west window is usually ideal. Water them regularly, feed them biweekly while they are actively growing, and maintain the surrounding humidity at about 50 percent. After they have bloomed, leave the tubers in their pots, and store them dry in a cool (55°F), dimly lit place. When they have rested for around three or four months, new growth will begin to appear, and at that point, repot the plants for a new season. For additional plants, plant seeds, take cuttings, or divide the tubers.

R. *cardinalis* (cardinal flower). Grows to 16 in. Has dark green, heart-shaped leaves and 2-in., brilliant red flowers.
R. *leucotricha* (Brazilian edelweiss). Grows to 14 in. Has hairy green leaves and 1-in. rose-coral flowers.
R. *lineata*. Grows to 14 in. Has hairy dark green leaves and clusters of small dark red flowers.
R. *macropoda*. Often confused with R. *cyclophylla*. Grows to 9 in. Has soft, heart-shaped, dark green leaves and brick red flowers.
R. *verticillata* (or R. *purpurea*) (double-decker plant). Grows to 24 in. Has pointed dark green leaves with serrated edges and an abundance of small pink flowers spotted with wine red.

Rehmannia angulata   *perennial*

This 3-ft. plant is evergreen in mild climates and deciduous in colder areas. It has coarse, toothed leaves and rosy red, foxglovelike flowers in the summer. Give it bright light or shade, water it regularly, and divide it if you want more plants.

Reseda odorata   *annual*   Mignonette

The mignonette has not-spectacular light green leaves but wonderfully fragrant flowers with yellow-white petals and saffron-colored anthers. It likes some shade and coolness, and a fair amount of water. The flowers come in the summer and fall; grow new plants from seed.

SUGGESTED VARIETY:
'Goliath'

Rhamnus   *shrub/tree*   Buckthorn

Buckthorns comprise a large group of either evergreen or deciduous shrubs and trees. They generally grow to about 15 ft. and are occasionally used in gardens, for their form and foliage. Buckthorns tolerate sun or part shade, some dryness, a poor soil, and wind—all desirable qualities.

R. cathartica (common buckthorn). Hardy to −50°F. Has shiny green leaves, thorny branches, and black berries.

R. frangula (alder buckthorn). Perhaps the most popular buckthorn. Hardy to −50°F. Has shiny dark green leaves and berries that turn from red to black.

RHAPIS *houseplant* Lady palm

These tough palms have fan-shaped fronds on tall cane stems. They are good plants to put in a north or west window. Plant them in 8- or 10-in. containers, and repot them only every three or four years. Soak the soil and then allow it to dry out before watering it again. In a mild climate, lady palms can be put outside, in the shade. Propagate them from offsets.

R. excelsa. Grows to 60 in. Has leathery, glossy green fronds with three to ten segments.

R. humilis. Slender, more graceful, and slightly smaller than *R. excelsa.*

RHIPSALIDOPSIS *houseplant* Easter cactus

Rhipsalidopsis is a mixed group of plants that are variously termed Thanksgiving cactus, Christmas cactus, and Easter cactus, depending on when they bloom. Most of these plants have arching, drooping, jointed, thick branches (no prickles) that double as leaves. The many flowers bloom at the tips and are usually some shade of pink or red. Put your cactus in a bright, but not sunny, window, and keep the soil moist but not soggy. Let the soil dry out slightly a few times a year, and forget the old admonition to keep it in darkness for a period in order for it to bloom (it's not true). It is easy to grow new plants from cuttings.

R. rosea. The most popular one. Grows to about 20 in. Produces pink flowers.

R. r. 'China Pink'. Has an abundance of flowers.

RHIPSALIS *houseplant* Chain cactus

This spineless (but otherwise resolute), pendant cactus grows to 36 in. and produces white flowers and then colorful berries in the winter. It is best potted in fir bark or a soil mix, given bright light, and kept moist in the summer and somewhat dry in the winter. Cuttings provide more cacti.

R. burchelli. Produces cream-colored flowers and pink berries.

R. capilliformis. Produces cream-colored flowers and white berries.

R. paradoxa. Has triangular stems and produces white flowers and red berries.

RHODODENDRON (including Azalea) *shrub*

Rhododendrons and azaleas are ornamental, either evergreen or deciduous, shrubs that produce spectacular flowers. There are hundreds of species of each. Both rhododendrons and azaleas thrive in a well-drained, acid soil and with lots of water. Too much sun, unless it is in a cool area, is generally not good; filtered sun or partial shade is ideal.

Plant rhododendrons in the early spring while they are blooming, and plant deciduous azaleas when they are dormant unless they are in cans. Plant evergreen azaleas at any time of year except in the late spring and summer, when the buds for the following year are developing.

Rhododendrons and azaleas are shallow rooted, so dry conditions are harmful. Therefore, keep the soil moist, especially in the early summer when the new growth is forming. Use an acid type of fertilizer. Remove dead flowers from rhododendrons so that seeds do not develop.

There are low-growing, spreading, and tall rhododendrons, and azaleas for both mild- and severe-winter climates. The many species, hybrids, and varieties of these plants offer a wide selection for all needs.

R. calophytum. Evergreen. Grows to 15 ft.; hardy to 20°F. Produces large clusters of flowers, white or pale pink with a crimson blotch.
R. laetevirens. An evergreen shrub. Grows to 4 ft.; hardy to −20°F. Produces small pink flowers.
R. luteum. A deciduous shrub. Grows to 12 ft.; hardy to −10°F. Produces fragrant yellow flowers.
R. mucronulatum (Korean rhododendron). A deciduous shrub. Grows to 5 ft.; hardy to −15°F. Produces purple flowers.

R. *obtusum.* A semievergreen shrub. Grows to 3 ft.; hardy to −5°F. Produces orange-to-red flowers.

R. *roseum elegans* (rose-shell rhododendron). Deciduous; grows to 9 ft.; hardy to −20°F. Produces fragrant pink flowers.

R. *schippenbachii* (royal azalea). A deciduous shrub. Grows to 4 ft.; hardy to −20°F. Produces large rose-pink flowers.

R. *strigillosum.* An evergreen shrub. Grows to 20 ft.; hardy to −10°F. Produces brilliant scarlet flowers.

R. *vaseyi* (pink-shell azalea). A deciduous shrub. Grows to 9 ft.; hardy to −10°F. Produces rose-pink flowers.

R. *wardii.* Grows to 10 ft.; hardy to −10°F. Produces yellow flowers.

R. *yedoense.* Deciduous. Grows to 5 ft.; hardy to −5°F. Produces purple flowers.

SUGGESTED VARIETIES:
'Albert'—white flowers
'Blue Diamond'—dark purple–blue flowers
'Britannia'—bright crimson red flowers
'Cadis'—large, fragrant, light pink flowers
'Cecile'—deep salmon-colored flowers with a yellow tinge
'Christmas Cheer'—pink flowers
'Crest'—primrose yellow flowers
'Elizabeth'—large bright rose-pink flowers
'Fedora'—small bright pink flowers
'Salmon Beauty'—large orange flowers
'Knapp Hill Hybrid'—orange or yellow-orange flowers
'Nancy Waterer'—golden yellow flowers
'Pink Pearl'—pink flowers
'Susan'—lavender-blue flowers

Rhoeo SPATHACEA *houseplant* Moses-in-the-cradle

Rhoeo can be grown outdoors in warm climates, but in most areas it is a houseplant. Moses-in-the-cradle has fleshy, olive green, lance-shaped leaves and produces little white flowers almost hidden by the enclosing, boat-shaped bracts. Give this plant bright light, and keep the soil moist. Grow new plants from seed.

R. *discolor.* Has a 12-in. rosette of stiff, dark green (almost black) leaves colored purple underneath.

R. *d. variegata.* Has green leaves with a white border.

Rhynchostylis *houseplant* Foxtail orchid

These large 30-in. orchids have long, leathery, dark green leaves and clusters of small, hanging, fragrant summer flowers. Pot foxtail orchids in fir bark constantly kept moist. Note that these plants do not need to rest; they can be in the full sun all the time. There are many varieties. Buy new orchids from specialists.

R. *gigantea.* Produces great plumes of pink-and-white flowers.

R. *retusa.* Has long stems with 1-in., rose-colored flowers.

Ribes *shrub* Currant/gooseberry

These deciduous or evergreen shrubs produce the familiar currants and gooseberries of jam fame. They can grow to 8 ft. or more. Plant them in sun to light shade, in almost any soil, and water them regularly.

R. odoratum. Hardy to −5°F. Has green leaves that turn bronze-brown in the fall, and good-tasting, small black currants.

R. ova-crispa (*R. grossularia*). This is the famous English gooseberry occasionally grown in the United States. Hardy to −5°F.

Ricinus communis *annual* Castor bean plant

Castor beans can grow rapidly to 15 ft., and thus, even though they are not particularly attractive, they are useful when a green cover is needed in a hurry. The leaves are large and lobed; the flowers are small and white and insignificant. Note, however, that the flowers produce the castor beans—large and mottled—which are poisonous. To prevent the seeds from developing, pinch off the seed capsules when they are small. But for this reason, the castor bean is not a plant to grow if you have young, inquisitive children.

Rivina humilis *houseplant* Rouge plant

One of the handful of species in this genus, the rouge plant has oval leaves, drooping clusters of white flowers, and red berries off and on during the year. Grow this 24-in. plant in a sunny window, and keep the soil moist. Take cuttings for new plants.

Robinia *shrub/tree* Locust

Locusts are deciduous trees or shrubs whose leaves are divided, fernlike, into many roundish leaflets and whose flowers are clusters of pink or white that bloom in the early summer. Locusts can tolerate heat and almost any soil, but their leaves do not change color in the fall, and they do not have interesting fruit. In addition, they are prey to locust borers, and they are difficult to propagate. Buy new plants if you still want them.

R. hispida (rose acacia). A shrub. Grows to 7 ft.; hardy to −10°F. Has oval leaves and rose-colored flowers.

R. nana. A shrub. Grows to 10 ft.; hardy to −10°F. Has small leaves.

R. pseudoacacia (black locust). A tree. Grows to 70 ft.; hardy to −10°F. Has thorny branchlets and fragrant white flowers.

R. viscosa. A tree. Grows to 40 ft.; hardy to −10°F. Produces pink flowers in May and June.

Rochea coccinea   *perennial*

This is a 2-ft. succulent with pointed leaves and tubular, fragrant, bright scarlet flowers that bloom in the late spring or summer. Although this plant is occasionally grown outside in mild climates (it is hardy to 40°F), it is generally considered best as a houseplant. Rochea prefers bright light or shade and little to moderate water.

Rodgersia podophylla   *perennial*   Bronze leaf plant

The 5-ft. bronze-leaf plant is grown, not surprisingly, for its bronze leaves, which are green when they first appear in the spring and then turn bronze in the summer. It also has creamy white flowers, making it a good background plant. Put it in a sunny place, and give it lots of water. Division is the best means of obtaining new plants.

Rohdea japonica   *houseplant*

This is a favorite houseplant in China and Japan (it can be grown outside in the shade in warm areas), with its white flowers and stiff dark green leaves that form a rosette. In the fall, red berries form from the flowers. It does best in bright light, with constantly moist soil. Rohdea grows slowly to 24 in. and can live for years without much attention. Wipe the leaves with a damp cloth once a month or so, and take cuttings for more plants.

R.j. marginata. Has dark green leaves with a white border.

Romneya coulteri   *perennial*   California tree poppy

These tall (to 8 ft.) plants are native to southern and Baja California. Their stems and deeply cut leaves are gray-green; their large crepe-papery, fragrant flowers are white. Matilija poppies thrive in the sun, in a place with excellent drainage and a bit on the dry side. They look best as accent plants. Divide them for new poppies.

R. c. trihocalyx. Produces saucer-shaped, white flowers with yellow centers.

SUGGESTED VARIETY:
'White Cloud'—white flowers

Rosa *perennial*   **Rose**

Roses are, without doubt, the most popular garden flower, if not the most popular flower, period. They are deciduous (there are a few evergreen ones for the warmest climates) and come in a variety of sizes and types (bushy or climbing). And of course, there are an abundance of colors, single or double flowers, and on and on. Very generally, roses need sun, regular watering, good drainage, good air circulation, fertilizer after each time they bloom, and a watchful eye for aphids, spider mites, and thrips, as well as such fungus diseases as mildew, rust, and black spot. They need to be insulated in the winter in freezing climates and severely cut back in milder climates. When you cut off the flowers, snip them just above a five-leaflet leaf; in that way the rose will send up new growth in its place. For new roses, buy bare-root plants if you can. The following are just a fraction of the roses available:

R. bracteata 'Mermaid'. Grows to 4 ft.; hardy to 10°F. Produces single, yellow, 9-in. flowers.

R. centifolia 'Muscosa' (moss rose). Grows to 6 ft.; hardy to −50°F. Produces very fragrant pink, white, or red flowers.

R. 'Charlotte Armstrong'. Produces blood red flowers.

R. 'Elizabeth of Glamis'. Produces deep salmon–colored flowers.

R. foetida. Grows to 10 ft.; hardy to −35°F. Has dark green leaves and single, yellow flowers.

R. gallica (French rose). Grows to 4 ft.; hardy to −10°F. Produces red or purple flowers.

R. 'Golden Rambler'. Produces fragrant yellow flowers in the early spring and summer.

R. 'Golden Slippers'. Produces red-yellow flowers.

R. hugonis (Father Hugo's rose). Grows to 8 ft.; hardy to −35°F. Has dark green leaves and bright yellow flowers.

R. moyesii (Moyes rose). Grows to 9 ft.; hardy to −5°F. Produces single, blood red flowers.

R. multiflora (Japanese rose). Grows to 10 ft.; hardy to −35°F. Produces clusters of small white flowers.

R. 'New Dawn'. A climbing rose. Produces pink flowers.

R. 'Royal Highness'. Produces large, fragrant, light pink flowers.

R. rugosa (rugosa rose). Grows to 6 ft.; hardy to −35°F. Has glossy green leaves and single or double flowers in a variety of colors.

R. spinosissima (Scotch rose). Grows to 3 ft.; hardy to −10°F. Produces single, pink, white, or yellow flowers.

R. 'Sutter's Gold'. Produces golden yellow flowers.

Rubus *shrub*

These shrubs are most often grown not for their looks but for their berries—such as blackberries and raspberries. Some varieties can reach 15 ft., need sun or light shade, moderate-to-less water, good drainage, and any soil. And they do need to be pruned regularly. Brambles have ruffled bright green leaves but no thorns. Before the berries come white flowers.

RUDBECKIA *perennial/annual* Gloriosa daisy, black-eyed susan

Growing to 36 in., these garden plants offer large, showy flowers in several colors. Once they begin blooming, they continue through the summer into the fall. Place them in the sun and in a loamy, well-drained soil, and water them regularly. The daisylike flowers are good for both background plants and cut flowers. Divide them for additional plants. There are many varieties.

R. gloriosa (gloriosa daisy). A black-eyed susan, with large, golden yellow flowers with a dark brown center.

R. laciniata (cut-leaf coneflower). Produces large yellow flowers marked inside with green.

SUGGESTED VARIETIES:
'Goldquelle'—bright orange flowers
'Goldstrum'—yellow-orange flowers
'Irish Eyes'—orange flowers
'Marmalade'—orange flowers

RUELLIA *houseplant*

Ruellias are graceful plants, with dark green leaves and pale pink, red, or white flowers from the fall through spring. They grow best in the full sun, with the soil kept barely moist. Indeed, too much water can harm them.

Ruellias look nice in baskets and also in a window. Take cuttings for additional plants.

R. amoena. Grows to 24 in. Has wavy oval leaves and red flowers.
R. macrantha. Grows to 40 in. Has dark green leaves and rose-colored flowers.
R. makoyana. Grows to 18 in. Has green leaves with silver veins and carmine red flowers.

RUMEX   *perennial*

This group of plants contains the sorrels, which can be used as a flavoring herb in salads and soups but are often considered weeds. In either case, rumex thrives in bright light, with a moderate amount of water, and blooms in the summer. For new plants (if you do not regard them as weeds), plant seeds.

R. acetosa. This is the common garden sorrel herb.
R. crispus. This is the common dock, considered a weed by all and highly undesirable in any garden.

SABAL PALMETTO   *tree*

This is a slow-growing fan palm, eventually reaching 20 ft., though it becomes much taller in its native southeastern states. The cabbage palm's long (5 to 8 ft.) fronds grow in a dense cluster at the top of the trunk. It needs sun and regular watering and does well in almost any soil. Cabbage palms can tolerate temperatures down to 40°F and can be divided for new plants.

SAGINA SUBULATA   *perennial*   Irish/Scotch moss

A tiny creeper, this mosslike plant is mainly used as a ground cover. Unlike the true mosses, however, this pseudomoss requires some sun (that is, only partial shade), ample water, good drainage, and a good soil. It grows only a few inches high and is often found between stepping-stones. Sagina's flowers are insignificant, but note that the difference between the Irish and Scotch types is that the Irish moss is green and the Scotch moss is golden green. Obtain new plants by means of division.

SAINTPAULIA IONANTHA   *houseplant*   African violet

There now are thousands of varieties of the familiar African violets, in countless leaf and flower shapes, colors, and sizes (including miniature). The leaves of African violets may be velvety or somewhat smooth; scalloped, smooth edged, or wavy; lance or heart shaped; or plain green or variegated.

The flowers, which bloom off and on during the year, may be single, double, or semidouble; small, medium sized, or large; and shades of red, blue, pink, purple, white, magenta, or lavender.

When potting African violets, be sure to use packaged sterilized soil, or buy soil specifically for them. Place them in the pot so that the crown is slightly above the soil line. Give them bright light in the spring and summer, some sun in the fall and winter, and always good air circulation. Keep the soil moist but never wet. And water your violets carefully, never allowing the crown to get wet (this will rot and then kill the plant). In addition, use only tepid water, as cold water will spot the leaves. Bottom watering (placing the pot in a saucer or bowl of water and letting the plant absorb it) is often advised, to ensure that the roots receive adequate moisture. Try alternating top and bottom watering. Be sure that the pot drains well; don't let it stand in water.

Propagate African violets from seed or leaf cuttings: Cut off a medium-sized leaf; in a pot of soil, make an angled hole about the size of the diameter of the stem; and insert the leaf (stem), with some stem still above the soil. Press the soil gently around the stem to hold it in place. Keep the leaf moist and in a bright light. After several weeks, you should see new growth beginning to peak above the soil. If this plant turns out to have multiple crowns, then later, when the plant is established and big enough to stand on its own, so to speak, you may want to separate them, carefully, potting each one in its own container. The following are just a few of the available varieties of African violets:

'Alakazam'—double lavender flowers
'Big Boy Blue'—double blue flowers
'Chateaugay'—double blue-purple flowers
'Cochise'—semidouble, star-shaped, red flowers
'Flash'—double rose-pink flowers
'Happy Time'—double pink flowers
'Lady Wilson'—double lavender-blue flowers edged with white
'Miniature White Girl'—single white flowers
'Pink Rook'—double pink flowers
'Purple Knight'—single dark purple flowers
'Red Honey'—double red flowers
'Spitfire'—single deep pink flowers fringed with white
'Tommie Lou'—double lavender flowers
'White Perfection'—immense double white flowers
'Zorro'—double lavender flowers

Salix   *shrub/tree*   Willow

Willows may be either trees or shrubs; they all are deciduous, like lots of water and moist conditions, are wide and spreading, and grow even in poor soils. They prefer cold winters. Although willows are graceful, lovely trees, they do have invasive roots and are prey to tent caterpillars, aphids, borers,

and spider mites. Keep your weapons at hand. Softwood and hardwood cuttings root easily.

S. babylonica (Babylon weeping willow). The best of the willows. Grows to 30 ft.; hardy to −5°F. Has long, pendulous branches and fine-textured foliage.

S. bebbiana. Grows to 40 ft.; hardy to 5°F. Has oval leaves.

S. caprea (goat willow). Grows to 27 ft.; hardy to −10°F. Has broad, dark green branches.

S. chrysoloma. Grows to 70 ft.; hardy to −10°F. Has golden yellow leaves.

S. discolor (pussy willow). Grows to 20 ft.; hardy to −20°F. Has bright green leaves.

S. fragilis. Grows to 60 ft.; hardy to −15°F. Has brittle twigs and long, toothed, bright green leaves.

S. lucida Grows to 20 ft.; hardy to −35°F. Has shiny, finely toothed, oval leaves.

S. matsudana 'Tortuosa' (corkscrew willow). Upright, pyramidal growth to 50 ft.; hardy to −20°F. Has narrow, bright green leaves.

SALPIGLOSSIS SINUATA   *annual*   Painted tongue

A member of the nightshade family, the painted-tongue grows to 20 in. and, in the summer, produces showy, funnel-shaped, dark purple or straw-colored, often striped, flowers. It does well in the sun and in a loamy soil with a moderate amount of water. These annuals are good in flower beds and also make good cut flowers. There are many varieties; grow new plants from seed.

'Bolero'—mixed colors
'Splash'—bright mixed colors
'Superbissima'—large flowers

SALVIA   *perennial/annual*   **Sage**

Salvia is a 36-in. plant that bears tiers of white, red, purple, or blue flowers in the summer. It needs a loamy, well-drained soil that is watered regularly, and sun, although it can also grow in shade. Salvias are good bedding plants and look best grown in clumps, by themselves. Divide the perennials, and plant seeds for the annuals.

S. haematodes. (perennial) Produces spires of blue flowers.
S. horminum. An annual. Produces tiers of purple flowers.
S. picherii. (azurea) (perennial) Produces large blue flowers.
S. splendens (scarlet sage). A shrubby perennial. Produces red flowers.
S. superba (violet sage). A perennial. Produces tall spires of blue-purple flowers.

SUGGESTED VARIETIES:
'Argent White'—white flowers
'East Friesland'—blue flowers
'Flamenco'—red flowers
'Victoria'—blue flowers
'Wrightii'—blue flowers

SAMBUCUS   *shrub*   **Elderberry**

These fast-growing shrubs (some trees) become large and rampant unless pruned. Their flowers are small and white and bloom in the spring, and the berries are blue, black, or red. Elderberries do well in either sun or shade and with an average amount of water—or a lot if the soil drains readily. The American elderberries are used for jams, and both the berries and the flowers can be made into wine. Improved varieties of the red and the American elder are available with larger flowers, and for a quick cover—or the ingredients for jam or wine—elderberries are useful. They are usually not bothered by insects, and softwood and hardwood cuttings root easily.

S. canadensis (American elder). Grows to 12 ft.; hardy to −35°F. Produces white flowers and blue-to-black berries.
S. racemosa 'Plumosa Aurea' (red elder). Grows to 12 ft.; hardy to −20°F. Has golden leaves and yellow berries.

SANGUINARIA CANADENSIS   *perennial*   **Bloodroot**

This harbinger of spring belongs to the poppy family. Bloodroots grow to only 8 in. or so and produce white, lilylike flowers in early spring—a welcome sight after a hard winter. The sap of bloodroots is red (hence their nickname) and is poisonous to both animals and humans. These little plants thrive in sun or shade and in a moist soil. They can withstand temperatures down to −35°F and can be divided.

SANSEVIERIA   *houseplant*   Snake plant

This is another of those houseplants for dark, difficult places and/or beginning or definitely untalented gardeners. It is nearly indestructible. The snake plant has sharply pointed, thick leaves that are variously mottled or marked. Some kinds grow upright, and others form a ground-hugging rosette. They survive in either sun or dark places, and they can accept either moisture or dryness—in the latter, however, remaining attractive but hardly changing in size. Mature plants produce tall sprays of fragrant, pink-white flowers. Propagate snake plants from offsets.

S. cylindrica. Grows to 60 in. Has arching, dark green leaves, several to a shoot.
S. ehrenbergii. Grows slowly to 18 in. Has blue leaves edged with white.
S. parva. Has a dense, 18-in.-wide rosette of green leaves with dark green crossbands.
S. trifasciata laurentii. Grows to 30 in. Has lance-shaped green leaves with yellow bands.

SANTOLINA CHAMAECYPARISSUS   *shrub*   Lavender cotton

Lavender cotton is a bushy shrub growing to 36 in., with very crowded, whitish gray (the lavender "cotton") leaves and small yellow flower heads that bloom in the summer. It is sometimes used as a ground cover or for edges or borders. Give this perennial sun and a moderate amount of water, and take cuttings in the spring for more plants.

SANVITALIA PROCUMBENS   *annual*   Creeping zinnia

This is not really a zinnia, creeping or otherwise, but it does look like one. It grows to only 4 to 6 in. high but can spread out a foot or more. The creeping zinnia's leaves look like miniature real zinnia leaves, and its flowers—yellow or orange with dark purple-brown centers—also look like zinnia flowers. Give this impostor plant sun and regular watering in a readily draining soil. It blooms from the summer through the fall; use it for those places where you want a low cover. Start new plants from seed.

SUGGESTED VARIETY:
'Goldbird'—yellow flowers

SAPONARIA   *perennial*   Soapwort

Saponarias come in two sizes, small (to 6 in.) and large (to 3 ft.). The small ones can be used in rock gardens, the large ones as background plants.

Soapworts prosper in the sun and with a moderate amount of water in a well-drained soil, and in the summer they bear pink flowers. Divide them for new plants.

S. ocymoides. A trailing soapwort with pink flowers.
S. officinalis. A tall soapwort with clusters of airy pink flowers.

Sarcococca ruscifolia   *shrub*

This evergreen shrub grows to about 6 ft. and has waxy, dark green, ruffle-edged leaves and fragrant white flowers in the early spring. It prefers the shade but will tolerate some sun in cool areas, and it needs an average amount of water in a rich soil. Watch out for scale on this plant, which can be divided. Sarcococca is often used in shaded areas where little else will grow. It is hardy down to −5°F.

Satureja   *perennial/annual*   Savory

This group of low-growing, aromatic herbs is a member of the mint family. Water savory regularly, and it will bloom from spring until fall, with small white or lavender-pink flowers. This herb also requires sun and a moist, rich, readily draining soil. Softwood cuttings provide more plants.

S. alpina (alpine savory). Branches and leaves stay green into the winter.
S. hortensis (common summer savory). Bushy growth and fragrant white flowers.
S. vulgaris (wild savory). Good for woodland gardens.

Saxifraga stolonifera   *houseplant*   Strawberry geranium

This is neither a strawberry nor a geranium, but it is an easy-to-grow houseplant. The strawberry geranium has geraniumlike leaves that are green with white veins and pink underneath, and it sends out runners, as strawberries do. The flowers are white. These trailing plants look good in baskets, dish gardens, or terrariums and on windowsills. Give them bright light and some shade, and a fair amount of water, though less in the winter. Mealybugs also like this plant; keep an eye out for them. Grow more strawberry geraniums by planting the runners.

S. sarmentosa. The most common species. Grows to 20 in. Has coarsely toothed, reddish leaves with white veins, and white flowers.
S. s. 'Tricolor'. Grows to 18 in. Has dark green-and-white leaves with rosy red edges and undersides.

SCABIOSA   *annual*   **Pincushion flower**

Pincushion flowers are so named because their stamens extend beyond the flower cluster, like pins sticking out of a pincushion. These annuals grow to 36 in. high, and their flowers, usually blue, rose, or white, bloom from the summer until the first frost. They like sun and a moderate amount of water in a well-drained, loamy soil. Pincushion flowers last a long time when cut, and they also look good in beds or massed by themselves. Obtain new plants from seed.

S. atropurpurea. Produces crimson flowers.
S. caucasica. Produces large, pale blue flowers.

SUGGESTED VARIETY:
'Floral Queen'—blue flowers

SCHEFFLERA   *houseplant*

Tough plants, scheffleras grow to 60 in., with leaves divided into leaflets that look like fingers on a hand. They prefer bright light, regular watering, and a rich soil. Scheffleras are good choices for public rooms, and when grown outside in warm climates, they may reach the size of small trees. New plants can be had from cuttings or half-ripened stems.

S. actinophylla. Brassaia (Queensland umbrella). Fast growing, with large, palmate, "umbrella" leaves and greenish flowers.
S. digitata. Has hairy yellow leaves with seven to ten "fingers," and greenish yellow flowers. Needs a cooler location than does *S. actinophylla.*

SCHIZANTHUS PINNATUS   *annual*   **Butterfly flower**

Also known as the poor man's orchid, this plant grows to 24 in. and produces huge quantities of small, orchidlike flowers in the spring. The flowers range in color from white to reddish brown. Give butterfly flowers shade, especially from the noon sun, an average amount of water, and cool conditions. For more flowers, plant seed.

SUGGESTED VARIETIES:
'Angel Wings'—white flowers
'Bouquet Series'—mixed colors
'Hit Parade'—mixed colors

SCHIZOSTYLIS COCCINEA   *bulb*   **Crimson flag**

This grassy plant from South Africa grows to 2 ft. and produces deep crimson flowers in the summer. It requires sun and lots of water and grows in almost any soil. Crimson flags are good accent plants. Divide them for more plants.

SUGGESTED VARIETIES:
'Grandiflora'—large flowers
'Sunrise'—pink flowers

SCHLUMBERGERA   *houseplant*   Christmas cactus

The Christmas cactus blooms at Christmastime, hence its name. It is not however a desert cactus, but an epiphytic plant that grows to 24 in. and has scalloped, jointed branches that double as leaves. Its flowers, which grow from the ends of the stems, may be pink, red, or salmon. In the fall and winter, give the Christmas cactus only a little water, keeping the soil barely moist. Then, in the spring and summer, give it lots of water. From mid October, put it in the sun during the day, and see that it has twelve hours of uninterrupted darkness at night, in a cool location (55°F), so that it can set its buds. The humidity should be around 60 percent. The Christmas cactus prefers a potting mixture of leaf mold, sand, and shredded osmunda. Take cuttings for more plants.

S. bridgesii. Produces red flowers.
S. b. 'Parna'. Produces small, bright red flowers.
S. b. 'Pink Perfection'. Produces large, bright clear red flowers.
S. b. 'Salmonea'. Produces scarlet flowers.

SCILLA   *bulb*   Bluebell

Good where masses of color are needed in the spring, these 10-in. plants bear blue (usually) flowers. They are easy to grow, requiring sun and regular

watering; they become dormant in the summer, however. There are species for all climates—check with your local nursery. Most scillas are planted in the fall, the bulbs spaced 5 in. apart and 3 in. deep. Use offsets for new plants.

S. hispanica. Usually produces blue flowers, although they can also be pink, rose-purple, white, or light salmon.
S. nutans (English bluebell). Produces white, purple, pink, or blue, bell-shaped flowers.
S. sibirica. Produces blue, bell-shaped flowers.

SCINDAPSUS   *houseplant*   Pothos

These vines, growing to 36 in. long, have smooth, heart-shaped, dark green leaves splashed with yellow, white, or silver. These plants are suitable for even difficult places: Give them bright but not strong light, a soil kept both moist and well drained, and some humidity. Scindapsus also looks good in a basket. Propagate it from cuttings.

S. aureus. Has 12-in., dark green leaves streaked with yellow.
S. a. 'Marble Queen'. Has dark green leaves streaked with white.
S. a. 'Orange Queen'. Has apricot-and-yellow leaves.
S. a. 'Silver Moon'. Has creamy yellow leaves.
S. pictus 'Argyraeus'. Has 6-in., satiny green leaves edged with silver.

SCUTELLARIA INTEGRIFOLIA   *perennial*   Skullcap

Skullcap is a 26-in.-tall plant that produces 1-in.-wide blue, violet, or red flowers in the summer. These perennials are good additions to a flower border or a rock garden. Besides sun and a moderate amount of water, they need a well-drained soil. Divide them to get more plants.

SEDUM   *perennial*   Stonecrop

This large group of plants generally does not grow over 12 in. high. They are particularly good for soil conditions in which nothing else can survive, and they are used mainly in rock gardens. Sedums are succulents from all regions of the world; some grow upright and others are trailing. The tiny varieties are used as a ground cover, and the larger ones can be grown in containers. Sedums bear small, sometimes brightly colored, star-shaped flowers in the summer and fall. They require sun and an average amount of water, but they can survive drought. Their stem cuttings root very readily, and there are many species and varieties.

S. acre (goldmoss sedum). Grows to 2 in. Makes a good mat or ground cover.
S. adolphii. Grows to 6 in. Has slightly curved leaves and white flowers.
S. morganianum (donkey tail). Often grown as a houseplant. Has pendulous stems of fleshy, overlapping, braided-seeming leaves.
S. sieboldii. Grows to 12 in. Produces pink flowers.

SELAGINELLA *houseplant* Club moss

Selaginella is a genus of small, ferny plants that are suitable for terrariums and dish gardens. Some are attractive hanging plants, and others are creepers good for covering the soil in the pots of larger plants. Grow club moss in a shady spot. Soak the soil, and then let it dry out between waterings, making sure not to spill any water on the leaves, as it will rot them. Take cuttings for new plants.

S. kraussiana. A creeper to 12 in., with tiny, bright green leaves.
S. lepidophylla (resurrection plant). A 6-in. ball of leaves. When dry, it is a dense mat; then when it is soaked, it revives.
S. martensii variegata. An upright grower to 12 in., with lacy, silver-tipped leaves.
S. uncinata. A creeper to 24 in., with blue-green leaves.
S. willdeovii. A climber to 10 in., with blue-green leaves.

SELENICEREUS *houseplant* Night-blooming cereus

Climbing to 7 ft. and bearing fragrant flowers in the summer (and at night, presumably), the night-blooming cereus can be allowed either to climb or hang on a support. Although it grows too large for a window, it can be put on a sun porch. Plant the night-blooming cereus in a sandy soil in a 5- or 6-in. pot, and give it sun in the winter and shade in the summer. Water it moderately in the fall and winter, and soak it the rest of the year. For more plants, take cuttings or buy them.

S. donkelaari. Produces 7-in. white flowers.
S. grandiflorus (queen-of-the-night). Produces 7-in. white or salmon pink flowers.
S. macdonaldiae. Produces 12-in. gold-and-white flowers.
S. pteranthus. Produces 12-in. white flowers.

SEMPERVIVUM *perennial* Hen-and-chickens

These succulents have stemless rosettes of leaves that measure from a half to 12 in. in diameter. They are good for rock gardens or wherever a covering is needed. Heads of white, yellow, or pink flowers open in the summer; then, when the flowering plants die, they are soon replaced by new ones. Give these succulents morning or afternoon sun and a moderately moist soil, and grow new plants from the offsets in the leaf axils.

S. arachnoideum (cobweb houseleek). A curiously nicknamed plant, with tiny gray-green rosettes growing to 4 in. across, joined by white hairs, cobweblike, and red flowers.
S. montanum. Has pointed, fleshy green rosettes growing to 6 in. across, and purple flowers.
S. tectorum calcareum (hen-and-chickens). Has leathery, light green rosettes growing to 12 in. across, and pink flowers. The "mother" rosette is soon joined by little "baby" rosettes.

SENECIO   *perennial*

These relatives of the daisy comprise a big group of plants, from the familiar dusty miller to cineraria to succulents, vines, and even shrubs. Most of these plants require cool conditions in bright light or shade, and an average amount of water in a loamy soil. They bloom in the spring and summer. Seeds are the best way to get new plants.

S. cineraria (dusty miller). Grows to 2.5 ft. Has small gray leaves and heads of white or yellow flowers.
S. cruentus. Grows to 3 ft. Produces masses of purplish red flowers.
S. elegans. Grows to 2 ft. Produces purple flowers with yellow centers.

SHEPHERDIA ARGENTEA   *shrub*   Silver buffaloberry

This deciduous shrub grows to about 5 or 6 ft. tall—good for hedges or as a background for flowers. Its leaves are long, oval, and silvery, and it bears bright red or orange berries in the fall. The silver buffaloberry is very tough, withstanding temperatures down to −50°F. Cuttings provide new plants.

SHORTIA GALACIFOLIA   *perennial*   Oconee bell

This ground cover grows to only 4 to 6 in. high. Its evergreen leaves turn bronze in the winter, and it produces white, bell-shaped flowers in the summer. Give it shade and lots of water in an acid soil. It reproduces itself by means of underground stems.

SIDALCEA CANDIDA   *perennial*   Prairie mallow

The prairie mallow grows to 48 in. tall, with palm-shaped leaves and, in the summer, branching spikes of cup-shaped, pink-to-crimson flowers. These plants need lots of sun and water and good drainage. Use them as border plants or in groups as accent plants. Prairie mallows spread quickly by themselves, but to hurry the process, divide them.

SILENE   *perennial*

There are many species of silene, some growing upright and others growing cushionlike. They all prefer sun with some shade and regular watering in a well-drained soil. In the summer, silene produces pink or lavender flowers. Grow new plants from seed.

S. armeria. Produces many clusters of pink flowers.
S. pendula. Produces fewer flowers than does *S. armeria*, and they are bluish white.

SINNINGIA *houseplant*   Gloxinia

These gesneriads from tropical Brazilian forests have single or double, tubular or slipper-shaped flowers in bright colors. Although some species are dormant in the winter, most of the newer hybrids bloom intermittently throughout the year. The tubers should be planted in the spring or fall: Put one tuber, hollow side up, in a 5-in. pot, and cover it with equal parts of sand, loam, and peat moss. Keep the pot in a warm place and the soil barely moist until the first leaves appear; then increase the water. Be sure not to get water on the leaves. Feed the plants regularly while they are actively growing. After the flowers have faded, gradually decrease the watering. Then cut off the tops of the plants, and store the tubers, in the pots, in a cool, dark place, again keeping the soil barely moist. Rest them for six to ten weeks (but no more, or they will lose their vitality). Repot the tubers in fresh soil in larger pots. For more plants, take cuttings or divide the roots.

S. barbata. Has bluish green leaves and white flowers streaked with red.
S. concinna. Produces small, tubular, lavender flowers with white throats.
S. pusilla. Perhaps the tiniest of all houseplants. Produces single, tubular, pale lavender flowers.
S. regina. Has velvety dark green leaves with white veins, and tubular, dark purple flowers.
S. speciosa. Has oval green leaves and slipper-shaped, pink or blue flowers.
S. s. 'Cinderella'. Produces single red flowers with white edges.
S. s. 'Dollbaby'. Produces single, tubular, lavender flowers.
S. s. 'Wyoming Glory'. Produces double bright red flowers with white edges.

SISYRINCHIUM ANGUSTIFOLIUM *perennial*   Blue-eyed grass

Blue-eyed grass is a member of the iris family and is often seen in flower borders. If it has sun and regular watering in almost any soil, it will produce flowers, generally in the spring, from purple to white to yellow. Blue-eyed grass can be divided and can tolerate temperatures down to −35°F.

SKIMMIA *shrub*

This evergreen shrub grows to about 4 ft. tall and has shiny green leaves, tiny white flowers, and red berries in the fall. It likes light to moderate shade (neither sun nor full shade) and an average amount of water. Skimmia is, however, susceptible to several insects, including thrips, skimmia mites, and red spider mites. Seed or division provides more plants. They are hardy down to −20°F.

SMITHIANTHIA *houseplant* Temple bells

Temple bells are gesneriads, with brightly colored leaves and bell-shaped flowers from November through May. In March or April, plant each rhizome 1 in. deep in soil, in a 4- or 5-in. pot. Grow the plants in an east or south window, and keep the soil moist and the surrounding humidity fairly high. After the plants have bloomed, store the rhizomes for about three months, dry, in their pots in a cool, shaded place. Then repot them and return them to a bright window. For additional temple bells, either plant seeds or divide the rhizomes.

S. cinnabarina. Grows to 16 in. Has serrated leaves covered with red hairs, and orange-red flowers.

S. multiflora. Grows to 20 in. Has deep green leaves and creamy, unspotted flowers.

S. zebrina. Grows to 30 in. Has round, dark green leaves marked with brown or purple and covered with silvery hairs, and bright red flowers spotted with darker red.

Cornell series hybrids. Produce flowers of various colors: apricot colored—'Cloisters'; peach colored—'Abbey'; red—'Carmel'; and straw yellow—'San Gabriel'.

SOLANDRA GUTTATA *vine* Cup-of-gold vine

A southern Florida plant, this vine can grow to 15 ft. long, and true to its name, it bears large, fragrant, yellow, cup-shaped flowers in the summer. The cup-of-gold vine needs warmth and sun and a moist soil. In frost-free areas, it is often used as an accent plant. Propagate this vine by means of air layering.

SOLANUM *houseplant*

Solanums are evergreen and deciduous shrubs and vines that include potatoes and eggplants. But the most popular nonedible solanums are the Jerusalem cherry and the potato vine—known not for potatoes but for its fragrant, star-shaped flowers. Both plants need bright light and a soil kept barely moist. In the winter, keep them cool, at about 50°F. If you want to keep them for more than one year, set them outside in the spring when the weather is fairly warm, and prune them down to about 10 in. You can also propagate solanums from seed.

S. jasminoides (potato vine). A shrubby climber to 72 in., with purplish green leaves, and fragrant white, or white tinged with blue, flowers in the fall or winter.

S. pseudocapsicum (Jerusalem cherry). Grows upright to 36 in. Produces white flowers, and red or yellow fruit in the fall and winter.

Solidago *perennial*   Goldenrod

First of all, goldenrod is not the plant that causes hayfever; it is often confused with ragweed, which is indeed the culprit and near which goldenrod sometimes grows. Indeed, goldenrod is a nice plant, growing to 36 in. with plumes of yellow flowers in the late summer. It does well in either sun or light shade, and it needs regular watering in a not-too-rich soil. Divide goldenrod for more plants.

Sollya heterophylla *vine*

An evergreen vine, sollya is grown mainly in the southern United States, where its clusters of long, brilliant blue, bell-shaped flowers bloom in the summer. With sun and regular watering, this vine can grow to 10 ft. Cuttings provide new plants.

Sophora *shrub/tree*

Sophoras can be either evergreen or deciduous, with leaves divided into leaflets, as well as fragrant, violet-blue or yellow flowers resembling sweet peas, followed by seed-bearing pods in the fall. Sophoras generally grow slowly (and hence they are shrubs, and not trees, for quite a while) and will grow even in a poor, sandy, dry soil. They are not usually bothered by insects and sometimes can be propagated by means of softwood cuttings.

S. microphylla. An evergreen. Grows to 40 ft.; hardy to −20°F. Has small leaflets and yellow flowers.
S. secundiflora (Texas mountain laurel). An evergreen. Grows upright to 20 ft.; hardy to −5°F. Produces violet-colored flowers in the early spring.
S. tetraptera. A deciduous, narrow tree. Grows to 40 ft.; hardy to 10°F. Produces yellow flowers in the spring; the leaves usually drop just before they bloom.

Sorbus *tree*   Mountain ash

These deciduous trees have long, oval, fernlike leaves, clusters of white flowers in the spring, and red berries in the fall. They require average conditions: sun or light shade, regular watering, and good drainage. Mountain ash trees also can tolerate heat, cold, and wind. They are, however, prey to borers, especially in the eastern United States, and they are difficult to propagate.

S. americana (American mountain ash). Grows to 30 ft.; hardy to −40°F. Has small leaflets and tiny flowers.
S. aucuparia (European mountain ash). Grows to 30 ft.; hardy to −35°F. Produces small white flowers in May and bright red berries in the fall.

S. cashmariana (Kashmir mountain ash). Grows to 40 ft.; hardy to −10°F. Produces pink flowers and red berries.

S. cuspidata. Grows to 20 ft.; hardy to −10°F. Produces creamy white flowers.

S. intermedia. Grows to 30 ft.; hardy to −10°F. Has grayish green leaves.

S. villmorinii. Grows to 20 ft.; hardy to −5°F. Produces small white flowers in the spring and red berries that turn to white in the fall.

SPARAXIS *bulb* Harlequin flower

The harlequin flower has narrow, sword-shaped leaves and, in the spring, spikes of small, funnel-shaped flowers in yellow, pink, purple, red, or white. In the fall, plant the bulbs just 1 in. deep, and at first, water them moderately. When they begin to send up leaves, increase the water. Be sure that the plants are in a sunny place, with the temperature at night not lower than 55°F or the flowers will wither. After the harlequin flowers have finished blooming, allow the leaves to dry up gradually. In the fall, add fresh soil. For more plants, either divide the bulbs or use offsets.

S. grandiflora. Produces yellow or purple flowers.

S. tricolor. Produces brown-purple flowers.

SPARMANNIA AFRICANA *shrub/tree* African linden

This evergreen shrub (or small tree) grows quickly to 10 or even 20 ft. It has hairy, pale green leaves and white flowers in the winter and spring (it is a warm-climate shrub). The African linden needs sun, plenty of water, and pruning, to keep it in bounds. It is vulnerable to spider mites. New shrubs can be started from stem-tip cuttings in the fall.

S. a. Produces single flowers.

S. a. forepleno. Produces double flowers.

SPATHIPHYLLUM *houseplant*

These 20-in. plants are from South America and have shiny green leaves and flowers carried in bracts called spathes, which resemble anthuriums. Spathiphyllums usually bloom in the winter, sometimes in the summer or fall. Put them in a bright spot, and keep the soil moist except in the winter when they should be kept fairly dry. Divide them for new plants.

S. cannaefolium. Grows to 24 in. Has leathery, black-green leaves.

S. clevelandii. Grows to 20 in. Has long leaves and white flowers.

S. communtatum. Grows to 30 in. Has broad, elliptical, green leaves.

S. floribundum. A dwarf, grows to only 14 in. Has green leaves and white flowers.

S. f. 'Marion Wagner'. Grows to 30 in. Has quilted, rich green leaves.

S. f. 'Mauna Loa'. Grows to 30 in. Has satiny, dark green leaves.

SUGGESTED VARIETIES:
'Petite'—dwarf
'Queen Amazonica'—large leaves

SPIREA   *shrub*

Spirea, a deciduous shrub, is easy to grow and, depending on the species, bloom with white, pink, or red flowers in the spring or summer. They also come in many sizes, from 2 to 8 ft. tall. All grow in sun or light shade, need an average amount of water, and thrive in all kinds of soils. Spirea requires little pruning and does not seem to be bothered by insects.

S. billiardii macrothyrsa (billiard spirea). A hybrid. Has arching branches and grows to 6 ft.; hardy to −10°F. Produces tiny, bright rose-colored flowers.
S. bumalda 'Anthony Waterer'. Grows to 2 ft.; hardy to −5°F. Has narrow, oval leaves and bright red flowers.
S. prunifolia 'Plena' (bridal wreath spirea). Grows to 6 ft.; hardy to −10°F. Has green leaves that turn orange in the fall, and double white flowers.
S. salcifolia. Grows to 6 ft.; hardy to −10°F. Has long, double-toothed, dark green leaves and pale rose or rose-white flowers.
S. thunbergii (Thunberg spirea). Grows to 5 ft.; hardy to −10°F. Has leathery branchlets and white flowers.
S. vanhouttei. The most valued spirea. Grows to 6 ft.; hardy to −10°F. Has arching branches and clusters of white flowers.
S. virginiana. Grows to 5 ft.; hardy to 10°F. Has slender branches.

SPREKELIA FORMOSISSIMA   *bulb*   Jacobean/Aztec lily

This lily, which grows to 20 in. high, has spectacular red flowers in the spring before its leaves appear. In the late winter or spring, plant one bulb to each 6-in. container. Put it in a sunny place, and keep the soil moist until September; then the soil should remain somewhat dry until December. The surrounding atmosphere should be quite humid. At repotting time, for more lilies, plant separately the small offset bulbs from the parent bulb.

STACHYS OLYMPICA   *perennial*   Lamb's ears

Lamb's ears have, not surprisingly, soft, thick, white, and rather woolly leaves, as well as small, purple flowers in the summer. They grow to a foot or more and are known mainly for their foliage—a good contrast plant in the garden. Lamb's ears do well in sun or light shade, with a moderate amount of water (but they also can tolerate some dryness) and in almost any readily draining soil. Divide them for new plants.

Stanhopea *houseplant*

The stanhopea is an orchid with 30-in. leaves and large, late-summer flower spikes, very colorful and very fragrant, though they last only a few days. Pot this orchid in fir bark in a slatted redwood basket, and place it in a humid spot. Give it plenty of water all year-round, sun in the winter and spring, and some shade in the summer and fall. Buy new plants from a specialist.

S. insignis. Produces one to four, 4-in., pale yellow flowers spotted with purple.
S. oculata. Produces three to seven, 6-in. flowers, usually yellow and orange.
S. wardii. Produces three to seven, 8-in. flowers, usually white with purple spots.

Stapelia *houseplant*

The starfish flower, or, less charitably, the carrion flower, is a rather bizarre succulent, with unusual, star-shaped flowers in various colors. Most of them also smell like carrion, but this is not offensive if they are outside. The starfish flower needs cool and dry conditions while they rest during the winter, and sun and an average amount of water in the summer. They can be divided for more plants.

Stephanotis Floribunda *vine* **Madagascar jasmine**

This is the flower made famous in bridal bouquets. It has evergreen, shiny, dark green leaves and waxy, white, very fragrant flowers in the summer and fall. Stephanotis likes a cool place and water about three times a week, except in the winter when once a week is enough. Mist it frequently, as well. This vine can grow to 15 ft. long and can be propagated from cuttings in the spring.

Sternbergia Lutea *bulb*

These little plants (to 12 in.) look like crocuses, with yellow-gold flowers and dark grassy green leaves, both in the fall. Plant them in the late summer, 6 in. apart and 4 in. deep, and give them sun and lots of water.

Stewartia Koreana *tree*

This tree can grow, though slowly, anywhere from 20 or 25 ft. to nearly 50 ft. It is rather narrow, with a pyramidal shape, white flowers in the summer, and dark green leaves turning orange or orange-red in the fall. It is all right in the sun unless it is very hot; then it needs some shade. Give it a fair amount of water, especially when it is young.

STOKESIA LAEVIS *perennial*   Stokes aster

Growing to 24 in., the blue flowers of this plant bloom in the summer and fall and last for a long time. It is happiest in the sun, with a moderate amount of water in a well-drained, loamy soil. Put these plants in a flower border, and divide them if you want more. Note that varieties with white, pink, and yellow flowers are also available.

SUGGESTED VARIETY:
'Silver Moon'—whitish yellow flowers

STRELITZIA *perennial*   Bird of paradise

Unless it is grown in a warm climate, this is a houseplant. The tropical bird of paradise has large, bananalike leaves and unusual, brightly colored flowers that, with some imagination, look like birds. If you are growing them outside, give them sun unless it is very hot, then light shade, and lots of water except during the winter when they may be kept drier and cooler (60°F). If you are growing them inside, the same requirements hold, but only mature plants with seven to ten leaves will bloom. The bird of paradise is a bit tricky to grow inside. Divide the rootstock for more plants.

S. nicolai. Grows to 48 in. or more, with white-and-purple flowers. Less showy than *S. reginae.*
S. reginae. The more popular of the two species. Grows slowly to 72 in., with orange-and-purple flowers.

STREPTOCARPUS *houseplant*   Cape primrose

The Cape primrose is a gesneriad with rich green leaves and funnel-shaped flowers ranging in color from pure white to pink to salmon to blue to deep violet. They do best in sun or bright light and in a soil that is kept moist. Feed them regularly while they are actively growing. The different species rest at different times, so watch for signs of dormancy, when they should not be fed or watered too much. Then, after a few months, new leaves will appear, at which time you should repot the plants. Propagate them from seed or cuttings.

S. dunnii. Generally has one large leaf and red flowers.
S. grandis. A curious, stemless plant with one large leaf to 36 in. long, and small, blue flowers.
S. rexii. Has 8-in. leaves and blue or white flowers.
S. saxorum. A trailer to 16 in. Has succulent leaves and 1.5-in., lavender flowers.

STROBILANTHES *perennial*

These perennials—not often seen but good for a sunny place—grow to about 24 in. tall. One species bears pinkish or pale purple flowers that look like foxgloves, and another is valued for both its violet flowers and its blue leaves tinged with silver. Keep the soil moist but not soggy. Despite their being labeled as perennials, these plants are good for only one season, so take cuttings in the spring for new plants.

S. dyeranus. Has 8-in., purple-green leaves and violet-colored flowers.
S. isophyllus. Has 4-in., willowy, toothed leaves and pinkish or blue-and-white flowers.

SWAINSONA *perennial*

This 36- to 48-in. semiclimber has white or red flowers that look like sweet peas, in the summer and lacy, light green leaves. Swainsona prefers the sun and lots of water until September; then keep the soil only fairly moist. Prune it after it has bloomed, and grow new plants from seed.

S. galegifolia. Produces red flowers.
S. g. albiflora. Produces pure white flowers.
S. g. violaceae. Produces rose-colored flowers.

SYMPHORICARPOS *shrub*   **Snowberry**

These low-growing, deciduous shrubs produce clusters of pink-tinged or white flowers in the early summer and then colored berries in the fall. Most have arching branches, making them a good choice where a horizontal mass is needed. They do well in sun or shade and can tolerate drought. Divide them for more plants.

S. albus (common snowberry). Grows to 6 ft.; hardy to −5°F. Produces pink flowers in May or June and white berries in the fall.
S. chenaultii (coral berry). Grows to 3 ft.; hardy to −10°F. Produces red berries.
S. doorenbosii. Grows to 10 ft.; hardy to −10°F. Has dark green leaves and large red berries.
S. occidentalis. Grows to 5 ft.; hardy to −35°F. Has oval, grayish green leaves and pink flowers.
S. orbiculatus (Indian currant). Grows quickly to 6 ft.; hardy to −50°F. Produces inconspicuous flowers and red berries.

SYMPHTUM OFFICINALE *perennial*   **Comfrey**

Comfrey, an herb, is sometimes grown in flower borders. It grows to 3 ft. tall and needs sun and a moist soil. The yellow flowers bloom in the summer and fall. Divide comfrey for more plants. But note that even though comfrey has sometimes been used as a medicinal tea, it does contain a poison and should not be eaten.

SUGGESTED VARIETY:
'Hidcote Blue'—blue flowers

SYMPLOCARPUS FOETIDUS   *perennial*   Skunk cabbage

The skunk cabbage, a 1-ft.-tall plant, is one of the first plants to come up in the spring. It is not, for obvious reasons, a garden plant: Its hooded flower is not attractive, but it is an American wildflower prevelant in some states.

SYNGONIUM PODOPHYLLUM   *houseplant*   Arrowhead

The arrowhead plant has long been a popular, easy-to-grow houseplant. It is a trailer, reaching 30 in. long, and has green or variegated leaves that may be small or large and lance or arrow shaped. Growing quickly, arrowheads do best in bright light or shade and in either soil or water. Cuttings provide new plants.

S. p. 'Emerald Gem'. Has smaller, rich green leaves.
S. p. 'Imperial White'. Has greenish white leaves.
S. p. wendlendii. A dainty creeper, with dark green, white-veined leaves.

SUGGESTED VARIETIES:
'Frostie'—green leaves with white variegation
'Maya Red'—green leaves with red variegation

SYRINGA   *shrub*   Lilac

Everyone loves the sweet-smelling lilacs, and there are many varieties from which to choose. Lilacs are deciduous, upright-growing shrubs valued both for their spring flowers and also as hedges or screens. They do well in sun or light shade, with an average amount of water (but they can tolerate some drought after they are established) and in an alkaline soil. Insects also like lilacs, but many of the new types are resistant to bugs and diseases. It is important to keep lilacs pruned, to keep them healthy. Trim them in the early spring, and they will still have a good crop of flowers. For the best results, take out one third of the old stems (of mature plants) one year, another third the next year, and the remaining third the third year. When you use this method, your lilacs will always look their best.

S. chinensis (Chinese lilac). A hybrid. Grows to 15 ft.; hardy to −5°F. Has fine-textured foliage and rose-purple flowers.
S. lacinata (cut-leaf lilac). Open growth to 6 ft.; hardy to −5°F. Has rich green foliage and pale purple flowers.
S. microphylla (little-leaf lilac). Grows to 6 ft.; hardy to −5°F. Produces pale purple flowers.

S. oblata dilatata (Korean early lilac). The earliest-blooming lilac. Grows to 12 ft.; hardy to −20°F. Produces pink flowers, and its leaves turn scarlet in the fall.

S. reflexa alba. Grows upright to 12 ft.; hardy to −20°F. Produces pale pink flowers.

S. velutina (Korean lilac). Grows to 20 ft.; hardy to −20°F. Produces pinkish or bluish lavender flowers.

S. vulgaris (common lilac). Bulky growth to 20 ft.; hardy to −10°F. Produces—what else?—lilac-colored flowers. Many varieties.

Tagets *annual*   Marigold

A useful and pretty group of plants, some marigolds are small—to 10 in.—and others are quite large—to 30 in. Their flowers are either single or double, yellow or orange, and will bloom from early summer until the first frost if the old flowers are kept cut off. Marigolds are easy to grow: Give them sun and lots of water, and almost any soil will do. Indeed, if you have space for only one kind of flower, marigolds should be your choice. *T. erecta* and *T. patula* make up the bulk of the varieties available today. Buy prestarted plants yearly.

T. erecta. Produces large yellow flowers.

Climbing roses make a statement in this garden and create a tower of color.

Ramblers add a dignified air to any rose garden.

PLATE 54

Many old fashioned yellow rose varieties are now available to collectors.

PLATE 55

The beautiful Scillas—an example of nature at her best; the blue color is always desirable in gardens.

PLATE 56

Strelitzia nicolai, a cousin of the popular bird-of-paradise (*Strelitzia reginae*) is often used to add dramatic height to indoor gardens.

PLATE 57

Salvia is red and bountiful, and makes a fine accent in gardens.

PLATE 58

Sparaxis hybrids are in demand because of their dark red color; bulbs bloom easily.

PLATE 59

Thalictrum is graceful and airy.

PLATE 60

Masses of marigolds for color and easily grown.

PLATE 61

The beauty of orchids is well displayed in this panorama of *Trichopila tortilis,* the corkscrew orchids because of the twisted flower petals.

PLATE 62

Vinca rosea, a symphony of pink.

PLATE 63

One of the popular bromeliads is *Vreisea cardinalis* which bears a stalk of orange bracts that last for weeks.

PLATE 64

One of the fine Vanda hybrids—many are grown as houseplants in the North; in southern Florida they can be grown outdoors.

PLATE 65

Veronica and Echinacea in the background create a handsome "waterfall" of color.

PLATE 66

Vanda coerulea, the famous blue orchid once a collector's item is now generally available from suppliers and grown as a houseplant.

PLATE 67

Yucca is generally an outdoor plant but it can be grown in large containers indoors as well.

PLATE 68

This cutting garden hosts a bunch of Zinnias, a favorite cut flower.

T. patula (French marigold). Produces yellow or orange flowers.
T. tenufolia. A dwarf. Produces small, golden orange flowers.

SUGGESTED VARIETIES:
'Baby Boy'—a dwarf, with yellow flowers
'Bonanza Yellow'—large yellow flowers
'Dainty Marietta'—pale orange and yellow flowers
'Disco'—bright orange flowers
'Lemon Gem'—butter yellow flowers
'Paprika'—yellow, orange, and red flowers
'Petite Sophia'—yellow and orange flowers

Tamarix   *shrub/tree*

Tamarisks are evergreen-appearing and deciduous shrubs or small trees that grow anywhere from 4 to 50 ft. They have feathery foliage and pink flowers that bloom either in just the spring or in the spring through the summer. Give tamarisks a lot of water and any soil that drains readily, and use them as background plants or hedges. New plants can be had from softwood or hardwood cuttings.

T. hispida. Hardy to 10°F. Has feathery, heathlike leaves. Will grow in dry soil.
T. parviflora. Hardy to 10°F. Produces small pink flowers; needs regular pruning.

Tanacetum vulgare *perennial*   Common tansy

A bunch of tansy hung at a window or door will discourage flies from entering. Its bright green, finely cut leaves are quite aromatic, and in the summer, tansy bears small, yellow, buttonlike flowers. If it is given bright light and an average amount of water, it will grow to be about 3 ft. tall. Divide tansy for more plants.

Taxus *shrub/tree*   Yew

Yews are dark green, evergreen shrubs and trees that are widely grown and thrive in almost any soil. Indeed, yews are tough and can tolerate neglect; deer seem to be their only enemy. Yews make excellent hedges, screens, and large accent plants, and in the fall they produce tiny red berrylike fruits that birds love. They are slow growing and do well even in the shade. Yews vary in size and growth style, and there also are dwarf yews available. They are difficult to propagate, so buy new plants. And yews may be attacked by vine weevils, scale, and spider mites. Keep your weapons at the ready.

T. baccata (English yew). Branching growth to 60 ft.; hardy to −5°F. Has dark green needles.
T. b. stricta (Irish yew). Very upright growth to 60 ft.; hardy to −5°F. Has very dark green needles.
T. cuspida (Japanese yew). Compact growth to 50 ft.; hardy to −10°F. Has dark green needles.
T. c. capitata. Grows to 20 ft.; hardy to −10°F.
T. media 'Hicksii'. Columnar or pyramidal growth to 40 ft.; hardy to −10°F.

TECOMARIA CAPENSIS   *vine/shrub*

The Cape honeysuckle is an evergreen, vining shrub (or shrubby vine) that, if supported, can grow to 25 ft. or, if pruned, can grow upright as a shrub. It has fine-textured foliage and bright orange, trumpet-shaped flowers that bloom in the fall through the winter. Cape honeysuckle needs bright light and a moderate amount of water in a well-drained, sandy soil; it is hardy to 40°F. Cuttings provide new plants.

TEUCRIUM CHAMAEDRYS   *shrub*   **Germander**

A member of the mint family, germander is low growing, to 1 ft., but spreads to about 2 ft. It has dense, toothed, dark green leaves and, in the summer, red-purple or white flowers. It likes sun and heat and tolerates drought but not a poorly draining soil. Divide it for new plants.

THALIA DEALBATA   *perennial*

This aquatic plant likes to grow in shallow pools. It has basal leaves and violet-colored flowers in the summer, growing on tall (about 5 ft.) stalks. This plant is strictly for a pool; pot it in a container that is then submerged in water. It can be divided.

THALICTRUM   *perennial*   **Meadowrue**

Meadow rue is a fine, lacy-leafed plant that grows to 40 in. and provides masses of tiny lavender or pink flowers in the summer and fall. It is ideal as a background plant in a border. Meadow rue needs sun or bright light, regular watering, and a loamy soil that drains well. Seed is the best way to get more plants. There are many species and varieties of meadow rue.

T. aquilegifolium. Produces lavender or pink flowers.
T. glaucum. Produces fragrant, fuzzy, yellow flowers.

SUGGESTED VARIETY:
'White Cloud'—white flowers

THERMOPSIS CAROLINIANA   *perennial*

This perennial has ovate 3-in. leaves and, in the summer, produces pea-shaped, yellow flowers on tall (30 in.) plants. It likes sun, a moderate amount of water, and a loamy soil and looks good in a rock garden or as an accent in background areas. Divide it for new plants.

THUJA   *shrub/tree*   **Arborvitae**

Arborvitae can be either a shrub or a tree; it has small, flat, needlelike, evergreen leaves. It actually is quite shrubby and somewhat pyramidal in shape and is used extensively in gardens. No arborvitae can tolerate dry conditions; they prefer moisture at the roots and in the air and usually grow quickly. Older arborvitae, however, lose their lower branches and hence their looks. They are difficult to propagate and may be attacked by insects. Nonetheless, they are very worthwhile additions to any garden.

T. occidentalis 'Douglasi Pyramidalis'. Columnar growth to 60 ft.; hardy to −35°F. Has bright green to yellowish green leaves.
T. o. fastigiata. Narrower and more columnar growth than that of *T. occidentalis*.
T. plicata (giant arborvitae). Narrow growth to 180 ft.; hardy to −5°F. Has scalelike leaves that do not turn brown in the winter.
T. standishii (Japanese arborvitae). Spreading growth to 40 ft.; hardy to −10°F.

THUNBERGIA   *vine*

Even though this tropical vine is a perennial, it grows fast enough to be treated as an annual, and it also cannot tolerate any but the mildest winters. Thunbergia is mainly known for its large, showy, yellow flowers that bloom in the summer; it also has triangular or heart-shaped leaves. Grow this vine in the full sun, and keep the soil moist. It should have some kind of support, such as a trellis. Plant seeds for new vines.

T. alata (black-eyed susan vine). Vining growth to 72 in. Produces darker-centered, yellow-orange or white flowers.

T. erecta. To many, the best species. Shrubby growth to 72 in. Has dark green leaves and blue flowers.

T. grandiflora (sky flower). Vining growth to 60 in. Produces large, pale blue flowers in the fall.

THYMOPHYLLA TENUILOBA   *annual*   Goldenfleece

A native of the American Southwest, the golden fleece grows to only 12 in. high and has divided, threadlike, dark green leaves and yellow, daisylike flowers in the summer. This plant looks good either as a ground cover or in masses. Golden fleeces like heat and sun and need a lot of water in a well-drained, loamy soil. New plants can be had from seed.

THYMUS   *perennial*

This well-known herb, besides being very useful in the kitchen, is an excellent, low-growing, evergreen (and, of course, fragrant) ground cover, with small, usually grayish green leaves. The flowers appear from May until the fall. If not in an herb garden, thyme does well planted between stepping-stones. It can be divided for more plants, and it is hardy to −20°F.

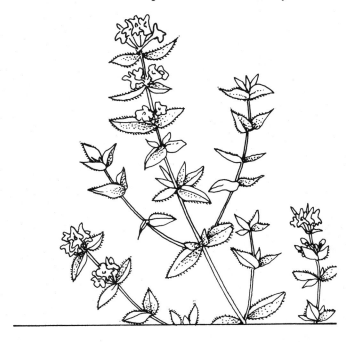

TIARELLA CORDIFOLIA *perennial* Foam flower

The foam flower grows to only 1 ft. high and has downy basal leaves and white flowers in the summer. It can be used as a ground cover or as an accent in a woodland garden. Grow it in the shade, with a moderate amount of water. Division provides new plants.

TIBOUCHINA SEMIDECANDRA *perennial* Princess flower

Despite being called a perennial, this is really a shrub or small tree, native to Brazil, that grows rather rapidly to as much as 18 ft. tall. Its evergreen leaves are oval, velvety, and ribbed, and its flowers are a brilliant purple, blooming in the summer. Give the princess flower—shrub—bright light or light shade and an average amount of water in a readily draining, acid soil. Take cuttings for new plants; they tolerate temperatures down to 10°F.

TIGRIDIA PAVONIA *bulb* Tiger flower

In the summer, tiger flowers produce large, triangular blossoms in orange, pink, red, yellow, or white. The leaves are rather long and narrow. Plant these bulbs in the spring, after the last frost, 4 in. apart and 4 in. deep. In cold climates, dig them up when the leaves are mature, and store them for the next year. Tiger flowers require sun and regular watering. Divide the bulbs for more plants.

TILIA *tree* Linden

Lindens are deciduous trees, with dense, compact crowns. Their leaves are heart shaped, and in the early summer they bear drooping clusters of fragrant, yellowish white flowers. Give these trees lots of water and a rich soil, and watch out for aphids. Buy new plants, as lindens are difficult to propagate.

T. americana (American linden). Grows to 60 ft.; hardy to −35°F. Has dark, dull green leaves.
T. platyphyllos (big-leaf linden). Rounded growth to 120 ft.; hardy to −20°F. Produces small, yellowish flowers.

TILLANDSIA *houseplant*

Tillandsia is a bromeliad with either tufted or palmlike foliage. Some of them are small—good for dish gardens—and others are large—best for a window. Both kinds need full sun and should be potted in a mixture of fir bark and soil, kept moist. Grow new plants from offsets.

T. argentea. Grows to 4 in. Has narrow, soft gray leaves and rose-colored leaves.

T. bulbosa. Grows to 6 in. Has a bulbous base and contorted, bright green leaves, and short, erect, red flower spikes.

T. circinnata. Grows to 8 in. Has an egg-shaped base and thick, contorted, grayish green leaves, and a pink flower spike.

T. cyanea. Grows to 30 in. Has palmlike, dark green leaves, and a pink flower spike with butterflylike purple flowers in the fall.

T. fasciculata. Grows to 30 in. Has tapering, gray-green leaves and a multicolored flower spike with violet-colored flowers.

T. ionanthe. Grows to 3 in. Has tufted leaves and red-and-violet flowers in the summer.

T. juneca. Grows to 12 in. Produces yellow-and-red flowers in the summer.

T. stricta. Grows to 6 in. Has curved, leathery, usually silvery leaves, and a yellow-white to rose-colored flower crown.

TITHONIA ROTUNDIFOLIA   *annual*   Mexican sunflower

A fast-growing, rather coarse plant, the Mexican sunflower can reach 6 ft. tall and produces spectacular, large, bright orange-red flowers in the summer. Although these plants can grow in any kind of soil, they need full sun and regular watering to do well. Mexican sunflowers look best as background plants.

TOLMIEA MENZIESII   *houseplant*   Piggyback plant

The piggyback plant is a creeper that produces new plants on the backs of mature leaves. Its toothed, fresh green foliage spreads to about 30 in., making it a good plant for a hanging basket. Give it filtered light, and keep the soil moist. (The piggyback plant also produces insignificant, reddish brown flowers.) For more plants, cut off a leaf with a budding piggy on top, and pot it in sand until it forms roots.

TORENIA FOURNIERI   *annual*   Wishbone flower

Although this plant grows to about 1 ft. high, it does not have a wishbone; only its flowers are shaped like one. Blooming in the summer and fall, these flowers are tricolored: light blue with darker blue markings and bright yellow throats. Plant wishbone flowers in the full sun unless it is especially hot, then in partial shade. Give them lots of water and a loamy soil. They are good in borders or in pots on the patio. Grow new plants from seed.

TRACHELOSPERMUM JASMINOIDES   *vine/shrub*   Star jasmine

This is the plant whose small white flowers smell like jasmine, even though it is not a true jasmine. Rather, it is a shrubby vine, with shiny, oval, bright green leaves, and it can either be pruned into a ground cover or trained on a trellis. Its spicy-smelling flowers appear in the early summer. Star jasmines do best in the sun and with the soil kept moist. They can withstand temperatures down to 40°F and can be propagated from cuttings in the spring.

Trachymene coerulea   *annual*   Blue lace flower

The blue lace flower grows to about 2 ft. tall, and its main feature is its numerous clusters of small, lavender-blue flowers that have a lacy appearance, as do its leaves. The flowers come in late spring or summer. Although these plants like sun, the flowers wilt quickly in hot weather; they are at their best in cool surroundings, with an average amount of water and a sandy soil. Blue lace flowers make excellent cut flowers. Grow new plants from seed.

Tradescantia   *houseplant*

This fast-growing, indestructible, small, trailing plant gets to be about 24 in. long, with oval, fleshy leaves in shades of cream, pink, mauve, red, gold, and dark green. Put it in either sun or shade and in soil that is allowed to dry out a bit between waterings. Grow new plants from cuttings.

T. blossfeldiana. Has green leaves with silver hairs, and pale purple flowers.
T. b. variegata. Has cream-and-green leaves.
T. fluminensis (wandering jew). Has green leaves and white flowers.
T. f. albo-vittata. Has bluish green-and-white leaves, and white flowers.
T. laekenensis. Has green-and-pink leaves and white flowers.
T. multiflora. Has dark green leaves and white flowers.
T. navicularis (chain plant). Has boat-shaped, coppery green leaves and clusters of rosy purple flowers.

Trapa natans   *perennial*

This aquatic herb grows in streams and ponds and also can be cultivated in a garden pool. It has both submerged and floating leaves and white flowers, in the summer. Buy new plants from specialists.

Trichocereus   *houseplant*

This is a group of large, slow-growing, columnar cacti. Most have gray-green stems and, when grown indoors, only occasionally produce their lovely, night-blooming flowers. In any case, grow them in a sandy soil that drains readily, and give them full sun, allowing them to dry out between waterings.

In the winter, keep these plants dry and cool (45°F). These cacti make good tub plants where space permits. Grow new plants from seed.

T. johnsonii. A deeply ribbed column growing to 60 in. Produces greenish white flowers.
T. spachianus. A closely ribbed column growing to 24 in. Produces white flowers.

TRICHOPILLA SUAVIS   *houseplant*

These orchids grow to 2 ft. tall and bear large (to 4 in.) flowers, trumpet shaped with corkscrew petals that are white and marked with rose. Pot them in fir bark, give them bright light, keep them moist all year-round, and keep them warm at night (above 55°F). Buy new plants from suppliers.

TRILLIUM   *perennial*

A popular wildflower, trilliums grow to about 1 ft. high and bear red, white, or yellow flowers in the early spring. Their leaves are a circle of three, at the top of each stem. Trilliums like shade and an-always moist soil.

TRITONIA CROCATA   *bulb*

These South African bulbs belong to the iris family. They grow to 36 in. high and have grassy foliage, and their flowers look like gladioli. The blossoms come in many shades of orange, pink, salmon, yellow, and apricot, and bloom in the summer. Plant the bulbs in a sunny location, 3 in. apart and 3 in deep, and water them regularly until the leaves die down. They can withstand some drought. Get new plants from offsets.

TROLLIUS   *perennial*   Globeflower

Globeflowers grow to 24 in. tall and have palmlike leaves and orange or yellow flowers in the spring and summer that look like ranunculus. Give them sun and plenty of water at the roots; be sure that they are in a loamy soil. For more globeflowers, either plant seeds or buy prestarted plants.

T. cultroum. Produces small, yellow-orange flowers.
T. europaeus. Produces orange flowers.
T. ledebouri. Produces an abundance of orange flowers.

SUGGESTED VARIETIES:
'Alabaster'—white flowers
'Canary Bird'—yellow flowers
'Orange Princess'—orange flowers

TROPAEOLUM *perennial/annual* Nasturtium

There are two kinds of nasturtiums, the vining type, growing to 6 ft., and the dwarf type, growing upright to 15 in. Both are easy to grow and bloom from summer until the first frost. The leaves are almost round, bright green, and are a good addition to salads, rather peppery like watercress. Nasturtium flowers come in several bright colors, maroon, red-brown, orange, yellow, red, and creamy white. Grow nasturtiums in the sun, in a sandy soil regularly watered and readily draining. Start new plants from seed (they often reseed themselves), or buy prestarted plants.

T. majus. The most popular nasturtium. A vining type, with orange-red flowers.
T. peregrinum. Produces yellow flowers, in a shape different from that of *T. majus.*
T. polyphyllum. Produces small, orange flowers.

SUGGESTED VARIETIES:
'Alaska'—white flowers
'Empress of India'—red flowers
'Peach Melba'—pink flowers

TSUGA *tree* Hemlock

Narrow, needlelike, evergreen leaves make hemlocks beautiful trees. They need lots of water, will tolerate some shade, but prefer some sun and an acid soil. There are many varieties of hemlocks from which to choose. They are difficult to propagate, so buy new plants.

T. canadensis (Canada hemlock). Grows to 90 ft.; hardy to −20°F. Has slender, horizontal branches and dark green leaves.
T. heterophylla (western hemlock). Grows to 125 ft.; hardy to −5°F. Has short, drooping branches and fine-textured, dark green to yellowish green leaves.

TULBAGHIA FRAGRANS *bulb* Society garlic

Society garlic grows to 24 in. and has long, narrow, medium green leaves and clusters of pink-lavender flowers on stalks rising above the leaves. Although they do look pretty (hence the *society* part of their name), they do smell like garlic when brushed. Use society garlic for accent plants. If you do not live in a warm-winter climate, plant the bulbs each year, 10 in. apart and 1 in. deep. Offsets provide new plants.

Tulipa   *bulb*   Tulip

There must be thousands of varieties of tulips, with different shapes, sizes, and colors. The selection is virtually limitless. The reason for their great popularity is that tulips are among the prettiest of all spring (or summer, for that matter) flowers. Tulips look wonderful planted in masses, but a few for a spot of color are nice, too. Plant tulips in a sunny location and in a sandy, well-drained soil, and water them regularly. Plant the bulbs in the fall, 2.5 times as deep as they are wide and 4 to 8 in. apart, depending on the ultimate size of the plant. Undoubtedly you get many gardening catalogs: Choose from them the varieties that seem appealing.

T. kaufmannia (waterlily tulip). Produces creamy yellow flowers marked with red on the outside and yellow at the center.

Tusillago farfara   *perennial*   Coltsfoot

The coltsfoot grows to 12 in. high, with basal leaves and, in the spring, bright yellow, daisylike flowers. Coltsfeet like bright light and a moderate amount of water, but be careful because their roots spread rapidly underground, and so they may become a nuisance.

TYPHA LATIFOLIA *perennial* Cat-tail

Cattails are tall, to about 5 ft., and grow in wet, marshy areas. Their "tails" are long, brown, cattail flowers that are sometimes used in dried arrangements. Cattails can be grown in a sunny, wet area in the garden, and they can be divided.

ULMUS *tree* Elm

Elms are very popular shade trees and once were the trees of choice to line streets. Sadly, however, we must use the past tense here, as Dutch elm disease has been slowly crossing the United States, killing virtually all the elms it attacks. In addition, elms are a favorite of many insects. Aside from all this, however, elms are fairly easy to grow, given normal watering and a reasonably good soil. They may have a columnar, vase, or weeping shape. And there are now new varieties available that seem to be more resistant to disease.

U. alata. Grows to 50 ft.; hardy to −10°F. Small leaves and flowers on pendant stalks.
U. americana (American elm). Grows to 120 ft.; hardy to −10°F. Has long leaves and flowers on pendant stalks.
U. parvifolia (Chinese elm). Grows to 50 ft.; hardy to −20°F. Open headed, with small leaves.
U. rubra. Grows to 40 ft.; hardy to −20°F. Open headed, with large leaves.

URSINIA ANETHOIDES *annual*

Ursinia grows to 16 in. high, with feathery foliage and orange flowers in the summer. It needs lots of sun, a moderate amount of water, and a sandy soil. Do not feed it, and grow new plants from seed. When planted in masses, ursinias make a nice color accent.

VACCINUM (HYBRIDS) *shrub* Blueberry

Anyone who likes to eat blueberries knows that they grow in many places throughout the United States but are generally considered a commercial crop rather than a garden shrub. Blueberries grow to be quite tall and are usually quite sprawling. There are varieties for both dry and wet soils, and most like an acid soil. Blueberries can tolerate temperatures down to −30°F.

VALERIANA OFFICINALIS *perennial* Garden heliotrope

Garden heliotrope grows to about 4 ft. tall and has light green leaves that come in pairs divided into smaller leaflets. The tiny, fragrant flowers bloom in the summer, can be white, pink, red, or lavender-blue, and appear as clusters at the tips of the stems. Garden heliotrope does well in either sun or light shade, with regular watering, and in almost any soil. For new plants, either divide them or plant seeds. Garden heliotrope is good in rock gardens.

VALLOTA SPECIOSA *bulb*   Scarborough lily

These lilies are native to South Africa, have strap-shaped, evergreen leaves, and, in the summer and early fall, clusters of funnel-shaped, bright orange-red flowers. The plants grow to about 2 ft. high, prefer light shade but will tolerate sun, and need regular watering except while dormant in the winter and spring, but they should not be allowed to dry out completely. Because these lilies do best when root bound, grow them in pots and divide them only when absolutely necessary.

VANDA *houseplant*

These orchids that made Hawaii famous actually come from the tropics of East Asia. Vandas have succulent, strap-shaped leaves and tall wands of flat flowers, about 5 in. in diameter. Plant them in fir bark in 6- or 7-in. pots, and do not disturb them for several years. Put the pots in a very sunny, humid place, and keep the soil moist at all times. Grow new plants from offsets.

V. caerulea (blue orchid). Grows to 30 in. Produces blue flowers in the fall.
V. rothschildiana. A hybrid, grows to 40 in. Produces blue flowers in the winter.
V. roxburghii. Grows to 26 in. Produces pale green-purple-and-brown flowers in the summer and sometimes in the spring, too.
V. tricolor. Grows to 30 in. Produces generally yellow-to-pink flowers at various times of the year.

VELTHEIMIA (VIRIDIFOLIA) *bulb*   Pineapple lily

The pineapple lily comes from South Africa, and its shiny, dark green, wavy-margined leaves make it a beautiful plant even when it is not in bloom. But when it is, it has rose-colored flowers that appear in the winter and early spring. Unless you live in a warm-winter climate, this plant must be grown indoors but may be set outside during the warm months. Grow it in the sun (but protect it from a too-hot sun), and keep the soil moist except during the summer, when it should rest dry for three to five weeks. Divide the bulbs for more plants.

Venidium fastuosum   *annual*

Large, bright orange, daisylike flowers and ferny foliage make this plant a good addition to the garden. It grows to 2 ft. high and needs sun and lots of water in a readily draining, sandy soil. Seeds provide new plants. Venidiums are good in either beds or borders.

Verbascum   *perennial*   **Mullein**

Mullein is a branched plant growing to 40 in., with fuzzy, rather weedy leaves and lavender flowers in the summer and fall. It is happiest in the sun, with an average amount of water in a well-drained soil. Mullein is a good background plant; divide it for more.

SUGGESTED VARIETY:
'Cotswold Gem'

Verbena hybrida   *perennial/annual*   **Verbena**

These 20- to 30-in. plants bear many clusters of white, pink, bright red, purple, and blue—and combinations thereof—flowers in the summer and fall. Grow verbenas in the sun; they are drought resistant and like a loamy, well-drained soil. Cuttings bring new plants. Try verbenas as a ground cover, in masses, or in a rock garden.

SUGGESTED VARIETIES:
'Derby'—violet-blue flowers
'Glowing Violet'—lavender-blue flowers

Veronica   *perennial*   **Speedwell**

Depending on the species, veronicas can be anywhere from 4 in. to 2.5 ft. tall, with white, rose, pink, or pale or dark blue flowers in the summer. They are good additions as background or border plants. Put them in a sunny place, in a loamy soil, and water them regularly. Divide veronicas for new plants.

V. incana (woolly speedwell). Produces blue flowers.
V. latifolia. Grows in clumps and produces dense clusters of lilac-colored flowers.

SUGGESTED VARIETIES:
'Crater Lake'—blue flowers
'Royal Blue'—blue flowers

Vɪʙᴜʀɴᴜᴍ   *shrub*

Viburnum can be either deciduous or evergreen. Some are valued most for their glossy, green leaves in the summer; others, for their often-fragrant flowers in the spring and sometimes brightly colored leaves and fruit in the fall. Almost all viburnums do well in either sun or shade, prefer ample water but will withstand some drought, and like a rich soil. They are rarely bothered by insects.

V. carlcephalum (fragrant snowball). A deciduous shrub. Grows to 9 ft.; hardy to −5°F. Has dull, grayish green leaves and fragrant white flowers.

V. carlesii (Korean spice viburnum). A deciduous shrub. Grows to 5 ft.; hardy to −10°F. Produces fragrant, pink flowers.

V. cassinoides. A deciduous shrub. Grows to 6 ft.; hardy to −35°F. Has clusters of creamy white flowers and bright red leaves in the fall.

V. davidii (David viburnum). An evergreen. Grows to 3 ft.; hardy to 5°F. Has dark green, deeply veined leaves and white flowers.

V. dentatum (arrowwood). A deciduous shrub. Grows to 15 ft.; hardy to −35°F. Has creamy white flowers and glossy red leaves in the fall.

V. japonicum (Japanese viburnum). An evergreen. Grows to 6 ft.; hardy to 5°F. Has glossy, dark green leaves and fragrant white flowers.

V. lantana (wayfaring tree). A deciduous shrub. Grows to 15 ft.; hardy to −20°F. Has tiny white flowers and red leaves in the fall.

V. opulus (European cranberry bush). A deciduous shrub. Grows to 12 ft.; hardy to −20°F. Has maple-shaped leaves that turn red in the fall, and clusters of white flowers.

V. plicatum (Japanese snowball). A deciduous shrub. Grows to 9 ft.; hardy to −10°F. Has dark green leaves and snowball clusters of white flowers.

V. p. tomentosum 'Mariesii'—large shrub

V. trilobum (American cranberry bush). A deciduous shrub. Grows to 12 ft.; hardy to −35°F. Similar to *V. opulus* but not so susceptible to aphids.

V. wrightii. A deciduous shrub. Grows to 9 ft.; hardy to −5°F. Has bright green leaves and small white flowers.

Vinca   *perennial*   Periwinkle, myrtle

Some kinds of vinca are small (*V. minor*), growing to only 8 in. high, and other kinds are the standard size (*V. major*), growing to 20 in. high. Vinca is a trailing plant, and indeed, the dwarf periwinkle is often used as a ground cover. The bigger variety is frequently found as a background plant. Both kinds have shiny, oval, dark green leaves and, in the summer and fall, have flat-faced lavender, magenta, or white-with-a-red-center flowers. Vinca prefers the shade but can tolerate some sun if it has a lot of water in a well-drained soil. Grow new plants from seed.

Viola   *perennial/annual*   Viola, violet, pansy

Violas, violets, and pansies all belong to the genus viola, and technically all of them are perennials, but some are treated as annuals. Most of these plants

grow to only 10 in. Violets usually are white or a shade of purple; violas and pansies come in many colors and color combinations. They all will bloom from spring through to the first frost if the dead flowers are picked off promptly. Plant all three in the sun, though in very hot regions they need some shade. All three like a rich, moist soil. Use these versatile plants almost anywhere in the garden for a spot of bright, dependable color. Dozens of new varieties. Choose from catalogs.

V. incognita (white violet). Has large leaves; white flowers.
V. odorata (sweet violet). Has heart-shaped green leaves and fragrant, purple flowers. Many varieties.
V. tricolor (johnny-jump-up). Produces purple-and-yellow flowers that resemble small pansies.
V. t. hortensis (pansy). An excellent strain with flowers in many different colors and color combinations.
V. williamsii. Produces violet-colored flowers.
V. wittrockiana. Produces brilliant red-purple flowers with purple blotches.

SUGGESTED VARIETY:
'Royal Robe'—violet, dark purple

VITEX   *shrub/tree*   Chaste tree

Vitex is a deciduous shrub/small tree, growing from about 6 ft. to about 25 ft., depending on the particular area. It is multitrunked, with dark green leaves that are gray underneath, and fragrant, lavender-blue flower spikes that appear in the late summer. Vitex can survive temperatures down to 5°F; it dies to the ground in some regions but soon revives.

Vitis coignetiae   *vine*

This is a fast-growing vine to 40 ft., valued for its bright red leaves in the fall. It thrives with sun and lots of water. Be warned, however, that this vine is invasive, so think carefully before you plant it, and put it only in a location where it can spread without infringing on anything else.

Vriesea   *houseplant*

Feathery, colorful flower plumes (bracts) that last for several months make this bromeliad ideal for a north window. Some kinds have pale green rosettes of leaves; others have dark green rosettes banded with brown. Pot them in equal parts of osmunda and soil, and keep their "vases" filled with water. Do not fertilize or spray them with insecticides. Buy new plants.

V. carinata (lobster claws). Grows to 18 in. Has a smooth, pale green rosette of leaves and a yellow-and-crimson flower plume.
V. hieroglyphica. Grows to 30 in. Has a banded green rosette of leaves with darker markings.
V. malzinei. Grows to 12 in. Has a plain green rosette of leaves and a cylindrical, orange flower plume.
V. splendens (flaming sword). Grows to 20 in. Has a green rosette of leaves with mahagony stripes, and bright red and yellow "swords" (flower plumes). Does not produce offsets, but new plants push up from the center of mature growth.

SUGGESTED VARIETIES:
'Kitteliana'—yellow bracts (plumes)
'Mariae'—yellow bracts
'Meyer's Favorite'—yellow bracts

Watsonia iridifolia   *bulb*

Watsonia, a native of South Africa, grows to 40 in. tall, with branched stems and masses of 3-in. pink or red flowers in the summer. Plant the bulbs in the late summer or fall, 6 in. apart and 4 in. deep, and in a sunny spot. Give them a moderate amount of water, and each year, dig them up, divide them, and replant them as soon as possible. Watsonias make good bedding or accent plants.

Weigela   *shrub*

These deciduous shrubs are native to East Asia. They produce an abundance of brightly colored flowers in the late spring through June. Weigela does best in the sun and with lots of water in a well-drained soil. Use it as a background plant, and propagate it by means of softwood or hardwood cuttings. Insects do not seem to be a problem.

W. florida (old-fashioned weigela). Many varieties. Grows to 6 ft.; hardy to −10°F.

SUGGESTED VARIETIES:
'Bristol Ruby'—ruby red flowers
'Bristol Snowflake'—white flowers
'Eva Rathke'—bright to deep crimson flowers
'Mont Blanc'—white flowers
'Vanicek'—red flowers
'Varigata'—fancy-leafed, multicolored form

WISTERIA FLORIBUNDA   *vine*   **Japanese wisteria**

This is one of the most popular vines, growing to 20 ft. long and bearing hanging clusters of fragrant, violet-colored flowers in the spring. Wisteria, which is deciduous, needs full sun and ample water, both when actively growing and in bloom. It is not fussy about soil. Wisteria can be trained

(pruned) either as a shrub or as a vine (given support such as a trellis). Cuttings provide new plants.

WOODWARDIA *perennial*

These stiff, leathery, broad-fronded ferns make a good contrast with the more delicate, feathery kinds. Grow them in the shade, and keep the soil moist. Chain ferns are large, some with fronds 4 to 8 ft. long and as much as 2 ft. wide. Divide the rootstock for new plants.

W. fimbriata (giant chain fern). Has leathery, broad, massive fronds.
W. orientalis. Has long, drooping, but stiff fronds.

XANTHISMA *annual*   Star of Texas

An easy-to-grow, 24-in. plant, the star of Texas has alternate leaves and, in the summer, bright yellow, daisylike flowers. It prefers sun but does not mind a poor, dry soil. Stars of Texas make good cut flowers and provide a spot of color in the garden. Grow new plants from seed.

Xanthosoma *houseplant*

These jungle plants from South America grow to 36 in. tall and have big, arrow-shaped leaves on long stalks. Their greenish or yellowish flowers are clustered on a spike and are more of an oddity than an attraction. Xanthosomas need bright light in humid surroundings and a moist, rich soil. Divide the tubers in the summer for more plants.

X. lindenii 'Magnificum'. Has 12-in., green-and-white leaves.
X. violaceum (violet-stemmed tara). Has dark green leaves with purple edges.

Xeranthemum annuum *annual*   **Everlasting**

Known for its "everlasting" flowers, these plants grow to 3 ft. tall and produce purple, violet, or rose-colored flower heads in the summer and fall. They like sun, regular watering, and a well-drained soil. Plant them in masses; the flowers are good cut and also dried. They last a long time, of course. Divide the plants if you want more of them.

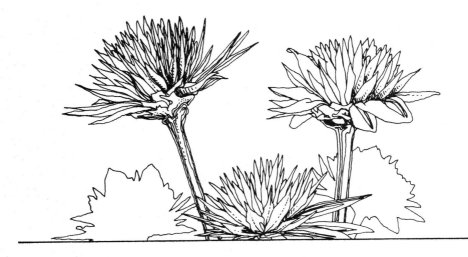

Yucca *perennial*

There are many species of yucca, some quite large, and they make good background plants. Some kinds of yucca have no stems, but others have stems that can reach tree size. They all have rosettes of stiff, sword-shaped leaves and tall, white flower spikes in the summer. Yuccas thrive in the full sun and in a well-drained, sandy soil. They can tolerate drought when established. Obtain new plants by means of air layering.

Y. aloifolia (Spanish bayonet). Has a 48-in. rosette of stiff, pointed, bluish green leaves.

Y. a. marginata. Has green leaves with yellow-cream markings.

Y. filamentosa. Has a nearly stemless, 40-in. rosette of bluish green leaves.

Y. whipplei. Has a stemless, 60-in. rosette of stiff, green leaves.

ZAMIA PUMILA   *houseplant*

These plants are native to Florida and Mexico. They have a short or completely submerged stem but a 2- to 4-ft.-wide crown of evergreen leaves. Each leaf has several pairs of rolled-edge leaflets, making the plant look somewhat like a fern. Zamia is very slow growing and likes bright light and a fair amount of water. If it has more than one crown, it can be divided for new plants.

ZANTEDESCHIA   *bulb*   Calla lily

Calla lilies grow to about 2 ft. tall and have basal, shiny, arrow- or lance-shaped leaves, and stalks with vase-shaped, white flower bracts that appear in the spring and summer. Give calla lilies sun or partial shade and plenty of water. Most soils are acceptable. Plant the bulbs 12 in. apart and 4 in. deep. Dig them up each year unless you live in a warm-winter region. Offsets are the source of new plants.

Z. aethiopica (common calla lily). Produces white flowers.
Z. elliottiana (golden calla lily). Produces golden yellow flowers.
Z. rehmannii (red or pink calla lily). Smaller than the others. Produces pink flowers.

SUGGESTED VARIETIES:
'Crowborough'—white flowers
'Green Goddess'—green flowers

ZEBRINA PENDULA   *houseplant*   Wandering jew

Trailing to about 3 ft. long, this plant has green leaves with white or yellow stripes; some varieties have stripes of other colors. Zebrina also bears small clusters of purplish or white flowers. Give it bright light and a moderate amount of water. Cuttings provide more plants.

ZEPHYRANTHES GRANDIFLORA   *bulb*   Rain lily

The rain lily's flowers, appearing in the late spring and early summer, look like small amaryllis; its leaves are bright green and rather grasslike. The plant itself grows to about 12 in. tall and needs full sun and lots of water. Plant the bulbs in the fall, 3 in. apart and 2 in. deep. Rain lilies look especially good in masses. Use offsets for new plants.

ZINNIA   *annual*

Zinnias bloom in the late summer and fall, and their flowers come in a variety of colors, sizes, and shapes. These plants are easy to please but do their best in the sun and in a good garden soil. To prevent mildew, always water the soil; do not sprinkle the plants. Zinnias like a moderate amount of water. They can be used in many ways and places: in borders, beds, or any place else you want dependable color. Seeds or prestarted plants are the best sources of more zinnias.

Z. elegans. Available in many colors: white, pink, rose, red, yellow, orange, and blue.
Z. linearis. Produces orange flowers into the late fall.

SUGGESTED VARIETIES:
'Dreamland'—mixed colors
'Marvel'—mixed colors
'Rosy Future'—pale pink flowers
'Starlet'—mixed colors

GLOSSARY

Annual   A plant that lives for only one seasonal cycle.

Biennial   A plant that lives for two seasonal cycles.

Broadcast   To scatter seeds rather than to sow them in rows.

Cambium   The layer of cells between the bark and the wood of some trees.

Chlorophyll   The substance that causes plants to be green.

Coniferous   Refers to a tree that bears woody cones containing naked seeds.

Cutting   A piece of leaf, stem, or root that is cut from a living plant to be used for propagation.

Damping-off   The decay of seedling stems that is caused by fungi.

Deciduous   Refers to a plant that drops its leaves each year at the end of its active growing season.

Dormant   Refers to a plant that is resting, that is, not growing actively or visibly.

Ecology   The study of the relationship between living organisms and their environment.

Epiphyte   A plant that is growing on an elevated support such as a tree.

Erosion   The washing away of sand or rock.

Flat   A shallow box used for young plants.

Forcing   A process that uses heat to hasten the development of plants.

Germination   The start of a plant's growth.

Grafting   The process of uniting one plant with another.

Habitat   The area where a plant can be found growing wild, that is, naturally.

Hardening off   The process of reducing moisture and lowering temperature in order to acclimate plants to colder surroundings.

Hardy   Refers to a plant that can survive temperatures down to a specified degree.

Inorganic   Refers to matter that is not derived from living organisms.

Leaching   The loss of nutrients from the soil.

Mulch   A material that is spread on the soil in order to keep it moist or cool.

Offset   A small bulb growing from the base of its parent bulb.

Organic   Refers to matter that is derived from living organisms.

pH   The measure by which a substance's acidity or alkalinity can be determined.

Perennial   A plant that can live for an indefinite number of seasonal cycles.

Pinching back   Removing the ends of new shoots in order to encourage branching or flower budding.

Propagation   The process of reproducing plants.

Species   Plants that possess one or more distinctive characteristics common to all of them.

Stolon A runner that is used to propagate a plant.

Subsoil The stratum of earth lying directly beneath the topsoil.

Succulent Refers to leathery or watery plant tissue.

Sucker A subsidiary plant growing from the base of the parent plant.

Topdressing The soil, compost, or fertilizer that is used on the surface of the ground without mixing it in.

Transplanting Moving seedlings or mature plants from one place to another.

PART THREE: LISTS, CHARTS, TABLES, AND SOURCES

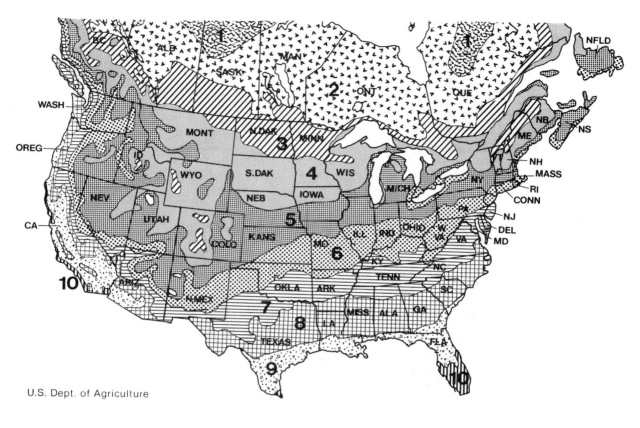

U.S. Dept. of Agriculture

Zone 1: below −50°	Zone 6: −10 to 0°
Zone 2: −50 to −40°	Zone 7: 0 to 10°
Zone 3: −40 to −30°	Zone 8: 10 to 20°
Zone 4: −30 to −20°	Zone 9: 20 to 30°
Zone 5: −20 to −10°	Zone 10: 30 to 40°

This is the Plant Hardiness Zone Map published by the U.S. Department of Agriculture. It is based on average annual low temperatures. A few other versions of zone maps are sometimes encountered and may differ from this one. However, this is the map that is generally used by growers and gardeners.

While this map (combined with zone information in the Botanical Names/Common Names Listing found on page 426) can help you decide which plants are best suited for your part of the country, microclimates can sometimes create vast temperature differences within a specific zone. For this reason, I have included temperature hardiness information for most trees and shrubs in the alphabetical listings.

COMMON NAMES/BOTANICAL NAMES

As we have said, the common names of many plants differ from one region of the country to another, and in addition, some plants are known in the same area by more than one name. For example, *Chlorophytum elatum* is called, depending on where one lives, airplane plant, spider plant, or friendship plant.

The following lists the most commonly used names of many plants, but nonetheless it may not include those plant names with which you are most familiar. However, by using the botanical names, you should be able to find the plants for which you are looking.

Please note that you will find entries in the dictionary section of this book for most of the plants in these lists, but not for all. This is a far more exhaustive listing, containing names of some rather obscure plants.

COMMON NAME	BOTANICAL NAME

A

Abyssinian sword lily	*Acidanthera*
Aconite	*Eranthis hyemalis*
Adder's tongue	Erythronium
Adonis African corn lily	*Adonis*
	Ixia
African daisy	*Arctotis grandis*
	Osteospermum (Ecklonis) hyoseroides
African iris	*Dietes iridioides*
African violet	*Saintpaulia ionantha*
Ageratum	*Ageratum houstonianum*
Alabama fothergilla	*Fothergilla monticola*
Aleppo pine	*Pinus halepensis*
Alkanet	Anchusa
	Anchusa myosotidiflora
Allegheny serviceberry	*Amelanchier laevis*
Allwood's pink	*Dianthus allwoodi*
Alpine poppy	*Papaver bursuri*
Alpine strawberry	*Fragaria vesca americana*
Amaryllis	*Hippeastrum*
Amazon lily	*Eucharis grandiflora*
American bittersweet	*Celastrus scandens*
American columbine	*Aquilegia canandensis*
American cranberry bush	*Viburnum trilobum*

COMMON NAME	BOTANICAL NAME
American elderberry	*Sambucus canadensis*
American elm	*Ulmus americana*
American holly	*Ilex opaca*
American linden	*Tilia americana*
American mountain ash	*Sorbus americana*
American strawberry	*Fragaria vesca*
Amur adonis	*Adonis amurensis*
Amur honeysuckle	*Lonicera maackii*
Anemone	Anemone
Angelica tree	Aralia
Angel's trumpet	Datura
Annual phlox	*Phlox drummondii*
	Phlox d. 'Blue Beauty'
	Phlox d. 'Dwarf Beauty Mix'
	Phlox d. 'Hybrid'
	Phlox d. 'Petticoat'
	Phlox d. 'Salmon Beauty'
Apostle plant	Neomarica
Aralia	Polyscias
Arctotis	*Arctotis stoechadifolia*
Arnold crabapple	*Malus arnoldiana*
Arrowhead	*Syngonium podophyllum*
Arrowwood	*Viburnum dentatum*
Aster	*Aster frikartii*
Astilbe	*Astilbe arendsii*
	Astilbe 'Fanal'
	Astilbe 'Federsee'
	Astilbe taquetti 'Superba'
Australian tea tree	*Leptospermum laevigatum*
Austrian black pine	*Pinus nigra*
Autumn adonis	*Adonis autumnalis*
Autumn crocus	*Colchicum autumnale*
Autumn elaeagnus	*Elaeagnus umbellata*
Autumn monkshood	*Aconitum autumnale*
Aztec lily	*Sprekelia formosissima*
Azure monkshood	*Aconitum fischeri*

B

Baboon flower	*Babiana stricta*
Baby blue eyes	*Nemophila menziesii*
Babylon weeping willow	*Salix babylonica*

Common Name	Botanical Name
Baby's breath	*Gypsophila paniculata*
Baby's tears	*Helxine soleiroii*
Bachelor's button	*Centaurea cyanus*
Bailey acacia	*Acacia baileyana*
Ball cactus	Notocactus
	Parodia
Balloonflower	*Platycodon grandiflorum*
Balloon vine	*Cardiospermum halicacabum*
Bamboo	Bambusa
	Phyllostachys
Bamboo palm	*Chamaedorea erumpens*
Banana	*Musa nana*
Barre/cactus	Echinocactus
Basket flower	*Centaurea americana*
Bayberry	*Myrica pennsylvanica*
Beach pine	*Pinus contorta*
Beach plum	*Prunus maritima*
Bearberry cotoneaster	*Cotoneaster dammeri*
Beardtongue	*Penstemon gloxinioides*
Bear's breech	*Acanthus mollis*
Beauty bush	*Kolwitzia amabilis*
Bedstraw	*Galium vernum*
Bee balm	*Monarda didyma*
Belladonna lily	*Amaryllis belladonna*
Bellflower	*Campanula*
	Campanula glomerata
Berlin poplar	*Populus berolinensis*
Bermuda buttercup	*Oxalis cernua*
Betel nut	*Areca lutescens*
Betony	*Stachys byzantina*
Big-leaf linden	*Tilia platyphyllos*
Billiard spirea	*Spiraea billiardii*
Bird of paradise	*Strelitzia reginae*
Bird's nest fern	*Aspleniumn nidus*
Bishop's hat	*Epimedium grandiflorum*
Blackberry lily	*Belamancanda chinensis*
Black-eyed Susan	*Rudbeckia fulgida*
	Rudbeckia hirta
	Thunbergia
	Thunbergia battiscombi
Black locust	*Robinia speudoacacia*
Black snakeroot	*Cimicifuga racemosa*

Blanket flower	*Gaillardia aristata*
	Gaillardia pulchella
	Gaillardia x grandiflora
Blazing star	*Mentzelia lindleyi*
Bleeding heart	*Dicentra spectabilis*
Blood cranesbill	*Geranium sanguineum*
Bloodflower	*Asclepias currassavica*
Bloodleaf	*Iresine herbstii*
Blood lily	Haemanthus
Bloodroot	*Sanguinaria canadensis*
Blue atlas cedar	*Cedrus atlantica* 'Glauca'
Bluebell	Scilla
Bluebell creeper	*Sollya heterophylla*
Bluebells	*Phaceliea*
	Phaceliea
Blueberry	Vaccinum
Blue daisy	*Felicia amelloides*
	Felicia a. 'White Felicia'
Blue-eyed grass	*Sisyrinchium bellum*
Blue globe thistle	*Echinops exaltabus*
Blue gum	*Eucalyptus globulus*
Blue lace flower	*Trachymene caerulea*
Blue lace flower	*Trachelium caeruleum*
Blue leaf wattle	*Acacia cyanophylla*
Blue lobelia	*Lobelia erinus*
	Lobelia siphilitica
Blue lungwort	*Pulmonaria angustifolia*
Blue poppy	*Meconopsis betonicifolia*
Blue sage	*Eranthemum pulchellum*
Bluets	*Houstonia longifolia*
Bog kalmia	*Kalmia polifolia*
Bog rosemary	Andromeda
Border forsythia	*Forsythia intermedia*
Border phlox	*Phlox paniculata*
Border pink	*Dianthus plumarius*
Bottle brush	*Callistemon lanceolatus*
Bowie oxalis	Oxalis
Box huckleberry	*Gaylussacia brachycera*
Brake fern	*Pteris cretica*
Bridal-wreath spirea	*Spiraea prunifolia*
Brodiaea	Brodiaea
Bronze leaf plant	*Rodgersia podophyllum*
Broom	Cytisus

Common Name	Botanical Name
Browallia	Browallia
	Browallia speciosa 'Marine Bells'
	Browallia s. 'Silver Bells'
Buckthorn	Rhamnus
Buffalo berry	Shepherdia
Bugbane	Cimicifuga
Bugleweed	*Ajuga reptans*
Bugloss	Echium
Bush cinquefoil	*Potentilla arbuscula*
Bush violet	*Browallia speciosa*
Butterfly bush	*Asclepias tuberosa*
	Asclepias curassavica
	Asclepias tuberosa
Butterfly flower	*Schizanthus pinnatus* 'Angel Wings'
	Schizanthus p. 'Hit Parade'
	Schizanthus wisetonensis
Butterfly iris	*Moraea iridioides*
Butterfly weed	
Button fern	*Pellaea rotundifolia*

C

Common Name	Botanical Name
Calendula	*Calendula officinalis*
	Calendula o. 'Fiesta Mix'
	Calendula o. 'Fiesta Yellow'
California bluebells	*Phacelia campanularia*
California poppy	*Eschscholzia californica*
California tree poppy	*Romneya coulteri*
Calla lily	Zantedeschia
Camas	Camassia
Campion; Catchfly	*Silene alpestris (quadrifida)*
Canada hemlock	*Tsuga canadensis*
Candle larkspur	*Delphinium elatum*
Candytuft	Iberis
Canna	*Canna hybrida*
Canoe birch	*Betula papyrifera*
Canterbury bells	*Campanula medium*
Cape cowslip	*Lachenalia tricolor*
Cape jasmine	*Gardenia jasminoides*
Cape marigold	*Dimorphoteca aurantiaca*
	Dimorphoteca hybrids

Common Name	Botanical Name
Cape primrose	Streptocarpus
Cardinal flower	*Lobelia cardinalis*
	Rechsteineria cardinalis
Carnation	*Dianthus caryophyllus*
Carnival orchid	Ascocentrum
Carolina jessamine	*Gelsemium sempervirens*
Carpet bugle	*Ajuga reptans*
Cast-iron plant	*Aspidistra elatior*
Castor bean plant	*Ricinus communis*
Catchfly	*Lychnis viscaria*
	Silene
Catmint	*Nepeta mussinii*
Cat-tail	*Typha latifolia*
Cedar of Lebanon	*Cedrus libani*
Century plant	*Agave americana*
Chain cactus	*Rhipsails burchelii*
Chalice vine	*Solandra guttata*
Chamomile	Anthemis
	Matricaria eximia
Charity	Polemonium
Chaste tree	*Vitex agnus-castus*
Checkerbloom	*Sidalcea malvaeflora*
Chenille plant	Acalypha
	Acalypha hispida
Cherry elaeagnus	*Elaeagnus multiflora*
Cherry laurel	*Prunus laurocerarus*
Chickweed	Cerostima
Chilean jasmine	*Mandevilla suaveolens*
China aster	*Callistephus chinensis*
Chin cactus	*Gymnocalycium mihanovichii*
China pink	*Dianthus chinensis*
Chincherinchee	*Ornithogalum thyrsoides*
Chinese bellflower	*Platycodon grandiflorum*
Chinese elm	*Ulmus parvifolia*
Chinese evergreen	*Agloanema commutum*
	Spathiphyllum
Chinese fountain palm	*Livistona chinensis*
Chinese forget-me-not	*Cynoglossum amabile*
Chinese ground orchid	*Betilla hyacinthina*
	Bletilla hyacinthina
Chinese hibiscus	*Hibiscus rosa-sinensis*
Chinese holly	*Ilex cornuta*
Chinese juniper	*Juniperus chinensis*
Chinese lantern	*Physalis alkengii*

Chinese larkspur	*Delphinium grandiflorum*
Chinese lilac	*Syringa chinensis*
Chinese peony	Paeonia
Chinese pieris	*Pieris forrestii*
Chinese poplar	*Populus lasiocarpa*
Chinese redbud	*Cercis chinensis*
Chinese witch hazel	*Hamamelis mollis*
Chokecherry	*Prunus virginiana*
Christmas cactus	Schlumbergera
Christmas rose	*Helleborus niger*
Chrysanthemum	Chrysanthemum
Cigar plant	*Cuphea ignea*
Cineraria	Senecio
	Senecio x hybridus
Cinquefoil	*Potentilla aurea*
	Potentilla fruticosa
Cladanthus	*Cladanthus arabicus*
Cliffbrake fern	*Pellaea rotundifolia*
Climbing bittersweet	*Celastrus scandens*
Climbing fern	*Lygodium palmatum*
Climbing lily	*Clematis* 'Nelly Moser'
Club moss	Selaginella
Coastal Juneberry	*Amelanchier obovalis*
Cockscomb	*Celosia argentea*
Coleus	*Coleus blumei*
Colorado spruce	*Picea pungens*
Coltsfoot	*Tusillago farfara*
Columbine	*Aquilegia alpina* 'Crimson star'
	Aquilegia a 'Harebell'
	Aquilegia hybrid
Comet orchid	Angraecum
Comfrey	*Symphtum officinalis*
Common American columbine	*Aquilegia canadensis*
Common box	*Buxus sempervirens*
Common camellia	*Camellia japonica*
Common catalpa	*Catalpa speciosa*
Common crocus	*Crocus vernus*
Common foxglove	*Digitalis purpurea*
Common geranium	*Pelargonium hortorum*
Common lavender	*Lavandula officinalis*
Common lilac	*Syringa vulgaris*
Common olive	*Olea europaea*
Common peony	*Paeonia officinalis*
Common privet	*Ligustrum vulgare*

Common Name	Botanical Name
Common star of Bethlehem	*Ornithogalum umbellatum*
Common stock	*Matthiola incana* 'Brompton Mix'
	Matthiola i. 'Excelsior Red'
	Matthiola i. 'Rose Midget'
Common sunflower	*Helianthus annuus*
Common tansy	*Tanacetum vulgare*
Common witch hazel	*Hamamelis virginiana*
Common yarrow	*Achillea millefolium*
Coneflower	*Echinacea purpurea*
	Echinacea p. 'White Luster'
Coral bean	*Erythrina herbacea*
Coral bell	*Heuchera sanguinea*
Coral berry	*Ardisia*
Coral drops	*Bessera elegans*
Coralvine	*Antigonon leptopus*
Corkscrew willow	*Salix matsudana* 'Toruosa'
Corncob	Lobivia
Corncockle	*Agrostemma githago*
Cornelian cherry	*Cornus mas*
Cornflower	*Centaurea cyanus*
	Centaurea montana
Cornflower aster	*Stokesia laevis*
Cornflower	*Rudbeckia hirta*
Corn lily	Ixia
Corn plant	*Dracaena massangeana*
Cosmos	Cosmos
Cowslip	*Primula officinalis*
Cranberry cotoneaster	*Cotoneaster apiculata*
Cranesbill	*Erodium chamaedryoides*
	Geranium cordatum
	Geranium grandiflorum
Crape myrtle	*Lagerstroemia indica*
Creeping gypsophila	*Gypsophila repens* 'Rosea'
Creeping Jacob's ladder	*Polemonium reptans*
Creeping zinnia	*Sanvitalia procumbens*
Crepe myrtle	*Lagerstromeria indica*
Crimson flag	*Schizostylis coccinea*
Croton	*Codiaeum variegatum*
Crown cactus	Rebutia
Crown imperial	*Fritillaria imperialis*
Cudweed	*Gnaphalium sylvaticum*
Cup-and-saucer vine	*Cobaea scandens*
Cup-of-flower	Nierembergia

COMMON NAME	BOTANICAL NAME
Cup-of-gold	*Solandra guttata*
Cupid's dart	*Catananche caerulea*
Cup sage	*Salvia farinacea*
Currant	*Ribes*
Cushion spurge	*Euphorbia epithymoides*
Cut-leaf coneflower	*Rudbeckia laciniata*
Cut-leaf lilac	*Syringa laciniata*
Cyclamen	Cyclamen

D

Daffodil	Narcissus
Dahlberg daisy	*Dyssoida tenuiloba*
Dahlia	Dahlia
Dancing lady orchid	Oncidium forbesi
	Oncidium ampliatum
Dandelion	*Taraxacum*
Date palm	*Phoenix dactylifera*
David viburnum	*Viburnum davidii*
Daylily	Hemerocallis
	Hemerocallis hybrid
	Hemerocallis 'Johanna'
Dead nettle	*Lamium variegatum*
Delicate lily	*Chlidanthus fragrans*
Deodar cedar	*Cedrus deodara*
Dill	Anthemum
Dill-leaf ursinia	*Ursinia anthemoides*
Dogtooth violet	*Erythronium dens canis*
Dollar plant	*Lunaria annua*
Dumbcane	*Dieffenbachia amoena*
Dusty miller	*Centaurea cineraria*
	Centaurea rutifolia
Dutch iris	*Iris hybrids*
Dutchman's pipe	*Aristolochia durior*
Dutch runner bean	*Phaseolus coccineus alba*
Dwarf flowering almond	*Prunus glandulosa*
Dwarf fothergilla	*Fothergilla gardenii*
Dwarf hinoki cypress	*Chamaecyparus obtussa 'Nana'*
Dwarf morning	*Convolvulus tricolor*

E

Earth star	Dyckia
Easter cactus	*Rhipsalideopsis*
Eastern redbud	*Cercis canadensis*
Eastern red cedar	*Juniperus virginiana*
Eastern white pine	*Pinus strobus*
Edelweiss	*Leontopodium alpinum*
Egyptian star flower	*Pentas lanceolata*
Elderberry	Sambucus
Elephant ears	Colocasia
	Colocasia esculenta
Emerald fern	*Alocasia*
	Asparagus sprengeri
English bluebell	*Scilla nutans*
English daisy	*Bellis perennis*
English hawthorn	*Crataegus oxyacantha*
English holly	*Ilex aquifolium*
English iris	*Iris xiphioides*
English monkshood	*Aconitum napellus*
English oak	*Quercus robur*
English wall flower	*Cheiranthus cheiri*
English yew	*Taxus baccata*
European alder	*Alnus glutonusa*
European ash	*Fraxinus excelsior*
European beech	*Fagus sylvatica*
European cranberry bush	*Viburnum opulus*
European mountain ash	*Sorbus aucuparia*
European silver fir	*Abies alba*
European white birch	*Betula pendula verucosa*
Evening primrose	*Gaura lindheimeri*
Evening primrose	*Primula vulgaris*
Evergreen candytuft	*Iberis sempervirens*
Everlasting	*Xeranthemum annuum*
Everlasting pea	Lathyrus

F

False aralia	Dizygotheca
False daisy	*Europys mauritanus*
False dragonhead	*Physostegia virginiana*
	Physostegia v. 'Summer Snow'
False indigo	Baptisia
	Baptisia australis

Common Name	Botanical Name
Farewell-to-spring	*Godetia amoena*
	Clarkia amoena
Father Hugo's rose	*Rosa hugonis*
Feather cockscomb	*Celosia plumosa* 'Apricot Brandy'
	Celosia p. 'New Look'
Fern-leafed beech	*Fagus sylvatica heterophylla*
Fern-leaved yarrow	*Achillea filipendula*
	Achillea filipendula
Fernleaf maple	*Acer japonicum* 'Aconitifolium'
Feverfew	*Chrysanthemum parthenium*
Fig	Ficus
Fig marigold	*Mesembryanthemum cordifolium*
Fire bush	*Kochia scoparia trichophila*
Firethorn	Pyracantha
Fireweed	Epilobium
Fishtail palm	*Caryota mitis*
Five-leaf akebia	*Akebia quinata*
Flame anemone	*Anemone fulgens*
Flame-of-the-woods	*Ixora coccinea*
Flamingo flower	Anthurium
Flax	Linum
Fleabane	Erigeron
	Erigeron glaucas
	Erigeron karvinskianus
Florist's cyclamen	*Cyclamen persicum*
Floss flower	*Ageratum houstonianum*
Flowering almond	*Prunus triloba*
Flowering ash	*Fraxinus ornus*
Flowering dogwood	*Cornus florida*
Flowering flax	Linum
Flowering maple	*Abutilon hybridum*
	Abutilon h. 'Golden Fleece'
	Abutilon megapotanicum
Flowering onion	Allium
	Allium schoenoprasum
Flowering quince	*Chaenomeles lagenaria*
Flowering tobacco	*Nicotiana alata grandiflora*
Flower-of-an-hour	*Hibiscus trionum*
Foam flower	*Tiarella cordifolia*
Forget-me-not	*Anchusa capensis*
	Myosotis sylvatica 'Blue Bird'
Fountain grass	*Pennisetum ruppelia*
Fountain plant	*Amaranthus salicifolius*

Four-o'clock	*Mirabilis jalapa*
Foxglove	Digitalis
	Digitalis purpurea
	Digitalis p. 'Alba'
	Digitalis p. 'Foxy Miss'
Foxtail orchid	*Rhyncostylis gigantea*
Fragrant snowball	*Viburnum carlcephalum*
Frangipani	*Plumeria vubra*
French buttercup	*Ranunculus asiaticus*
French marigold	*Tagetes patula*
French rose	*Rosa gallica*
Fringe tree	*Chionanthus virginica*
Full-moon maple	*Acer japonicum*

G

Garden heliotrope	*Valeriana officinalis*
Garden pansy	*Viola x wittrockiana*
Garden verbena	*Verbena hortensis 'Polaris'*
Gas plant	*Dictamnus albus*
	Dictamus fraxinella rubra
Gay feather	Liatris
	Litatris spicata
	Liatris s. 'Alba'
Gazania	*Gazania langiscapa*
Gentian	*Gentiana asclepiadea*
Geranium	*Geranium dalmaticum*
	Pelargonium
	Pelargonium sanguineum
Germander	*Teucrium chamaedrys*
German statice	*Limonium dumosum*
German violet	*Exacum affine*
Giant arborvitae	*Thuja plicata*
Giant Burmese honeysuckle	*Lonicera hildebrandiana*
Giant onion	*Allium giganteum*
Giant summer hyacinth	*Galtonia candicans*
Ginger lily	Hedychium
	Hedychium coronarium
Ginkgo	*Ginkgo biloba*
Ginseng	*Panax quinquifolius*

Common Name	Botanical Name
Gladiola	Gladiolus
Globe amaranth	*Gomphrena globosa*
Globe candytuft	*Iberis umbellata*
Globeflower	Trollius
	Trollius europaeus
Gloriosa daisy	*Rudbeckia gloriosa*
Glory bower	*Clerodendrum thompsoniae*
Glorybush	*Tibouchina urvilleana*
Glory lily	*Gloriosa rothschildiana*
Glory-of-the-snow	*Chionodoxa sardensis*
Gloxinia	*Sinningia speciosa*
Goatsbeard	*Aruncus sylvester*
Goat willow	*Salix caprea*
Gold dust plant	*Aucuba japonica*
Golden centaurea	*Centaurea macrocephala*
Golden columbine	*Aquilegia chrysanta*
Golden chain tree	*Laburnum*
Golden coreopsis	*Coreopsis tinctoria*
Golden crocus	*Crocus chrysanthus*
Goldenfleece	*Thymophylla ternuiloba*
Golden Irish yew	*Taxus baccata* 'Fastigiata Aureomarginata'
Golden lantern	*Calochortus pulchellus*
Golden marguerite	*Anthemis tinctoria*
Golden privet	*Ligustrum* 'vicaryi'
Goldenrain tree	*Koelreuteria paniculata*
Goldenrod	Solidago
	Solidago x hybrida
Golden spider lily	*Lycoris african*
Golden star	*Chrysogonum virginiana*
Golden-yellow sweet pea	*Crotalaria retusa*
Goldfish plant	*Hypocyrta nummularia*
	Hypocyrta strigillosa
Gooseneck loosestrife	*Lysimachia clethroides*
Grape holly	*Mahonia aquifolium*
Grape hyacinth	*Muscari botryoides*
Grape-leaf anemone	*Anemone vitifolia*
Gray poplar	*Populus canescens*
Grecian urn plant	*Acanthus mollis*
Greek anemone	*Anemone blanda*
Greek juniper	*Juniperus excelsa*
Greek valerian	Polemonium
Green ash	*Fraxinus pennsylvanica*
Ground ivy	*Nepeta hederaceae*
Ground morning glory	*Convolvulus mauritanicus*

H

Hackberry	Celtis
Hanging begonia	*Begonia pendula*
Hardy willow-leaf cotoneaster	*Cotoneaster salicifolia floccosa*
Harlequin flower	*Sparaxis tricolor*
Hart's tongue fern	*Phyllitis scolopendrium*
Harvest brodiaea	*Brodiaea elegans*
Hawk's beard	*Crepis rubra*
Heart-leaved bergenia	*Bergenia cordifolia*
Heath	Erica
Heather	*Calluna vulgaris*
Hedgehog cactus	Echinocereus
Hedge maple	*Acer campestre*
Helen's flower	*Helenium autumnale*
Heliotrope	*Heliotropium*
	Heliotropium arborescens
	Heliotropium a. 'Black Prince'
Hen and chickens	Selaginella
	Sempervivum
Himalayan foxtail lily	Eremurus
Himalayan primrose	*Primula denticulata*
Hinoki false cypress	*Chamaecyparis obtusa*
Holly	*Ilex aquifolium*
Hollyfern	Polystichum
Hollyhock	*Althaea rosea*
	Altheae r. 'Majorette Hybrid'
	Malva alcea
Holly-leaf osmanthus	*Osmanthus heterophyllus*
Holly oak	*Quercus ilex*
Honesty plant	*Lunaria annua*
Honey bell	*Mahernia verticillata*
Horsetail plant	*Equisetum hymale*
Hungarian oak	*Quercus frainetto*
Hyacinth	Hyacinthus

I

Ibolium ligustrum	*Ligustrum ibolium*
Iceland poppy	*Papaver nudicaule*

Common Name	Botanical Name
Ice plant	*Cephalophyllum hybrid*
	Dorotheanthus bellidiflorus
	Mesembryanthemum crystallinum
	Mesembryanthemum c. (red)
Inch plant	*Tradescantia virginiana*
Indian crocus	Pleione
Indian currant	*Symphoricarpos orbiculatus*
Indian hawthorn	*Raphiolepis indica*
Indian mock strawberry	*Duchesnea indica*
Indigo	*Indigofera tinctoria*
Inkberry	*Ilex glabra*
Iris	Iris
Irish moss	*Sagina subulata*
Irish yew	*Taxus baccata stricta*
Italian aster	*Aster amellus*
Italian stone pine	*Pinus pinea*
Ivy arum	Scindapsus
	Scindapsus aureus
Ivy geranium	*Pelargonium peltatum*

J

Common Name	Botanical Name
Jacobean lily	*Sprekelia formosissima*
Japanese andromeda	*Pieris japonica*
Japanese anemone	*Anemone japonica*
Japanese arborvitae	*Thuja standishii*
Japanese barberry	*Berberis thunbergii*
Japanese black pine	*Pinus thunbergiana*
Japanese cedar	*Cryptomenia japonica*
Japanese dogwood	*Cornus kousa*
Japanese holly	*Ilex crenata*
Japanese iris	*Iris kaempferi*
Japanese maple	*Acer palmatum*
Japanese primrose	*Primula japonica*
Japanese privet	*Ligustrum japonicum*
Japanese quince	*Chaenomeles japonica*
Japanese red pine	*Pinus densiflora*
Japanese rose	*Rosa multiflora*

Common Name	Botanical Name
Japanese snowball	*Viburnum plicatum*
Japanese spurge	*Pachysandra terminalis*
Japanese viburnum	*Viburnum japonicum*
Japanese white pine	*Pinus parviflora*
Japanese winterberry	*Ilex serrata*
Japanese wisteria	*Wisteria floribunda*
Japanese yew	*Taxus cuspidata*
Jasmine	*Jasminum officinale*
Job's tears	*Coix lacryma-jobi*
Johnny-jump-up	*Viola tricolor*
Joseph's coat; Love-lies-bleeding	*Amaranthus tricolor*
Judas tree	*Cercis siliquastrum*

K

Common Name	Botanical Name
Kaffir lily	*Clivia miniata*
Kashmir mountain ash	*Sorbus cashmariana*
King's crown	Jacobinia
Kite orchid	*Masdevallia coccinea*
Knotweed	*Polygonum capitaltum*
Korean barberry	*Berberis koreana*
Korean early lilac	*Syringa oblata dilatata*
Korean lilac	*Syringa velutina*
Korean rhododendron	*Rhododendron mucronulatum*
Korean spice viburnum	*Viburnum carlesii*
Kudzu vine	*Peuraria lobata*

L

Common Name	Botanical Name
Laceleaf Japanese maple	*Acer palmatum 'Dissectum'*
Lady-of-the-night	*Brassavola nodosa*
Lady palm	*Rhapis exelsa*
Lady's eardrops	Fuchsia
Lady slipper orchid	Paphiopedilum
Lady Washington geranium	*Pelargonium domesticum*
Lamb's ear	*Stachys byzantina*
Lantana	Lantana
Large flowering cotoneaster	*Cotoneaster multiflora*
Large fothergilla	*Fothergilla major*

COMMON NAME	BOTANICAL NAME
Larkspur	*Consolida ambigua*
	Delphinium
Laurel oak	*Quercus laurifolia*
Lavender	*Lavandula angustifolia*
Lavender cotton	*Santolina chamaecypaus*
Lawson false cypress	*Chamaecyparus lawsoniana*
Lazy daisy	*Aphanostephus skirrobasis*
Leadwort	*Ceratostigma plumbaginoides*
Leatherleaf viburnum	*Viburnum rhytidophyllum*
Lemoine deutzia	*Deutzia lemoinei*
Lemon vine	*Pereskia aculeata*
Lenten rose	*Helleborus niger*
	Helleborus orientalis
Leopard plant	*Ligularia dentata*
Leopard's bane	*Doronicum caucasicum*
Lilac honeysuckle	*Lonicera syringanthar*
	Cuphea ignea
Lily	Lilium
Lily leek	*Allium moly*
Lily magnolia	*Magnolia liliflora*
Lily of the Nile	*Agapanthus africanus*
Lily of the valley	*Convallaria majalis*
Lily-of-the-valley tree	*Clethra arborea*
Lily turf	*Ophiopogon japonica*
Linden viburnum	*Viburnum dilatatum*
Lion's ear	*Leonotis leonurus*
Lipstick plant	*Aesychnanthus speciosa*
Littleleaf box	*Buxus microphylla*
Littleleaf lilac	*Syringa microphylla*
Live oak	*Quercus virginiana*
Living-rock plant	Lithops
Living rocks	*Neoregelia carolinae*
Living-vase plant	*Aechmea fasciata*
	Neoregelia
	Lithops
Lobelia	Lobelia
Loblolly tree	*Gordonia lasianthus*
Locust	Robinia
Lombardy poplar	*Populus nigra* 'Italica'
London plane tree	*Platanus acerifolia*
Loosestrife	*Lysimachia punctata*
Loquat	*Eriobotyra japonica*
Lovage	*Levisticum officinalis*

Love-in-a-mist	*Nigella damascena*
Lungwort	*Pulmonaria angustifolia*
Lupine	*Lupinus*
	Lupinus hybrid 'Little Lulu'
	Lupinus polyphyllus

M

Macedonian pine	*Pinus peuce*
Madagascar jasmine	*Stephanotis floribunda*
Madagascar periwinkle	*Catharanthus r.* 'Little Blanche'
	Cartharanthus r. 'Magic Carpet Mix'
Madonna lily	*Lilium candidum*
Magellan barberry	*Berberis buxifolia*
Maidenhair fern	Adiantum
Mallow	*Malva maritima*
Mallow-wort	*Malope trifida*
Maltese cross	*Lychnis chalcedonica*
Mango	*Mangifera indica*
Marguerite	*Chrysanthemum frutescens*
Marigold	Tagetes
	Tagetes 'Baby Boy'
	Tagetes 'Bonanza Yellow'
	Tagetes 'Dainty Marietta'
	Tagetes 'Disco'
	Tagetes 'Gold Buy'
	Tagetes 'Golden Gem'
	Tagetes 'Lemon Gem'
	Tagetes 'Nugget'
	Tagetes 'Paprika'
	Tagetes 'Queen Sophia'
	Tagetes 'Scarlet Sophie'
Mariposa lily	Calochortus
Marsh marigold	*Caltha palustris*
Mask flower	*Alonsoa warscewiczii*
Masterwort	*Astrantia major*
May apple	*Podophyllum peltatum*
Meadowrue	*Thalictrum diffusiflorum*
Meadow saffron	*Colchicum speciosum*
Mexican firecracker	*Maettia bicolor*
Mexican foxglove	*Allophytum mexicanum*

COMMON NAME	BOTANICAL NAME
Mexican love vine	Dipladenia
Mexican sunflower	*Tithonia rotundifolia*
Mexican tree fern	*Cibotium scheidei*
Michelmas daisy	Aster
	Aster novae-angliae
Mignonette	*Reseda odorata*
Milkweed	*Euphorbia lophogora*
Miniature flag plant	*Acorus gramineus*
Miniature holly	*Malpighia coccigera*
Miniature hollyhock	Sidalcea
Mist flower	*Eupatorium coelestinum*
Mock orange	*Carpenteria californica*
	Philadelphus
Mock strawberry	*Duchesnea indica*
Monarch	*Venidium fastuosum*
Mondo grass	*Liriope muscari*
Money plant	*Lunaria annua*
Moneywort	*Lysimachia punctata*
Monkey flower	*Mimulas guttata*
	Mimulus g. 'Malibu Orange'
	Mimulus guttatas 'Malibu Yellow'
	Mimulus variegatus
Montbretia	*Crocosmia crocosmiiflora*
	Crocosmia (montbretia) crocosmiiflora
	Crocosmia (montbretia) masoniorum
Moon flower	*Phalaenopsis amabilis*
Moonflower	*Calonyction aculeatum*
Morning glory	Convolvulus
	Ipomoea purpurea
	Ipomoea p. 'Early Call'
	Ipomoea p. 'Heavenly Blue'
Moses-in-a-cradle	*Rheo discolor*
Moss campion	*Silene schafta*
Moss phlox	*Phlox subulata*
Moss pink	*Phlox subulata*
Moss rose	*Helianthemum nummularium*
	Portulaca grandiflora
	Rosa centifolia 'Muscosa'
Moth orchid	*Phalaenopsis amabilis*
Mountain ash	*Sorbus vilmorinii*
Mountain laurel	*Kalmia latifolia*
Moyes rose	*Rosa moyesii*
Mugwort	*Artemesia schmidtiana*

COMMON NAME	BOTANICAL NAME
Mullein	Verbascum
	Verbascum chaixii
Mullein pink	*Lychnis coronaria*

N

Nanking cherry	*Prunus tomentosa*
Naples onion	*Allium neapolitanum*
Nasturtium	Tropaeolum
	Tropaeolum majus
Neapolitanum cyclamen	*Cyclamen neapolitanum*
Nemesia	*Nemesia strumosa*
New Zealand flax	*Phormium tenax*
Night blooming cactus	Selenicereus
Night blooming cereus	*Hylocereus undatus*
Night-blooming cereus	*Hylocereus undatus*
Night jasmine	Cestrum
Nippon chrysanthemum	*Chrysanthemum nipponicum*
Nordmann fir	*Abies nordmanniana*
Norfolk Island pine	*Auraucaria heterophylla*
Norway maple	*Acer platanoides*
Norway spruce	*Picea abies*

O

Oak-leafed hydrangea	*Hydrangea quercifolia*
Old-fashioned weigela	*Weigela florida*
Old man cactus	Cephalocereus
	Cephalocereus senilis
Oleander	Nerium
	Nerium oleander
Orange-eye butterfly bush	*Buddleia davidii*
Orange jasmine	*Murraya exotica*
Orchid cactus	Epiphyllum
Orchid tree	Bauhinia
Oriental plane tree	*Platanus orientalis*
Oriental poppy	*Papaver orientale*
Oriental spruce	*Picea orientalis*

Common Name	Botanical Name
Ox-tongue plant	*Gasteria lingulata*
Ozark sundrop	*Oenothera missouriensis*

P

Common Name	Botanical Name
Pacific Coast iris	*Iris douglasiana*
Pacific dogwood	*Cornus nuttallii*
Painted daisy	*Chrysanthemum coccineum*
	Pyrethrum roseum
Painted leaf plant	Coleus
Painted tongue	*Salpiglossis sinuata*
	Salpiglossis s. 'Splash'
Pampas grass	Cortaderia
Pansy	*Viola tricolor hortensis*
Pansy orchid	Miltonia
Papaya	*Carica papaya*
Paper flower	*Bougainvillea glabra*
Partridge berry	*Mitchella repens*
Passion flower	*Passiflora caerulea*
	Passiflora 'Coral Seas'
	Passifora edulis
Patience plant	Impatiens
Peach-leaved bellflower	*Campanula persicifolia* 'White Star'
Peacock flower	*Tigrida pavonia*
Peacock plant	Episcia
	Kaempfera roscoeana
	Kaempfera roscoeana
Pearly everlasting	*Anaphalis margaritacea*
Peegee hydrangea	*Hydrangea paniculata* 'Grandiflora'
Penstemon	*Penstemon gloxinoides*
	Penstemon g. 'Firebrand'
	Penstemon g. 'Huntington Pink'
	Penstemon g. 'Ruby King'
Pepper plant	*Capsicum annuum*
Perennial flax	*Linum perenne*
Periwinkle	*Vinca rosea*
Persian centaurea	*Centaurea dealbata*
Persimmon	*Diospyros virginiana*
Peruvian lily	*Alstroemeria aurantiaca*
Petunia	Petunia
Phlox	Phlox

Common Name	Botanical Name
Photinia	*Photinia villosa*
Piggy-back plant	*Tolmiea*
	Tolmiea menzenii
Pimpernel	Anagallis
	Anagallis linifolia
Pincushion	*Mammillaria*
	Scabiosa caucasica
Pin-cushion cactus	Mammillaria
Pincushion flower	*Scabiosa barbata*
	Scabiosa atro purpurea
	Scabiosa caucasica
Pineapple	Ananas
Pineapple lily	*Veltheimia viridifolia*
Pink	Dianthus
	Dianthus plumarius
Pink calla	*Zantedeschia rehmannii*
Pink-flowered yarrow	*Achillea m. 'Roseum'*
Pink-sand verbena	*Abronia umbellata*
Pink-shell azalea	*Rhododendron vaseyi*
Pin oak	*Quercus palustris*
Plantain lily	*Hosta alba-margarinata*
	Hosta 'Krossa Regal'
	Hosta venusta
Plum	Prunus
Plumbago vine	Plumbago
Plume poppy	*Macleaya cordata*
Pocketbook plant	*Calceolaria herbeohybrida*
	Calceolaria integrifolia
Poinsettia	*Euphorbia pulcherrima*
Polypody fern	Polypodium
	Polypodium aureum
Pomegranate	*Punica granatum*
Pond weed	Aponogeton
Poppy	*Callirhoe involucrata*
Poppy-flowered anemone	*Anemone coronaria*
Poppy mallow	*Callirhoe involucrata*
Porcelain vine	*Ampelopsis brevipedunculata*
Pothos	*Scindapus*
Pot marigold	*Calendula officinalis*
Prairie gentian	*Lisanthus grandiflorum*
Prairie mallow	Sidalcea
Prickly pear	Opuntia
	Opuntia microdays

COMMON NAME	BOTANICAL NAME
Prickly poppy	*Argemone grandiflora*
Primrose	*Oenothera speciosa*
	Primula
	Primula x obconica
	Primula x polyantha
Primrose jasmine	*Jasminum mesnyi*
Prince's-feather	*Amaranthus hypochondriacus*
Princess flower	*Tibouchina semidecandra*
Punch-and-Judy orchid	Gongora
Punch-and-Judy orchid	*Gongora bufonia*
Purple beech	*Fagus sylvatica purpurea*
Purple coneflower	*Echinacea purpurea* 'Shooting Star'
Purple-leaf sand cherry	*Prunus cistena*
Purple loosestrife	*Lythrum salicaria*
Pussy ears	Cyanotis
Pussy willow	*Salix discolor*

Q

Queen of the prairie	*Flipendula rubra*
Queensland umbrella	*Schefflera actinophylla*
Queen's wreath	*Petrea volubilis*

R

Ragwort	*Ligularia dicorum*
Rainbow cactus	Echinocereus
Rainbow flower	Achimenes
	Achimenes
Rain lily	*Zephyranthes grandiflora*
Red elderberry	*Sambucus racemosa*
Red-hot poker	*Knifphofia a.* 'Vanilla'
	Kniphofia aloides
	Kniphofia uvaria
	Kniphofia a. 'Border Ballet'
Red maple	*Acer rubrum*
Red pepper plant	*Capsicum frutescens*
Red pine	*Pinus resinosa*
Redtwig dogwood	*Cornus stolonifera*
Red valerian	*Centranthus valerian ruber*

Reed grass	*Arundo donax*
Regal lily	*Lilium regale*
Rock purslane	*Calandrinia umbellata*
Rock rose	*Helianthemum nummularium* 'Fire Dragon'
Rock-spray cotoneaster	*Cotoneaster horizontalis*
Rocky Mountain columbine	*Aquilegia caerulea*
Rocky Mountain garland	*Clarkia elegans*
Rosary vine	Ceropegia
Rose acacia	*Robinia hispida*
Rosebud cherry	*Prunus subhirtella*
Rose campion	*Lychnis coronaria*
Rose mallow	Hibiscus
Rosemary	*Rosmarinus officinalis*
Rose moss	*Portulaca grandiflora*
Rose-of-Sharon	*Hibiscus syriacus*
Rose-shell rhododenron	*Rhododendron roseum elegans*
Rouge plant	*Rivina humilis*
Round-leaf Juneberry	*Amelanchier sanguinea*
Royal azalea	*Rhododendron schlippenbachii*
Rugosa rose	*Rosa rugosa*
Running Juneberry	*Amelanchier spicata*
Russian olive	*Elaeagnus angustifolia*

S

Sage	Salvia
Sago palm	*Cycas revoluta*
Saint Johnswort	*Hypericum moserianum*
Sand cherry	*Prunus susquehanae*
Sargent crabapple	*Malus sargentii*
Sasanqua camellia	*Camellia sasanqua*
Satin flower	Godetia
Saucer magnolia	*Magnolia soulangana*
Savory	*Satureja montana*
Sawara false cypress	*Chamaecyparis pisifera*
Scarab Lawson cypress	*Chamaecyparis lawsoniana* 'Allumii'
Scarborough lily	*Vallota speciosa*
Scarlet flax	*Linum grandiflorum*
Scarlet flowering gum	*Eucalyptus ficifolia*
Scarlet oak	*Quercus coccinea*
Scarlet runner bean	*Phaseolus caracalla*

COMMON NAME	BOTANICAL NAME
Scarlet sage	*Salvia splendens*
Scarlet trumpet honeysuckle	*Lonicera brownii*
Scotch crocus	Crocus
Scotch moss	*Sagina subulata*
Scotch pine	*Pinus sylvestris*
Scotch rose	*Rosa spinosissima*
Screw pine	*Pandanus veitchii*
Sea holly	*Eryngium oliverianium*
Sea lavender	*Limonium latifolium*
Sea pink	Armeria
	Armeria maritima
Sea poppy	Glaucium
	Glaucium corniculatum
Sea urchin cactus	Echinopsis
Self-heal plant	*Prunella webbiana*
Serbian spruce	*Picea omorika*
Shadblow serviceberry	*Amelanchier canadensis*
Shasta daisy	*Chrysanthemum maximum*
Shell flower	Alpinia
	Tigridia pavonia
Shirley poppy	*Papaver rhoeas*
Shooting star	*Cyclamen coum*
Short-tubed lycoris	*Lycoris radiata*
Showy primrose	*Oenothera speciosa* 'Berlandier'
Shrimp plant	*Belorpone guttata (Justicia)*
Siberian dogwood	*Cornus alba* 'Sibirica'
Siberian iris	*Iris siberica*
Siberian wallflower	*Cheiranthus*
Sieber crocus	*Crocus sieberii*
Silk flower	*Abelmoschus moschatos*
Silk tassel	*Garrya elliptica*
Silver buffaloberry	*Shepardia argentea*
Silk tree	*Albizia julibrissin*
Silverbells	*Halesia carolina*
Silver mound	*Artemesia schmidtiana*
Silver red cedar	*Juniperus virginiana* 'Glauca'
Single-seed hawthorn	*Crataegus monogyna*
Sitka spruce	*Picea sitchensis*
Skullcap	*Scutellaria baicalensis*
Skunk cabbage	*Symphlocarpus foetidus*
Slender deutzia	*Deutzia gracilis*
Small leafed cotoneaster	*Cotoneaster microphylla*
Snake plant	*Sansieveria trifasciata*

Snake's head	*Fritillaria meleagris*
Snapdragon	*Antirrhinum majus*
Sneezeweed	*Achillea ptarmica*
	Helenium autumnale
Sneezewort	*Achillea ptarmica*
Snowberry	*Symphoricarpos albus*
Snowdrop	*Galanthus nivalis*
	Oenothera
Snowflake	*Leucojum vernum*
Snow-in-summer	*Cerastium tomentosum*
Snow-on-the-mountain	*Euphorbia marginata*
Soapwort	*Saponaria ocymoides*
Society garlic	*Tulbaghia fragrans*
Solomon's seal	*Polygonum biflorum*
Sourwood	*Oxydendrum arboreum*
Southern catalpa	*Catalpa bignonioides*
Southern magnolia	*Magnolia grandiflora*
Southern yew	*Podocarpus nagi*
Spanish iris	*Iris xiphium*
Speckled alder	*Alnus incana*
Speedwell	Veronica
	Veronica incana 'Crater Lake'
	Veronica i. 'Royal Blue'
Spider flower	*Cleome spinosa*
Spider lily	*Hymenocallis*
	Hymenocallis narcissifolia
	Lycoris radiata
Spider orchid	*Ansellia africana*
Spider plant	*Chlorophytum elatum*
Spiderwort	*Tradescantia virginiana*
Spiral ginger	Costus
	Costus igneus
Spreading cotoneaster	*Cotoneaster divaricata*
Spring adonis	*Adonis vernalis*
Spring meadow saffron	*Bulbocodium vernum*
Spurge	Euphorbia
	Euphorbia lophogora
	Pachysandra terminalis
Staghorn fern	*Platycerium grandiflorum*
Star cactus	Astrophytum
	Astrophytum asterias
Star flower	*Huernia pillansi*

Common Name	Botanical Name
Star glory	Quamoclit
Star jasmine	*Trachelospermum jasminoides*
Star magnolia	*Magnolia stellata*
Star of Bethlehem	Ornithogalum
Star of Persia	*Allium christophii*
Star of Texas	*Xanthisma texanum*
Star plant	*Cryptanthus zonatus*
Stock	*Matthiola incana*
Stoke's aster	*Stokesia laevis*
Stonecrop	*Sedum spectabile*
Strawberry geranium	*Saxifraga soarentosa*
Strawberry guava	Psidium
Strawflower	*Helichrysum bracteatum*
Striped squill	*Puschkinia scilloides*
Sugar maple	*Acer saccharum*
Summer adonis	*Adonis aestrivalis*
Summer forget-me-not	*Anchusa capensis*
Summer phlox	*Phlox paniculata*
Summer sweet	*Clethra alnifolia*
Sun cactus	Heliocereus
	Heliocereus undatus
Sundrops	Oenothera
	Oenothera tetragona
Sunflower	Helianthus
Sun rose	*Helianthemum nummularium*
Sunshine daisy	*Gamolepis tagetes*
Swamp Juneberry	*Amelanchier intermedia*
Swan River daisy	*Brachycome iberidifolia*
Swedish ivy	Plectranthus
Sweet alyssum	*Lobularia maritima*
Sweet bay	*Magnolia virginiana*
Sweet gum	*Liquidambar styaciflua*
Sweet locust	*Gleditsia triacanthos*
Sweet mock orange	*Philadelphus coronarius*
Sweet mountain pine	*Pinus mugo*
Sweet olive	*Osmanthus fragrans*
Sweet pea	*Lathyrus odoratus*
Sweet rocket	*Hesperis matronalis*
Sweet shrub	*Calycanthus floridus*
Sweet sultan	*Cantaurea moschata*
Sweet violet	*Viola odorata*
Sweet William	*Dianthus barbatus*

COMMON NAME	BOTANICAL NAME
Sweet William phlox	*Phlox divaricata*
Swiss cheese plant	*Monstera deliciosa*
Swiss stone pine	*Pinus cembra*

T

Table fern	*Pteris cretica*
Tahoka daisy	*Aster tanacetifolius*
Tassel flower	*Amaranthus caudatus*
	Emilia flammea
Tatarian dogwood	*Cornus alba*
Tatarian honeysuckle	*Lonicera tatarica*
Temple bells	Smithiantha
Texas bluebonnet	*Lupinus subcaornosus*
Texas mountain laurel	*Sophora secundiflora*
Thread cypress	*Chamaecyparis pisifera* 'Filifera'
Threadleaf coreopsis	*Coreopsis verticillata*
	Coreopsis v. 'Moonbeam'
Thrift	Armeria
	Armeria maritima
Thunberg spirea	*Spiraea thunbergii*
Tickseed	Coreopsis
	Tigrida pavonia
Tidytips	*Layia campestris*
Ti plant	*Cordyline terminalis*
Tiger flower	*Tigrida pavonia*
Toadflax	*Linaria maroccana*
Toad lily	*Tricyrtis hirta*
Transvaal daisy	*Gerbera jamesonii*
Tree fern	Blechnum
Tree mallow	*Lavatera trimestris*
Tree-of-heaven	*Ailanthus altissima*
Tricolor beech	*Fagus sylvatica* 'Tricolor'
True primula	*Primula vulgaris*
Trumpet crater	*Campsis tagliabuana*
Trumpet flower	*Beaumontia grandiflora*
	Datura metel
Trumpet vine	*Allamanda cathartica*
	Bignonia capreolata
	Doxantha unguis-cati
Tuberose	*Polyanthes tuberosa*
Tuberous begonia	*Begonia tuberhybrida*

COMMON NAME	BOTANICAL NAME
Tulip tree	*Liriodenron tulipifera*
Turkey oak	*Quercus cerris*
Tussock bellflower	*Campanula carpatica*
Twinspur	*Diascia barberae*

U
Umbrella plant	*Cyperus alternifolia*

V
Veitch magnolia	*Magnolia veitchii*
Venus flytrap	*Dionaea muscipula*
Verbena	*Verbena hortensis*
Vervain	*Verbena venosa*
Violet	Viola
	Viola cornuta
Violet boltonia	*Boltonia latisquama*
Violet sage	*Salvia superba*
Virginia stock	*Malcomia maritima*
Virgin's bower	Clematis
Volcano plant	*Bromelia balanse*

W
Wall rockcress	*Arabis caucasia*
Wandering Jew	*Tradescantia virginiana*
Wand flower	*Dierama pulcherrimum* Sparaxis *Sparaxis tricolor*
Warty barberry	*Berberis verruculosa*
Water lily	*Nymphaea*
Water arum	*Calla palustria*
Watsonia	Watsonia
Wax begonia	*Begonia semperflorens*
Wax plant	*Hoya bella*

Common Name	Botanical Name
Wayfaring tree	*Viburnum lantana*
Weeping forsythia	*Forsythia suspensa*
Western catalpa	*Catalpa speciosa*
Western hemlock	*Tsuga heterophylla*
Western sand cherry	*Prunus besseyi*
White ash	*Fraxinus americana*
White fir	*Abies concolor*
White ironbark	*Eucalyptus leucoxylon*
White mariposa	*Calochortus venustus*
White oak	*Quercus alba*
White poplar	*Populus alba*
White Rockcress	*Arabis albida (cancasica)*
White spruce	*Picea glauca*
Wild ginger	Asarum
Wild indigo	*Baptisia tinctoria*
Wild lilac	*Ceanothus*
Willow bellflower	*Campanula persicifolia*
Windflower	*Anemone japonica*
	Anemone j. 'September Charm'
	Anemone vitifolia 'Robustissima'
Winged euonymus	*Euonymus alatus*
Winged everlasting	*Ammobium alatum*
Winterberry	*Ilex verticillata*
Wintergreen	*Gaultheria procumbens*
Wintergreen barberry	*Berberis julianae*
Winter honeysuckle	*Lonicera fragrantissima*
Winter jasmine	*Jasminum nudiflorum*
Winter Savory	*Satureja montana*
Wishbone flower	*Torenia fournierii*
Wishbone plant	Torenia
	Torenia fournierii
Witch hazel (Chinese)	*Hamamelis mollis*
Wolfsbane	*Aconitum vulparia*
Woodland forget-me-not	*Myosotis sylvatica*
Woolly speedwell	*Veronica incana*
Woolly yarrow	*Achillea tomentosa*

Y

Yarrow	Achillea
Yellow cosmos	*Cosmos sulphureus*
Yellow flag	*Iris pseudacorus*
Yellow foxglove	*Digitalis grandiflora*

COMMON NAME	BOTANICAL NAME
Yellow moraea	Moraea
	Morea bicolor
Young's weeping birch	*Betula pendula 'Youngii'*
Yulan magnolia	*Magnolia denudata*

Z
Zinnia	Zinnia

BOTANICAL NAMES/COMMON NAMES

NOTE: Annual plants are not given a zone designation here. They are sold by most nurseries only for specific climates and in specific seasons.

BOTANICAL NAME	COMMON NAME	ZONE

A

BOTANICAL NAME	COMMON NAME	ZONE
Abelmoschus moschatos	Silk flower	5–7
Abies alba	European silver fir	4
Abies concolor	White fir	4
Abies nordmanniana	Nordmann fir	4
Abronia umbellata	Pink-sand verbena	8
Abutilon hybridum	Flowering maple	9–10
Abutilon h. 'Golden Fleece'	Flowering maple	9–10
Abutilon megapotanicum	Flowering maple	9–10
Acacia baileyana	Bailey acacia	10
Acacia cyanophylla	Blue leaf wattle	10
Acalypha hispida	Chenille plant	10
Acanthus mollis	Bear's breech	8
	Grecian urn plant	8
Acer campestre	Hedge maple	8
Acer japonicum 'Aconitifolium'	Fernleaf maple	6
Acer japonicum	Full-moon maple	6
Acer palmatum 'Dissectum'	Laceleaf Japanese maple	6
Acer palmatum	Japanese maple	6
Acer platanoides	Norway maple	4
Acer rubrum	Red maple	4
Acer saccharum	Sugar maple	4
Achillea	Yarrow	2–3
Achillea filipendula	Fern-leaved yarrow	2–3
Achillea millefolium	Common yarrow	2–3
Achillea m. 'Roseum'	Pink-flowered yarrow	2–3
Achillea ptarmica	Sneezeweed	2–3
	Sneezewort	2–3
Achillea tomentosa	Woolly yarrow	2–3
Achimenes	Rainbow flower	9–10
Achimenes	Rainbow flower	9–10
Acidanthera	Abyssinian sword lily	10
Aconitum autumnale	Autumn monkshood	4

BOTANICAL NAME	COMMON NAME	ZONE
Aconitum fischeri	Azure monkshood	2–3
Aconitum napellus	English monkshood	2–3
Aconitum vulparia	Wolfsbane	2–3
Acorus gramineus	Miniature flag plant	5
Adiantum	Maidenhair fern	9
Adonis	Adonis African corn lily	2–3
Adonis aestrivalis	Summer adonis	2–3
Adonis amurensis	Amur adonis	2–3
Adonis autumnalis	Autumn adonis	2–3
Adonis vernalis	Spring adonis	2–3
Aechmea fasciata	Living-vase plant	10
Aesychnanthus speciosa	Lipstick plant	10
Agapanthus africanus	Lily of the Nile	9
Agave americana	Century plant	6
Ageratum houstonianum	Ageratum	6
	Floss flower	6
Agloanema commutum	Chinese evergreen	10
Agrostemma githago	Corncockle	8
Ailanthus altissima	Tree-of-heaven	5
Ajuga reptans	Bugleweed	5
	Carpet bugle	5
Akebia quinata	Five-leaf akebia	4
Albizia julibrissin	Silk tree	6
Allamanda cathartica	Trumpet vine	10
Allium	Flowering onion	4–7
Allium christophii	Star of Persia	4
Allium giganteum	Giant onion	5
Allium moly	Lily leek	2–3
Allium neapolitanum	Naples onion	7
Allium schoenoprasum	Flowering onion	2–3
Allophytum mexicanum	Mexican foxglove	10
Alnus glutonusa	European alder	5
Alnus incana	Speckled alder	2
Alocasia	Emerald fern	10
Alonsoa warscewiczii	Mask flower	—
Alpinia	Shell flower	10
Alstroemeria aurantiaca	Peruvian lily	7
Althaea rosea	Hollyhock	5
Altheae r. 'Majorette Hybrid'	Hollyhock	5
Amaranthus caudatus	Tassel flower	5
Amaranthus hypochondriacus	Prince's-feather	—
Amaranthus salicifolius	Fountain plant	—
Amaranthus tricolor	Joseph's coat; Love-lies-bleeding	—
Amaryllis belladonna	Belladonna lily	9

BOTANICAL NAME	COMMON NAME	ZONE
Amelanchier canadensis	Shadblow serviceberry	9
Amelanchier intermedia	Swamp Juneberry	4
Amelanchier laevis	Allegheny serviceberry	4
Amelanchier obovalis	Coastal Juneberry	4
Amelanchier sanguinea	Round-leaf Juneberry	5
Amelanchier spicata	Running Juneberry	4
Ammobium alatum	Winged everlasting	—
Ampelopsis brevipedunculata	Porcelain vine	4–8
Anagallis	Pimpernel	—
Anagallis linifolia	Pimpernel	—
Ananas	Pineapple	10
Anaphalis margaritacea	Pearly everlasting	4–8
Anchusa capensis	Forget-me-not	4
	Summer forget-me-not	4
Anchusa	Alkanet	4
Anchusa myosotidiflora		4
Andromeda	Bog rosemary	2
Anemone blanda	Greek anemone	6
Anemone	Anemone	6
Anemone coronaria	Poppy-flowered anemone	7
Anemone fulgens	Flame anemone	6
Anemone japonica	Japanese anemone	6
Anemone j. 'September Charm'	Windflower	6
Anemone vitifolia 'Robustissima'	Windflower	6
Anemone vitifolia	Grape-leaf anemone	5
Angraecum	Comet orchid	10
Ansellia africana	Spider orchid	10
Anthemis	Chamomile	4
Anthemis tinctoria	Golden marguerite	4
Anthemum	Dill	—
Anthurium	Flamingo flower	10
Antigonon leptopus	Coralvine	9
Antirrhinum majus	Snapdragon	7
Aphanostephus skirrobasis	Lazy daisy	5
Aponogeton	Pond weed	10
Aquilegia alpina 'Crimson star'	Columbine	4
Aquilegia a 'Harebell'	Columbine	4
Aquilegia caerulea	Rocky Mountain columbine	4
Aquilegia canadensis	Common American columbine	4
Aquilegia canandensis	American columbine	4
Aquilegia chrysanta	Golden columbine	4
Aquilegia hybrid	Columbine	4
Arabis albida (cancasica)	White Rockcress	4
Arabis caucasia	Wall rockcress	4

Botanical Name	Common Name	Zone
Aralia	Angelica tree	10
Arctotis grandis	African daisy	10
Arctotis stoechadifolia	Arctotis	10
Ardisia	Coral berry	10
Areca lutescens	Betel nut	10
Argemone grandiflora	Prickly poppy	8
Aristolochia durior	Dutchman's pipe	10
Armeria	Sea pink	4
	Thrift	4
Armeria maritima	Sea pink	4
	Thrift	4
Artemesia schmidtiana	Silver mound	4
Artemesia schmidtiania	Mugwort	4
Aruncus sylvester	Goatsbeard	4
Arundo donax	Reed grass	6
Asarum	Wild ginger	3
Asclepias curassavica	Butterfly bush	4
Asclepias currassavica	Bloodflower	4
Asclepias tuberosa	Butterfly bush	4
Ascocentrum	Carnival orchid	10
Asparagus sprengeri	Emerald fern	10
Aspidistra elatior	Cast-iron plant	9
Aspleniumn nidus	Bird's nest fern	10
Aster	Michelmas daisy	4–7
Aster amellus	Italian aster	4
Aster frikartii	Aster	5
Aster novae-angliae	Michelmas daisy	5
Aster tanacetifolius	Tahoka daisy	5
Astilbe arendsii	Astilbe	7
Astilbe taquetti 'Superba'	Astilbe	7
Astilbe 'Fanal'	Astilbe	7
Astilbe 'Federsee'	Astilbe	7
Astrantia major	Masterwort	7
Astrophytum asterias	Star cactus	10
Astrophytum	Star cactus	10
Aucuba japonica	Gold dust plant	10
Auraucaria heterophylla	Norfolk Island pine	10

B

Botanical Name	Common Name	Zone
Babiana stricta	Baboon flower	8
Bambusa	Bamboo	7–9
Baptisia australis	False indigo	7
Beaumontia grandiflora	Trumpet flower	10

BOTANICAL NAME	COMMON NAME	ZONE
Baptisia		
Baptisia tinctoria	Wild indigo	7
Bauhinia	Orchid tree	7
Begonia pendula	Hanging begonia	10
Begonia semperflorens	Wax begonia	10
Begonia tuberhybrida	Tuberous begonia	10
Belamancanda chinensis	Blackberry lily	5
Bellis perennis	Shrimp plant	10
Belorpone guttata (Justicia)	English daisy	4
Berberis buxifolia	Magellan barberry	5
Berberis julianae	Wintergreen barberry	6
Berberis koreana	Korean barberry	6
Berberis thunbergii	Japanese barberry	5
Berberis verruculosa	Warty barberry	6
Bergenia cordifolia	Heart-leaved bergenia	4
Bessera elegans	Coral drops	9
Betilla hyacinthina	Chinese ground orchid	10
Betula papyrifera	Canoe birch	3
Betula pendula verucosa	European white birch	2
Betula pendula 'Youngii'	Young's weeping birch	2
Bignonia capreolata	Trumpet vine	10
Blechnum	Tree fern	10
Bletilla hyacinthina	Chinese ground orchid	10
Boltonia latisquama	Violet boltonia	4
Bougainvillea glabra	Paper flower	10
Brachycome iberidifolia	Swan River daisy	—
Brassavola nodosa	Lady-of-the-night	10
Brodiaea	Brodiaea	8
Brodiaea elegans	Harvest brodiaea	8
Bromelia balanse	Volcano plant	10
Browallia	Browallia	—
Browallia speciosa 'Marine Bells'	Browallia	—
Browallia speciosa	Bush violet	—
Browallia s. 'Silver Bells'	Browallia	—
Buddleia davidii	Orange-eye butterfly bush	6
Bulbocodium vernum	Spring meadow saffron	6
Buxus microphylla	Littleleaf box	6
Buxus sempervirens	Common box	6

C

Calandrinia umbellata	Rock purslane	—
Calceolaria herbeohybrida	Pocketbook plant	—
Calceolaria integrifolia		—

BOTANICAL NAME	COMMON NAME	ZONE
Calendula officinalis	Calendula	—
	Pot marigold	—
Calendula o. 'Fiesta Mix'	Calendula	—
Calendula o. 'Fiesta Yellow'	Calendula	—
Calla palustris	Water arum	3
Callirhoe involucrata	Poppy mallow	4
	Poppy	4
Callistemon lanceolatus	Bottle brush	9
Callistephus chinensis	China aster	—
Calluna vulgaris	Heather	4–5
Calochortus	Mariposa lily	4
Calochortus pulchellus	Golden lantern	4
Calochortus venustus	White mariposa	4
Calonyction aculeatum	Moonflower	8
Caltha palustris	Marsh marigold	4
Calycanthus floridus	Sweet shrub	6
Camassia	Camas	6
Camellia japonica	Common camellia	7–8
Camellia sasanqua	Sasanqua camellia	7–8
Campanula carpatica	Turkey oak	4
Campanula glomerata	Bellflower	4
Campanula medium	Canterbury bells	—
Campanula persicifolia 'White Star'	Peach-leaved bellflower	4
Campanula persicifolia	Willow bellflower	4
Campanula	Bellflower	4
Campsis tagliabuana	Trumpet crater	5
Canna hybrida	Canna	7
Cantaurea moschata	Sweet sultan	5
Capsicum annuum	Pepper plant	10
Capsicum frutescens	Red pepper plant	10
Cardiospermum halicacabum	Balloon vine	10
Carica papaya	Papaya	10
Carpenteria californica	Mock orange	6
Cartharanthus r. 'Magic Carpet Mix'	Madagascar periwinkle	10
Caryota mitis	Fishtail palm	10
Catalpa bignonioides	Southern catalpa	5
Catalpa speciosa	Common catalpa	5
	Western catalpa	5
Catananche caerulea	Cupid's dart	—
Catharanthus r. 'Little Blanche'	Madagascar periwinkle	10
Ceanothus	Wild lilac	5
Cedrus atlantica 'Glauca'	Blue atlas cedar	5–6
Cedrus deodara	Deodar cedar	5–6
Cedrus libani	Cedar of Lebanon	5–6

Botanical Name	Common Name	Zone
Celastrus scandens	American bittersweet	3
	Climbing bittersweet	3
Celosia argentea	Cockscomb	3
Celosia plumosa 'Apricot Brandy'	Feather cockscomb	—
Celosia p. 'New Look'	Feather cockscomb	—
Celtis	Hackberry	5
Centaurea americana	Basket flower	5–7
Centaurea cineraria	Dusty miller	5–7
Centaurea cyanus	Bachelor's button	5–7
	Cornflower	5–7
Centaurea dealbata	Persian centaurea	5–7
Centaurea macrocephala	Golden centaurea	5–7
Centaurea montana	Cornflower	5–7
Centaurea rutifolia	Dusty miller	5–7
Centranthus valerian ruber	Red valerian	5
Cephalocereus	Old man cactus	10
Cephalocereus senilis	Old man cactus	10
Cephalophyllum hybrid	Ice plant	9–10
Cerastium tomentosum	Snow-in-summer	3–4
Ceratostigma plumbaginoides	Leadwort	8
Cercis canadensis	Eastern redbud	5
Cercis chinensis	Chinese redbud	6
Cercis siliquastrum	Judas tree	6
Ceropegia	Rosary vine	10
Cerostima	Chickweed	—
Cestrum	Night jasmine	10
Chaenomeles japonica	Japanese quince	5
Chaenomeles lagenaria	Flowering quince	5
Chamaecyparis lawsoniana 'Allumii'	Scarab Lawson cypress	5–6
Chamaecyparis obtusa	Hinoki false cypress	4–5
Chamaecyparis pisifera 'Filifera'	Thread cypress	5–6
Chamaecyparis pisifera	Sawara false cypress	4–5
Chamaecyparus lawsoniana	Lawson false cypress	4–5
Chamaecyparus obtussa 'Nana'	Dwarf hinoki cypress	10
Chamaedorea erumpens	Bamboo palm	—
Cheiranthus cheiri	English wall flower	—
Cheiranthus	Siberian wallflower	—
Chionanthus virginica	Fringe tree	5
Chionodoxa sardensis	Glory-of-the-snow	5
Chlidanthus fragrans	Delicate lily	9
Chlorophytum elatum	Spider plant	10
Chrysanthemum	Chrysanthemum	3–4
Chrysanthemum coccineum	Painted daisy	3–4
Chrysanthemum frutescens	Marguerite	3–4

BOTANICAL NAME	COMMON NAME	ZONE
Chrysanthemum maximum	Shasta daisy	3–4
Chrysanthemum nipponicum	Nippon chrysanthemum	3–4
Chrysanthemum parthenium	Feverfew	3–4
Chrysogonum virginiana	Golden star	7
Cibotium schiedei	Mexican tree fern	10
Cimicifuga	Bugbane	3–4
Cimicifuga racemosa	Black snakeroot	3–4
Cladanthus arabicus	Cladanthus	—
Clarkia amoena	Farewell-to-spring	—
Clarkia elegans	Rocky Mountain garland	—
Clematis	Virgin's bower	5–9
Clematis 'Nelly Moser'	Climbing lily	5–9
Cleome spinosa	Spider flower	—
Clerodenrum thompsoniae	Glory bower	10
Clethra alnifolia	Summer sweet	4–6
Clethra arborea	Lily-of-the-valley tree	4–6
Clivia miniata	Kaffir lily	10
Cobaea scandens	Cup-and-saucer vine	—
Codiaeum variegatum	Croton	10
Coix lacryma-jobi	Job's tears	—
Colchicum autumnale	Autumn crocus	6–7
Colchicum speciosum	Meadow saffron	6–7
Coleus blumei	Coleus	10
Coleus	Painted leaf plant	10
Colocasia	Elephant ears	10
Colocasia esculenta	Elephant ears	10
Consolida ambigua	Larkspur	—
Convallaria majalis	Lily of the valley	3–4
Convolvulus	Morning glory	10
Convolvulus mauritanicus	Ground morning glory	10
Convolvulus tricolor	Dwarf morning	10
Cordyline terminalis	Ti plant	10
Coreopsis	Tickseed	—
Coreopsis tinctoria	Golden coreopsis	6–7
Coreopsis verticillata	Threadleaf Coreopsis	6–7
Coreopsis v. 'Moonbeam'	Threadleaf Coreopsis	6–7
Cornus alba 'Sibirica'	Siberian dogwood	3
Cornus alba	Tatarian dogwood	3
Cornus florida	Flowering dogwood	5
Cornus kousa	Japanese dogwood	6
Cornus mas	Cornelian cherry	5–6
Cornus nuttallii	Pacific dogwood	5–6
Cornus stolonifera	Redtwig dogwood	3–4
Cortaderia	Pampas grass	8

BOTANICAL NAME	COMMON NAME	ZONE
Cosmos	Cosmos	—
Cosmos sulphureus	Yellow cosmos	—
Costus igneus	Spiral ginger	10
Costus	Spiral ginger	10
Cotoneaster apiculata	Cranberry cotoneaster	5
Cotoneaster dammeri	Bearberry cotoneaster	5–6
Cotoneaster divaricata	Spreading cotoneaster	5–6
Cotoneaster horizontalis	Rock-spray cotoneaster	5–6
Cotoneaster microphylla	Small leafed cotoneaster	5–6
Cotoneaster multiflora	Large flowering cotoneaster	5–6
Cotoneaster salicifolia floccosa	Hardy willow-leaf cotoneaster	6
Crataegus monogyna	Single-seed hawthorn	5–6
Crataegus oxyacantha	English hawthorn	5–6
Crepis rubra	Hawk's beard	—
Crocosmia crocosmiiflora	Mimulus variegatus	10
Crocosmia (montbretia) crocosmiiflora	Montbretia	10
Crocosmia (montbretia) masoniorum	Montbretia	10
Crocus	Scotch crocus	7
Crocus chrysanthus	Golden crocus	7
Crocus sieberii	Sieber crocus	7
Crocus vernus	Common crocus	7
Crotalaria retusa	Golden-yellow sweet pea	9
Cryptanthus zonatus	Star plant	10
Cryptomeria japonica	Japanese cedar	5
Cuphea ignea	Cigar plant	—
	Lilac honeysuckle	—
Cyanotis	Pussy ears	10
Cycas revoluta	Sago palm	10
Cyclamen	Cyclamen	4–5
Cyclamen coum	Shooting star	5
Cyclamen neapolitanum	Neapolitanum cyclamen	5
Cyclamen persicum	Florist's cyclamen	9
Cynoglossum amabile	Chinese forget-me-not	—
Cyperus alternifolia	Umbrella plant	10
Cytisus	Broom	6–7

D

BOTANICAL NAME	COMMON NAME	ZONE
Dahlia	Dahlia	10
Datura	Angel's trumpet	10
Datura metel	Trumpet flower	—
Delphinium	Larkspur	3–4
Delphinium elatum	Candle larkspur	3–4
Delphinium grandiflorum	Chinese larkspur	3–4

| --- | --- | --- |
Deutzia gracilis	Slender deutzia	5–6
Deutzia lemoinei	Lemoine deutzia	5–6
Dianthus allwoodi	Allwood's pink	—
Dianthus barbatus	Sweet William	8
Dianthus caryophyllus	Carnation	8
Dianthus	Pink	—
Dianthus chinensis	China pink	4
Dianthus plumarius	Border pink	4
	Pink	—
Diascia barberae	Tussock bellflower	3–4
Dicentra spectabilis	Bleeding heart	3–4
Dictamnus albus	Gas plant	3–4
Dictamus fraxinella rubra	Gas plant	3–4
Dieffenbachia amoena	Dumbcane	10
Dierama pulcherrimum	Wand flower	10
Dietes iridioides	African iris	9–10
Digitalis	Foxglove	4–5
Digitalis grandiflora	Yellow foxglove	4–5
Digitalis purpurea	Common foxglove	4–5
	Foxglove	4–5
Digitalis p. 'Alba'	Foxglove	4–5
Digitalis p. 'Foxy Miss'	Foxglove	4–5
Dimorphoteca aurantiaca	Cape marigold	10
Dimorphoteca hybrids	Cape marigold	10
Dionaea muscipula	Venus flytrap	10
Diospyros virginiana	Persimmon	10
Dipladenia	Mexican love vine	10
Dizygotheca	False aralia	10
Doronicum caucasicum	Leopard's bane	5
Dorotheanthus bellidiflorus	Ice plant	9–10
Doxantha unguis-cati	Trumpet vine	9–10
Dracaena massangeana	Corn plant	10
Duchesnea indica	Mock strawberry	6
Duchesnea indica	Indian mock strawberry	6
Dyckia	Earth star	10
Dyssoida tenuiloba	Dahlberg daisy	10

E

Echinacea purpurea 'Shooting Star'	Purple coneflower	4
Echinacea purpurea	Coneflower	4
Echinacea p. 'white luster'	Coneflower	4
Echinocactus	Barre/cactus	10
Echinocereus	Hedgehog cactus	10
	Rainbow cactus	10

BOTANICAL NAME	COMMON NAME	ZONE
Echinopsis	Sea urchin cactus	10
Echinops exaltabus	Blue globe thistle	4
Echium	Bugloss	—
Elaeagnus angustifolia	Russian olive	3
Elaeagnus multiflora	Cherry elaeagnus	5
Elaeagnus umbellata	Autumn elaeagnus	4
Emilia flammea	Tassel flower	—
Epilobium	Fireweed	4
Epimedium grandiflorum	Bishop's hat	4
Epiphyllum	Orchid cactus	10
Episcia	Peacock plant	10
Equisetum hymale	Horsetail plant	10
Eranthemum pulchellum	Blue sage	9
Eranthis hyemalis	Aconite	5
Eremurus	Himalayan foxtail lily	4–5
Erica	Heath	6
Erigeron	Fleabane	—
Erigeron glaucas	Fleabane	4
Erigeron karvinskianus	Fleabane	9
Eriobotyra japonica	Loquat	10
Erodium chamaedryoides	Cranesbill	6–7
Eryngium oliverianium	Sea holly	3–4
Erythrina herbacea	Coral bean	10
Erythronium	Adder's tongue	4–5
Erythronium dens canis	Dogtooth violet	4–5
Eschscholzia californica	California poppy	10
Eucalyptus ficifolia	Scarlet flowering gum	8–10
Eucalyptus globulus	Blue gum	8–10
Eucalyptus leucoxylon	White ironbark	8–10
Eucharis grandiflora	Amazon lily	10
Euonymus alatus	Winged euonymus	4
Eupatorium coelestinum	Mist flower	5–6
Euphorbia	Spurge	5
Euphorbia epithymoides	Cushion spurge	5
Euphorbia lophogora	Milkweed	5
	Spurge	5
Euphorbia marginata	Snow-on-the-mountain	5
Euphorbia pulcherrima	Poinsettia	10
Europys mauritanus	False daisy	—
Exacum affine	German violet	10

F

Fagus sylvatica heterophylla	Fern-leafed beech	5
Fagus sylvatica purpurea	Purple beech	5

BOTANICAL NAME	COMMON NAME	ZONE
Fagus sylvatica 'Tricolor'	Tricolor beech	5
Fagus sylvatica	European beech	5
Felicia amelloides	Blue daisy	—
Felicia a. 'White Felicia'	Blue daisy	—
Ficus	Fig	10
Flipendula rubra	Queen of the prairie	3–4
Forsythia intermedia	Border forsythia	5–6
Forsythia suspensa	Weeping forsythia	5–6
Fothergilla gardenii	Dwarf fothergilla	6
Fothergilla major	Large fothergilla	6
Fothergilla monticola	Alabama fothergilla	6
Fragaria vesca americana	Alpine strawberry	6–7
Fragaria vesca	American strawberry	6–7
Fraxinus americana	White ash	4
Fraxinus excelsior	European ash	4
Fraxinus ornus	Flowering ash	4
Fraxinus pennsylvanica	Green ash	4
Fritillaria imperialis	Crown imperial	6
Fritillaria meleagris	Snake's head	6
Fuchsia	Lady's eardrops	10

G

BOTANICAL NAME	COMMON NAME	ZONE
Gaillardia aristata	Blanket flower	3–4
Gaillardia pulchella	Blanket flower	—
Gaillardia x grandiflora	Blanket flower	—
Galanthus nivalis	Snowdrop	5
Galium vernum	Bedstraw	3–4
Galtonia candicans	Giant summer hyacinth	6
Galtonia	Giant summer hyacinth	6
Gamolepis tagetes	Sunshine daisy	—
Gardenia jasminoides	Cape jasmine	10
Garrya elliptica	Silk tassel	8
Gasteria lingulata	Ox-tongue plant	10
Gaultheria procumbens	Wintergreen	4–7
Gaura lindheimeri	Evening primrose	6
Gaylussacia brachycera	Box huckleberry	6
Gazania langiscapa	Gazania	—
Gelsemium sempervirens	Carolina jessamine	7
Gentiana asclepiadea	Gentian	6
Geranium cordatum	Cranesbill	6–8
Geranium dalmaticum	Geranium	6–8
Geranium grandiflorum	Cranesbill	6–8
Geranium sanguineum	Blood cranesbill	6–8

Botanical Name	Common Name	Zone
Gerbera jamesonii	Transvaal daisy	8
Ginkgo biloba	Ginkgo	5
Gladiolus	Gladiola	7–8
Glaucium	Sea poppy	—
Glaucium corniculatum	Sea poppy	—
Gleditsia triacanthos	Sweet locust	5
Gloriosa rothschildiana	Glory lily	10
Gnaphalium sylvaticum	Cudweed	—
Godetia	Satin flower	—
Godetia amoena	Farewell-to-spring	—
Gomphrena globosa	Globe amaranth	—
Gongora bufonia	Punch-and-Judy orchid	10
Gongora	Punch-and-Judy orchid	10
Gordonia lasianthus	Loblolly tree	8
Gymnocalycium mihanovichii	Chin cactus	10
Gypsophila paniculata	Baby's breath	6–7
Gypsophila repens 'Rosea'	Creeping gypsophila	6–7

H

Botanical Name	Common Name	Zone
Haemanthus	Blood lily	10
Halesia carolina	Silverbells	6
Hamamelis mollis	Chinese witch hazel	5
	Witch hazel (Chinese)	5
Hamamelis virginiana	Common witch hazel	5
Hedychium	Ginger lily	10
Hedychium coronarium	Ginger lily	10
Helenium autumnale	Helen's flower	4
	Sneezeweed	4
Helianthemum nummularium 'Fire Dragon'	Rock rose	6–7
Helianthemum nummularium	Moss rose	6–7
	Sun rose	6–7
Helianthus annuus	Common sunflower	6–7
Helianthus	Sunflower	6–7
Helichrysum bracteatum	Strawflower	5–6
Heliocereus	Sun cactus	10
Heliocereus undatus	Sun cactus	10
Heliotropium a. 'Black Prince'	Heliotrope	10
Heliotropium arborescens	Heliotrope	10
Heliotropium	Heliotrope	10
Helleborus niger	Christmas rose	6–7
	Lenten rose	6–7
Helleborus orientalis	Lenten rose	6–7

BOTANICAL NAME	COMMON NAME	ZONE
Helxine soleiroii	Baby's tears	10
Hemerocallis	Daylily	6–7
Hemerocallis hybrid	Daylily	6–7
Hemerocallis 'Johanna'	Daylily	6–7
Hesperis matronalis	Sweet rocket	3–4
Heuchera sanguinea	Coral bell	5
Hibiscus	Rose mallow	9–10
Hibiscus rosa-sinensis	Chinese hibiscus	9–10
Hibiscus syriacus	Rose-of-Sharon	9–10
Hibiscus trionum	Flower-of-an-hour	9–10
Hippeastrum	Amaryllis	10
Hosta alba-margarinata	Plantain lily	3–4
Hosta venusta	Plantain lily	3–4
Hosta 'Krossa Regal'	Plantain lily	3–4
Houstonia longifolia	Bluets	5
Hoya bella	Wax plant	10
Huernia pillansi	Star flower	10
Hyacinthus	Hyacinth	7
Hydrangea paniculata 'Grandiflora'	Peegee hydrangea	5–7
Hydrangea quercifolia	Oak-leafed hydrangea	5–7
Hylocereus undatus	Night blooming cereus	10
Hymenocallis narcissifolia	Spider lily	10
Hymenocallis	Spider lily	10
Hypericum moserianum	Saint Johns wort	6–7
Hypocyrta nummularia	Goldfish plant	10
Hypocyrta strigillosa	Goldfish plant	10

I

BOTANICAL NAME	COMMON NAME	ZONE
Iberis	Candytuft	4
Iberis sempervirens	Evergreen candytuft	4
Iberis umbellata	Globe candytuft	4
Ilex aquifolium	English holly	5–6
	Holly	5–6
Ilex cornuta	Chinese holly	6–7
Ilex crenata	Japanese holly	6–7
Ilex glabra	Inkberry	4
Ilex opaca	American holly	3
Ilex serrata	Japanese winterberry	5
Ilex verticillata	Winterberry	3–4
Impatiens	Patience plant	—
Indigofera tinctoria	Indigo	6
Ipomoea purpurea	Morning glory	10

| --- | --- | --- |
Ipomoea p. 'Early Call'	Morning glory	10
Ipomoea p. 'Heavenly Blue'	Morning glory	10
Iresine herbstii	Bloodleaf	10
Iris	Iris	4–8
Iris douglasiana	Pacific Coast iris	8
Iris hybrids	Dutch iris	8
Iris kaempferi	Japanese iris	5
Iris pseudacorus	Yellow flag	6
Iris siberica	Siberian iris	4
Iris xiphioides	English iris	7
Iris xiphium	Spanish iris	7
Ixia	Adonis African corn lily	7–8
	Corn lily	7–8
Ixora coccinea	Flame-of-the-woods	10

J

Jacobinia	King's crown	10
Jasminum mesnyi	Primrose jasmine	6–8
Jasminum nudiflorum	Winter jasmine	6–8
Jasminum officinale	Jasmine	6–8
Juniperus chinensis	Chinese juniper	4–5
Juniperus excelsa	Greek juniper	4–5
Juniperus virginiana 'Glauca'	Silver red cedar	4–5
Juniperus virginiana	Eastern red cedar	4–5

K

Kaempfera roscoeana	Peacock plant	10
Kalmia latifolia	Mountain laurel	3
Kalmia polifolia	Bog kalmia	3
Knifphofia a. 'Vanilla'	Red-hot poker	7
Kniphofia aloides	Red-hot poker	7
Kniphofia a. 'Border Ballet'	Red-hot poker	7
Kniphofia uvaria	Red-hot poker	7
Kochia scoparia trichophila	Fire bush	—
Koelreuteria paniculata	Goldenrain tree	6
Kolwitzia amabilis	Beauty bush	5

L

Laburnum	Golden chain tree	5–6
Lachenalia tricolor	Cape cowslip	9

BOTANICAL NAME	COMMON NAME	ZONE
Lagerstroemria indica	Crape myrtle	10
Lagerstromia indica	Crepe myrtle	10
Lamium variegatum	Dead nettle	3–4
Lantana	Lantana	9–10
Lathyrus	Everlasting pea	—
Lathyrus odoratus	Sweet pea	—
Lavandula angustifolia	Lavender	6
Lavandula officinalis	Common lavender	6
Lavatera trimestris	Tree mallow	—
Layia campestris	Tidytips	—
Leonotis leonurus	Lion's ear	9–10
Leontopodium alpinum	Edelweiss	6
Leptospermum laevigatum	Australian tea tree	9
Leucojum vernum	Snowflake	5–6
Levisticum officinalis	Lovage	6–7
Liatris	Gay feather	4–6
Liatris s. 'Alba'	Gay feather	4–6
Ligularia dentata	Leopard plant	6–7
Ligularia dicorum	Ragwort	6–7
Ligustrum ibolium	Ibolium ligustrum	5–6
Ligustrum japonicum	Japanese privet	5–6
Ligustrum vulgare	Common privet	5–6
Ligustrum 'vicaryi'	Golden privet	5–6
Lilium	Lily	5–6
Lilium candidum	Madonna lily	5–6
Lilium regale	Regal lily	5–6
Limonium dumosum	German statice	5–6
Limonium latifolium	Sea lavender	—
Linaria maroccana	Tiger flower	—
	Toadflax	—
Linum	Flax	5–6
	Flowering flax	5–6
Linum grandiflorum	Scarlet flax	5–6
Linum perenne	Perennial flax	5–6
Liquidambar styaciflua	Sweet gum	6
Liriodenron tulipifera	Tulip tree	10
Liriope muscari	Mondo grass	6–7
Lisanthus grandiflorum	Prairie gentian	—
Litatris spicata	Gay feather	—
Lithops	Living-rock plant	10
Livistona chinensis	Living-vase plant	10
Lobelia		—

| --- | --- | --- |
Lobelia cardinalis	Cardinal flower	3
Lobelia erinus	Blue lobelia	—
Lobelia siphilitica	Blue lobelia	6
Lobivia	Corncob	10
Lobularia maritima	Sweet alyssum	—
Lonicera brownii	Scarlet trumpet honeysuckle	6
Lonicera fragrantissima	Winter honeysuckle	6
Lonicera hildebrandiana	Giant Burmese honeysuckle	9
Lonicera maackii	Amur honeysuckle	3
Lonicera syringantha	Lilac honeysuckle	5
Lonicera tatarica	Tatarian honeysuckle	4
Lunaria annua	Dollar plant	—
	Honesty plant	—
	Money plant	—
Lupinus	Lupine	—
Lupinus hybrid 'Little Lulu'		—
Lupinus polyphyllus	Lupine	4
Lupinus subcaornosus	Texas bluebonnet	—
Lychnis chalcedonica	Maltese cross	4
Lychnis coronaria	Mullein pink	—
	Rose campion	—
Lychnis viscaria	Catchfly	4
Lycoris african	Golden spider lily	10
Lycoris radiata	Short-tubed lycoris	10
	Spider lily	10
Lygodium palmatum	Climbing fern	10
Lysimachia clethroides	Gooseneck loosestrife	4
Lysimachia punctata	Loosestrife	4–5
	Moneywort	4–5
Lythrum salicaria	Purple loosestrife	4

M

Macleaya cordata	Plume poppy	4
Maettia bicolor	Mexican firecracker	10
Magnolia denudata	Yulan magnolia	6
Magnolia grandiflora	Southern magnolia	7
Magnolia liliflora	Lily magnolia	3
Magnolia soulangana	Saucer magnolia	5–6
Magnolia stellata	Star magnolia	6
Magnolia veitchii	Veitch magnolia	7–8
Magnolia virginiana	Sweet bay	6
Mahernia verticillata	Honey bell	10
Mahonia aquifolium	Grape holly	10

BOTANICAL NAME	COMMON NAME	ZONE
Malcomia maritima	Virginia stock	—
Malope trifida	Mallow-wort	—
Malpighia coccigera	Miniature holly	10
Malus arnoldiana	Arnold crabapple	5
Malus sargentii	Sargent crabapple	5
Malva alcea	Hollyhock	5
Malva maritima	Mallow	5
Mammillaria	Pin-cushion cactus	10
Mammillaria	Pincushion	10
Mandevilla suaveolens	Chilean jasmine	10
Mangifera indica	Mango	10
Masdevallia coccinea	Kite orchid	10
Matricaria eximia	Chamomile	5
Matthiola incana 'Brompton Mix'	Common stock	—
Matthiola incana	Stock	—
Matthiola i. 'Excelsior Red'	Common stock	—
Matthiola i. 'Rose Midget'	Common stock	—
Meconopsis betonicifolia	Blue poppy	7
Mentzelia lindleyi	Blazing star	—
Mesembryanthemum cordifolium	Fig marigold	10
Mesembryanthemum crystallinum	Ice plant	10
Mesembryanthemum c. (red)	Ice plant	10
Miltonia	Pansy orchid	10
Mimulas guttata	Monkey flower	6
Mimulus guttatas 'Malibu Yellow'	Monkey flower	6
Mimulus g. 'Malibu Orange'	Monkey flower	6
Mimulus variegotus	Monkey flower	6
Mirabilis jalapa	Four-o'clock	—
Mitchella repens	Partridge berry	4
Monarda didyma	Bee balm	5
Monstera deliciosa	Swiss cheese plant	10
Moraea	Yellow moraea	10
Moraea iridioides	Butterfly iris	10
Morea bicolor	Yellow moraea	10
Murraya exotica	Orange jasmine	10
Musa nana	Banana	5
Muscari botryoides	Grape hyacinth	—
Myosotis sylvatica 'Blue Bird'	Forget-me-not	—
Myosotis sylvatica	Woodland forget-me-not	3
Myrica pennsylvanica	Bayberry	

N
| Narcissus | Daffodil | 5–6 |

BOTANICAL NAME	COMMON NAME	ZONE
Nemesia strumosa	Nemesia	—
Nemophila menziesii	Baby blue eyes	9–10
Neomarica	Apostle plant	10
Neoregelia carolinae	Living rocks	10
Neoregelia	Living-vase plant	10
Nepeta hederaceae	Ground ivy	4
Nepeta mussinii	Catmint	4
Nerium	Oleander	10
Nerium oleander	Oleander	10
Nicotiana alata grandiflora	Flowering tobacco	—
Nierembergia	Cup-of-flower	7
Nigella damascena	Love-in-a-mist	—
Notocactus	Ball cactus	10
Nymphaea	Water lily	10

O

BOTANICAL NAME	COMMON NAME	ZONE
Oenothera	Snowdrop	4–6
	Sundrops	4–6
Oenothera missouriensis	Ozark sundrop	5
Oenothera speciosa 'Berlandier'	Showy primrose	6
Oenothera speciosa	Primrose	4
Oenothera tetragona	Sundrops	4
Olea europaea	Common olive	9
Oncidium ampliatum	Dancing lady orchid	10
Oncidium forbesi	Dancing lady orchid	10
Ophiopogon japonica	Lily turf	7
Opuntia	Prickly pear	7–10
Opuntia microdays	Prickly pear	7–10
Ornithogalum	Star of Bethlehem	5
Ornithogalum thyrsoides	Chincherinchee	5
Ornithogalum umbellatum	Common star of Bethlehem	4–5
Osmanthus fragrans	Sweet olive	6
Osmanthus heterophyllus	Holly-leaf osmanthus	6
Osteospermum (Ecklonis) hyoseroides	African daisy	—
Oxalis cernua	Bermuda buttercup	9–10
Oxalis	Bowie oxalis	9–10
Oxydendrum arboreum	Sourwood	5

P

BOTANICAL NAME	COMMON NAME	ZONE
Pachysandra terminalis	Japanese spurge	6
	Spurge	6

BOTANICAL NAME	COMMON NAME	ZONE
Paeonia	Chinese peony	4
Paeonia officinalis	Common peony	4
Panax quinquifolius	Ginseng	4
Pandanus veitchii	Screw pine	10
Papaver bursuri	Alpine poppy	4
Papaver nudicaule	Iceland poppy	3
Papaver orientale	Oriental poppy	3–4
Papaver rhoeas	Shirley poppy	—
Paphiopedilum	Lady slipper orchid	10
Parodia	Ball cactus	10
Passiflora caerulea	Passion flower	7–10
Passiflora 'Coral Seas'	Passion flower	7–10
Passifora edulis	Passion flower	7–10
Pelargonium	Geranium	9–10
Pelargonium domesticum	Lady Washington geranium	9–10
Pelargonium hortorum	Common geranium	9–10
Pelargonium peltatum	Ivy geranium	9–10
Pelargonium sanguineum	Geranium	9–10
Pellaea rotundifolia	Button fern	10
	Cliffbrake fern	10
Pennisetum ruppelia	Fountain grass	7–8
Penstemon gloxinioides	Beardtongue	6–7
Penstemon gloxinoides	Penstemon	6–7
Penstemon g. 'Firebrand'	Penstemon	6–7
Penstemon g. 'Huntington Pink'	Penstemon	6–7
Penstemon g. 'Ruby King'	Penstemon	6–7
Pentas lanceolata	Egyptian star flower	10
Pereskia aculeata	Lemon vine	10
Petrea volubilis	Queen's wreath	10
Petunia	Petunia	—
Peuraria lobata	Kudzu vine	10
Phacelia campanularia	California bluebells	—
Phaceliea	Bluebells	—
Phalaenopsis amabilis	Moon flower	10
	Moth orchid	10
Phaseolus caracalla	Scarlet runner bean	—
Phaseolus coccineus alba	Dutch runner bean	—
Philadelphus	Mock orange	4
Philadelphus coronarius	Sweet mock orange	4
Phlox	Phlox	4
Phlox divaricata	Sweet William phlox	4
Phlox drummondii	Annual phlox	—
Phlox d. 'Blue Beauty'	Annual phlox	—
Phlox d. 'Dwarf Beauty Mix'	Annual phlox	—

BOTANICAL NAME	COMMON NAME	ZONE
Phlox d. 'Hybrid'	Annual phlox	—
Phlox d. 'Petticoat'	Annual phlox	—
Phlox d. 'Salmon Beauty'	Annual phlox	—
Phlox paniculata	Border phlox	5
	Summer phlox	5
Phlox subulata	Moss phlox	5
	Moss pink	5
Phoenix dactylifera	Date palm	10
Phormium tenax	New Zealand flax	9
Photinia villosa	Photinia	7
Phyllitis scolopendrium	Hart's tongue fern	10
Phyllostachys	Bamboo	7–8
Physalis alkengii	Chinese lantern	3–4
Physostegia virginiana	False dragonhead	3–4
Physostegia v. 'Summer Snow'	False dragonhead	3–4
Picea abies	Norway spruce	2–3
Picea glauca	White spruce	2–3
Picea omorika	Serbian spruce	2–3
Picea orientalis	Oriental spruce	5
Picea pungens	Colorado spruce	2–3
Picea sitchensis	Sitka spruce	5
Pieris forrestii	Chinese pieris	5
Pieris japonica	Japanese andromeda	4–5
Pinus cembra	Swiss stone pine	2–3
Pinus contorta	Beach pine	7
Pinus densiflora	Japanese red pine	5
Pinus halepensis	Aleppo pine	9
Pinus mugo	Sweet mountain pine	4
Pinus nigra	Austrian black pine	5
Pinus parviflora	Japanese white pine	5
Pinus peuce	Macedonian pine	5
Pinus pinea	Italian stone pine	9
Pinus resinosa	Red pine	2–3
Pinus strobus	Eastern white pine	2–3
Pinus sylvestris	Scotch pine	2–3
Pinus thunbergiana	Japanese black pine	6
Platanus acerifolia	London plane tree	5
Platanus orientalis	Oriental plane tree	6
Platycerium grandiflorum	Staghorn fern	10
Platycodon grandiflorum	Balloonflower	4
	Chinese bellflower	4
Plectranthus	Swedish ivy	9
Pleione	Indian crocus	8
Plumbago	Plumbago vine	9

BOTANICAL NAME	COMMON NAME	ZONE
Plumeria vubra	Frangipani	10
Podocarpus nagi	Southern yew	9
Podophyllum peltatum	May apple	3–4
Polemonium	Charity	2–3
	Greek valerian	2–3
Polemonium reptans	Creeping Jacob's ladder	2–3
Polyanthes tuberosa	Tuberose	9
Polygonum biflorum	Solomon's seal	3–4
Polygonum capitaltum	Knotweed	3–4
Polypodium aureum	Polypody fern	9–10
Polypodium	Polypody fern	9–10
Polyscias	Aralia	8–9
Polystichum	Hollyfern	10
Populus alba	White poplar	4
Populus berolinensis	Berlin poplar	2–3
Populus canescens	Gray poplar	5–6
Populus lasiocarpa	Chinese poplar	5–6
Populus nigra 'Italica'	Lombardy poplar	2–3
Portulaca grandiflora	Moss rose	—
	Rose moss	—
Potentilla arbuscula	Bush cinquefoil	3
Potentilla aurea	Cinquefoil	—
Potentilla fruticosa	Cinquefoil	—
Primula	Primrose	5–6
Primula denticulata	Himalayan primrose	5–6
Primula japonica	Japanese primrose	5–6
Primula officinalis	Cowslip	4–5
Primula vulgaris	Evening primrose	5–6
	True primula	5–6
Primula x obconica	Primrose	5–6
Primula x polyantha	Primrose	2–3
Prunella webbiana	Self-heal plant	4
Prunus	Plum	4–6
Prunus besseyi	Western sand cherry	4
Prunus cistena	Purple-leaf sand cherry	2–3
Prunus glandulosa	Dwarf flowering almond	4–5
Prunus laurocerasus	Cherry laurel	7
Prunus maritima	Beach plum	3–4
Prunus subhirtella	Rosebud cherry	6
Prunus susquehanae	Sand cherry	5
Prunus tomentosa	Nanking cherry	2–3
Prunus triloba	Flowering almond	4–5
Prunus virginiana	Chokecherry	6
Psidium	Strawberry guava	10

BOTANICAL NAME	COMMON NAME	ZONE
Pteris cretica	Brake fern	10
	Table fern	10
Pulmonaria angustifolia	Blue lungwort	3–4
	Lungwort	3–4
Punica granatum	Pomegranate	9
Puschkinia scilloides	Striped squill	5
Pyracantha	Firethorn	7–8
Pyrethrum roseum	Painted daisy	3–4

Q

Quamoclit	Star glory	10
Quercus alba	White oak	3
Quercus cerris	Oak	6
Quercus coccinea	Scarlet oak	5
Quercus frainetto	Hungarian oak	5
Quercus ilex	Holly oak	4
Quercus laurifolia	Laurel oak	7
Quercus palustris	Pin oak	4–5
Quercus robur	English oak	6
Quercus virginiana	Live oak	7–8

R

Ranunculus asiaticus	French buttercup	8
Raphiolepis indica	Indian hawthorn	9
Rebutia	Crown cactus	10
Rechsteineria cardinalis	Cardinal flower	10
Reseda odorata	Mignonette	—
Rhamnus	Buckthorn	2–3
Rhapis exelsa	Lady palm	10
Rheo discolor	Moses-in-a-cradle	10
Rhipsalidopsis	Easter cactus	10
Rhipsails burchelii	Chain cactus	10
Rhododendron mucronulatum	Korean rhododendron	5
Rhododendron roseum elegans	Rose-shell rhododenron	4–5
Rhododendron schlippenbachii	Royal azalea	5
Rhododendron vaseyi	Pink-shell azalea	5
Rhyncostylis gigantea	Foxtail orchid	10
Ribes	Currant	6
Ricinus communis	Castor bean plant	—

BOTANICAL NAME	COMMON NAME	ZONE
Rivina humilis	Rouge plant	9
Robinia	Locust	5–6
Robinia hispida	Rose acacia	5–6
Robinia speudoacacia	Black locust	5–6
Rodgersia podophyllum	Bronze leaf plant	6–7
Romneya coulteri	California tree poppy	10
Rosa centifolia 'Muscosa'	Moss rose	2–3
Rosa gallica	French rose	5–6
Rosa hugonis	Father Hugo's rose	5–6
Rosa moyesii	Moyes rose	5–6
Rosa multiflora	Japanese rose	5–6
Rosa rugosa	Rugosa rose	2–3
Rosa spinosissima	Scotch rose	5
Rosmarinus officinalis	Rosemary	6
Rudbeckia fulgida	Black-eyed Susan	5
Rudbeckia gloriosa	Gloriosa daisy	4
Rudbeckia hirta	Black-eyed Susan	—
	Cornflower; Black-eyed Susan	—
Rudbeckia laciniata	Cut-leaf coneflower	4

S

BOTANICAL NAME	COMMON NAME	ZONE
Sagina subulata	Irish moss	5
	Scotch moss	5
Saintpaulia ionantha	African violet	10
Salix babylonica	Babylon weeping willow	6
Salix caprea	Goat willow	5
Salix discolor	Pussy willow	4
Salix matsudana 'Toruosa'	Corkscrew willow	4–5
Salpiglossis sinuata	Painted tongue	—
Salpiglossis s. 'Splash'	Painted tongue	—
Salvia	Sage	—
Salvia farinacea	Cup sage	—
Salvia splendens	Scarlet sage	—
Salvia superba	Violet sage	6
Sambucus canadensis	American elderberry	4
Sambucus	Elderberry	4
Sambucus racemosa	Red elderberry	5
Sanguinaria canadensis	Bloodroot	5
Sansieveria trifasciata	Snake plant	10
Santolina chamaecypaus	Lavender cotton	6–7
Sanvitalia procumbens	Creeping zinnia	—
Saponaria ocymoides	Soapwort	2–3

BOTANICAL NAME	COMMON NAME	ZONE
Saturjea montana	Winter Savory	6
Satureja montana	Savory	6
Saxifraga soarentosa	Strawberry geranium	10
Scabiosa atropurpurea	Pincushion flower	—
Scabiosa barbata	Pincushion flower	—
Scabiosa caucasica	Pincushion flower	2–3
	Pincushion	2–3
Schefflera actinophylla	Queensland umbrella	10
Schizanthus pinnatus 'Angel Wings'	Butterfly flower	—
Schizanthus p. 'Hit Parade'	Butterfly flower	—
Schizanthus wisetonensis	Butterfly flower	9
Schizostylis coccinea	Crimson flag	10
Schlumbergera	Christmas cactus	10
Scilla	Bluebell	5
Scilla nutans	English bluebell	5
Scindapus aureus	Ivy arum	10
Scindapsus	Ivy arum	10
Scindapus	Pothos	10
Scutellaria baicalensis	Skullcap	4
Sedum spectabile	Stonecrop	10
Selaginella	Club moss	10
	Hen and chickens	10
Selenicereus	Night blooming cactus	10
Sempervivum	Hen and chickens	5
Senecio	Cineraria	10
Senecio x hybridus	Cineraria	10
Shepardia argentea	Silver buffaloberry	2–3
Shepherdia	Buffalo berry	2–3
Sidalcea	Miniature hollyhock	5–6
	Prairie mallow	5–6
Sidalcea malvaeflora	Checkerbloom	5–6
Silene alpestris (quadrifida)	Campion; Catchfly	5
Silene	Catchfly	5
Silene schafta	Moss campion	10
Sinningia speciosa	Gloxinia	2–3
Sisyrinchium bellum	Blue-eyed grass	
Smithiantha	Temple bells	10
Solandra guttata	Chalice vine	10
	Cup-of-flower	10
Solidago	Goldenrod	3–4
Solidago x hybrida	Goldenrod	3–4
Sollya heterophylla	Bluebell creeper	—
Sophora secundiflora	Texas mountain laurel	5
Sorbus americana	American mountain ash	2–3

|---|---|---|
Sorbus aucuparia	European mountain ash	2–3
Sorbus cashmariana	Kashmir mountain ash	5
Sorbus vilmorinii	Mountain ash	5
Sparaxis tricolor	Harlequin flower	10
	Wand flower	10
Sparaxis	Wand flower	10
Spathiphyllum	Chinese evergreen	10
Spiraea billiardii	Billiard spirea	5
Spiraea prunifolia	Bridal-wreath spirea	5
Spiraea thunbergii	Thunberg spirea	5
Sprekelia formosissima	Aztec lily	10
	Jacobean lily	10
Stachys byzantina	Betony	4
	Lamb's ear	4
Stephanotis floribunda	Madagascar jasmine	10
Stokesia laevis	Cornflower aster	6
	Stoke's aster	6
Strelitzia reginae	Bird of paradise	10
Streptocarpus	Cape primrose	10
Symphlocarpus foetidus	Skunk cabbage	2–3
Symphoricarpos albus	Snowberry	6
Symphoricarpos orbiculatus	Indian currant	2–3
Symphtum officinalis	Comfrey	4
Syngonium podophyllum	Arrowhead	10
Syringa chinensis	Chinese lilac	6
Syringa laciniata	Cut-leaf lilac	6
Syringa microphylla	Littleleaf lilac	6
Syringa oblata dilatata	Korean early lilac	6
Syringa velutina	Korean lilac	3–4
Syringa vulgaris	Common lilac	5

T

Tagetes	Marigold	—
Tagetes patula	French marigold	—
Tagetes 'Baby Boy'	Marigold	—
Tagetes 'Bonanza Yellow'	Marigold	—
Tagetes 'Dainty Marietta'	Marigold	—
Tagetes 'Disco'	Marigold	—
Tagetes 'Golden Gem'	Marigold	—
Tagetes 'Gold Buy'	Marigold	—
Tagetes 'Lemon Gem'	Marigold	—
Tagetes 'Nugget'	Marigold	—

Tagetes 'Paprika'	Marigold	—
Tagetes 'Queen Sophia'	Marigold	—
Tagetes 'Scarlet Sophie'	Marigold	—
Tanacetum vulgare	Common tansy	3–4
Taraxacum	Dandelion	2–3
Taxus baccata stricta	Irish yew	6–7
Taxus baccata 'Fastigiata Aureomarginata'	Golden Irish yew	6–7
Taxus baccata	English yew	6–7
Taxus cuspidata	Japanese yew	4–5
Teucrium chamaedrys	Germander	5–6
Thalictrum diffusiflorum	Meadowrue	2–3
Thuja plicata	Giant arborvitae	2–3
Thuja standishii	Japanese arborvitae	5
Thunbergia battiscombi	Black-eyed Susan	—
Thunbergia	Black-eyed Susan	—
Thymophylla ternuiloba	Goldenfleece	—
Tiarella cordifolia	Foam flower	4
Tibouchina semidecandra	Princess flower	9
Tibouchina urvilleana	Glorybush	9
Tigrida pavonia	Peacock flower	6–7
	Tickseed	6–7
	Toad flax	6–7
	Shell flower	6–7
Tilia americana	American linden	2–3
Tilia platyphyllos	Big-leaf linden	2–3
Tithonia rotundifolia	Mexican sunflower	—
Tolmiea menzenii	Piggy-back plant	10
Tolmiea	Piggy-back plant	10
Torenia	Wishbone plant	—
Torenia fournierii	Wishbone flower	—
	Wishbone plant	—
Trachelium caeruleum	Blue lace flower	8
Trachelospermum jasminoides	Star jasmine	8
Trachymene caerulea	Blue lace flower	—
Tradescantia virginiana	Inch plant	5
	Spiderwort	5
Tradescantia	Wandering Jew	5
Tricyrtis hirta	Toad lily	7–8
Trollius	Globeflower	4–5
Trollius europaeus	Globeflower	4–5
Tropaeolum majus	Nasturtium	—
Tropaeolum	Nasturtium	—

BOTANICAL NAME	COMMON NAME	ZONE
Tsuga canadensis	Canada hemlock	4
Tsuga heterophylla	Western hemlock	9
Tuberose		—
Tulbaghia fragrans	Society garlic	10
Tulip tree		10
Tusillago farfara	Coltsfoot	3–4
Typha latifolia	Cat-tail	3–4

U

Ulmus americana	American elm	5–6
Ulmus parvifolia	Chinese elm	4
Ursinia anthemoides	Dill-leaf ursinia	—

V

Vaccinum	Blueberry	2–3
Valeriana officinalis	Garden heliotrope	4
Vallota speciosa	Scarborough lily	10
Veltheimia viridifolia	Pineapple lily	10
Venidium fastuosum	Monarch	—
Verbascum	Mullein	4–6
Verbascum chaixii	Mullein	4–6
Verbena hortensis 'Polaris'	Garden verbena	—
Verbena hortensis	Verbena	—
Verbena venosa	Vervain	—
Veronica	Speedwell	4–5
Veronica incana 'Crater Lake'	Speedwell	4–5
Veronica incana	Woolly speedwell	4–5
Veronica i. 'Royal Blue'	Speedwell	4–5
Viburnum carlcephalum	Fragrant snowball	5–6
Viburnum carlesii	Korean spice viburnum	5
Viburnum davidii	David viburnum	7
Viburnum dentatum	Arrowwood	2–3
Viburnum dilatatum	Linden viburnum	5–6
Viburnum japonicum	Japanese viburnum	7
Viburnum lantana	Wayfaring tree	4
Viburnum opulus	European cranberry bush	4
Viburnum plicatum	Japanese snowball	5
Viburnum rhytidophyllum	Leatherleaf viburnum	6

BOTANICAL NAME	COMMON NAME	ZONE
Viburnum trilobum	American cranberry bush	2–3
Vinca rosea	Periwinkle	4–5
Viola	Violet	6
Viola cornuta	Violet	6
Viola odorata	Sweet violet	6
Viola tricolor hortensis	Pansy	5
Viola tricolor	Johnny-jump-up	5
Viola x wittrockiana	Garden pansy	—
Vitex agnus-castus	Chaste tree	7–8

W
Watsonia	Watsonia	10
Weigela florida	Old-fashioned weigela	5–6
Wisteria floribunda	Japanese wisteria	5

X
Xanthisma texanum	Star of Texas	—
Xeranthemum annuum	Everlasting	—

Z
Zantedeschia	Calla lily	9–10
Zantedeschia rehmannii	Pink calla	9–10
Zephyranthes grandiflora	Rain lily	9–10
Zinnia	Zinnia	—

SEED SOWING AND GERMINATION TIMES FOR ANNUALS AND PERENNIALS

COMMON (AND BOTANICAL) NAME	ANNUAL OR PERENNIAL	SOW SEED OUTDOORS AFTER LAST FROST	SOW SEED INDOORS	GERMINATION (IN DAYS)
Ageratum	A		X	21
Alyssum	P	X		14
Amaranthus	A	X		14
Anemone	P	X		14–21
Arabis	P	X		21–28
Arctotis	A		X	8–10
Argemone	A	X		14–21
Armeria	P	X		21–28
Aster, China (Callistephus chinensis)	A		X	14–21
Aubrietia	P	X		14–21
Baby's breath (Gypsophila paniculata)	A, P	X		7–14
Balsam (Impatiens balsamina)	A		X	14–21
Bee balm (Monarda didyma)	P		X	7–10
Begonia	P		X	14–21
Bells of Ireland	A		X	14–21
Blanket flower (Gaillardia aristata)	P	X		14–21
Blue lace flower (Trachymene caerulea)	A		X	7–10
Boltonia	P		X	14–21
Browallia (Browallia viscosa)	A		X	14–21
Butterfly weed (Aslepias tuberosa)	P	X		10–14
Calendula (Calendula officinalis)	A		X	14–21
California tree poppy (Romneya coulteri)	P		X	14–20

COMMON (AND BOTANICAL) NAME	ANNUAL OR PERENNIAL	SOW SEED OUTDOORS AFTER LAST FROST	SOW SEED INDOORS	GERMINATION (IN DAYS)
Calliopsis	A		X	14–28
(Coreopsis tinctoria)				
Candytuft	P	X		14–21
(Iberis sempervirens)				
Canterbury bells	A		X	5–7
(Campanula medium)				
Cerastium	P	X		14–28
(Cerastium tomentosum)				
Chinese bellflower	P		X	14–21
(Platycodon grandiflorum)				
China pink	A		X	7–10
(Dianthus chinensis)				
Chrysanthemum	P	X		14–35
(Chrysanthemum carinatum)				
Columbine	P	X		21–48
(Aquilegia)				
Coreopsis	P	X		14–21
(Coreopsis grandiflora)				
Cornflower	P	X		10–15
(Centaurea)				
Cosmos	A, P		X	14–28
(Cosmos bipinnatus)				
Dahlia	A		X	14–21
(Dahlia pinnata)				
Datura	A		X	14–21
(Datura suaveolens)				
Delphinium	P	X		14–28
(Delphinium elatum)				
Dimorphoteca	A		X	10–15
Dodecatheon	P		X	7–14
Dusty miller	A		X	14–21
(Centaurea gymocarpa or Senecio cineraria)				
English daisy	P	X		7–14
(Bellis perennis)				
Feverfew	P	X		14–21
(Chrysanthemum parthenium)				
Fleabane	P		X	14–21
(Erigeron)				
Forget-me-not	P	X		21–28
(Myosotis)				
Foxglove	P	X		14–21
(Digitalis purpurea)				

COMMON (AND BOTANICAL) NAME	ANNUAL OR PERENNIAL	SOW SEED OUTDOORS AFTER LAST FROST	SOW SEED INDOORS	GERMINATION (IN DAYS)
Gaillardia	A		X	14–21
(Gaillardia picta)				
Gas plant	P		X	7–14
(Dictamus)				
Gerbera	P	X		20–30
Geum	P	X		20–30
Globe amaranth	A	X		14–21
(Gomphrena globosa)				
Godetia	A	X		14–21
Helenium	P		X	10–15
Helianthemum	P		X	10–21
Heliopsis	P		X	4–7
Hollyhock	A	X		14–21
(Althaea rosea)				
Italian bellflower	P	X		10–15
(Campanula isophylla)				
Kochia	A		X	15–20
Larkspur	A	X		21–28
(Delphinium ajacis)				
Leopard's bane	P	X		14–21
(Doronicum caucasicum)				
Liatris	P	X		7–14
Limonium	P	X		7–14
Linaria	A		X	14–21
(Linaria maroccana)				
Lobelia, blue	A		X	14–21
(Lobelia erinus)				
Lobelia, red	P	X		7–10
(Lobelia cardinalis)				
Lupine	A, P	X		21–28
(Lupinus polyphyllus)				
Marigold	A		X	7–14
(Tagetes species)				
Mignonette	A	X		14–21
(Reseda odorata)				
Morning glory	A		X	21–28
(Ipomoea purpurea)				
Nasturtium	A	X		14–21
(Tropaeolum majus)				
Nemesia	A		X	7–14
Nicotiana	A, P		X	14–18
Nierembergia	A		X	10–14

COMMON (AND BOTANICAL) NAME	ANNUAL OR PERENNIAL	SOW SEED OUTDOORS AFTER LAST FROST	SOW SEED INDOORS	GERMINATION (IN DAYS)
Oenothera	P	X		15–20
Pansy	A	X		14–21
(Viola tricolor)				
Patience plant	A		X	14–18
(Impatiens)				
Penstemon	P	X		14–20
Petunia	A		X	7–14
(Petunia hybrida)				
Phlox	A		X	14–21
(Phlox drummondii)				
Pink	P	X		10–25
(Dianthus deltoides)				
Polemonium	P		X	12–15
Poppy	P		X	7–14
(Papaver orientale)				
Primrose	P		X	21–30
(Primula)				
Pyrethrum	P	X		12–15
(Chrysanthemum coccineum)				
Red-hot poker	P	X		21–28
(Kniphofia aloides)				
Rose mallow	P		X	18–24
(Hibiscus moscheutos)				
Rudbeckia	A		X	20–25
Salpiglossis	A		X	14
(Salpiglossis sinuata)				
Salvia	A		X	15–20
Scabiosa	A		X	7–10
Schizanthus	A		X	15–20
Shasta daisy	P	X		15–20
(Chrysanthemum maximum)				
Sidalcea	P		X	12–15
Snapdragon	A		X	7–14
(Antirrhinum majus)				
Speedwell	P	X		15–20
(Veronica)				
Stock	A		X	14
(Matthiola incana)				
Stokesia	P		X	15–20
Strawflower	A		X	7–10
(Helichrysum bracteatum)				

COMMON (AND BOTANICAL) NAME	ANNUAL OR PERENNIAL	SOW SEED OUTDOORS AFTER LAST FROST	SOW SEED INDOORS	GERMINATION (IN DAYS)
Sunflower (Helianthus)	P	X		14–21
Swan River daisy (Brachycome iberidifolia)	A		X	7–10
Sweet alyssum (Lobularia maritima)	A		X	14–21
Sweet rocket (Hesperis matronalis)	P	X		20–30
Thunbergia	A		X	8–10
Tithonia (Tithonia rotundifolia)	P		X	14–21
Torenia	A		X	14–21
Trollius	P	X		21–30
Verbena (Verbena hortensis)	A		X	21–28
Vinca rosea	P		X	14–21
Violet (Viola cornuta)	P	X		14–21
Wallflower (Cheiranthus cheiri)	P	X		10–15
Zinnia (Zinnia elegans)	A		X	4–7

FLOWERING, SEED-DISPERSAL TIMES, AND GERMINATION OF TREES

COMMON AND BOTANICAL NAMES	FLOWERING	SEED DISPERSAL	GERMINATION*
Alder, red (Alnus rubra)	Early spring	November–December	a
Ash, green (Fraxinus pennsylvanica)	May	October–May	a
Ash, white (F. americana)	April–May	September–December	a
Basswood (Tilia americana)	June–July	Fall–spring	b
Beech, American (Fagus grandifolia)	April–May	After first heavy frost	a
Birch, gray (Betula populifolia)	April–May	October–January	a
Birch, paper (B. papyrifera)	April–June	September–April	a
Birch, sweet (B. lenta)	April–May	September–November	a
Box elder (Acer negundo)	March–May	September–March	a
Douglas fir (Pseudotsuga menziesii)	Spring–summer	August–September	a
Fir, balsam (Abies balsamea)	May	September–November	a
Fir, California red (A. magnifica)	June	September–October	a
Fir, Pacific silver (A. amabilis)	Spring	October	a
Fir, white (A. concolor)	May–June	September–October	a

a = Stratify 2 to 3 months at 32° to 45° F.
b = Soak seed in hot water, and then stratify 3 to 5 months at 32° to 45° F.
c = Stratify 2 to 4 months at 68° to 80° F, and then stratify 2 to 4 months at 32° to 45° F.
d = Scarify seed coat (nick the seed with a knife).

COMMON AND BOTANICAL NAMES	FLOWERING	SEED DISPERSAL	GERMINATION*
Hackberry (*Celtis occidentalis*)	April–May	October–winter	a
Hemlock, eastern (*Tsuga canadensis*)	May–June	September–winter	a
Hemlock, western (*T. heterophylla*)	Spring	September	a
Hickory, mockernut (*Carya tomentosa*)	April–May	September–December	c
Hickory, pignut (*C. glabra*)	April–May	September–December	c
Hickory, shagbark (*C. ovata*)	April–June	September–December	c
Hickory, shellbark (*C. laciniosa*)	April–June	September–December	c
Honey locust (*Gleditsia triacanthos*)	May–June	September–February	d
Larch, western (*Larix occidentalis*)	Spring	August–September	a
Locust, black (*Robinia pseudoacacia*)	May–June	September–April	d
Maple, red (*Acer rubrum*)	February–May	April–July	a
Maple, silver (*A. saccharinum*)	February–April	April–June	a
Maple, sugar (*A. saccharum*)	March–May	October–December	a
Oak, black (*Quercus velutina*)	April–May	September–November	a
Oak, northern red (*Q. rubra*)	April–May	September–October	a
Oak, scarlet (*Q. coccinea*)	April–May	September–October	a
Oak, southern red (*Q. falcata*)	April–May	September–October	a
Pecan (*Carya illinoensis*)	March–May	September–October	a
Pine, eastern white (*Pinus strobus*)	April–June	September–October	a
Pine, jack (*P. banksiana*)	May	Fall–several years	a
Pine, loblolly (*P. taeda*)	March–April	Fall–spring	a

COMMON AND BOTANICAL NAMES	FLOWERING	SEED DISPERSAL	GERMINATION*
Pine, ponderosa (*P. ponderosa*)	April–June	Fall–spring	a
Pine, western white (*P. monticola*)	Spring	Fall–spring	a
Red cedar, eastern (*Juniperus virginiana*)	March–May	February–March	c
Red cedar, western (*Thuja plicata*)	April	August–October	c
Redwood (*Sequoia sempervirens*)	November–March	Fall	a
Spruce, black (*Picea mariana*)	May–June	October	a
Spruce, red (*P. rubens*)	April–May	September	a
Spruce, white (*P. glauca*)	May	August–November	a
Sweet gum (*Liquidambar styraciflua*)	March–May	September–November	a
Sycamore, American (*Platanus occidentalis*)	May	September–May	a
Walnut, black (*Juglans nigra*)	May–June	Fall	a
Yellow poplar (*Liriodendron tulipifera*)	April–June	October–January	a

a = Stratify 2 to 3 months at 32° to 45° F.
b = Soak seed in hot water, and then stratify 3 to 5 months at 32° to 45° F.
c = Stratify 2 to 4 months at 68° to 80° F., and then stratify 2 to 4 months at 32° to 45° F.
d = Scarify seed coat (nick the seed with a knife).

SEED DISPERSAL TIMES FOR SHRUBS

SHRUB	SEED DISPERSAL	REMARKS
Barberry	Fall or spring	Stratify 2 to 6 weeks at 40° F.
Camellia	Fall	Sow before seed coat hardens.
Ceanothus	Spring or fall	Soak seed in hot water.
Cotoneaster	Spring or fall	Stratify 3 to 4 months at 70° F, and then stratify for 3 months at 32° F.
Euonymus	Late fall	Stratify 3 to 4 months at 32° to 50° F.
Holly	Spring	Stratify 3 to 4 months at 32° to 50° F.
Oleander	Late fall	Plant immediately.
Pittosporum	Spring	Soak seed in hot water for 2 hours
Plumbago	Late winter	Germinates easily.
Privet	Late fall	Stratify 2 to 3 months at 45° F.
Rose	Spring or fall	Stratify 3 to 6 months at 35° F.
Spirea	Late summer	Germinates easily.
Viburnum	Fall	Stratify 3 to 6 months at 40° F., and then stratify 2 to 4 months at 70° to 80° F.

WET SOIL CONDITIONS:

TREES

DECIDUOUS

Acer rubrum (red maple)
Alnus glutinosa (European alder)
Betula populifolia (gray birch)
Gleditsia aquatica (water locust)
Liquidambar styraciflua (sweet gum)
Plantanus occidentalis (buttonwood)
Quercus palustris (pin oak)
Salix alba (white willow)
Tilia americana (American linden)

EVERGREEN

Abies balsamea (balsam fir)
Thuja occidentalis (arborvitae)
Tsuga canadensis (Canada hemlock)

SHRUBS

Alnus (various) (alders)
Amelanchier canadensis (shadblow serviceberry)

Andromeda species (andromeda)
Aronia arbutifolia (red chokeberry)
Calluna vulgaris (heather)
Clethra alnifolia (summer sweet)
Cornus alba (Tatarian dogwood)
Cornus sanguinea (bloodtwig dogwood)
Cornus stolonifera (red osier)
Hypericum densiflorum (dense hypericum)
Ilex glabra (inkberry)
Ilex verticillata (winterberry)
Kalmia angustifolia (sheep laurel)
Ligustrum amurense (amur privet)
Pieris floribunda (mountain andromeda)
Rhododendron (rhoodendron)
Sabal minor (dwarf palmetto)
Salix (various) (willow)
Spiraea menziesii (spiraea)
Spiraea tomentosa (hardhack)
Vaccinum corymbosum (highbush blueberry)
Viburnum alnifolium (hobblebush)
Viburnum cassinoides (white rod)
Viburnum dentatum (arrowwood)
Viburnum lentago (nannyberry)
Viburnum sieboldii (Siebold viburnum)

PERENNIALS

Aruno 'Donax' (giant reed)
Asclepias incarnata (swamp milkweed)
Caltha palustris (marsh marigold)
Equisetum hyemale (horsetail plant)
Gentiana asclepiadea (willow gentian)
Helenium (various) (Helen's flower)
Hibiscus moscheutos (swamp rose mallow)
Iris pseudacorus (yellowflag)
Iris versicolor (blue flag)
Lobelia cardinalis (cardinal flower)
Lythrum (various) (loosestrife)
Monarda didyma (bee balm)
Myosotis scorpioides (true forget-me-not)
Oenothera (various) (evening primrose)
Sarracenia purpurea (pitcher plant)
Saxifraga (saxifrage)
Vinca (periwinkle)

DRY-SOIL CONDITIONS:

TREES

DECIDUOUS

Acer ginnala (Amur maple)
Acer tataricum (Tatarian maple)
Ailanthus altissima (tree of heaven)
Betula pendula (European birch)
Betula populifolia (gray birch)
Carya glabra (pignut)
Cotinus coggygria (smoke tree)
Populus alba (white poplar)
Populus tremuloides (quaking aspen)
Prunus cerasus (sour cherry)
Prunus serotina (black cherry)
Quercus suber (cork oak)
Robinia pseudoacacia (black locust)

EVERGREEN

Juniperus chinensis (Chinese juniper)
Juniperus virginiana (eastern red cedar)
Picea alba (Canadian spruce)
Picea abies (excelsa) (Norway spruce)
Pinus mugo (Swiss mountain pine)
Pinus rigida (pitch pine)
Pinus strobus (white pine)
Pinus sylvestris (Scots pine)

SHRUBS

Acacia
Arbutus unedo (strawberry tree)
Arctostaphylos uva-ursi (bearberry)
Berberis, several (barberry)
Betula glandulosa
Betula nana
Buddleia alternifolia (fountain buddleia)
Ceanothus americanus (New Jersey tea)
Cotoneaster (cotoneaster)

Cytisus (broom)
Elaeagnus angustifolia (Russian olive)
Elaeagnus longpipes (goumi)
Euonymus japonica (evergreen euonymus)
Genista tinctoria (dyer's greenweed)
Hamamelis virginiana (common witch hazel)
Hypericum spathalatum (shrubby Saint Johnswort)
Juniperus communis (juniper)
Juniperus horizontalis (creeping juniper)
Kolkwitzia amabilis (beauty bush)
Ligustrum vulgare (common privet)
Nerium oleander (oleander)
Pittosporum tobira (Japanese pittosporum)
Potentilla fruticosa (cinquefoil)
Prunus besseyi (western sand cherry)
Prunus maritima (beach plum)
Pyracantha coccinea (scarlet firethorn)
Raphiolepis umbellata (yeddo hawthorn)
Rhamnus alaternus
Rhamnus frangula (alder buckthorn)
Rhus (various) (sumac)
Robinia hispida (rose acacia)
Robinia pseudoacacia (locust)
Robinia viscosa (clammy locust)
Rosa (various) (rose)
Salix tristis (dwarf gray willow)
Tamarix species (tamarix)
Viburnum lantana (wayfaring tree)
Viburnum lentago (nannyberry)

PERENNIALS

Achillea (various) (yarrow)
Ajuga reptans (carpet bugle)
Anthemis tinctoria (golden marguerite)
Artemisia pycnocephala
Asclepias tuberosa (butterfly weed)
Aster novae-angliae (New England aster)
Callirhoe involucrata (poppy mallow)
Cerastium tomentosum (snow-in-summer)
Coreopsis grandiflora (tickseed)
Dianthus (various) (pink)
Echinops exaltatus (globe thistle)

Echium
Gazania hybrids
Geranium grandiflorum (cranesbill)
Gypsophila paniculata (baby's breath)
Helianthus (various) (sunflower)
Limonium latifolium (statice, sea lavender)
Papaver nudicaule (Iceland poppy)
Phlox subulata (moss pink)
Potentilla atrosanguinea (cinquefoil)
Rudbeckia hirta (coneflower)
Veronica (various) (speedwell)
Yucca filamentosa (Adam's needle)

ANNUALS

Arctotis stoechadifolia grandis (African daisy)
Browallia americana (browallia)
Centaurea cyanus (bachelor's button, cornflower)
Convovulus tricolor (dwarf morning glory)
Coreopsis tinctoria (calliopsis)
Cryophytum crystallinum (ice plant)
Delphinium ajacis (larkspur)
Dimorphoteca (various) (Cape marigold)
Eschscholzia californica (California poppy)
Euphorbia marginata (snow-on-the-mountain)
Gaillardia pulchella (rose-ring gaillardia)
Gypsophila elegans (baby's breath)
Helianthus annuus (sunflower)
Ipomoea purpurea (morning glory)
Mirabilis jalapa (four-o'-clock)
Phlox drummondii (annual phlox)
Portulaca grandiflora (rose moss)
Salvia splendens (scarlet sage)
Zinnia elegans (giant-flowered zinnia)

SHADY PLACES:

TREES

DECIDUOUS

Acer circinatum (vine maple)
Acer ginnala (Amur maple)
Acer palmatum (Japanese maple)
Acer spicatum (mountain maple)
Albizia julibrissin (silk tree)
Alnus species (alder)
Betula papyrifera (canoe birch)
Cercis canadensis (redbud)
Cornus alba
Cornus kousa (Chinese dogwood)
Cornus mas (Cornelian cherry)
Crataegus oxyacantha 'Paul's Scarlet' (hawthorn)
Elaeagnus angustifolia (Russian olive)
Franklinia alatamaha (franklinia)
Fraxinus holotricha
Magnolia stellata (star magnolia)
Malus species and hybrids (flowering crabapple)
Prunus (various) (flowering cherry and others)
Sorbus (various) (mountain ash)

EVERGREEN

Magnolia soulangiana (saucer magnolia)
Pinus bungeana (lacebark pine)
Taxus species (yew)
Thuja species (arborvitae)
Tsuga species (hemlock)

SHRUBS

Acanthopanax pentaphyllus
Amelanchier (various) (serviceberry)
Aronia (various) (chokeberry)
Azalea nudiflorum (Pinxter flower)
Caenothus americanus (New Jersey tea)
Cephlanathus occidentalis (buttonbush)

Chionanthus virginica (fringe tree)
Clethra alnifolia (summer sweet)
Cornus alba 'Sibirica' (Tatarian dogwood)
Cornus mas (Cornelian cherry)
Euonymus fortunei (winter creeper)
Hamamelis virginiana (common witch hazel)
Hypericum (various) (Saint Johnswort)
Ilex glabra (inkberry)
Ilex verticillata (winterberry)
Kalmia latifolia (mountain laurel)
Leucothoe catesbaei (drooping leucothoe)
Mahonia aquifolium (Oregon grape)
Mahonia bealei (leatherleaf grape)
Pieris floribunda (mountain andromeda)
Rhododendron (various)
Rhus canadensis (fragrant sumac)
Ribes alpinum (alpine currant)
Ribes sanguineum (flowering currant)
Vaccinium corymobosum (highbush blueberry)
Viburnum (various) (viburnum)

PERENNIALS (semishade)

Acontium anthora (monkshood)
Ajuga (bugle)
Althaea rosea (hollyhock)
Anemone hupehensis japonica (Japanese anemone)
Anemonella thalictroides (rue anemone)
Aquilegia hybrids (columbine)
Asperula (woodruff)
Campanula rotundifolia (harebell)
Convallaria majalis (lily of the valley)
Cornus canadensis (bunchberry)
Dicentra spectabilis (bleeding heart)
Dictamus albus (gas plant)
Epimedium grandiflorum (bishop's hat)
Geranium grandiflorum (cranesbill)
Helleborus niger (Christmas rose)
Hemerocallis (various) (daylily)
Hepatica
Heuchera sanguinea (coral bell)
Hibiscus moscheutos (swamp rose mallow)
Hosta (various) (plantain lily)
Hypericum (Saint Johnswort)

Iberis sempervirens (evergreen candytuft)
Lobelia cardinalis (cardinal flower)
Mertensia virginica (Virginia bluebell)
Monarda didyma (bee balm)
Phlox divaricata (sweet William phlox)
Platycodon grandiflorum (balloon flower)
Primula (various) (primrose)
Trollius europeaus (globeflower)

ANNUALS (light shade)

Ageratum houstonianum (floss flower)
Bellis perennis (English daisy)
Catharanthus roseus (Madagascar periwinkle)
Celosia 'Plumosa' (plume cockscomb)
Centaurea americana (basket flower)
Centaurea moschata (sweet sultan)
Clarkia elegans (clarkia)
Cryophytum crystallinum (ice plant)
Delphinium ajacis (larkspur)
Euphorbia marginata (snow-on-the-mountain)
Gerbera jamesoni (Transvaal daisy)
Godetia amoena (farewell to spring)
Impatiens balsamina (balsam)
Lobelia erinus (lobelia)
Lobularia maritima (sweet alyssum)
Lupinus hartwegii (lupine, annual)
Myosotis sylvatica (forget-me-not)
Nicotiana sanderae (flowering tobacco)
Phlox drummondii (annual phlox)
Primula malacoides (fairy primrose)
Salpiglossis sinuata (painted tongue)
Viola tricolor hortensis (pansy)

VINES

Akebia quinata (fiveleaf akebia)
Ampelopsis breviped-unculata (porcelain ampelopsis or blueberry climber)
Aristolochia durior (Dutchman's pipe)
Celastrus scandens (American bittersweet)
Clytosoma (Bignonia capreolata) (cross vine or trumpet vine)
Euonymus fortunei (wintercreeper)

Fatshedera lizei
Ficus pumila (repens) (creeping fig)
Gelsemium sempervirens (Carolina jessamine)
Hedera helix (English ivy)
Hydrangea petiolaris (climbing hydrangea)
Jasminum nudiflorum (winter jasmine)
Jasminum officinale (white jasmine)
Lonicera hildebrandiana (Burmese honeysuckle)
Lonicera japonica 'Halliana' (Hall's honeysuckle)
Parthenocissus quinqefolia (Virginia creeper)
Pueraria thunbergiana (kudzu vine)
Smilax rotundifolia (horse brier)
Trachelospermum jasminoides (star jasmine)
Vitis coignetiae (glory grape)

BULBS (semishade)

Achimenes (rainbow flower)
Anemone
Begonia (tuberous)
Caladium
Camassia (camas)
Chionodoxa (glory of snow)
Colchicum (meadow of saffron)
Colocasia esculenta (taro)
Convallaria (lily of the valley)
Crocus
Cyclamen (various) (cyclamen)
Eranthis (winter aconite)
Erythronium (dogtooth violet)
Frittilaria

CITY CONDITIONS (plants that withstand pollution):

TREES

DECIDUOUS

Acer platanoides (Norway maple)
Aesculus carnea (red horse chestnut)
Ailanthus altissima (tree of heaven)
Betula alba (white birch)

Carpinus betulus (European hornbeam)
Catalpa speciosa (western catalpa)
Cornus florida (flowering dogwood)
Crataegus oxyacantha (English hawthorn)
Crataegus phanopyrum (Washington hawthorn)
Elaeagnus angustifolia (Russian olive)
Euonymus europaea (spindle tree)
Fraxinus americana (white ash)
Ginkgo biloba (maidenhair tree, gingko tree)
Gleditsia triancanthos (honey locust)
Ilex opaca (American holly)
Magnolia (various)
Malus species (flowering crabapple)
Phellodendron amurense (Amur corktree)
Platanus acerifolia (plane tree)
Populus nigra italica (Lombardy popular)
Prunus subhirtella (rosebud cherry)
Quercus borealis (red oak)
Rhamnus davurica (davurica buckthorn)
Sophora japonica (Japanese pagoda tree)
Styrax japonica (snowbell tree)
Syringa pekinensis (Peking lilac)
Tilia cordata (small-leafed linden)
Ulmus pumila (dwarf elm)

EVERGREEN

Abies concolor (white fir)
Picea pungens (Swiss mountain pine)
Pinus mugo (Swiss mountain pine)
Taxus cuspidata (Japanese yew)
Thuja occidentalis (American arborvitae)
Tsuga caroliniana (Carolina hemlock)

SHRUBS

Abelia grandiflora (abelia)
Acanthopanax pentaphyllum
Aesculus parviflora (bottlebrush buckeye)
Aralia elata
Azalea (many)
Berberis thunbergii (Japanese barberry)

Buddleia davidii (butterfly bush)
Buxus microphylla Koreana (Korean boxwood)
Chaenomeles japonica (Japanese quince)
Clematis paniculata
Cornus paniculata (gray dogwood)
Cornus sanguinea (bloodtwig dogwood)
Cornus stolonifera (red-osier dogwood)
Cotoneaster horizontalis (rock spray)
Deutzia gracilis
Deutzia scabra 'Candidissima" (snowflake deutzia)
Elaeagnus angustifolia (Russian olive)
Euonymus (many)
Fatsia japonica
Forsythia (all species)
Hibiscus syriacus (rose of Sharon)
Hydrangea quercifolia (oakleaf hydrangea)
Ilex crenata (Japanese holly)
Ilex glabra (inkberry)
Juniperus chinensis 'Pfitzeriana' (Pftizer juniper)
Kalmia latifolia (mountain laurel)
Kerria japonica (kerria)
Lagerstroemia indica (crape myrtle)
Ligustrum (various) (privet)
Lonicera species (honeysuckle)
Mahonia aquifolium (Oregon grape)
Malus sargentii (Sargent crabapple)
Myrica caroliniensis (bayberry)
Nandina domestica (heavenly bamboo)
Osmanthus aquifolium (holly olive)
Philadelphus (mock orange)
Pieris japonica (Japanese andromeda)
Potentilla fruticosa (cinquefoil)
Prunus subhirtella (rosebud cherry)
Pyracantha coccinea (scarlet firethorn)
Rhododendron carolinianum
Rhododendron hybrids
Rhus contius (smoke tree)
Rosa multiflora (Japanese rose)
Rosa rugosa (rugosa rose)
Spiraea thunbergii (Thunberg spiraea)
Spiraea vanhouttei (Vanhoutte's spiraea)
Symphoricarpos albus (snowberry)
Syringa vulgaris (common lilac)
Tamarix (various)
Viburnum dentatum (arrowwood)

Viburnum lantana (wayfaring tree)
Vitex agnus-castus (chaste tree)
Weigela hybrids
Wisteria sinensis (Chinese wisteria)

PERENNIALS

Astilbe japonica
Bergenia
Chrysanthemum
Coreopsis
Dianthus barbatus (sweet William)
Gaillardia
Hemerocallis (daylily)
Heuchera sanguinea (coral bells)
Hosta plantaginea (plantain lily)
Iris (bearded iris)
Paeonia (peony)
Phlox
Sedum (stonecrop)

ANNUALS

Ageratum
Antirrhinum (snapdragon)
Cleome
Lobelia erinus (lobelia)
Lobularia
Mirabilis
Nicotiana
Petunia
Phlox
Salvia
Tagetes (marigold)
Verbena
Zinnia

VINES

Akebia quinta (five-leaf akebia)
Clematis paniculata

Cobaea scandens (cup-and-saucer vine)
Hedera helix (English ivy)
Lonicera Japonica 'Halliana' (Hall's honeysuckle)
Parthenocissus quinquefolia (Virginia creeper)
Parthenocissus tricuspidata (Boston ivy)
Phaseolus coccineus (scarlet runner bean)
Polygonum auberti (China fleece vine)

SOIL BETWEEN PAVED AREAS (Creepers):

SHRUBS

Cotoneaster dammeri
Juniperus (many) (juniper)
Santolina
Thymus
Thymus serpyllum lanuginosus (mother-of-thyme)
Thymus serpyllum vulgaris (lemon thyme)

PERENNIALS

Ajuga reptans (carpet bugle)
Anthemis nobilis (chamomile)
Arabis alpina (mountain rockcress)
Arenaria montana
Arenaria verna
Armeria maritima (sea pink or thrift)
Bellis perennis
Campanula glomerata accaulis
Dianthus (pink)
Gypsophila repens
Iberis sempervirens (edging candytuft)
Phlox subulata (moss pink)
Sedum acre (stonecrop)
Sempervivum arachnoideum (cobweb houseleek)
Veronica repens (creeping speedwell)
Veronica rupestris
Veronica serpyllifolia
Vinca minor (common periwinkle)

PURPOSE IN THE GARDEN TO PROVIDE SHADE:

TREES

Acer (various) (maple)
Aesculus carnea (red horse chestnut)
Callistemon citrinus (bottlebrush)
Catalpa speciosa (western catalpa)
Celtis occidentalis (hackberry)
Cinnamomum camphora (camphor tree)
Crataegus oxyacantha (English hawthorn)
Crataegus phaenopyrum (Washington hawthorn)
Fagus sylvatica (European beech)
Fraxinus americana (white ash)
Ginkgo biloba (ginkgo tree or maidenhair tree)
Gleditsia triacanthos (sweet honey locust)
Koelreuteria paniculata (goldenrain tree)
Liquidambar styraciflua (sweet gum)
Magnolia grandiflora (southern magnolia)
Malus (crabapple)
Platanus acerifolia (London plane tree)
Populus alba (white poplar)
Populus nigra 'Italica' (Lombardy poplar)
Prunus sargentii (Sargent cherry)
Quercus (various) (oak)
Sophora japonica (Japanese pagoda tree)
Sorbus aucuparia (mountain ash)
Syringa japonica (Japanese tree lilac)
Tilia americana (American linden)
Tilia cordata (small-leafed linden)
Ulmus americana (American elm)
Zelkova serrata (Japanese zelkova)

SHRUBS FOR HEDGES:

DECIDUOUS (to 5 ft.)

Berberis koreana (Korean barberry)
Berberis menotorensis (mentor barberry)
Berberis thunbergii 'Erecta' (Japanese barberry)
Cotoneaster lucida (hedge cotoneaster)
Euonymus alata 'Compacta' (winged euonymus)
Ligustrum vulgare 'Lodense' (privet)

Rosa species (rose)
Salix purpurea Gracillis (dwarf purple osier)

EVERGREEN (to 5 ft.)

Berberis juliane (wintergreen barberry)
Berberis sempervirens suffruticosa (dwarf box)
Berberis verruculosa (warty barberry)
Euonymus fortunei
Euonymus kiautschovica
Ilex crenata (Japanese holly)
Ilex crenata 'Microphylla'
Thuja occidentalis varieties (American arborvitae)

DECIDUOUS (to 30 ft.)

Acer ginnala (Amur maple)
Crataegus species (hawthorn)
Hibiscus syriacus (shrub althea)
Lonicera maackii (Amur honeysuckle)
Lonicera tatarica (Tatarian honeysuckle)
Philadelphus coronarius (mock orange)
Spiraea prunifolia (bridal wreath spirea)
Spiraea thunbergii
Syringa persica (Persian lilac)
Syringa vulgaris (common lilac)
Viburnum lantana (wayfaring tree)
Viburnum sieboldii (Siebold viburnum)

EVERGREEN (to 30 ft.)

Abelia grandiflora (glossy abelia)
Buxus sempervirens (common boxweed)
Photinia serrulata (Chinese photinia)
Pittosporum tobira (Japanese pittosporum)
Podocarpus macrophyllus
Pyracantha coccinea (firethorn)

FOR EDGING:

PERENNIALS

Achillea tomentosa (woolly yarrow)
Ajuga reptans (carpet bugle)
Alyssum saxatile (alyssum or basket of gold)
Arabis alpina (mountain rockcress)
Arabis caucasica (wall rockcress)
Armeria maritima (sea pink or thrift)
Aubrietia deltoide (common aubrieta)
Bellis perennis (English daisy)
Campanula carpatica (bellflower)
Cerastium tomentosum (snow-in-summer)
Dianthus plumarius (grass pink)
Festuca ovina 'Glauca' (blue fescue)
Heuchera sanguinea (coral bells)
Iberis sempervirens (evergreen candytuft)
Papaver nudicaule (Iceland poppy)
Phlox procumbens (hairy phlox)
Phlox subulata (moss pink)
Primula (various) (primrose)
Sedum (various) (stonecrop)
Veronica (various) (speedwell)
Viola (various)

ANNUALS

Ageratum (various)
Antirrhinum (dwarf kinds) (snapdragon)
Begonia semperflorens (wax begonia)
Brachycome iberidifolia (Swan River daisy)
Browallia americana (browallia)
Calendula officinalis (calendula or marigold)
Celosia (various) (cockscomb)
Centaurea cineraria (dusty miller)
Coreopsis tinctoria (calliopsis)
Cryophytm crystallinum (ice plant)
Dianthus chinensis (China pink)
Eschscholzia californica (California poppy)
Iberis umbellata (globe candytuft)
Linum grandiflorum 'Rubrum' (scarlet flax)
Lobelia erinus (lobelia)

Petunia (various) (petunia)
Phlox drummondii (annual phlox)
Portulaca grandiflora (rose moss)
Tagetes (marigold)
Tropaeolum majus (nasturtium)
Verbena (various)

FOR BEST GROUND COVER:

SHRUBS

Akebia quinata (fiveleaf akebia)
Arctostaphylos uva-ursi (bearberry)
Calluna vulgaris (heather)
Cotoneaster dammeri
Cotoneaster horizontalis (rock spray)
Euonymus radicans (various) (wintercreeper)
Hedera helix (English ivy)
Hypericum calycinum (Saint Johnswort)
Jasminum nudiflorum (winter jasmine)
Juniperus chinesis 'Pftizeriana' (Pftizer juniper)
Juniperus communis depressa (spreading juniper)
Juniperus conferta (shore juniper)
Juniperus horizontalis (creeping juniper)
Lantana montevidensis (trailing lantana)
Lonicera japonica 'Halliana' (Hall's honeysuckle)
Rhus aromatica (fragrant sumac)
Rosa multiflora (Japanese rose)
Rosa virginiana (Virginia rose)
Spiraea tomentosa (hardhack)
Thymus (thyme)
Thymus serpyllum lanuginosis (mother-of-thyme)
Thymus serpyllum vulgaris (lemon thyme)

PERENNIALS

Ajuga reptans (carpet bugle)
Anthemis nobilis (chamomile)
Arabis alpina (mountain rock cress)
Campanula (bellflower)
Cerastium tomentosum (snow-in-summer)
Convallaria majalis (lily of the valley)

Drosanthemum floribundum
Gazania splendens (gazania)
Iberis sempervirens (evergreen candytuft)
Lampranthos spectablis (trailing ice plant)
Malephora croceum (ice plant)
Mentha requienii (mint)
Myosotis (forget-me-not)
Nepeta mussinii
Pachysandra terminalis (Japanese pachysandra)
Phlox divaricata (sweet William phlox)
Phlox subulata (moss pink)
Sedum acre (stonecrop)
Vinca minor (common periwinkle)

ROCK GARDEN PLANTS:

(WHITE)

Achillea (silver alpine yarrow)
Arabis albida (wall rockcress)
Arabis alpina (mountain rockcress)
Arenaria grandiflora (showy sandwort)
Cerastium tomentosum (snow-in-summer)
Claytonia caroliniana (spring beauty)
Convallaria majalis (lily of the valley)
Helleborus niger (Christmas rose)
Iberis sempervirens (evergreen candytuft)
Potentilla fruticosa (cinquefoil)
Saxifraga (saxifrage)
Sedum album (stonecrop)
Silene maritima (catchfly)

(BLUE)

Ajuga reptans (carpet bugle)
Campanula carpatica (bellflower)
Centaurea montana (mountain bluet)
Gentiana acaulis (stemless gentian)
Iris cristata (crested iris)
Iris pumila (dwarf bearded iris)
Linum alpinum (alpine flax)
Linum lewisii (prairie flax)
Linum perenne (blue flax)

Lithodora diffusa
Myosotis sylvatica (forget-me-not)
Phlox divaricata (sweet William phlox)
Phlox subulata (moss pink)
Platycodon grandiflorum (balloon flower)
Plumbago (leadwort)
Veronica rupestris (creeping speedwell)

(LILAC)

Campanula carpatica (bellflower)
Campanula rotundifolia (harebell)
Iris cristata (crested iris)
Iris pumila (dwarf bearded iris)
Phlox divaricata (sweet William phlox)
Viola cornuta (tufted viola)

(PURPLE)

Anemone pulsatilla (pasque flower)
Aster alpinus (rock aster)
Aubrieta deltoidea (common aubrieta)
Platycodon grandiflorum (balloon flower)

(CARMINE)

Dianthus deltoides (maiden pink)
Phlox stolonifera (creeping phlox)

(RED)

Aquilegia caerula (Colorado columbine)
Aquilegia canadensis (American columbine)
Epimedium rubrum
Hypericum repens (Saint Johnswort)
Sempervivum tectorum (houseleek)

(ROSE)

Claytonia caroliniana (spring beauty)
Dianthus plumarius (grass pink)
Dicentra spectabilis (bleeding heart)
Helleborus niger (Christmas rose)
Heuchera sanguinea (coral bell)
Sedum stoloniterum (stonecrop)

(PINK)

Geranium grandifolium (cranesbill)
Gypsophila repens (creeping baby's breath)
Phlox subulata (moss pink)
Saxifraga (saxifrage)
Sedum album (stonecrop)
Sedum sieboldii

(YELLOW)

Achillea tomentosa (woolly yarrow)
Alyssum argenteum (silver alyssum)
Alyssum saxatile (alyssum, basket of gold)
Alyssum saxatile compactum (dwarf goldentuft)
Aster alpinus (rock aster)
Draba olympica
Hypericum repens (Saint Johnswort)
Iris pumila (drawf bearded iris)
Sedum acre (stonecrop)
Sedum sarmentosum
Sempervivum tectorum (houseleek)

FOR COLORFUL AUTUMN FOLIAGE:

TREES

(PURPLE)

Fraxinus americana (white ash)
Liquidamber styraciflua (sweetgum)

(RED)

Acer ginnala (Amur maple)
Acer japonicum (Japanese maple)
Acer rubrum (red maple)
Acer saccharum (sugar maple)
Crataegus phaenopyrum (Washington thorn)
Liquidambar styraciflua (sweetgum)
Oxydendrum arboreum (sourwood)
Quercus coccinea (scarlet oak)

(YELLOW)

Acer rubrum (red maple)
Acer saccharum (sugar maple)
Carya glabra (pignut)
Cercidiphyllum japonicum (katsura tree)

SHRUBS

(PURPLE)

Cornus racemosa (gray dogwood)
Viburnum (various)

(RED, CRIMSON, ROSE, SCARLET)

Acer circinatum (vine maple)
Amelanchier canadensis (shadblow serviceberry)
Aronia arbutifolia (red chokeberry)
Azalea mucronulata (Korean azalea)
Azalea obtusa kaempferi
Berberis (various) (barberry)
Cotoneaster horizontalis (rock spray)
Enkianthus campanulatus (bellflower)
Euonymus alatus (winged euonymus)
Hydrangea quercifolia (oakleaf hydrangea)
Nandina domestica (heavenly bamboo)
Photinia serrulata (Chinese photinia)
Rhus (various) (sumac)
Ribes alpinum (alpine currant)
Vaccinum corymbosum (highbush blueberry)
Viburnum (various)

(YELLOW, ORANGE, BRONZE)

Acanthopanax pentaphyllum
Chionanthus virginica (fringetree)
Enkianthus campanulatus (bellflower)
Fothergilla
Hamamelis (witch hazel)
Leucothoe catesbaei (drooping leucothoe)
Mahonia aquifolium (Oregon grape)
Mahonia species (holly grape)
Pieris floribunda (mountain andromeda)
Pieris japonica (Japanese andromeda)
Rhododendron
Spiraea prunifolia (bridal wreath spiraea)
Spiraea thunbergli (thunberg spiraea)
Viburnum dentatum (arrowwood)

SHRUB FLOWERING CALENDAR

SPRING

Amelanchier canadensis (serviceberry)
Amelanchier grandiflora (apple serviceberry)
Andromeda polifolia (bog rosemary)
Chaenomeles japonica (Japanese quince)
Chaenomels speciosa (flowering quince)
Cornus mas (Cornelian cherry)
Enkianthus perulatus
Forsythia intermedia (forsythia)
Jasminum nudiflorum (winter jasmine)
Lonicera fragrantissima (winter honeysuckle)
Mahonia species (grape holly)
Pieris floribunda (mountain andromeda)
Pieris japonica (Japanese andromeda)
Rhodondendron

SUMMER

Albelia grandiflora (glossy abelia)
Kalmia latifolia (mountain laurel)
Kolkwitzia amabilis (beauty bush)
Philadelphus (various) (mock orange)
Potentilla fruticosa (bush cinquefoil)
Rosa (shrub type) (rose)
Spiraea (various)

FALL

Clethra alnifolia (summer sweet)
Hamamelis virginiana (common witch hazel)
Hibiscus syriacus (althea or hibiscus)
Hydrangea (various)
Prunus subhirtella
Spiraea billiardi (billiard spirea)
Tamarix (various)

FLOWERS

TREES, SHRUBS, AND VINES FOR FLOWERS:

TREES

Acacia baileyana (Bailey acacia)
Aesculus glabra (Ohio buckeye)
Albizia julibrissin (silk tree)
Catalpa speciosa (catalpa)
Cercis canadensis (redbud)
Cornus florida (dogwood)
Cornus kousa chinensis
Franklinia alatamaha
Jacaranda acutifolia
Koelreuteria paniculata (goldenrain tree)
Magnolia grandiflora (southern magnolia)
Magnolia stellata (star magnolia)
Malus species (crabapple)
Prunus species (fruit trees)
Sophora japonica (Japanese pagoda tree)

SHRUBS

Azalea
Buddleia davidii (butterfly bush)
Callistemon citrinus (bottlebrush)
Calluna vulgaris (heather)
Camellia
Carpenteria californica (mock orange)
Chaenomeles speciosa (flowering quince)
Daphne odora (fragrant daphne)
Forsythia intermedia (border forsythia)
Fothergilla major
Hamamelis virginiana (common witch hazel)
Hibiscus syriacus (shrub althaea)
Kalmia latifolia (mountain laurel)

Lagerstroemica indica (crape myrtle)
Rhododendron
Rosa (rose)
Spiraea
Syringa chinesis
Syringa vulgaris (common lilac)
Viburnum
Weigela

VINES

Bignonia capreolata (cross vine)
Bougainvillaea
Clematis species
Clytosoma
Hydrangea petiolaris (climbing hydrangea)
Mandevilla suaveolens (Chilean jasmine)
Passiflora caerulea (passion flower)
Plumbago capensis (plumbago)
Rosa (rose)
Stephanotis floribunda (Madagascar jasmine)
Trachelospermum species (star jasmine)
Wisteria floribunda (Japanese wisteria)

FOR CUT FLOWERS:

SHRUBS

Buddleia
Chaenomeles (quince)
Cornus mas (Cornelian cherry)
Corylus maxima (filbert)
Deutzia
Forsythia
Philadelphus (mock orange)
Prunus
Salix caprea (French pussy willow)
Salix discolor (pussy willow)
Spiraea
Syringa (lilac)
Tamarix

PERENNIALS

Achillea (various) (yarrow)
Anemone japonica (Japanese anemone)
Aster (various)
Chrysanthemum morifolium (florists' chrysanthemum)
Delphinium (various)
Dianthus barbatus (sweet William)
Gaillardia grandiflora (blanket flower)
Paeonia (various) (peony)
Rudbeckia hirta (coneflower)

ANNUALS

Amaranthus caudatus (love-lies-bleeding)
Antirrhinum majus (snapdragon)
Arctotis stoechadifolia grandis (African daisy)
Browallia speciosa (major) (browallia)
Calendula officinalis (calendula or pot marigold)
Callistephus chinensis (aster or China aster)
Centaurea moschata (sweet sultan)
Chrysanthemum
Clarkia elegans (clarkia)
Coreopsis tinctoria (calliopsis)
Cosmos
Delphinium ajacis (larkspur)
Dianthus chinensis (China pink)
Dimorphoteca (various) (African daisy, Cape marigold)
Eschscholzia californica (California poppy)
Gaillardia
Gomphrena globosa (globe amaranth)
Gypsophila
Helianthus annuus (sunflower)
Helichrysum bracteatum (strawflower)
Lathyrus odoratus (sweet pea)
Lupinus (lupine)
Mathiola bicornis (night-scented stock)
Matthiola incana (stock)
Nicotiana sanderae (flowering tobacco)
Nigella damescena (love-in-a-mist)
Papaver glaucum (tulip poppy)
Papaver rhoeas (Shirley poppy)
Phlox drummondii (annual phlox)
Polygonum orientale (princess feather)
Reseda odorata (mignonette)
Salpiglossis sinuata (painted tongue)

Scabiosa atropurpurea (pincushion flower)
Senecio elegans (purple ragwort)
Tagetes (marigold)
Verbena hybrida (hortensis) (garden verbena)
Zinnia elegans (small-flowered zinnia)
Zinnia haageana (orange zinnia)

FOR FRAGRANCE:

SHRUBS

Abelia grandiflora (glossy abelia)
Ceanothus americanus (New Jersey tea)
Clethra alnifolia (summer sweet)
Daphne odora (winter daphne)
Deutzia gracilis (slender dautzia)
Fothergilla (several) (fothergilla)
Gardenia jasminoides (gardenia)
Jasminum officinale (common white jasmine)
Lonicera (several) (honeysuckle)
Osmanthus heterophyllus (holly olive)
Philadelphus coronarius (sweet mock orange)
Raphiolepsis umbellata (yeddo hawthorn)
Rosa (rose)
Skimmia japonica

PERENNIALS

Anthemis nobilis (chamomile)
Arabis (various) (rock cress)
Artemisia abrotanum (southernwood)
Asperula odorata (sweet woodruff)
Convallaria majalis (lily of the valley)
Dianthus (various) (pink)
Dictamnus albus (gas plant)
Heliotropium arborescens (heliotrope)
Hemerocallis (various) (daylily)
Hesperis matronalis (sweet rocket)
Hosta plantaginea (plaintain lily)
Lathyrus grandiflorus (everlasting pea)
Monarda didyma (bee balm)
Oenothera (various) (evening primrose)
Paeonia (various) (peony)
Phlox (various)

Rosa species (roses)
Viola cornuta (tufted viola)
Viola odorata (sweet violet)

ANNUALS

Ageratum houstonianum (floss flower)
Antirrhinum majus (snapdragon)
Calendula officinalis (calendula or pot marigold)
Centaurea moschata (sweet sultan)
Delphinium ajacis (larkspur)
Iberis umbellata (globe candytuft)
Lathyrus odoratus (sweet pea)
Lobularia maritima (sweet alyssum)
Lupinus luteus (yellow lupine)
Matthiola bicornis (night-scented stock)
Matthola incana (stock)
Nicotiana sanderal (flowering tobacco)
Oenothera biennis (evening primrose)
Petunia
Phlox drummondii (annual phlox)
Reseda odorata (mignonette)
Scabiosa atropurpurea (pincushion flower)
Tagetes (marigold)
Tropaeolum majus (nasturtium)
Verbena (various)
Viola tricolor hortensis (pansy)

BULBS

Acidanthera
Convallaria
Freesia
Hedychium (ginger lily)
Hemerocallis (daylily)
Lillium (lily)
Lycoris
Muscari (grape hyacinth)
Narcissus
Puschkinia (white)

VINES

Akebia quinata (five-leaf akebia)
Gelsemium sempervirens (Carolina yellow jessamine)

BY COLOR:

PERENNIALS
(WHITE)

Achillea ptarmica (yarrow)
Althaea rosea (hollyhock)
Anemone hupehensis japonica (Japanese anemone)
Anemone thalictroides (rue anemone)
Aquilegia (columbine)
Arabis alpina (mountain rockcress)
Arabis caucasica (wall rockcress)
Arctotis
Artemisia frigida (fringed wormwood)
Asperula odorata (sweet woodruff)
Aster
Astilbe
Bellis perennis (English daisy)
Bergenia cordiflora (heartleaf bergenia)
Campanula persicifolia (peach-leafed bellflower)
Cerastium tomentosum (snow-in-summer)
Chrysanthemum coccineum (painted daisy)
Chrysanthemum maximum (Shasta daisy)
Chrysanthemum morifolium (florists' chrysanthemum)
Convallaria majalis (lily of the valley)
Cornus canadensis (bunch berry)
Delphinium hybrid (Connecticut Yankee and Pacific giant)
Deltoides plumarius (grass pink)
Dianthus barbatus (sweet William)
Dianthus deltoides (maiden pink)
Dicentra spectabilis (bleeding heart)
Dictamnus albus (gas plant)
Gypsophila paniculata (baby's breath)
Heliotropium arborescens (heliotrope)
Helleborus niger (Christmas rose)
Hemerocallis (daylily)
Hesperis matronalis (sweet rocket)
Heuchera sanguinea (coral bell)
Hosta plantaginea (plantain lily)
Iberis sempervirens (evergreen candytuft)
Iris kaempferi (Japanese iris)
Kniphofia uvaria (torch lily)
Lathyrus latifolius (perennial pea)
Limonium latifolium (statice, sea lavender)
Monarda didyma (bee balm)

Paeonia (various) (peony)
Papaver orientale (oriental poppy)
Pelargonium domesticum (Lady Washington geranium)
Penstemon (various) (beard tongue)
Phlox divaricata (sweet William phlox)
Phlox paniculata (summer phlox)
Phlox subulata (moss pink)
Platycodon grandiflorum (balloon flower)
Primula malacoides (fairy primrose)
Polygonatum multiflorum (Solomon's seal)
Rudbeckia hirta (coneflower)
Saxifraga (saxifrage)
Scabiosa caucasica (pincushion flower)
Viola cornuta (tufted viola)
Viola ordorata (sweet violet)
Yucca filamentosa (Adam's needle)

(BLUE)

Anchusa capensis (summer forget-me-not)
Aquilegia (columbine)
Aquilegia alpina (dwarf columbine)
Aster frikartii (aster)
Aster novae-angliae (New England aster)
Aubrieta deltoidea (common aubrieta)
Campanula carpatica (bellflower)
Campanula rotundifolia (harebell)
Delphinium hybrid (Connecticut Yankee and Pacific giant)
Echinops exaltatus (globe thistle)
Felicia amelloides (blue marguerite)
Gentiana asclepiadea (willow gentian)
Heliotropium arborescens (heliotrope)
Limonium latifolium (statice, sea lavender)
Linum perenne (blue flax)
Lithodora diffusa (gromwell)
Lupinus polyphyllus (lupine)
Mertensia virginica (Virginia bluebell)
Myosotis scorpioides (true forget-me-not)
Penstemon (various) (beard tongue)
Phlox divaricata (sweet William phlox)
Phlox subulata (moss pink)
Platycodon grandiflorum (balloon flower)
Primula malacoides (fairy primrose)
Primula polyantha (polyanthus)
Salvia patens (blue salvia, meadow sage)

Veronica (speedwell)
Viola cornuta (tufted viola)

(LAVENDER)

Althaea rosea (hollyhock)
Anemone pulsatilla (prairie windflower, pasque flower)
Aquilegia (columbine)
Aster frikartii (aster)
Aster novae-angliae (New England aster)
Aubrieta deltoidea (common aubrieta)
Bergenia crassifolia
Chrysanthemum morifolium (florists' chrysanthemum)
Dianthus (pink)
Digitalis purpurea (foxglove)
Hesperis matronalis (sweet rocket)
Hosta plantaginea (plantain lily)
Iris dochotoma (vesper iris)
Paeonia (peony)
Pelargonium domesticum (Lady Washington geranium)
Phlox subulata (moss pink)
Primula malacoides (fairy primrose)
Primula polyantha (polyanthus)
Tulbaghia fragrans
Valeriana officinalis (common valerian)
Vinca minor (common periwinkle)
Viola cornuta (tufted viola)

(VIOLET)

Anemone pulsatilla (prairie windflower, pasque flower
Delphinium hybrid (Connecticut Yankee and Pacific giant)
Epimedium grandiflorum (bishop's hat)
Gentiana asclepiadea (willow gentian)
Iris kaempferi (Japanese iris)

(LILAC)

Acanthus mollis (Grecian urn)
Althaea rosea (hollyhock)

(PURPLE-LAVENDER)

Bergenia crassifolia

(PURPLE-VIOLET)

Aquilegia (columbine)
Aster novae-angliae (New England aster)
Aubrieta deltoidea (common brieta)
Chrysanthemum morifolium (florists' chrysanthemum)
Dianthus (pink)
Digitalis purpurea (foxglove)
Heliotropium arborescens (heliotrope)
Helleborus niger (Christmas rose)
Pelargonium domesticum (Lady Washington geranium)
Platycodon grandiflorum (balloon flower)
Primula polyantha (polyanthus)
Viola cornuta (tufted viola)
Viola odorata (sweet violet)

(PURPLE)

Althaea rosea (hollyhock)
Armeria maritima (sea pink or thrift)
Iris kaempferi (Japanese iris)
Liatris pycnostacha (gayfeather)
Lupinus polyphyllus (lupine)
Lythrum (loosetrife)
Phlox paniculata (summer phlox)
Scabiosa caucasica (pincushion flower)

(RED-PURPLE)

Callirhoe involucrata (poppy mallow)
Lathyrus grandiflorus (everlasting pea)
Lathyrus latifolius (perennial pea)

(RED)

Althaea rosea (hollyhock)
Anemone hupehensis japonica (Japanese anemone)
Aquilegia (columbine)
Aster
Astilbe (various) (meadowsweet)
Aubrieta deltoidea (common brieta)
Digitalis purpurea (foxglove)
Epimedium grandiflorum (bishop's hat)
Gaillardia grandiflora (blanket flower)
Geranium grandiflorum (cranesbill)
Hemerocallis (daylily)

Heuchera sanguinea (coral bell)
Iris kaempferi (Japanese iris)
Kniphofia (various) (torch lily)
Lobelia cardinalis (cardinal flower)
Lupinus polyphyllus (lupine)
Monarda didyma (bee balm)
Paeonia (peony)
Papaver nudicaule (Iceland poppy)
Papaver orientale (oriental poppy)
Pelargonium domesticum (Lady Washington geranium)
Penstemon (various) (beard tongue)
Phlox paniculata (summer phlox)
Phlox subulata (moss pink)
Primula malacoides (fairy primrose)
Primula polyantha (polyanthus)
Saxifraga (saxifrage)
Sedum spectabile (stonecrop)
Senecio (cineraria)
Viola cornuta (tufted viola)

(ROSE)

Acanthus mollis (Grecian urn)
Althaea rosea (hollyhock)
Bellis perennis (English daisy)
Bergenia cordifolia (heartleaf bergenia)
Bergenia crassifolia
Dianthus deltoides (maiden pink)
Dianthus plumarius (grass pink)
Dicentra spectabilis (bleeding heart)
Hibiscus moscheutos (swamp rose mallow)
Iris kaempferi (Japanese iris)
Lythrum (various) (loosestrife)
Phlox paniculata (summer phlox)
Physostegia virginiana (false dragonhead)

(PINK)

Althaea rosea (hollyhock)
Anemone hupehensis japonica (Japanese anemone)
Anemonella thalictroides (rue anemone)
Aquilegia (columbine)
Armeria martima (sea pink or thrift)
Aster
Astilbe (various) (meadowsweet)
Aubrieta deltoidea (common aubrieta)

Bellis perennis (English daisy)
Campanula carpatica (bellflower)
Chrysanthemum coccineum (painted daisy)
Dianthus barbatus (sweet William)
Dianthus deltoides (maiden pink)
Dianthus plumarius (grass pink)
Dicentra spectabilis (bleeding heart)
Digitalis purpurea (foxglove)
Helborus niger (Christmas rose)
Hemerocallis (daylily)
Heuchera sanguinea (coral bell)
Iris (bearded iris)
Iris kaempferi (Japanese iris)
Limonium latifolium (statice, sea lavender)
Lupinus polyphyllus (lupine)
Monarda didyma (bee balm)
Paeonia (peony)
Papaver nudicaule (Iceland poppy)
Papaver orientale (oriental poppy)
Pelargonium domesticum (Lady Washington geranium)
Penstemon (various) (beard tongue)
Phlox divaricata (sweet William phlox)
Phlox paniculata (summer phlox)
Phlox subulata (moss pink)
Platycodon grandiflorum (balloon flower)
Primula malacoides (fairy primrose)
Primula polyantha (polyanthus)
Rudbeckia hirta (coneflower)
Saxifraga (saxifrage)
Sedum spectabile
Senecio (cineraria)
Tulbaghia fragrans
Veronica (speedwell)
Viola odorata (sweet violet)

(SALMON)

Papaver orientale (oriental poppy)

(ORANGE)

Althaea rosea (hollyhock)
Asclepias incarnata (swamp milkweed)
Asclepias tuberosa (butterfly weed)
Chrysanthemum morifolium (florists' chrysanthemum)
Dianthus (pink)

Erysimum asperum (Siberian wallflower)
Gazania hybrids
Geum chiloense (coccineum) (geum)
Helenium (Helen's flower)
Heliopsis (various) (orange sunflower)
Hemerocallis (various) (daylily)
Kniphofia (torch lily)
Linaria vulgaris (toadflax)
Papaver nudicaule (Iceland poppy)
Papaver orientale (oriental poppy)
Penstemon (various) (beard tongue)
Phlox paniculata (summer phlox)
Primula polyantha (polyanthus)
Rudbeckia hirta (coneflower)
Strelitzia reginae (bird of paradise)
Viola cornuta (tufted viola)

(YELLOW)

Achillea tomentosa (woolly yarrow)
Aconitum anthora (monkshood)
Althaea rosea (hollyhock)
Alyssum saxtile (alyssum, basket of gold)
Anthemis nobilis (chamomile)
Anthemis tinctoria (golden marguerite)
Aquilegia chrysantha (golden columbine)
Artemisia abrotanum (southernwood)
Caltha palustris (marsh marigold)
Centaurea gymnocarpa (dusty miller)
Chrysanthemum morifolium (florists' chrysanthemum)
Coreopsis grandiflora (tickseed)
Dianthus (pink)
Digitalis purpurea (foxglove)
Gaillardia grandiflora (blanket flower)
Gazania hybrids
Geum chiloense (coccineum) (geum)
Helenium (Helen's flower)
Helianthus decapetalus multiflorus (sunflower)
Heliopsis (various) (orange sunflower)
Hemerocallis (various) (daylily)
Hypericum (Saint Johnswort)
Kniphofia (torch lily)
Oenothera (various) (evening primrose)
Paeonia (various) (peony)
Papaver nudicaule (Iceland poppy)

Primula polyantha (polyanthus)
Rudbeckia hirta (coneflower)
Saxifraga (saxifrage)
Solidago (various) (goldenrod)
Viola cornuta (tufted viola)

ANNUALS

(WHITE)

Ageratum houstonianum (floss flower)
Antirrhinum majus (snapdragon)
Arctotis stoechadifolia grandis (African daisy)
Begonia semperflorens (wax begonia)
Brachycome iberidifolia (Swan River daisy)
Browallia americana (browallia)
Calendula officinalis (calendula or pot marigold)
Callistephus chinesis (aster or China aster)
Campanula mediuim (Canterbury bell)
Catharanthus roseus (vinca rosea) (Madagascar periwinkle)
Centaurea cyanus (bachelor's button, cornflower)
Centaurea imperialis (royal sweet sultan)
Chrysanthemum
Clarkia amoena (farewell-to-spring)
Clarkia elegans (clarkia)
Clarkia unguiculata (mountain garland)
Cleome spinosa (spider flower)
Cosmos bipannatus (cosmos)
Delphinium ajacis (larkspur)
Dianthus species (pink)
Dimorphotheca sinuata (Cape marigold, African daisy)
Echium
Euphorbia marginata (snow-on-the-mountain)
Gomphrena globosa (globe amaranth)
Gypsophila elegans (baby's breath)
Helichrysum bracteatum (strawflower)
Iberis amara (rocket candytuft)
Iberis umbellata (globe candytuft)
Impatiens balsamina (balsam)
Ipomoea purpurea (morning glory)
Lathyrus odoratus (sweet pea, summer)
Limonium bonduellii (statice, sea lavender)
Lobelia erinus (lobelia)
Lobularia maritima (sweet alyssum)
Lupinus mutabilis (lupine)
Matthiola incana (stock)

Mirabilis jalapa (four-o'clock)
Nemesia strumosa (nemesia)
Nicotiana alata
Nicotiana sanderae (flowering tobacco)
Nicotiana sylvestris
Nigella damascena (love-in-a-mist)
Oenothera biennis (evening primrose)
Papaver nudicaule (Iceland poppy)
Papaver rhoeas (Shirley poppy)
Petunia hybrids
Phlox drummondii (annual phlox)
Physalis alkekengi (Chinese lantern)
Portulaca grandiflora (rose moss)
Primula malocoides (fairy primrose)
Scabiosa atropurpurea (pincushion flower)
Schizanthus pinnatus (butterfly flower)
Senecia elegans (purple ragwort)
Tropaeolum majus (nasturtium)
Verbena hybrida (hortensis) (garden verbena)
Viola tricolor hortensis (pansy)
Zinnia angustifolia (Mexican zinnia)
Zinnia elegans (small-flowered zinnia, giant-flowered zinnia)

(BLUE)

Ageratum houstonianum (floss flower)
Browallia americana (browallia)
Callistephus chinensis (aster, China aster)
Campanula medium (Canterbury bell)
Centaurea cyanus (bachelor's button or cornflower)
Convolvulus tricolor (dwarf morning glory)
Cosmos
Delphinium ajacis (larkspur)
Echium
Ipomoea purpurea (morning glory)
Limonium bonduellii (statice, sea lavender)
Linaria maroccana (baby snapdragon)
Lobelia erinus (lobelia)
Matthiola incana (stock)
Myosotis sylvatica (forget-me-not)
Nemesia strumosa (nemesia)
Nierembergia caerulea (blue cupflower)
Nigella damascena (love-in-a-mist)
Papaver rhoeas (Shirley poppy)
Salvia (sage)
Scabiosa atropurpurea (pincushion flower)

Trachymene caerulea (blue lace flower)
Verbena hybrids
Viola tricolor hortensis (pansy)
Zinnia elegans (giant-flowered zinnia)

(LAVENDER)

Callistephus chinensis (aster, China aster)
Centaurea cyanus (bachelor's button, cornflower)
Clarkia elegans (clarkia)
Delphinium ajacis (larkspur)
Limonium bonduellii (statice, sea lavender)
Lobularia maritima (sweet alyssum)
Zinnia elegans (small-flowered zinnia)

(VIOLET)

Antirrhinum majus (snapdragon)
Gomphrena globosa (globe amaranth)
Ipomoea purpurea (morning glory)
Lobelia erinus (lobelia)
Trachymene caerulea (blue lace flower)
Zinnia elegans (giant-flowered zinnia)

(MAUVE)

Impatiens
Schizanthus pinnatus (butterfly flower)

(LILAC)

Browallia speciosa major (browallia)
Cosmos
Iberis umbellata (globe candytuft)
Lathyrus odoratus (sweet pea)
Lupinus (lupine)
Matthiola bicornus (night-scented stock)
Petunia hybrids
Phlox drummondii (annual phlox)

(PURPLE)

Antirrhinum majus (snapdragon)
Browallia americana (browallia)
Browallia speciosa major
Dianthus chinensis (China pink)

Echium
Impatiens
Ipomoea purpurea (morning glory)
Lathyrus odoratus (sweet pea)
Linaria maroccana (baby snapdragon)
Lobularia maritima (sweet alyssum)
Lupinus (lupine)
Matthiola bicornus (night-scented stock)
Matthiola incana (stock)
Nemesia strumosa (nemesia)
Petunia hybrids
Phlox drummondii (annual phlox)
Salpiglossis sinuata (painted tongue)
Scabiosa atropurpurea (pincushion flower)
Schizanthus pinnatus (butterfly flower)
Senecio elegans (purple ragwort)
Verbena hybrids
Viola tricolor hortensis (pansy)
Zinnia elegans (giant-flowered zinnia)

(MAGENTA)

Impatiens

(WINE)

Centaurea cyanus (bachelor's button, cornflower)
Gaillardia pulchella (rose-ring gaillardia)

(MAROON)

Coreopsis tinctoria (calliopsis)
Gaillardia pulchella (rose-ring gaillardia)
Tropaeolum majus (nasturtium)
Zinnia angustifolia (Mexican zinnia)

(CARMINE)

Delphinium ajacis (larkspur)

(SCARLET)

Linum grandiflorum 'Rubrum' (scarlet flax)
Salvia splendens (scarlet sage)
Verbena hybrida (hortensis) (garden verbena)
Zinnia elegans (small-flowered zinnia, giant-flowered zinnia)

(CRIMSON)

Amaranthus caudatus (love-lies-bleeding)
Gomphrenia globosa (globe amaranth)
Linaria maroccana (baby snapdragon)
Matthiola incana (stock)
Nicotiana
Papaver rhoeas (Shirley poppy)
Portulaca grandiflora (rose moss)
Tropaeolum majus (nasturtium)

(RED)

Antirrhinum majus (snapdragon)
Brachycome iberidifolia (Swan River daisy)
Callistephus chinensis (aster, China aster)
Convolvulus
Helichrysum bracteatum (strawflower)
Impatiens balsamina (balsam)
Ipomoea purpurea (morning glory)
Mirabilis jalapa (four-o'clock)
Papaver glaucum (tulip poppy)
Primula malocoides (fairy primrose)
Salpiglossis sinuata (painted tongue)

(ROSE)

Begonia semperflorens (wax begonia)
Centaurea moschata (sweet sultan)
Clarkia amoena (farewell-to-spring)
Clarkia elegans (clarkia)
Cosmos bipannatus (cosmos)
Delphinium ajacis (larkspur)
Dianthus barbatus (sweet William)
Eschscholzia californica (California poppy)
Gypsophila elegans (baby's breath)
Iberis umbellata (globe candytuft)
Impatiens balsamina (balsam)
Lathyrus odoratus (sweet pea)
Limonium bonduellii (statice, sea lavender)
Linum grandiflorum 'Rubrum' (scarlet flax)
Lobularia maritima (sweet alyssum)
Matthiola incana (stock)
Nemesia strumosa (nemesia)
Nigella damascena (love-in-a-mist)
Oenothera biennis (evening primrose)

Petunia hybrids
Phlox drummondii (annual phlox)
Polygonum orientale (princess feather)
Primula malacoides (fairy primrose)
Salvia splendens (scarlet sage)
Scabiosa atropurpurea (pincushion flower)
Schizanthus pinnatus (butterfly flower)
Senecio elegans (purple ragwort)
Viola tricolor hortensis (pansy)

(PINK)

Ageratum houstonianum (floss flower)
Antirrhinum majus (snapdragon)
Begonia semperflorens (wax begonia)
Callistephus chinensis (China aster)
Campanula (Canterbury bell)
Catharanthus roseus (vinca rosea) (Madagascar periwinkle)
Celosia 'Plumosa' (plume cockscomb)
Centaurea cyanus (bachelor's button, cornflower)
Clarkia elegans (clarkia)
Cleome spinosa (spider flower)
Cosmos bipinnatus (cosmos)
Cryophytum crystallinum (ice plant)
Delphinium ajacis (larkspur)
Dianthus chinensis (China pink)
Eschscholzia californica (California poppy)
Gypsophila elegans (baby's breath)
Helichrysum bracteatum (strawflower)
Iberis umbellata (globe candytuft)
Impatiens balsamina (balsam)
Ipomoea purpurea (morning glory)
Lathyrus odoratus (sweet pea)
Linaria maroccana (baby snapdragon)
Lobelia erinus (lobelia)
Lupinus hartwegii (lupine, annual)
Matthiola incana (stock)
Mirabilis jalapa (four-o'clock)
Myosotis sylvatica (forget-me-not)
Nemesia strumosa (nemesia)
Papaver rhoeas (Shirley poppy)
Petunia hybrids
Polygonum orientale (princess feather)
Primula malocoides (fairy primrose)
Salpiglossis sinuata (painted tongue)

Salvia splendens (scarlet sage)
Tropaeolum majus (nasturtium)
Verbena hybrida (hortensis) (garden verbena)

(SALMON)

Delphinium ajacis (larkspur)
Dimorphoteca sinuata (African daisy, Cape marigold)
Iberis umbellata (globe candytuft)
Papaver rhoeas (Shirley poppy)

(ORANGE)

Antirrhinum majus (snapdragon)
Calendula officinalis (calendula, pot marigold)
Chrysanthemum
Clarkia
Coreopsis tinctoria (calliopsis)
Eschscholzia californica (California poppy)
Gerbera jamesonii (Transvaal daisy)
Nemesia strumosa (nemesia)
Papaver rhoeas (Shirley poppy)
Portulaca grandiflora (rose moss)
Salpiglossis sinuata (painted tongue)
Tagetes (marigold)
Tithonia rotundifolia (Mexican sunflower)
Viola tricolor hortensis (pansy)
Zinnia angustifolia (Mexican zinnia)
Zinnia elegans (small-flowered zinnia, giant-flowered zinnia)

(BRONZE)

Chrysanthemum

(GOLD)

Calendula officinalis (calendula, pot marigold)
Celosia 'Plumosa' (plume cockscomb)
Eschscholzia californica (California poppy)
Gomphrena globosa (globe amaranth)
Helianthus annuus (sunflower)
Tagetes (marigold)

(YELLOW)

Antirrhinum majus (snapdragon)
Calendula officinalis (calendula or pot marigold)

Callistephus chinensis (aster, China aster)
Celosia 'Plumosa' (plume cockscomb)
Centaurea moschata (sweet sultan)
Chrysanthemum
Clarkia
Coreopsis tinctoria (calliopsis)
Cosmos sulphureus (yellow cosmos)
Dimorphoteca sinuata (African daisy, Cape marigold)
Eschscholzia californica (California poppy)
Gaillardia pulchella (rose-ring gaillardia)
Gerbera jamesonii (Transvaal daisy)
Limonium sinuatum (statice, sea lavender)
Linaria maroccana (baby snapdragon)
Lupinus luteus (yellow lupine)
Lupinus mutabilis (lupine)
Matthiola incana (stock)
Mirabalis jalapa (four-o'-clock)
Nemesia strumosa (nemesia)
Oenothera biennis (evening primrose)
Portulaca grandiflora (rose moss)
Reseda odorata (mignonette)
Rudbeckia bicolor (coneflower)
Salpiglossis sinuata (painted tongue)
Tagetes (marigold)
Thunbergia alata (clockvine)
Tropaeolum majus (nasturtium)
Viola tricolor hortensis (pansy)
Zinnia angustifolia (Mexican zinnia)
Zinnia elegans (small-flowered zinnia, giant-flowered zinnia)

BULBS
(WHITE)

Acidanthera
Agapanthus (lily-of-the-Nile)
Anenome coronaria (poppy-flowered anemone)
Begonia (tuberous)
Calochortus (mariposa lily)
Camassia (camas)
Canna
Chionodoxa (glory of snow)
Colchicum autumnale (autumn crocus)
Crocus
Cyclamen (hardy)
Dahlia
Erythronium (dogtooth violet)

Freesia
Frittilaria
Galanthus
Gladiolus (gladiola)
Hemerocallis (daylily)
Hippeastrum (amaryllis)
Hyacinthus orientalis (common hyacinth)
Iris (bearded iris)
Iris tingitana (Dutch iris)
Lilium (lily)
Lycoris
Muscari (grape hyacinth)
Narcissus
Scilla hispanica (Spanish bluebell)
Sparaxis tricolor (wand flower)
Tulipa (tulip)
Watsonia
Zantedeschia (calla)
Zephyranthes (zephyr lily)

(BLUE)

Agapanthus (lily-of-the-Nile)
Anenome coronaria (poppy-flowered anemone)
Calochortus (mariposa lily)
Camassia (camas)
Chionodoxa (glory of snow)
Crocus
Freesia
Hyacinthus orientalis (common hyacinth)
Iris (bearded iris)
Iris tingitana (Dutch iris)
Muscari (grape hyacinth)
Scilla hispanica (Spanish bluebell)
Sparaxis tricolor (wand flower)

(LAVENDER)

Anenome coronaria (poppy-flowered anemone)
Calochortus (mariposa lily)
Colchicum autumnale (autumn crocus)
Crocus
Dahlia
Erythronium (dogtooth violet)
Freesia
Gladiolus (gladiola)

Hyacinthus orientalis (common hyacinth)
Iris (bearded iris)
Iris kaempferi (Japanese iris)
Iris tingitana (Dutch iris)
Lilium (lily)
Muscari (grape hyacinth)
Sparaxis tricolor (wand flower)
Tulipa (tulip)

(VIOLET, PURPLE)

Agapanthus (lily-of-the-Nile)
Anemone coronaria (poppy-flowered anemone)
Calochortus (mariposa lily)
Colchicum autumnale (autumn crocus)
Crocus
Dahlia
Erythronium (dogtooth violet)
Freesia
Frittilaria
Gladiolus (gladiola)
Hyacinthus orientalis (common hyacinth)
Iris (bearded iris)
Iris kaempferi (Japanese iris)
Iris tingitana (Dutch iris)
Lilium (lily)
Muscari (grape hyacinth)
Scilla hispanica (Spanish bluebell)
Sparaxis tricolor (wand flower)

(RED)

Anemone coronaria (poppy-flowered anemone)
Begonia (tuberous)
Canna
Cyclamen (hardy)
Dahlia
Eremurus (desert candle)
Freesia
Frittilaria
Gladiolus (gladiola)
Hemerocallis (daylily)
Hyacinthus orientalis (common hyacinth)
Iris (bearded iris)
Iris kaempferi (Japanese iris)
Lilium (lily)

Lycoris radiata
Ranunculus asiaticus (turban buttercup)
Sparaxis tricolor (wand flower)
Tigrida (tiger flower)
Tulipa (tulip)
Watsonia
Zantedeschia (calla)
Zephryanthes (zephyr lily)

(PINK)

Amaryllis belladonna (belladonna lily)
Aneome coronoria (poppy-flowered anemone)
Begonia (tuberous)
Canna
Colchicum autumnale (autumn crocus)
Crocus
Cyclamen (hardy)
Dahlia
Erythronium (dogtooth violet)
Freesia
Gladiolus (gladiola)
Hemerocallis (daylily)
Hippeastrum (amaryllis)
Hyacinthus orientalis (common hyacinth)
Iris (bearded iris)
Iris kaempferi (Japanese iris)
Lilium (lily)
Lycoris squamigera
Ranunculus asiaticus (turban buttercup)
Scilla hispanica (Spanish bluebell)
Tigrida pavonia (tiger flower)
Tulipa (tulip)
Watsonia
Zantedeschia rehmanni (pink calla)
Zephyryathes (zephyr lily)

(ORANGE)

Begonia (tuberous)
Canna
Clivia miniata (kaffir lily)
Dahlia
Freesia
Fritillaria
Gladiolus (gladiola)

Hemerocallis (daylily)
Hippeastrum (amaryllis)
Hyacinthus orientalis (common hyacinth)
Iris (bearded iris)
Iris tingitana (Dutch iris)
Lilium (lily)
Narcissus
Ranunculus asiaticus (turban buttercup)
Tigridia pavonia (tiger flower)
Tulipa (tulip)
Zantedeschia (calla)

(YELLOW)

Begonia (tuberous)
Calochortus (mariposa lily)
Canna
Clivia miniata (kaffir lily)
Crocus
Dahlia
Eranthis (winter aconite)
Eremurus (desert candle)
Erythronium (dogtooth violet)
Freesia
Frittilaria
Gladiolus (gladiola)
Hemerocallis (daylily)
Hyacinthus orientalis (common hyacinth)
Iris (bearded iris)
Iris tingitana (Dutch iris)
Lilium (lily)
Lycoris
Narcissus
Ranunculus asiaticus (turban buttercup)
Sparaxis tricolor (wand flower)
Sternbergia lutea
Tulipa (tulip)
Zantedeschia (calla)
Zantedeschia ellottiana (golden calla)

PLANT SOCIETIES

You can write to these plant societies for information on membership, which usually includes a bulletin or magazine (monthly or semi-monthly). Some societies have library books available, distribute seed, and hold conventions.

Prices listed are membership fees as of January, 1992.

American Boxwood Society ($15)
Blandy Experimental Farm
P.O. Box 85
Boyce, VA 22620

American Camellia Society ($17.50)
Dr. C. David Schiebert
P.O. Box 1217
Fort Valley, GA 31030-1217

American Conifer Society ($20)
Maxine Schwarz
P.O. Box 242
Severna Park, MD 21146

American Dahlia Society ($8)
Michael Martinolich
159 Pine St.
New Hyde Park, NY 11040

American Fuchsia Society ($12.50)
San Francisco County Fair Bldg.
Ninth Ave. & Lincoln Way
San Francisco, CA 94122

American Hemerocallis Society ($18)
Elly Launius
1454 Rebel Dr.
Jackson, MS 39211

American Hibiscus Society ($13)
P.O. Drawer 321540
Cocoa Beach, FL 32932

American Hosta Society ($12.50)
Jack A. Freedman
3103 Heatherhill Dr.
Huntsville, AL 35802

American Iris Society ($9.50)
Carol Ramsey
6518 Beachy Ave.
Wichita, KS 67206

American Peony Society ($7.50)
Greta M. Kessenich
250 Interlachen Rd.
Hopkins, MN 55343

American Rhododendron Society ($25)
Paula L. Cash
14885 S.W. Sunrise Ln.
Tigard, OR 97224

American Rose Society ($25)
P.O. Box 30,000
Shreveport, LA 71130

Azalea Society of America ($15)
Marjorie Taylor
P.O. Box 6244
Silver Spring, MD 20901

Cactus & Succulent Society of America ($20)
Virginia F. Martin
2631 Fairgreen Ave.
Arcadia, CA 93130

The Delphinium Society ($6)
Shirley E. Bassett Takakkaw
Ice House Wood
Oxted, Surrey, RH8 9DW, England

Gardenia Society of America ($5)
Lyman Duncan
P.O. Box 879
Atwater, CA 95301

Herb Society of America ($35)
9019 Kirtland Chardon Rd.
Mentor, OH 44060

Hobby Greenhouse Association ($10)
Janice L. Hale
8 Glen Terr.
Bedford, MA 01730

Hydroponic Society of America ($25)
Gene Brisbon
P.O. Box 6067
Concord, CA 94524

International Camellia Society ($9)
Edith Mazzei
1486 Yosemite Cir.
Concord, CA 94521

International Clematis Society
Hildegard Widmann-Evison
Buford House, Tenbury Wells
Worcester WR15 8HQ, England

International Geranium Society ($12.50)
Mrs. Robin Schultz
5861 Walnut Dr.
Eureka, CA 95501

International Lilac Society, Inc. ($10)
Walter W. Oakes
P.O. Box 315
Rumford, ME 04276

Magnolia Society ($15)
Phelan A. Bright
907 S. Chestnut St.
Hammond, LA 70403-5102

National Chrysanthemum Society ($12)
Galen L. Goss
5012 Kingston Dr.
Annandale, VA 22003

National Fuchsia Society ($14)
Mrs. Mildred Elliott
15103 McRae
Norwalk, CA 90650

North American Lily Society ($12.50)
Dorothy B. Schaefer
P.O. Box 476
Waukee, IA 50263

Perennial Plant Association ($35)
Steven Still
3383 Schirtzinger Rd.
Columbus, OH 43026

FOR MORE PLANT INFORMATION

The following groups are also good sources of information on plant conservation and general horticultural subjects. Write them for membership information and fees.

Brooklyn Botanic Garden
1000 Washington Ave.
Brooklyn, NY 11225

The Farallones Institute
The Rural Center
15290 Coleman Valley Rd.
Occidental, CA 95465

Gardens for All
Dept. FG
180 Flynn Ave.
Burlington, VT 05401

Herb Society of America
300 Massachusetts Ave.
Boston, MA 02115

National Audubon Society
950 Third Ave.
New York, NY 10022

National Wildlife Federation
1412 16th St., N.W.
Washington, DC 20036

Sierra Club
530 Bush St.
San Francisco, CA 94108

STATE AGRICULTURAL EXTENSION SERVICES

This service is the combined effort of the county government, the state college or university responsible for agriculture, and the U.S. Department of Agriculture. Telephone numbers and addresses for these services will be found under the county government listings in your local telephone directories. The Agricultural Extension Service is the most up-to-date and extensive source of information on horticultural subjects in the United States. Circulars or bulletins answering frequently asked questions about gardening are generally available in printed form for the asking. Addresses of these offices follow:

Auburn University
Auburn, Alabama 36830

College of Agriculture
University of Arizona
Tucson, Arizona 85721

University of Arkansas
Box 391
Little Rock, Arkansas 72203

Agricultural Extension Service
2200 University Ave.
Berkeley, California 94720

Colorado State University
Fort Collins, Colorado 80521

College of Agriculture
University of Connecticut
Storrs, Connecticut 06268

College of Agricultural Sciences
University of Delaware
Newark, Delaware 19711

University of Florida
217 Rolfs Hall
Gainesville, Florida 32601

College of Agriculture
University of Georgia
Athens, Georgia 30602

University of Hawaii
2500 Dole St.
Honolulu, Hawaii 96822

College of Agriculture
University of Idaho
Moscow, Idaho 83843

College of Agriculture
University of Illinois
Urbana, Illinois 61801

Agricultural Administration Building
Purdue University
Lafayette, Indiana 47907

Iowa State University
Ames, Iowa 50010

Kansas State University
Manhattan, Kansas 66502

College of Agriculture
University of Kentucky
Lexington, Kentucky 40506

Louisiana State University
Knapp Hall, University Station
Baton Rouge, Louisiana 70803

Department of Public Information
University of Maine
Orono, Maine 04473

University of Maryland
Agricultural Division
College Park, Maryland 20742

Stockbridge Hall
University of Massachusetts
Amherst, Massachusetts 01002

Department of Information Service
109 Agricultural Hall
East Lansing, Michigan 48823

Institute of Agriculture
University of Minnesota
St. Paul, Minnesota 55101

Mississippi State University
State College, Mississippi 39762

1-98 Agricultural Building
University of Missouri
Columbia, Missouri 65201

Office of Information
Montana State University
Bozeman, Montana 59715

Dept. of Information
College of Agriculture
University of Nebraska
Lincoln, Nebraska 68503

Agricultural Communications Service
University of Nevada
Reno, Nevada 89507

Schofield Hall
University of New Hampshire
Durham, New Hampshire 03824

College of Agriculture
Rutgers, State University
New Brunswick, New Jersey 08903

New Mexico State University
Drawer 3AI
Las Cruces, New Mexico 88001

State College of Agriculture
Cornell University
Ithaca, New York 14850

North Carolina State University
State College Station
Raleigh, North Carolina 27607

North Dakota State University
State University Station
Fargo, North Dakota 58102

Ohio State University
2120 Fyffe Road
Columbus, Ohio 43210

Oklahoma State University
Stillwater, Oklahoma 74074

Oregon State University
206 Waldo Hall
Corvallis, Oregon 97331

Pennsylvania State University
Armsby Building
University Park, Pennsylvania 16802

University of Rhode Island
16 Woodwall Hall
Kingston, Rhode Island 02881

Clemson University
Clemson, South Carolina 29631

South Dakota State University
University Station
Brookings, South Dakota 57006

University of Tennessee
Box 1071
Knoxville, Tennessee 37901

Texas A & M University
Services Building
College Station, Texas 77843

Utah State University
Logan, Utah 84321

University of Vermont
Burlington, Vermont 05401

Virginia Polytechnic Institute
Blacksburg, Virginia 24061

Washington State University
115 Wilson Hall
Pullman, Washington 99163

West Virginia University
Evansdale Campus
Appalachian Center
Morgantown, West Virginia 26506

University of Wisconsin
Madison, Wisconsin 53706

University of Wyoming
Box 3354
Laramie, Wyoming 82070

Federal Extension Service
U.S. Department of Agriculture
Washington, D.C. 20250

MAIL-ORDER SUPPLIERS

Write to these suppliers for information on prices, shipping, and available plants and products. Catalogs are generally free, but send a self-addressed stamped envelope.

PLANTS, GENERAL

Burgess Seed & Plant Co.
905 Four Seasons Rd.
Bloomington, IL 61701

Henry Field's Heritage Gardens
1 Meadow Ridge Rd.
Shenandoah, IA 51601-0700

Gurney Seed & Nursery Co.
Yankton, SD 57079

Herbst Brothers Seedsmen, Inc.
1000 N. Main St.
Brewster, NY 10509

International Growers Exchange, Inc.
16785 Harrison
Livonia, MI 48154

Inter-State Nurseries
Hamburg, IA 51644

J. W. Jung Seed & Nursery Co.
335 S. High St.
Randolph, WI 53957

Kelly Nurseries
P.O. Box 800
Dansville, NY 14437-0800

Krider Nursery
Box 29
Middlebury, IN 56540

Louisiana Nursery
Rt. 7, Box 43
Opelousas, LA 70570

May Nursery Company
P.O. Box 1312
2115 W. Lincoln Ave.
Yakima, WA 98907

Earl May Seed & Nursery Co.
Shenandoah, IA 51603

J. E. Miller Nurseries
Canandaigua, NY 14424

Nichols Garden Nursery
1190 North Pacific Highway
Albany, OR 97321

Spring Hill Nurseries
6523 N. Galena Rd.
P.O. Box 1758
Peoria, IL 61656

Stern Nurseries
Geneva, NY 14456

Tennessee Nursery & Seed Co.
Tennessee Nursery Rd.
Cleveland, TN 37311

Wayside Gardens Co.
Hodges, SC 29695

White Flower Farm
Litchfield, CT 06759

SPECIALTY PLANT SUPPLIERS

Begonias

Antonelli Bros.
2545 Capitola Rd.
Santa Cruz, CA 95062

Fairyland Begonia and Lily Garden
1100 Griffith Rd.
McKinleyville, CA 95521

Bulbs, Corms, Tubers

P. DeJager & Sons, Inc.
188 Asbury St.
S. Hamilton, MA 01982

John Scheppers, Inc.
63 Wall St.
New York, NY 10005

Chrysanthemums

Dooley Gardens
Rt. 1
Hutchinson, MN 55350

Huff's Gardens
P.O. Box 187
Burlington, KS 66839

Sunnyslope Gardens
8638 Huntington Dr.
San Gabriel, CA 91775

Thon's Garden Mums
4811 Oak St.
Crystal Lake, IL 60012

Daylilies

American Daylily & Perennials
P.O. Box 210
Grain Valley, MO 64029

Lenington-Long Gardens
7007 Manchester Ave.
Kansas City, MO 64133

Saxton Gardens
1 First St.
Saratoga Springs, NY 12866

Seawright Gardens
134 Indian Hill
Carlisle, MA 01741

Wimberlyway Gardens
7024 N. W. 18th Ave.
Gainesville, FL 32605-3237

Fruits, Berries, Nuts

Ahrens Strawberry Nursery
R.R. 1
Huntingburg, IN 47542

Allen Co.
P.O. Box 310
Fruitland, MD 21826-0310

Ames' Orchard & Nursery
6 E. Elm St.
Fayetteville, AR 72703

Brittingham Plant Farms
P.O. Box 2538
Salisbury, MD 21801

Chestnut Hill Nursery
Rt. 3, Box 267
Alachua, FL 32615

Cumberland Valley Nurseries, Inc.
P.O. Box 471
McMinnville, TN 37110

Dean Foster Nurseries
511 S. Center St.
P.O. Box 127
Hartford, MI 49057

Hollydale Nursery
P.O. Box 26
Pelham, TN 37366

Johnson Orchard & Nursery Co.
Rt. 5, Box 29J
Ellijay, GA 30540

Nourse Farms, Inc.
Box 485 RFD
S. Deerfield, MA 01373

Raintree Nursery & Northwoods Nursery
391 Butts Rd.
Morton, WA 98356

Rayner's
P.O. Box 1617
Salisbury, MD 21801
   (berries)

Stark Brothers Nurseries
Box X9851G
Louisiana, MO 63353

Gesneriads

Fischers Greenhouses
Linwood, NJ 08221

Lyndon Lyon
14 Mutchier St.
Dolgeville, NY 13329

Gladiolus

Michigan Bulb Co.
1950 Waldorf N. W.
Grand Rapids, MI 49550

Noweta Gardens
St. Charles, MN 55972

Pleasant Valley Glads
P.O. Box 494
Agawam, MA 01001

Waushara Gardens
Plainfield, WI 54966

Houseplants

Alberts & Merkel Bros, Inc.
P.O. Box 537
Boynton Beach, FL 33435

Cook's Geraniums
712 N. Grand
Lyons, KS 67554

Fischer Greenhouse
Oak Ave.
Linwood, NJ 08221
   (African violets)

Glasshouse Works
Church St., Box 97
Stewart, OH 45778-0097

Greenlife Gardens
101 County Line Rd.
Griffin, GA 30223

Grigsby Cactus Gardens
2354 Bella Vista Dr.
Vista, CA 92084

Robert B. Hamm
10065 River Mist Way
Rancho Cordova, CA 95670

Kartuz Greenhouses
1408 Sunset Dr.
Vista, CA 92083

Lauray of Salisbury
Undermountain Rd.
Rt 41
Salisbury, CT 06068

Logee's Greenhouses
55 North St.
Danielson, CT 06239

Lyndon Lyon Greenhouses
14 Mutchler St.
Dolgeville, NY 13329-0249
   (African violets)

Merry Gardens
P.O. Box 595
Camden, ME 04843

Rainbow Gardens
1444 E. Taylor St.
Vista, CA 92084

Rhapis Gardens
105 Rhapis Rd.
Box 287
Gregory, TX 78359

Shady Hill Gardens
821 Walnut St.
Batavia, IL 60510
   (geraniums)

Sunset Nurseries (bamboo)
4007 Elrod Ave.
Tampa, FL 33616

Tinari Greenhouses
Box 190
2325 Valley Rd.
Huntingdon Valley, PA 19006
   (African violets)

Volkmann Brs. (African violets)
2714 Minert St.
Dallas, TX 75219

Irises

Comanche Acres Iris Gardens
R.R. 1, Box 258
Gower, MO 64454

Cooley's Gardens, Inc.
Box 126
Silverton, OR 97381

Mid-America Iris Gardens
P.O. Box 12982
Oklahoma City, OK 73157

Schreiner's Gardens
3625 Quinaby Rd. N.E.
Salem, OR 97303

Gilbert H. Wild & Sons
Sarcoxie, MS 64862

Lilies

B & D Lilies
330 P St.
Port Townsend, WA 98368

Borbeleta Gardens
15974 Canby Ave., Rt. 5
Fairbault, MN 55021

Fairyland Begonia and Lily Garden
1100 Griffith Rd.
McKinleyville, CA 95521

Oregon Bulb Farms
14071 N. E. Arndt Rd.
Aurora, OR 97002

Rex Bulb Farms
P.O. Box 774
Port Townsend, WA 98368

Orchids

Fennell Orchid Jungle
26715 S. W. 157th Ave.
Homestead, FL 33031

Arnold J. Klehm
44 W. 637 Rt. 72
Hampshire, IL 60140

Oakhill Gardens
Box 25
Binnie Rd.
Dundee, IL 6061X

Rod McLellan Co.
1450 El Camino Real
South San Francisco, CA 94080

Orchids by Hausermann, Inc.
2N-134 Addison Rd.
Villa Park, IL 60181

Perennials

Bluebird Nursery
Box 460
Clarkson, NE 68629

Bluestone Perennials
7211 Middle Ridge Rd.
Madison, OH 44057

Busse Gardens
Rt. 2, Box 238
Cokato, MN 55321
   (peonies, hostas, daylilies, perennials)

Caprice Farm Nursery
15425 S. W. Pleasant Hill Rd.
Sherwood, OR 97140
   (tree peonies, hostas, daylilies)

Carroll Gardens
P. O. Box 310
Westminster, MD 21157

Crownsville Nursery
P. O. Box 797
Crownsville, MD 21032

Fairway Enterprises
114 The Fairway
Albert Lea, MN 56007

Holbrook Farm and Nursery
Rt. 2, Box 223B
Fletcher, NC 28732

Klehm & Son Nursery
Rt. 5, Box 197 Penny Rd.
S. Barrington, IL 60010

Lamb Nurseries
E. 101 Sharp Ave.
Spokane, WA 99202

Milaegers
4838 Douglas Ave.
Racine, WI 53402

Putney Nursery, Inc.
Rt. 5
Putney, VT 05346

Rice Creek Gardens
1315 66th Ave. N.E.
Minneapolis, MN 55432

Rocknoll Nursery
9210 U.S. 50
Hillsboro, OH 45133-8546

Savory's Gardens
5300 Whiting Ave.
Edina, MN 55435
   (hostas)

Siskiyou Rare Plant Nursery
2825 Cummings Rd.
Medford, OR 97501

Spring Hill Nurseries
6523 N. Galena Rd.
P. O. Box 1758
Peoria, IL 61656

Gilbert H. Wild & Son
Sarcoxie, MO 64862
   (peonies, daylilies)

Rhododendrons, Azaleas

The Bovees Nursery
1737 S. W. Coronado
Portland, OR 97219

Cardinal Nursery
Rt. 1, Box 316
State Rd., NC 28676

Carlson's Gardens
Box 305
South Salem, NY 10590

Greer Gardens
1280 Goodpasture Island Rd.
Eugene, OR 97401

Roses

Armstrong Nurseries
Ontario, CA 91764

Fred Edmunds Roses
6235 S. W. Kahle Rd.
Wilsonville, OR 97070

Jackson & Perkins Co.
Medford, OR 97501

The Mini Farm
Rt. 1, Box 501
Bon Aqua, TN 37025

Mini-Roses
P. O. Box 4255, Station A
Dallas, TX 75208

Moore Miniature Roses
2519 Visalia Ave.
Visalia, CA 93277

Nor'East Miniature Roses, Inc.
58 Hammond St.
Rowley, MA 01969
P.O. Box 473
Ontario, CA 91762

Pixie Treasures Miniature Rose Nursery
4121 Prospect Ave.
Yorba Linda, CA 92686

Roses of Yesterday and Today
802 Brown's Valley Rd.
Watsonville, CA 95076

Star Roses
West Grove, PA 19390

Water lilies

Lilypons Water Gardens
301 Flower Rd.
Lilypons, MD 21717
or
301 Lilypons Rd.
Brookshire, TX 77423
or
301 Lilypons Way
P.O. Box 1130
Thermal, CA 92274
 (use nearest address)

Paradise Gardens
16 May St.
Whitman, MA 02382

Perry's Water Gardens
191 Leatherman Gap Rd.
Franklin, NC 28734

S. Scherer & Sons
Waterside Rd.
Northport, NY 11768

Slocum Water Gardens
1101 Cypress Gardens Blvd.
Winter Haven, FL 33880-6099

Three Springs Fisheries
120 Main Rd.
Lilypons, MD 21717

William Tricker Inc.
Box 398
Saddle River, NJ 07458
or
Box 7845
Independence, OH 44131

Van Ness Water Gardens
2460 North Euclid Ave.
Upland, CA 91786

OTHER SPECIALTY SUPPLIERS

Fox Hill Farm
444 W. Michigan Ave.
Box 9
Parma, MI 49269
 (herbs)

John Messelaar Bulb Co., Inc.
P.O. Box 269
Ipswich, MA 01938

Mohn's, Inc.
P.O. Box 2301
Atascadero, CA 93423
 (perennial hybrid poppies)

Musser Forests, Inc.
P.O. Box 340
Indiana, PA 15701
 (evergreen & hardwood seedling trees)

Plumeria People
P.O. Box 820014
Houston, TX 77282-0014

Prairie Nursery
P.O. Box 365
Westfield, WI 53964
 (prairie flowers, grasses)

Sandy Mush Herb Nursery
Rt 2
Leicester, NC 28748

Shady Oaks Nursery
700 19th Ave. N.E.
Waseca, MN 56093
 (northern & shade plants)

Swan Island Dahlias
P.O. Box 800
Canby, OR 97013

TyTy Plantation
Box 159
TyTy, GA 31795
   (cannas, southern bulbs)

Mary Walker Bulb Co.
P.O. Box 256
Omega, GA 31775
   (southern specialties)

SEEDS, GENERAL

Banana Tree
715 Northampton St.
Easton, PA 18042
   (tropical ornamentals)

John Brudy Exotics
3411 Westfield
Brandon, FL 33511-7736
   (unusual tropicals)

W. Atlee Burpee & Co.
300 Park Ave.
Warminster, PA 18974

The Cook's Garden
Box 65
Londonderry, VT 05148
   (salad & imported vegetables)

The Country Garden
Rt. 2, Box 455A
Crivitz, WI 54114
   (cut flowers)

Henry Field Seed & Nursery Co.
407 Sycamore St.
Shenandoah, IA 51602

Gurney Seed & Nursery Co.
Yankton, SD 57079

Harris Seeds Garden Trends, Inc.
961 Lyell Ave.
Rochester, NY 14606

Hastings
P.O. Box 4274
Atlanta, GA 30302-4274

Jackson & Perkins Co.
P.O. Box 1028
Medford, OR 97501

Le Jardin du Gourmet
Box 32
West Danville, CT 05873
   (herbs, shallots)

J. W. Jung Seed & Nursery Co.
335 S. High St.
Randolph, WI 53957

Kitazawa Seed Company
356 West Taylor St.
San Jose, CA 95110

Liberty Seed Co.
P.O. Box 806
New Philadelphia, OH 44663

Earl May Seed & Nursery Co.
208 N. Elm St.
Shenandoah, IA 51603

Nichols Garden Nursery
1190 N. Pacific Hwy.
Albany, OR 97321
   (vegetables)

George W. Park Seed Co.
P.O. Box 31
Greenwood, SC 29647

Pinetree Garden Seeds
R.R. 1, Box 397
New Gloucester, ME 04260
   (small quantity vegetables)

Clyde Robin Seed Co., Inc.
P.O. Box 2855
Castro Valley, CA 94546

Select Seeds
81 Stickney Hill Rd.
Union, CT 06076
   (heritage perennials and annual flowers)

Shepherd's Garden Seeds
7839 W. Zayante Rd.
Felton, CA 95018
   (European vegetables)

R. H. Shumway's
P.O. Box 1
Graniteville, SC 29829
      or
P.O. Box 777
Rockford, IL 61105
(use near address)

Stokes Seeds
Stokes Bldg
Buffalo, NY 14240

Thompson & Morgan, Inc.
Jackson, NJ 08527

Otis S. Twilley Seed Co.
P.O. Box 65
Trevose, PA 19047

Wildflower Seed Co.
P.O. Box 406
St. Helena, CA 94574
   (specialty wildflower seed mixtures)

BENEFICIAL INSECTS

The following insectaries provide natural enemies of insect pests:

American Biological Supply Co.
1330 Dillon Heights Ave.
P.O. Box 3149
Baltimore, MD 21228

Beneficial Insectary
14751 Oak Run Rd.
Oak Run, CA 96069

BioLogic
Box 177 Springtown Rd.
Willow Hill, PA 17271

Carolina Biological Supply Co.
Burlington, NC 27215

Nature's Control
Box 35
Medford, OR 97501

Rincon Vitova
Box 45
Oak View, CA 93022

GARDEN TOOLS AND EQUIPMENT

Country Home Products
Box 89
Cedar Beach Rd.
Charlotte, VT 05445

Cumberland General Store
Rt. 3
Crossville, TN 38555

Denman & Co.
2913 Saturn St.
Brea, CA 92621

John Houchins & Sons, Inc.
801 N. Main
Schulenburg, TX 78956

LaMotte Chemical Co.
P.O. Box 329
Chestertown, MD 21620

A. M. Leonard
6665 Spiker Rd.
Piqua, OH 45356

Mantis Mfg.
1458 County Line Rd.
Huntingdon Valley, PA 19006

Walter Nicke
19 Columbus Tpk.
Hudson, NY 12534

Smith & Hawken Tool Co.
68 Homer
Palo Alto, CA 94301

Troy Bilt Mfg.
102nd St. & 9th Ave.
Troy, NY 12180

Yardman
5389 W. 130th
Cleveland, OH 44111

BOOKS FOR FURTHER READING

The books in the following list are the ones that I have referred to over and over through the years. Some are old classics, some are revised editions, and some are relatively new. Most are available at libraries and at bookstores with good gardening sections. If you have trouble locating any, you may try checking with a local plant society; they often make books available or can refer you to places to find them. Because of space I cannot list all the books I would like to, especially the recent plethora of big color garden books, so if your favorite book is missing it is not deliberate. What you will find here are the books that I have found to be most helpful in my many years of gardening.

LANDSCAPING AND PLANNING BOOKS

Brookes, John. *The Book of Garden Design.* New York: Macmillan Publishing Co., 1991.

Eckbo, Garrett. *Urban Landscape Design.* New York: MaGraw-Hill, 1964.

Hyams, Edward. *English Cottag Gardens.* New York: Viking Penguin, 1988.

Ireys, Alice Recknagel. *Garden Design.* Englewood Cliffs, NJ: Prentice Hall, 1991.

Ireys, Alice Recknagel. *Designs for American Gardens: A Guide with Complete Plans, Growing Information, and Hundreds of Recommended Plants.* Englewood Cliffs, NJ: Prentice Hall, 1991.

Johnson, Hugh. *The Principles of Gardening.* New York: Simon & Schuster, 1984.

Malitz, Jerome. *Personal Landscapes.* Portland, OR: Timber Press, 1989.

Nelson, William R. *Planning Design: A Manual of Theory and Practice.* Champaign, IL: Stipes Publishing Co., 1985.

Reader's Digest, ed. *Reader's Digest Practical Guide to Home Landscaping*. Pleasantville, NY: Reader's Digest Association, 1972.

Saito, Katsuo. *Japanese Gardens*. New York: Tuttle, Charles E., Company, 1971.

Smith, Ken. *Home Landscaping in the Northeast & Midwest*. New York: Price Stern Sloan, Inc., 1985.

Smith, Ken. *Southern Home Landscaping*. New York: Price Stern Sloan, Inc., 1982.

TREES AND SHRUBS

Bird, Richard. *Flowering Trees & Shrubs*. Hauppauge, NY: Barron's Educational Series, Inc., 1989.

Frederick, William H., Jr. *100 Great Garden Plants*. Portland, OR: Timber Press, 1986.

Gardiner, James M. *Magnolias*. Chester, CT: Globe Pequot, 1989.

Harris, Richard W. *Arboriculture: Care of Trees, Shrubs & Vines in the Landscape, 2nd ed.* Englewood Cliffs, NJ: Prentice Hall, 1991.

Hessayon, D. G. *The Tree & Shrub Expert*. New York: Sterling Publishing Company, Inc., 1990.

The Hillier Manual of Trees & Shrubs. North Pomfret, VT: Trafalgar Square, 1991.

Taffler, Stephen. *Climbing Plants & Wall Shrubs*. North Pomfret, VT: Trafalgar Square, 1991.

Wyman, Donald. *Trees for American Gardens*. New York: Macmillan Publishing Co., 1969.

Zucker, Isabel. *Flowering Shrubs and Small Trees*. New York: Grove/Weidenfeld, 1990.

REGIONAL BOOKS

Foley, Daniel J. *Gardening by the Sea*. Orleans, MA: Parnassus Imprints, 1982.

Hunt, William L. *Southern Garden, Southern Gardening*. Durham, NC: Duke University Press, 1982.

Schuler, Stanley, *How to Grow Almost Everything*. New York: Evans & Co., 1965.

PERENNIALS AND ANNUALS

Clausen, Ruth Rogers, and Nicholas H. Ekstrom. *Perennials for American Gardens*. New York: Random House, 1989.

Garden Way Staff. *Using Annuals & Perennials*. Longmeadow Press, 1990.

McGourty, Frederick. *The Perennial Gardener*. Boston: Houghton Mifflin, 1991.

McGourty, Frederick. *Perennials & Their Uses*. Brooklyn, NY: Brooklyn Botanic Garden, 1989.

Sunset Magazine & Book Editors. *Garden Color: Annuals & Perennials*. Menlo Park, CA: Sunset Publishing Corp., 1981.

Wilson, Helen Van Pelt. *New Perennials Preferred*. New York: Macmillan Publishing Co., 1992.

VINES, GROUND COVERS, AND LAWNS

Foley, Daniel J. *Ground Covers for Easier Gardening*. Mineola, NY: Dover Publications, 1972.

Fretwell, Barry O. *Clematis*. Deer Park, WI: Capability's Books, 1989.

Wyman, Donald. *Shrubs and Vines for American Gardens*. New York: Macmillan Publishing Co., 1970.

BULBS

Glattstein, Judy. *The Gardener's World of Bulbs*. Brooklyn, NY: Brooklyn Botanic Garden, 1991.

Horton, Al. *All About Bulbs*. San Ramon, CA: Ortho Books, 1986.

James, Theodore. *Flowering Bulbs Indoors & Out*. New York: Macmillan Publishing Co., 1991.

Whiteside, Katherine. *Classic Bulbs: Hidden Treasures for the Modern Garden*. New York: Random House, 1992.

LILIES

Bird, Richard. *Lilies.* Book Sales, Inc., 1991.

Brown, M. Jefferson. *A Plantsman's Guide to Lilies.* New York: Sterling Publishing Co., 1991.

Jefferson-Brown, Michael. *The Lily: For Garden, Patio & Display.* North Pomfret, VT: Trafalgar Square, 1988.

VEGETABLES AND FRUITS

Garden Way Staff. *Fruits & Vegetables: One Thousand and One Gardening Questions Answered.* Powmall, VT: Storey Communications, Inc., 1990.

Hagy, Fred. *The Practical Garden of Eden: Beautiful Landscaping with Fruits & Vegetables.* New York: Overlook Press, 1990.

Hill, Lewis. *Fruits and Berries for the Home Garden, revised edition.* Powmall, VT: Storey Communications, Inc. 1992.

Rogers Gessert, Kate. *The Beautiful Food Garden: Creative Landscaping with Vegetables, Herbs, Fruits & Flowers.* Powmall, VT: Storey Communications, Inc., 1987.

Solomon, Steve. *Growing Vegetables West of the CAscades.* Seattle, WA: Sasquatch Books, 1989.

WATER GARDENING

Leverett, Brian. *Water Gardens: Step by Step to Success.* North Pomfret, VT: Trafalgar Square, 1991.

Swindells, Philip. *The Water Garden.* New York: Sterling Publishing Co., 1990.

Uber, William C. *Water Gardening Basics.* Upland, CA: Dragonfly Press, 1988.

DISEASES AND PESTS

Carr, Anna. *Rodale's Color Handbook of Garden Insects.* Emmaus, PA: Rodale Press, 1983.

Chaube, H. S. *Plant Disease Management: Principles & Practice.* Boca Raton, FL: CRC Press, Inc., 1991.

Debach, Paul. *Biological Control of Natural Enemies, Second Edition.* Cambridge, UK: Cambridge University Press, 1991.

Hart, Rhonda M. *Bugs, Slugs & Other Thugs: Controlling Garden Pests Organically.* Powmall, VT: Storey Communications, Inc., 1991.

Ware, George W. *The Pesticide Book.* Thomson Publications, 1989.

PLANT PROPAGATION

Clarke, Graham & Alan Toogood. *The Complete Book of Plant Propagation.* New York: Sterling Publishing Co., Inc., 1990.

Hartmann, Hudson T. and Dale E. Kester. *Plant Progagation—Principles and Practices, Fifth Edition.* Englewood Cliffs, NJ: Prentice-Hall, 1990.

Hill, Lewis. *Secrets of Plant Propagation.* Powmall, VT: Storey Communications, Inc., 1985.

Thompson, Peter. *Creative Propagation: A Grower's Guide.* Portland, OR: Timber Press, 1989.

ORGANIC GARDENING

Blake, Francis. *Organic Farming & Growing.* North Pomfret, VT: Trafalgar Square, 1991.

Hamilton, Geoff. *Organic Gardening.* New York: Random House, 1992.

Pike, Dave. *Organic Gardening: Step by Step to Growing Success.* Trafalgar Square, 1991.

Smith, Keith. *Backyard Organic Gardener.* Lothian Publishers, 1990.

Sunset Editors. *An Illustrated Guide to Organic Gardening.* Menlo Park, CA: Sunset Publishing Corp., 1991.

PATIO GARDENING

Kramer, Jack. *Patio Gardening.* New York: Price Stern Sloan, Inc., 1980.

Williams, Robin. *The Complete Book of Patio & Container Gardening.* New York: Sterling Publishing Co., Inc., 1991.

Yang, Linda. *The Terrace Gardener's Handbook: Raising Plants on a Balcony, Terrace, Rooftop, Penthouse or Patio.* Portland, OR: Timber Press, 1982.

CONTAINER GARDENING

Hillier, Malcolm. *Book of Container Gardening.* New York: Simon & Schuster, 1991.

Joyce, David. *Hanging Baskets, Window Boxes, & Other Container Gardens: A Guide to Creative Small-Scale Gardening.* New York: Summit Books, 1991.

Taloumis, George. *Container Gardening.* New York: Brooklyn Botanic Garden, 1989.

CITY GARDENING

Colby, Deirdre. *City Gardening.* New York: Simon & Schuster, 1988.

Riker, Tom. *City & Suburban Gardens: Frontyards, Backyards, Terraces, Rooftops & Window Boxes.* Englewood Cliffs, NJ: Prentice-Hall, 1977.

Young, Linda, *The City Gardener's Handbook.* New York: Random House, 1990.

GREENHOUSE GARDENING

Edwards, Jonathan. *Greenhouse Gardening: Step by Step to Growing Success.* North Pomfret, VT: Trafalgar Square, 1991.

Hessayon, D. G. *Be Your Own Greenhouse Expert.* New York: Sterling Publishing Co., Inc., 1991.

INDOOR GARDENING

Crockett, James. *Crockett's Indoor Garden.* Boston, MA: Little Brown & Co., 1978.

herwig, Rob. *How to Grow Healthy Houseplants.* Los Angeles, CA: Price Stern Sloan, 1979.

Herwig, Rob. *Growing Houseplants.* New York: Facts on File, Inc., 1992.

Herwig, Rob. *The Tresury of Houseplants.* New York: Macmillan, 1979.

ORCHIDS

Kramer, Jack. *The World Wildlife Fund Book of Orchids*. New York, Abbeville Press, 1989.

Leroy-Terquem, Gerald & Parisot, Jean. *Orchids: Care & Cultivation*. New York: Sterling Publishing Co., Inc., 1991.

Northern, Rebecca. *Home Orchid Growing, Fourth Edition*. Englewood Cliffs, NJ: Prentice-Hall, 1990.

Rentoul, J. N. *Expanding Your Orchid Collection*. Lothian Publishers, 1990.

ROSES

Ray, Richard & MacCaskey, Michael. *Roses*. New York: Price Stern Sloan, Inc., 1984.

Ross, Dean. *The Ross Guide to Rose Growing*. Lothian Publishers, 1991.

Toogood, Alan. *Roses in Gardens*. New York: Sterling Publishing Co., Inc., 1990.

PRUNING

Cook, Alan D. *Pruning Techniques*. Brooklyn, NY: Brooklyn Botanic Gardens, 1991.

Joyce, David. *The Complete Guide to Pruning & Training Plants*. New York: Simon & Schuster, 1992.

Rudman, Jack. *Climber & Pruner*. Syosset, NY: National Learning Corp., 1991.

Plant names change frequently as taxonomists continue their work with plants. No doubt by the time this book goes to press, there may be some changes in botanical names. For our reference we have used HORTUS III, 1976 Edition, Macmillan Publishers.

Every effort has been made by the author and the publisher to provide accurate, up-to-date information in the lists of sources. The publisher welcomes responses from readers on any additions or changes. Please send letters to:

Jack Kramer
2225 Crayton Rd.
Naples, FL 33940

The author gratefully acknowledges the following for permission to reprint illustrations, photographs and color plates in this book.

Illustrations and Photographs

Architectural Pottery: Page 118
Jerry Bagger: Pages 2, 112
Matthew Barr: Pages 6, 20, 35, 48, 52, 56, 60, 92, 93 top and
                            bottom, 94, 95, 121

Hedrich Blessing: Page 26
California Redwood Assoc: Page 114
Bob Johnson: Pages 9, 22, 24, 25, 28, 32, 33, 61, 62, 78, 81, 84,
                            88, 96, 97, 98, 99, 100, 104, 105, 108, 117, 130

Jack Kramer: Pages 7, 34, 35, 41, 53, 64, 65, 66, 68, 75 top, 91,
                            113, 116, 120, 122, 123, 124, 125, 126, 127, 128,
                            129

Adrian Martinez: Pages 3, 11, 15, 16, 21, 29, 31, 37, 38, 49, 50, 80,
                            85, 87, 102, 103

Ken Molino: Pages 12, 82, 101, 111
USDA: Pages 4, 40, 59 top and bottom, 69, 115
Van Ness Water Gardens: Pages 109, 110
Michael Valdez: Pages 42, 43, 44, 45, 51, 55, 131, 132, 133, 134, 135,
                            136, 137, 138, 139

Western Wood Products: Pages 7, 23, 54, 94, 107
J.R.Wilson: Pages 75 bottom, 76, 119

COLOR PLATES
Molly Adams: 31
Matthew Barr: 6, 9, 10, 14, 26, 30, 31, 32, 33, 34, 36, 53
Cindy Gilberg: 2, 22, 25, 65
Bob Jones: 19
Jack Kramer: 4, 8, 13, 15, 17, 19, 20, 21, 27, 37, 38, 39, 40, 41, 43, 47, 48, 50, 51,
    54, 55, 56, 58, 60, 61, 66, 67, 68
Hermann Pigors: 42
George Taloumis: 1, 3, 5, 7, 11, 12, 16, 18, 23, 24, 28, 29, 31, 44, 45, 46, 49, 52, 57,
    59, 62

All drawings in the Gardening Dictionary are by Bob Johnson.

INDEX

Dyckia, 224

Firethorn, 333
Fireweed, 228
Fishtail palm, 192–93
Fittonia, 239
Five-leaf akebia, 153–54
Flame-of-the-woods, 271
Flamingo flower, 163
Flats, 8, 390
   planting from, 80
   sowing seeds in, 78
Flax, 283–84
Fleabane, 232
Floss flower, 152
Flowering maple, 144
Flowering onion, 154–55
Flowering quince, 197–98
Flowering tobacco, 303
Flowers. *See also* Annuals; Bulbs;
     Perennials
   shrubs for, 487–88
   trees for, 460–62, 487
   vines for, 488
Foam flower, 370
Forcing, 390
Forget-me-not, 299
   Chinese, 215
Formal garden, 32–33
Forsythia, 239–40
Forsythia suspensa, 105
Fothergilla, 240
Fountain grass, 315
Four o'clock, 297
Foxglove, 221
   Mexican, 155
Foxtail orchid, 339
Fragaria vesca, 240
Fragrance
   annuals for, 491
   bulbs for, 491
   perennials for, 490–91
   shrubs for, 490
   vines for, 491
Frangipani, 327
Franklinia alatahama, 240
Fraxinus, 240–41
Freesia hybrids, 241
Fremontia mexicana, 241
Fringe tree, 199
Fritillaria, 241
Fuchsia, 242
Fungus, 75

G *Gaillardia aristata*, 243
Gaillardia grandiflora, 96
Gail midge, 70
Galanthus, 244
Galax aphylla, 244
Galium verum, 244
Galtonia candicans, 244
Gamolepis tagetes, 244
Garden design, 19–34
   for arcs, 34
   for beds, 27, 30
   for borders, 27, 30
   for drifts, 34
   drought-resistant garden plan, 24
   landscape symbols in, 20
   for late summer/fall garden, 24
   for narrow backyard, 31
   for side yard, 29
   for spring garden, 22
   for summer/early fall garden, 28
Garden gloves, 17
Garden heliotrope, 376–77
Gardenia, 245
Garden(s). *See also* Plants
   assembling container, 52–57
   building vertical, 47–51
   climate zones in, 7
   color in. *See* Color in garden
   mail order suppliers, 517–26
   mulches in, 6, 39–40
   pruning in, 14–16
   soil in, 35–40
   sources of information on, 513
   tools in, 17–18
   watering, 37, 40–47
Garrya elliptica, 245
Gas plant, 221
Gasteria, 245
Gaultheria, 246
Gaura lindheimeri, 246
Gay feather, 281
Gaylussacia brachycera, 246
Gazania, 82, 246
Gelsemium sempervirens, 247
Gentian, 247
Gentiana asclepiadea, 247
Geranium, 91, 232, 247, 313–15
   strawberry, 349
Geranium grandiflorum, 247
Gerbera jamesonii, 248
Germander, 367
German violet, 236